Opinionated Women In the Land of Steady Habits

EDITED BY JAMES HERBERT SMITH

Elm Grove Press, LLC
PO Box 153, Old Mystic, CT 0637

ALSO BY JAMES HERBERT SMITH

- A Passion for Journalism, A Newspaper Editor Writes to his Readers
- Wah-say-lan, A Tale of the Iroquois in the American Revolution
- Wah-say-lan, Seneca Warrior (Young Adult)
- A Boy's Life in the Baby Boom, True Tales from Small Town America

ELM GROVE

Elm Grove Press, LLC
PO Box 153
Old Mystic, CT 06372
www.elmgrovepress.org

Printed in USA. Published 2018

ISBN: 978-1-940863-10-8

Dedication

This book is dedicated to

Barbara Ann, Stephanie, Sarah and Rebecca

Introduction

My daughter Barbara Ann was born May 19, 1969, six years after Betty Friedan's "Feminine Mystique" and two years before Gloria Steinem's "Ms." magazine. In my mind and heart that day I pledged that no boy, no man was going to stand in the way of my daughter's ambitions and desires, and American society would have to change to accommodate a new generation of girls who could become the women they wanted to be.

All four of my daughters found their own way, a generation after their mothers couldn't, for example, play high school varsity sports. They could be cheerleaders though and cheer on the boys.

Barbara Ann and her sister Stephanie played high school varsity sports. All four of them became what they wanted to become: an advertising executive, a senior editor, a school social worker and mother, and a teacher and mother. They succeeded in doing what they wanted to do.

In that spirit, we present to you this book of accomplished women writing a cacophony of ideas and opinions – antidotes, perhaps to the Land of Steady Habits, a moniker Connecticut adopted in the early 1800s reflecting the practice of repeatedly electing the same male officials to office.

Women who found niches to present their views in "features" departments, before they were generally admitted to the ranks of newsmen in the newsroom. Women who invaded newsrooms when they were a man's domain in the early 1970s. We give you here Opinionated Women from every daily newspaper in Connecticut writing eloquently on politics, current events, war and peace, race relations, sports, journalism itself, gardening, friendship, dance, theater, books, film, fashion, dining – all manner of life in our world. I had the privilege and the pleasure of working with many of them in Hartford, Meriden, Danbury, New London and elsewhere.

We have 63 opinionated women. Some of them are good friends with each other. They are all journalistic colleagues. They span decades, even centuries. They don't all think alike, they have separate passions, but they have this in common: a desire and ability to write clearly, to make you think, to entertain and to persuade.

We present them in alphabetical order by their last names, with one exception. With the 'w' on her last name, Barbara White was always toward the end of any list. I worked with her in her later years, and like so many others, was influenced by her common sense, her drive for a depth of understanding in the words she wrote, her eloquent defense of a free press, her generous nature especially to the newest in the newsroom of her Record-Journal in Meriden.

So with an editor's prerogative, I present Mrs. White first. And apologies to anyone I have missed. A couple women opted out but I did my best to track down the state's opinionated daily newspaperwomen and I hope I found them all, but perhaps not.

I should thank the editors and publishers of all of Connecticut's dailies for permission to reprint their columnists. I also thank Joe Nunes, retired from The Hartford Courant and author of a history of the newspaper; Angel Diggs of the New Haven Register for her dogged assistance in going through old files to uncover writers from decades past; Patricia Watson and Oneil Cormier of the New Britain Public Library for help in their archives on the writings of the late Judith Brown, owner of the New Britain Herald; former Courant colleague Henry J. McNulty for his photo of Irene Driscoll, and the National Baseball Hall of Fame in Cooperstown for permission to reprint its photo of Claire Smith.

James Herbert Smith, Bethel, CT

Opinionated Women

Barbara C. White	Record-Journal Meriden
Jennifer Abel	The Bristol Press, Middletown Press, New Britain Herald
Ginny Apple	The Hartford Courant
Ann Baldelli	The Day New London
Gina Barreca	The Hartford Courant
Betty Barrett	The Hartford Courant
Lynn Uhlfelder Berman	Greenwich Time
Judith Brown	New Britain Herald
Susan Campbell	The Hartford Courant
Angela Carella	The Advocate Stamford
Jacqueline S. Carlsen	New Haven Register
Maura Casey	The Day New London, The Hartford Courant
Lisa Chedekel	New Haven Register
Maureen E. Croteau	The Hartford Times, The Hartford Courant, The Day New London
Elizabeth G. Curren	New Haven Register
Donna Doherty	New Haven Register
Phyllis Donovan	Record-Journal Meriden
Irene Driscoll	The Hartford Courant
Bethe Dufresne	The Day New London
Mary Ellen Fillo	The Hartford Courant

Jenifer Frank .... The Hartford Courant
Robin Glassman .... New Haven Register, Connecticut Post
Barbara Grady .... New Haven Register
Deborah Hornblow .... The Hartford Courant
Marge Hoskin .... Norwich Bulletin
Karen Hunter .... The Hartford Courant
Michele Jacklin .... The Hartford Courant
Kate F. Jennings .... New Haven Register
Terese Karmel The Hartford Courant, The Willimantic Chronicle
Linda Tuccio-Koonz .... The News-Times Danbury
Kathleen V. Kudlinski .... New Haven Register
Donna Larcen .... The Hartford Courant
Dolores Laschever .... Torrington Register Citizen
Wendy Lecker .... Stamford Advocate
Sarah Wesley Lemire .... The Hartford Courant
Sarah Darer Littman .... Greenwich Time
Carolyn Lumsden .... The Hartford Courant
Carrie MacMillan .... Waterbury Republican-American
Karen Mamone .... The Hartford Courant
Vivian B. Martin .... The Hartford Courant
Lisa McGinley .... The Day New London
Meg (Angus-Smith) McGuire .... The News-Times Danbury

Faith Vincent Middleton................. Journal Inquirer Manchester
Kathy O'Connell .... Record-Journal Meriden
Kyrie O'Connor .... The Hartford Courant
Maxine Olderman .... New Haven Register
Tracey O'Shaughnessy.................... Waterbury Republican-American
Amy Pagnozzi .... The Hartford Courant
Nancy Pappas Metcalf .... The Hartford Courant
Barbara Parent .... Record-Journal Meriden
Carol King Platt .... The Day New London,
Record-Journal Meriden
Barbara Roessner .... The Hartford Courant
Susan Schoenberger......................... The Hartford Courant
Sandi Kahn Shelton .... New Haven Register
Lisa Siedlecki .... The News-Times Danbury
Lydia Huntley Sigourney................ The Hartford Courant
Claire Smith .... The Hartford Courant
Jacqueline Smith .... The News-Times Danbury,
Record-Journal Meriden
Jane Stern .... Connecticut Post
Ernestine Stodelle .... New Haven Register
Helen Ubiñas .... The Hartford Courant
Deb Waldman .... New Haven Register
Katharine Weber .... New Haven Register

BARBARA C. WHITE

Barbara C. White was the editor of the Record-Journal of Meriden from 1978 to 1988. The magna cum laude English literature major at Radcliffe College, married Harvard Law School grad Carter H. White, whose family owned the Meriden Record (later merged with the Journal).

Barbara started at the Record in 1946 writing book and theater reviews and travel features. For decades her restaurant reviews decorated the walls of New England restaurants. In the 1950s she was a columnist and editorial writer, later becoming editor of the editorial page. She served as a Pulitzer juror, was an active member of the American Society of Newspaper Editors, the New England Society of Newspaper Editors and the National Conference of Editorial Writers. She also was an officer of the Meriden League of Women Voters, the Meriden College Club, AAUW and the city wide PTA. She is a member of the Connecticut Society of Professional Journalists Hall of Fame. She died in 2009. Her son, Eliot C. White, is president and publisher of the Record-Journal and her grand daughter Elizabeth White is executive vice-president and assistant publisher.

It's Hard To Hate Or Fear A Friend

By Barbara C.White Record-Journal Meriden Dec. 17 1988

A cherished, long-time friend of mine died recently. A musician by profession, she was a well-loved teacher, a voracious reader, an ardent nature lover and conservationist, a witty talker and a person of exquisite charm and sensitivity. She was also a lesbian.

More than half a century ago, when I first knew her, I didn't know the word or what it meant. I was only vaguely aware of what a homosexual was – the word "gay" had not come into use. But there were several people with these orientations among the two dozen or so teachers and students at the music camp next to my aunt's farm in Maine.

My sister and I were friendly with everybody at the camp, especially the young men who provided a reliable dating pool. I was puzzled initially when one or another of those who were gay would ask me out, spend a wonderful evening with me obviously enjoying my company, but never acting like a "date," not even bothering to hold my hand. Finally my sister, younger but more knowledgeable, with a steady boyfriend from among the group, enlightened me that these were boys "who liked boys better." I was glad to learn that it wasn't simply that I was unattractive. They were already my friends and we continued to respect and enjoy each other.

My mother, who was even less informed than I, was vaguely uneasy about the whole set-up; she didn't trust musicians much. But my aunt, to whom we were entrusted for two weeks at a time, was totally unruffled. A professional musician herself, she had her own shrewd ideas of when and whether we were endangered. The more people, the more different kinds of people we got to know, the better our judgment would be, she declared. "It's all grist for the mill," she would say after I'd brought back a particularly flamboyant character.

She had a sharp eye, however, for where threats might come from. Even when we were little girls, she kept her eye on the camp director, a booming-voiced, emotional man they called Poppa, who had a loving way with him, "Don't ever sit on Poppa's lap," she warned. "And if he puts his hands on you, tell him to stop and come right home."

My friend-to-be, Shelley I will call her, was not one of the musically inspired, frequently overheated students. She was a pianist, a teacher-coach of great musical knowledge and skill, some 20 years older than I. She traveled with a companion, a woman I'll call Jane. Theirs was an open, established and devoted relationship, acknowledged and respected by the musical community. Shelly was an Englishwoman who had been married for some years and had decided that marriage did not suit her. Her alliance with Jane was of several years' standing, a variant of what used to be known in New England as a Boston marriage.

The years passed, and the camp was discontinued. My sister married her baritone boy-friend, and we kept in touch, sometimes, with the youngsters from the camp, many of whom were based around Boston. The war came. I heard later that Bobby, one of the gayest of the gay, who used to convulse us all with imitations of Franklin D. Roosevelt, was killed in the Battle of the Bulge.

Shelly and Jane had bought from Poppa a piece of land on the edge of the water even closer to our house than the camp had been. On it they built a weathered, low cottage in the blueberry field just up from the wide, flat rocks. Its windows commanded the sweep of the Georges River, up towards Thomaston and all the way down to the open ocean. Seagulls swooped in their front yard, and sometimes a harbor seal could be seen on the reef that the low tide bared.

The two ladies lived there peaceably summer after summer. Shelley taught voice in the music shack, a small shed next to the cottage, equipped with a grand piano, because the sound of the constant singing in the house bothered Jane. When November came they moved up to town to an equally modest, compact house where Jane tended the home fires and Shelley devoted time to the art museum and to whatever cultural activities Rockland had to offer.

Every year we came up with our kids, a noisy, aggressive bunch who were interested only in houses that had other kids in them. When they were young teens, a group of them became aware of Shelley and Jane and got the idea they were weird. It certainly wasn't the ladies' lifestyle, which was quiet and inoffensive in the extreme. But probably some of the kids had heard talk at home, and the ladies' elderly precision, combined with Shelley's clipped British accent marked them as different. There were a few night raids on their woodpile, whoops, and hollers as kids raced through their yard, and snickers in the corners.

We declared that property off-limits and grounded the offenders for a few nights. At the same time we saw to it that one kid or another get sent next door to deliver a piece of blueberry cake or a book, or to ask if any errands needed doing at the store. Our children eventually became their good friends.

Jane died when both ladies were in their 80s. She had used a pacemaker for several years, and there was a long illness at the end. Shelley cared for her devotedly, grumbling humorously about how bad-tempered sickness can make people. She grieved deeply when Jane died, and kept a picture of her on the mantel.

Shelley lived on alone, cared for by a devoted neighbor who came in by the day, companioned by a temperamental Siamese cat, and visited often by former friends and pupils. Never did I visit her that she didn't have a new, stimulating book in her hand or some wonderful music, a symphony or a song, on her tape recorder. She was 97 when she died, still independent, still charming and opinionated.

I have Shelley and the boys at Poppa's camp to thank that I have never felt dislike, distrust or revulsion for people whose sexual orientations are different from mine. Concern, yes, now that AIDS and other sexually transmitted diseases have cast their shadow on all sexual contacts, some more endangering than others. I reserve my distrust, and warn young people against those of either sex or any orientation who try to force their attentions on others or to exploit others.

And I have my Aunt Laura to thank for trusting me enough and giving me the opportunity to find out for myself about all kinds of people, how they are like me and how they are different.

If You Don't Get Arrested, Your Name Won't Be Printed

By Barbara C. White Record-Journal Meriden Feb. 21, 1987

Wallingford reporter Darryl Campagna wrote a news story recently about the town's police blotter. That's the daily record of arrests and charges, which the police keep and which by law is available for the public inspection.

As the story noted, the police blotter is one of the best-read features in the paper. People read it as news but also as a kind of entertainment, almost like gossip. Many readers in each of our towns don't put the paper down until they check on which one of their friends and neighbors has gotten tagged for sliding through a stop sign, letting a dog roam, or some more serious offense.

Also noted in the story is the pressure applied by people who have been caught and who try to keep their names out of the paper. The police have come to understand, as have we, that in many cases the publication of the name is a more dreaded penalty than the fine or other official punishment.

Wallingford Police Lt. William Birney acknowledged as much when he told our reporter of the requests that he gets to keep out both names and ages. He can't censor the blotter, he tells them. It would be illegal to do so when a legitimate arrest is made.

"What we always do is refer them to the paper and that kind of gets them off our back," he added.

It gets them off the backs of the police, but it puts them right on our backs. We don't get as many calls as we used to, requesting that names in arrests not be run; most people know our policy. But we do get some, and some that we get are truly impassioned.

We must tell them that the only way to keep their names out of the paper is not to get arrested. We are no more able than the police to censor the police log, but for a very different reason. It's a matter of fairness, of honest reporting. Once we have decided to run the police log, at all (and we believe that, for other reasons than that it is well read, it is important that it be run) we must carry it in its entirely, as it appears at the station, with all names and charges included.

Each person, naturally enough, believes he or she is an exception. We have been asked to exclude some names because their owners claim they didn't do what they were accused of doing. We have been urged to drop others because they are friends of a staff member or are prominent advertisers or politicians. Many call claiming publication would result in loss of job or other grief. If we agreed to one exception, in fairness we would have to agree to others. Pretty soon we wouldn't be running the police log any more.

Our editors have been the recipients of bitter arguments and passionate appeals, even threats in connection with this policy. I have been accused of standing in judgment on people who may have made a mistake but whom the paper is punishing. My answer is that by treating all names alike and everybody equally we are refusing to stand in judgment. It is up to the police to make and record the arrest, which is then public knowledge, available to all who care to see it. It is up to the courts to pass judgment. We also report that judgment in the same form as the arrest. To pick and choose, deciding who is worthy of special treatment – that would be standing in judgment.

We have been threatened by people who say they intend to commit suicide if their names appear, and that we will be guilty of their death. So far none of them has committed suicide. We have been entreated by people, among them respectable middle-aged women picked up on shop-lifting charges, who claim their lives will be ruined. I have seen some of them later, their heads still high. Politicians and officials have exerted extreme pressure to quash a drunk driving charge. If it is on the blotter it has gone in, and after an initial flurry life has gone on.

The police blotter is a fact of life in which most of us – including my own family – sooner or later usually find our names. It's not the end of the world. The arrested person's guilt or innocence will be duly recorded in the court disposition column. People have short memories and more humanity than they are sometimes given credit for.

One of my favorite police blotter stories concerns my fellow-worker Carter White, the Record-Journal publisher. He was picked up in Wallingford one Sunday morning for violating posted speed limits; the incident was duly reported in the paper's police blotter. He hoped it would go unnoticed, but no. He got sympathy cards from three of his friends.

My other favorite story is about a friend who got pinched by police for letting her dog roam. Not only were her name and address printed, but her age too appeared. She thought it was unfair; they should have printed the dog's age instead.

Always A New Technique For Keeping Meetings Secret

By Barbara C.White Record-Journal Meriden Feb. 4, 1989

Just about everybody thinks the public has a Right to Know, and that laws enforcing this right are a good thing. But when it comes to officials and their own conduct of public business, a lot of them just can't accept that it applies to them. Public agencies and officials come up with some of the darnedest dodges for keeping their meetings and records secret.

The latest to surface is the so-called walking quorum. The East Baton Rouge Parish School Board in Baton Rouge, La., developed it to get around an FOI law, which forbids most closed meetings.

As in Connecticut, a meeting must have a quorum to be official. Seven of a 12-member board constituted a quorum. The board got around the restriction by holding sequential meetings of four members each, at which members walked in and out of the closed meeting, taking turns discussing such topics as school transportation, racial imbalance, finances and school renovations.

The State-Times and Morning Advocate sued the board and a judge has issued a temporary restraining order, pending a hearing.

In this state the closed-door caucus loophole is still legal and very much in use; in Meriden it made its reappearance once more this year. A party caucus is not at present an official meeting in the FOI sense of the word. It is, according to FOI law, an "assembly of the enrolled members of a single political party who are members of a public agency . . ."

It's used, especially in City Council meetings, to inform party members and get some kind of consensus of a party position before the regular council meeting. It's abused when all the arguments, all the positions are explored, and all the decisions are taken so that when the members go out on the floor they simply ram the decision through.

It is also abused when items not on the regular agenda are brought into the caucus and then popped through the subsequent meeting with no chance for the opposing party to develop and present a position.

Caucus abuse happens more commonly when the body is over-weighted by one party; Meriden's present 18-2 tilt of the council toward the

Democrats is a case in point. It has happened in the past when the council was overwhelmingly Republican.

There's more than party involved here; there's respect for the public. Last November a Democratic council caucus lasted 90 minutes. Members of the public as well as the one Republican in attendance had to wait, and then were denied effective floor debate.

An alert Record-Journal reporter has managed to narrow the loophole a little by challenging the right of Corporation Counsel Lawrence Kendzior to be present at these caucuses. The Democrats acknowledged the violation and now the caucus must work on its own. Some questions and legal opinions are pushed out to the open floor.

Mitchell Pearlman, the FOIC's executive director, would like to see legislation to close the loophole altogether, a change that deserves support.

Record for the biggest, most unexpected loophole in the history of Connecticut's FOI laws goes to the "lawyer-client privilege" relationship, which slipped into place in 1984. It hinges on a ruling by Judge Samuel J. Friedman that public agencies and lawyers could meet privately for any reason, on the grounds that the client-attorney relationship is "privileged." The case concerned a closed meeting of the North Haven Zoning Board of Appeals which the FOIC had ruled illegal.

Used to its full potential, this loophole could have closed any public meeting in the state at will. Agencies would need only to express their intent to meet with their attorney and the door would slam. A resident attorney, ready to consult on demand, would be standard equipment for any well-managed board or office.

Fortunately for whatever reason, agencies were slow to avail themselves of this loophole. Maybe they weren't aware of it, although newspapers in particular gave it big play. Maybe they just couldn't believe their good fortune. Maybe most of them didn't have the conscience to operate in all that much secrecy; they just wanted to make a few more of their own rules.

In any case, in the two years that the loophole was open, in only a handful of instances was it used. In 1986 the legislature, alerted to the danger, acted decisively to declare that the FOI law superseded the attorney-client relationship in public bodies.

There was a narrow squeak, however, with a smaller loophole that some legislators wanted to leave open and some officials are still aiming for. The law as it stands allows a closed meeting only when there is to be a discussion of litigation, which is actually in process. An attempt was made to stretch this to allow executive sessions to discuss "reasonably anticipated claims or litigation." It was knocked out by opponents who pointed out that "reasonably" could be stretched to mean just about anything.

There are still a lot of people, many of them lawyers, who would like to see that exception. The Southington Water Board is citing it to justify the closed session which the Record-Journal is challenging and it sounds as though Cheshire's Public Building Commission Town Hall subcommittee is using the same reasoning. This last year Wallingford's Mayor William Dickinson expressed frustration at the idea of being barred from closing a meeting when legal counsel was called for.

The good news is that, especially on the state level, municipal officials are learning to live with the law and to understand its guidelines. Even the dodges and the searches for loopholes show more knowledge of and respect for its restrictions. Reporters and editors who used to come up against a blank wall when they cited public rights of access now often find more willing co-operation. Many officials and records-keepers have found that they can live with it.

The not-so-good news is that in towns that are run by many boards and commissions that change membership at every election, every year is a new challenge. The process of getting the word out is never over.

He Was Sure He Was Going To Win, But …

By Barbara C. White Record-Journal Meriden Jan. 1 1976

He came for the flavor; last week he died for the taste.

He was 51 years old when lung cancer caught up with him, and he had been smoking ever since he was 14. In the last few years it was a consistent two packs a day. He was my brother.

It wasn't the right time for him to die. He was a big, strong fellow and had always been in good health. He had been a varsity athlete in school, and lately his enthusiasm was all for tennis. When they took his right lung out last summer, he worried that the pain and scar tissue would damage his serve.

His death came at a bad time for his family. He had been struggling for some years to make a small business successful. This year for the first time it made a profit. Without him, its chances are questionable.

He left two girls in their middle teens, both needing the financial help that the business could provide as they head toward college, as well as the love and closeness that they had enjoyed with him. He left a beautiful wife, and what should have been the best years of his life.

My mother always worried about his smoking. But back 20 years ago he could say to her that nobody had ever proved it did anybody any harm.

Last summer after the loss of the lung he admitted that he had counted too much on beating the odds. "All my life I've been lucky," he told me. "I didn't think it could happen to me."

Still he was sure he was going to win, and fought bitterly against the pain and the weakness that never quite left him. Until a week before Christmas he believed that the persistent pain in his shoulder was bursitis, left over from an old lacrosse injury. And even then he admitted that it was hard denying himself the smoke from those cigarettes.

Now, when one of my children or someone I care for lights a cigarette, I feel a little sick.

Today is "Connecticut No Smoking Day." If you are one of those who are trying to make it through for the first time without a smoke, do this when you feel the urge: Stand up, take a big, full breath, and give thanks inside yourself that you still have lungs healthy enough to enjoy the good air.

Not everybody is so lucky.

JENNIFER ABEL

Jennifer Abel was a reporter and columnist for The Bristol Press and New Britain Herald. Her work has appeared in Playboy, the Guardian, Salon, Consumer Affairs, Mashable and a variety of other print and online publications.

Quitting Cigarettes No Help For State Budget Woes

By Jennifer Abel New Britain Herald and Bristol Press March 15, 2009

Do you find your wallet depressingly light compared to a year ago? If so, take heart in knowing it's not just you; the whole state's broke these days. Connecticut's facing a budget deficit of $8.7 billion over the next two years, and that deficit will only grow deeper after what I did last week.

Before discussing my responsibility for the state's budget woes, I'll point out that the human brain has a hard time grasping such abstractly huge numbers as "eight point seven billion." Maybe this will help you picture it: if you made a million dollars a day, weekends and holidays included, amassing $8.7 billion would take almost 24 years.

How did a rich state like Connecticut wind up in such a fiscal mess? Charles Dickens figured it out over a century ago, when he had Mr. Micawber tell David Copperfield: "Annual income 20 pounds, annual expenditure nineteen, nineteen and six, result happiness. Annual income twenty pounds, annual expenditure twenty pounds ought and six, result misery."

In other words, don't spend more than you have. But if you change pounds to dollars, and make the numbers exponentially bigger, you'll describe what happened to us. During the go-go bubble years, when property values and the tax assessments on them reached the stratosphere, not one local government – neither the guys running my town, nor the guys running yours – thought, "Hey, let's take this opportunity to pay down some debt and build up savings." Instead, they spent every dollar they had and borrowed even more, with the vague idea of paying off this debt sometime in the future.

Which would have been a fine plan, if not for the future's nasty habit of eventually becoming the present. In Connecticut's case, this happened at the exact moment the bubble popped. Now the state faces bills much higher than the twenty-ought-six Mr. Micawber warned against, and these revenue problems are compounded by my decision, last week, to stop paying state cigarette taxes.

There's multiple ways to do this. You can buy tax-free smokes on New York State Indian reservations (disclaimer: this is extremely illegal if you get caught), or you can buy tobacco and roll your own, but I took the simpler method known as "Buy nicotine patches and quit smoking altogether."

Naturally, this made my non-smoking friends turn Supportive with a capital S. "Congratulations!" they gushed. "Statistically speaking, you've just increased your life span by seven years!"

Which, in turn, only intensifies the government's budget woes. The problem with increasing your lifespan by seven years is that those years are added to the wrong end of your life. I won't get to spend seven extra years in my 30s; instead, I'll spend additional time in the "retired old person collecting checks from the government" phase of my existence. I did a quick calculation on the back of an envelope: assuming Social Security and Medicare still exist, then between lost cigarette tax revenues and increased old-age payout, my decision to quit smoking will cost the state and federal governments over 600,000 dollars, not counting inflation.

So, to all you people suffering in the wake of severed state budget cuts: I sincerely apologize for making your troubles worse. I was tempted to keep smoking, for the sake of The Children, but ultimately I'm just too selfish.

Who Do You Call To Get A Better Job?

By Jennifer Abel The Bristol Press, The Middletown Press New Britain Herald Dec. 28, 2008

The other night I tried selling my soul to Satan in exchange for a secure, fulfilling job offering a decent salary and opportunities for advancement (yes, America, that is what it takes nowadays).

Unfortunately, the growing world economic crisis has even hurt the soul market. With so many souls offered for sale, prices are dropping even faster than the real estate and stock markets combined. Forget about making a profit on any sales; you'll be lucky if you get enough to cancel out your losses.

"I'm cutting back on personal spending these days," the Devil said to me. "Who isn't? If you're selling your soul for a job, the most I can afford to offer right now is a temp gig warming office seats for big-industry CEOs while they fly to Congress to collect their bailout checks. Pays 20 bucks an hour plus travel costs. No bennies."

I'm not desperate enough to even consider such an insulting offer. Yet. "Come back in a few months," I told him. "Maybe I should see how the new year and new president work out, before committing to anything drastic."

"Suit yourself," Satan said. "The longer you wait to sell, the less you'll get when you do. And that's not even counting what inflation will do to the value of the dollar. C'mon. I can have you on a plane flying to Detroit tomorrow. Just sign here."

But I shook my head, in lieu of saying "No," and Lucifer vanished in a sulfurous puff of smoke.

The moral of this story is: Don't try selling your soul to Satan, because whatever he offers won't be worth it. And yet, the more I think about it, the more I like the idea.

The idea of leading a major company, I mean. I don't suppose anyone reading this belongs to the board of directors of some huge corporation looking to hire a high-ranking executive officer? If so, look no further than me.

Granted, I have no idea how to run such a business. If you put me at the helm of your company, I'll probably drive it into the ground, flush its stock value down the toilet and add most of its work force to the unemployment rolls.

What everyone else is doing, in other words. So why hire me instead of them?

Most corporate executives who trash their companies charge hundreds of millions of dollars each year for their services. I'm willing to trash your company for a mere half-million, plus health and dental.

This enormous salary differential could shore up your stock value. Preserve hundreds of jobs. Or fund your next round of executive bonuses and corporate retreats in Maui.

Also: I am a woman who was raised in the South. This means I know how to shed realistic-looking tears on demand. Maybe I can use this skill to finagle an extra few hundred billion out of the (mostly male) members of Congress when I visit Washington and tell them why the taxpayers need to pay for my company's bailout.

Of course, "Trashing the economy and using taxpayer money to do it" is the sort of job you can't take unless you sell your soul first. I'll call Satan again tomorrow morning

---

Of Shooting Galleries and Gun-Free Zones

By Jennifer Abel The Bristol Press The Middletown Prsss and New Britain Herald
Dec. 14, 2008

You know those amusement-park shooting galleries where you use an air rifle to knock down multiple rows of moving mechanical ducks? The way they work is, you shoot at the targets all you want, and none of the targets can shoot back. Most schools and workplaces operate on the same principle. Aside from that, they're quite different from arcade gun ranges. When you read about shooting sprees in gun-free zones, you'll notice that the shooters wield weapons far more lethal than any air rifle. And they don't fire at plastic ducks, either. Behold one of the great paradoxes of modern criminal psychology: Signs that say things such as "This is a gun-free zone" or "Guns are absolutely not allowed here" don't deter the sort of people who are already ignoring society's much-stricter prohibitions against mass murder. Too bad. Gun-free shootings are common enough that English has evolved clichés to describe them: post-office fatalities gave Americans the phrase "Going postal," while "School shooting" even has its own Wikipedia entry. But don't panic. School shootings that lead to fatalities occur in America roughly once every two months, on average. That's statistically negligible, in a country of more than 300 million. Even when you add office and workplace shootings to the equation, you're still more likely to die in a car accident than from a bullet fired in a gun-free zone. Yet the shootings draw interest in ways that car accidents don't. Why's that? Maybe the sense of legally enforced helplessness has something to do with it. Accidents happen all the time. Everyone accepts that. As for deliberate attacks ... it's unlikely some nut on the highway will come gunning for you in his car. But if one does, well, at least you'd be in a car, too. There's no defensive-driving equivalent to the gun-free zone, no legal requirement that grants attackers advantages over their victims.

And no shortage of well-meaning people who think disarming law-abiding citizens will make it harder for criminals to shoot people. The Second Amendment to the Constitution guarantees "the right to keep and bear arms." Of all freedoms in the Bill of Rights, it's the only one that Americans can't legally exercise without written permission from the government. If you're looking to get this permission for yourself, I can't tell you how to do it, since the requirements vary from state to state and even city to city. But whatever the gun laws in your locality, I can tell you this: If you're unlucky enough to get shot, the guy who did it was probably ignoring those laws anyway.

No matter how many speeches a politician gives in favor of gun control, it's a safe bet that his own bodyguards are still packing heat. Even if he's giving a speech at a school or post office or other gun-free zone. The Secret Service and other professional-bodyguard types apparently don't trust the ability of "No guns allowed" signs to keep shooters from hitting their targets.

That's the difference between public servants and the public they serve. Our servants' lives are considered much too valuable to risk in a gun-free zone.

Ginny Apple interviewing Ivan Lendl

Ginny Apple was The Courant's first fulltime woman sports writer. She graduated from the University of Oklahoma in 1973 where she was sports editor of the student newspaper, the Oklahoma Daily. She has an M.A. in creative writing from the University of Bridgeport. She served as assistant tennis pro and coach at Point O'Pines Camp for girls, Brant Lake, NY. Among other awards, she took second place in 1978 in the national Associated Press Sports Editors competition for a column about pro players Betty Stove and Tracy Austin.

Holding a Czech On Outside World

By Ginny Apple The Hartford Courant Dec. 19, 1982

Ivan Lendl is a complex puzzle. To obtain an adequate reading of his personality one must painstakingly search for and separate the individual pieces of his life.

He shuns the press. He does not socialize with anyone outside a small circle of friends. His telephone is set up only for outgoing calls, it does not ring in his house.

Since his first appearance on the professional tennis scene in 1978, Lendl has been shrouded in mystery. Few have been able to crack his cloak of secrecy.

Though he has alienated fans and press, Lendl still maintains silence. He does what he wants and talks to whom he wants.

His life is a one-way mirror into which no one can see.

Why is he so secretive?

"I prefer to have the privacy," he said.

Why?

"Just because I prefer it."

What makes Lendl interesting, of course, is his ability on the tennis court. Had he been a run-of-the-mill player no one would have bothered. But during the past 1½ years Lendl has been phenomenal. Since the 1981 U.S. Open, Lendl has won 182 tournament matches, losing only 18. During that time he had victory streaks of 45, 26, and 12 matches. Ranked third in the world, he has dominated John McEnroe, the world's top-ranked player, beating him six consecutive times.

And through all this Lendl has kept to himself.

He would prefer if things were always as they are when he plays Davis Cup matches in Czechoslovakia. There, no one is allowed to speak to him privately. The Czech captain sees that this rule is not broken.

"The captain is guiding us," Lendl explained. "No one can talk to us, he doesn't let anyone through. There's the press conference and that's the end of it. That's the way it's supposed to be because you are there to practice and to play the matches and not to talk to the press for six hours."

Perhaps it is his background. The Czechoslovakian has said that Europeans have an entirely different mentality from Americans, that they are not as public with their personal lives.

Or perhaps he's still a youngster who achieved fame and fortune too quickly.

Yet, at times Ivan Lendl lets go, if only for a moment. He has a quick wit and quite often jokes in press conferences. A constant glint in his eye reveals a hidden warmth, creating a yearning to know more about this strange young man who hits the tennis ball with the force of a cannon.

"I just want to have my own personal life," he said, "and the word private is there because it's supposed to be private.

"Nobody's asking you what you prefer besides your job. And, I don't see any reason why they should be asking tennis players. Nobody's asking a doctor what he likes to do if he goes out or if he likes discos or not."

His image has made Lendl the scapegoat of the crowd at most tournaments. Though they "ooh and ahh" at many of his shots, they constantly ride him. To them Lendl is brusque, cold and just plain mean. Lendl says this doesn't bother him. He says he really does not hear the crowd.

"If I concentrate I really don't hear it as much," he said. "If I concentrate really well, and that's what I try to do, you can tell they are there, but still you concentrate, so that makes the end of it."

He seems to have a personal vendetta against the press. He often skips interviews and later says he knew nothing about them.

"If they're fair, I don't mind the press," he said. "If they write what I say it's fine. But if they take half a quote and put it together, then it makes a completely different sentence. That's what I really mind."

On the tour Lendl spends most of the time in his room. He believes going shopping or poking around town drains energy and disturbs concentration. At most tournaments he won't even play golf, his latest love.

"You've just got to keep your energy and concentration," he said. "I just sleep and eat and watch TV and sleep and eat and read and sleep. So it's pretty boring. That's all you can if you want to win."

Lendl travels with his friend and adviser Wojtek Fibak of Poland to many of the tournaments. They both maintain homes in Greenwich. Lendl likes Connecticut because he says, "it's nice and quiet."

He does not make many friends on tour partly because that makes it more difficult to go out and crush them on the court, but also because the hectic schedule prevents it.

"There really is no time to make friends," he said. "It's just switching so much around so many guys and so many tournaments. It's very difficult to find a very good friend. I'm friendly with most of the guys, but it's not likely they will be my best friends."

Lendl is not a member of the Association of Tennis Professionals. It was Lendl who was outspoken when Bjorn Borg was told he must qualify for Grand Prix tournaments if he didn't play a designated minimum.

"I agree with Borg," said Lendl. "I mean you're self employed and you're not working for the pro council, so they have no right to tell you how many tournaments and where to play."

On court Lendl is calculating and impenetrable, rarely displaying emotion. He works very hard at maintaining this tough exterior.

"If I would be vulnerable to what everybody says about me," he said, "I couldn't live probably. It's not that I don't care, It's just you can't be bothered about it.

"Anything you do, you always please some people and some people get angry at you," he said. "What I try to do is just please more people than make people angry."

Perhaps this, more than anything, is the hidden piece in his puzzle.

Magical Dorothy Hamill Brings A Smile To Your Heart

By Ginny Apple The Hartford Courant Oct. 6, 1976

New Haven -- There was silence all around. But it was a magical, electrifying silence filled with zealous anticipation. A nervous, charming young lady stood in the wings of the ice arena in her angelic white outfit. Then the music skipped its way around the cavernous building and a dancing beam of light landed on the ethereal Dorothy Hamill.

Almost instantly, as if prompted by some invisible cue man, the 19-year-old Olympic Gold Medal Figure Skating champion, glided onto the ice to a near-deafening tumult of applause.

This was their heroine, their darling, their ice princess.

It was one of those times when even the most hardened cynic would have trouble digesting the lump in his throat.

Dorothy Hamill was on top of the world and with her she had lifted thousands of people up into the world of sparkle and glitter.

And this performance, a free-skating exhibition, which preceded the close of the Winter Olympics, was one that would be remembered for years by old and young alike.

It wasn't coincidental that the vivacious Miss Hamill skimmed across the ice to the strains to "How Lucky Can You Get." For if anyone recognizes how fortune has smiled upon her, it is Dorothy Hamill. And as the music continued the people were hypnotized by the fluid, deer-like movements of this girl from Riverside, Conn. In less than a week the disarmingly friendly young princess had captivated audiences and sprinkled her magic upon all who gazed upon her.

And no one minded. They simply oohed and aahed at her elegance and were glad to be her enthralled subjects.

After her whirlwind jaunts around the world, in which she collected an Olympic Gold Medal and a World Figure Skating Championship, Dorothy Hamill has returned to New England for her professional debut. To the consternation of many of her followers, she has signed a pro contract with the Ice Capades and left the aesthetic world of amateur figure skating behind.

But the professional Dorothy Hamill is still the same enchanting athlete who cried when she saw her country's flag raised in honor of her accomplishments. Storybook princesses somehow never lose their original purity. And though Miss Hamill will never again thrill Olympic audiences, she will spread her refreshing innocence all over the land.

After receiving the key to the city of New Haven Tuesday, where she will be performing in the Ice Capades through Sunday, the humble Miss Hamill gratefully, almost tearfully accepted an official proclamation from Gov. Grasso. According to the governor, "Dorothy Hamill is truly a child of our state . . . She has continued to bring hope and encouragement to all young and old who dare to dream dreams and dare to aspire." With that the governor declared Oct. 5-10 as Dorothy Hamill week in Connecticut.

The Olympic star explained her entrance into the pro ranks as an extension of her skating aspirations. She said in the United States young skaters are encouraged as Olympic prospects. Then she smiled, impishly, and joked, "You see, in four years, I'll be considered over the hill."

The magnanimity of this petite, 5' 3" brunette is instantly overwhelming. All of her laurels are secondary to the people who have supported her and believed in her. Reflecting upon her emotional moments on the Olympic pedestal, the blue-eyed skater said, "I can't tell you how I had chills and goose bumps all over. It was an incredible feeling. All the things I'd wished for and all the people who had sacrificed for me – I couldn't believe my dream came true."

Then someone walked up and placed her gold medal around her neck. She looked down at it admiringly, smiled, then shook her head in disbelief. "Oh," she said, "I haven't seen this for a long while." It was as if she'd seen it for the first time ever.

When Dorothy ends her ice skating career she hopes to work with the blind. "I would like to start a program to teach the blind children how to skate," she said sincerely. She revealed how'd she seen a blind boy skate in Wilmington, Del., and was extremely "touched." That's the kind of person she is – filled with total selflessness. You get the idea that the only reason she is skating professionally is so all her fans in America can see her skate first-hand.

Dorothy feels that as a member of the Ice Capades, she is more of an entertainer than a sports figure. She finds performing much harder because she must produce night after night. Her six-hour-a-day practice time has been reduced to one hour. "I can't let down now," she admitted. "I used to have only one major competition a year to worry about and I could let down saying I had another two months to go. But not now."

Her much publicized fall in Pittsburgh was more a result of foreign matter on the ice than nerves. "When you are out there skating after the other acts," she said, "you have to pray you don't step on a feather." Miss Hamill will continue to perform her Olympic routine as long as the physical demands can be met.

Dorothy Hamill's the type of person who plants a song in your heart and a smile on your face when you take her leave. It's a magic that even Snow White would have trouble conveying.

Proposed Football Stadium Is No 'Field of Dreams'

By Ginny Apple The Hartford Courant Sept. 26, 1993

With the euphoria sweeping the Hartford area over the prospect of bringing a National Football League team here, it is hard for well-intentioned sports fans to sort out the clear pattern that has emerged.

It seems that we have taken very seriously the "Field of Dreams" statement – "Build it and they will come" – so much so that we have thrown out reason.

In a state whose major cities – Hartford, New Haven and Bridgeport – are struggling desperately for economic and social survival, is it clear thinking, or illusion, that draws us to the sports dream maker as he tosses a football before us.

Has anyone thought to look at recent events surrounding the concessions the state made to keep the Whalers hockey team in Hartford? Some people questioned the motives of Whalers owner Richard Gordon when he traveled to Minneapolis. Was he seeking a prospective home for his financially bereft team? It is true that Gordon has made his millions and invested millions in Greater Hartford. But was his visit to Minneapolis intended to scare Connecticut into giving him a better deal on his lease, on improvements to the Civic Center and, ultimately, on his bottom line?

When you have lots of money and the ability to get more, contracts become pieces of paper easily tattered. Bill Bidwell broke his lease with the city of St. Louis. Many other owners have done the same.

Is businessman Francis W. Murray's courtship of Connecticut, in effect, smoke-and-mirror theatrics to force a commitment from the city of Boston or the state of Massachusetts?

This is not a new technique. Al Davis convinced the city of Oakland to take his Raiders back, although the deal eventually backfired.

An even more flagrant example involved the San Francisco Giants baseball team. The city of St. Petersburg, Fla., built a major league baseball stadium on the hope and promise that the Giants would relocate there, only to find that the city had been duped by both the team's owners and by major league baseball.

Whence goes that field of dreams?

Dreams come easy when your buddies are wealthy and your toys are major league sports franchises. But what about the dreams of fans? What is in their best interest?

Research has proved the value of sports in uplifting society – in providing vicarious thrills and accomplishments. Who wouldn't welcome football powerhouses such as the Buffalo Bills and Miami Dolphins in our backward?

It is an exciting prospect. Certainly, recent polls show few people oppose the move of the Patriots to Hartford. It doesn't seem to matter that the team has been a loser since its 55-10 shellacking by the Chicago Bears in the 1986 Super Bowl.

When Walter O'Malley skipped town with his beloved Brooklyn Dodgers, moving them to Los Angeles, who lost out? The fans. When Robert Irsay packed up the Baltimore Colts football team and moved it to Indianapolis, who lost out? The fans. When Davis moved his Raiders from Oakland to Los Angeles, who lost out? The fans. When Bidwell uprooted the St. Louis Cardinals football team and moved it to Phoenix, who lost out? The fans.

And that's the rub. No matter what the cost to fans, to traditions, to the economics of a region, the wheelers and dealers of the sports franchise world are programmed to "win" in their negotiations at any cost.

The world of major league franchises is sophisticated, greedy and, ultimately, filled with scant regard for the fan. Murray has made it clear that he anticipates that Hartford fans will be willing to pay the highest price for tickets in the NFL. What a deal.

When Bidwell moved his cardinals to Arizona, he not only raised ticket prices to the highest in the NFL at the time, but he also charged $40,000 each for 60 air-conditioned luxury boxes that, in the minds of local corporations and investors, were lofty temples to their success. (Of course, these "ego boxes," as Howard Cosell calls them, are built in remote spaces that would not even be occupied by cheap seats.) But, they are profitable for owners, and, if they are not sold, as Richard Gordon learned at the Civic Center, they become embarrassing monuments to frivolity.

There's no doubt that the construction of a $252.1 million stadium would created thousands of jobs and generate income for the state service industry. But what happens if, two years after the stadium is built, Murray comes to the state and says he is unable to pay the $5 million annual lease? And if the state does not reduced the lease, he will take his team elsewhere? What will the state do then?

Where does that leave local fans who have pledged their allegiance to this major league team?

Does a city riddled with street violence, cutbacks in its school budget and a growing image problem need a quarter of a billion dollars invested within its borders in a "field of dreams" that might be used only 10 or 12 times a year?

Wouldn't the region be better served if that money were channeled into building a center for industry, or an international trade center to keep pace with the increase economic globalization? Why not use some of the money as economic incentives to entice businesses to Hartford or provide tax relief for small business already here? Wouldn't the people of this area benefit more from better schools, more students' sports teams and greater access to sophisticated education equipment?

Despite the excitement over the prospect of securing a National Football League team for Hartford and despite the promising economic forecasts by consultants, state and city officials and fans alike should take a step back and ask: is this really a good idea?

After all, what makes a city major league? Cleveland has its Browns, Indians and Cavaliers, but do these sports teams make it any more a major league city than its symphony?

Let's not be distracted by high-tech video projections of a beautiful stadium and happy throngs at the gate.

It's clear that Hartford and Connecticut face challenges that the New England Patriots can't solve for them no matter how much we wish they could.

ANN BALDELLI

Ann Baldelli retired in the winter of 2017 as a reporter and editor at The Day, New London. Over a 39-year career there, she wrote and edited thousands of stories on a variety of topics, including breaking news, state and municipal government, politics, personality profiles, lifestyle, business, gaming and entertainment, food and leisure, health and exercise, and general interest. Baldelli covered almost every beat at the newspaper and worked as associate editorial page editor, assistant managing editor for local news, city editor, night city editor, and community editor. She wrote an opinion column at various times over the decades. A resident of Stonington, she is a graduate of St. Michael's College in Vermont.

Don't Forget Life Quality In Reform

By Ann Baldelli The Day New London Sept. 13. 2009

It's been five years since Ray Hocking scratched an itch, brushed his teeth or tied his shoes. Friday was the fifth anniversary of Hocking's freak fall in the kitchen of his Norwich condominium that left him a quadriplegic.

He's paralyzed from the chest down, without use of his arms or legs; dependent on others for virtually every single need. As Americans debate the issue of health care reform and whether this country can do better for its sick and disabled citizens, they should look to Ray Hocking for inspiration to make changes.

For all but four months of the time since he broke his neck, Hocking, now 66, has lived in a small room at Haven Health Center, a Norwich convalescent home. It's not where Hocking belongs, but it's where the career power-company lineman ended up because under rigid Medicaid rules, it's what he can afford and where he is the safest.

Hocking worked 38 years stringing wire and digging ditches before his fall on Sept. 11, 2004. He had "good" insurance, but the catastrophic injury forced him onto Title XIX - Medicaid - the government insurance program for people with limited resources, or in Hocking's case, extraordinary medical bills.

He would still like to go home, and some quadriplegics do, but for the Hockings, it's financially impossible. Medicaid covers a certain level of care, and Sandra Hocking, who continues to work full time as a credit executive at Mohegan Sun, would have to leave her job to care for him and still hire additional help, which she can't afford to do. So her husband lives at Haven Health, and in reality, she does, too.

Evenings after her casino shift ends, Sandra goes "home" to Haven Health Center. In her husband's cramped second-floor room, the couple shares a snack while rehashing the day's news and watching television. Before they turn the lights out at 11 p.m., she brushes his teeth before brushing her own. Then they turn in. She has spent every night with her husband at Haven Health, except for the few times when he's been hospitalized or two short visits she's made to see her grown daughter in Minnesota.

Sandra is there when aides come in at 2 a.m. and again at 5 to turn Ray so he won't develop bedsores. And she's there in the morning to make coffee and feed him breakfast. Then she leaves for the Route 82 condominium that the couple shared, the place where Ray either snapped his neck and fell, or fell and snapped his neck. He's still not sure which happened first. The last thing he remembers is closing the refrigerator door.

She's at the condo just long enough to shower and change her clothes, check her e-mail, and do some laundry before heading off to work. Even on her days off, she spends most of her time at Haven Health, keeping Ray company.

The Hockings have grown to appreciate Haven Health and the care that Ray receives there. But their case is just one of many examples of how health care in this country can be improved.

Nursing home care is expensive - in this state out-of-pocket residents pay $9,000 to $13,000 monthly, depending on where they are and the care they receive. The government insurances negotiate better rates, but it is still expensive.

President Obama has pledged to preserve Medicare and Medicaid, but to eliminate the waste and fraud associated with the programs. And he should. But it's also time to break the cookie-cutter mold of government insurance programs and make them adaptable and flexible.

I believe it would not only be less expensive, but also more humane, to house Ray Hocking in his home, even if Medicaid footed the bill to provide his wife with assistance and the equipment she needs to care for him. And I believe the same would be true for the nation's elderly, many of whom are forced to spend down their life's savings to qualify for convalescent home assistance in their waning days. They would be happier, and perhaps healthier too, if they could stay in their homes with help.

Health care needs to be reformed, and rethinking long-held rules and practices might not just save money, but could improve the quality of living for people like Ray Hocking.

Just Stop All This Counting!

By Ann Baldelli The Day New London June 27, 2010

Someone please tell the 2010 Census people to leave us alone.

Since the official once-every-decade count of every American resident kicked off more than three months ago, census takers have counted my family of four at least three times - not that the enumerators believe that.

Despite filling out the official 2010 Census form and promptly mailing it back in early April, a Census worker found his way to our door a few weeks later and insisted we answer the 10-question survey for him. We complied, begrudgingly.

About a month later the U.S. Census called one night, explaining that it is essential that the agency count every person and that our family needed to enumerated. The Census worker was ready do it right then over the phone.

"We've already been counted," I said. Twice in fact. But the caller refused to believe it. She insisted on counting us again.

Anyone who's been counted at their door or over the phone knows that the enumerators ask their 10 questions in robot-like fashion. Maybe once it is OK, but the second time is a hassle and third time a reason for resentment. Don't skip ahead, don't rush your answers and, by all means, don't try to synthesize the information.

Name. Sex. Age. Date of birth. Race. Household relationships. Do you rent? Do you own? It gets repetitious real fast when you repeat identical answers over and over about spouses and children.

After providing the information for the third time my husband and I agreed to take a stand. We would not be counted again, no matter what. Not that we thought it likely they'd try to count us again.

Alas, they did.

About two weeks ago I answered the phone one evening and what sounded like a young man identified himself as a worker for the 2010 Census who was calling to count our household.

"You've got to be kidding," I said. "No way are you counting us again." He tried to reason, used his charm, and told me several times how important it is that every person is counted.

"Put your supervisor on the phone," I said.

When she got on the line I told her our story. We filled out and mailed in the original form. We answered questions when a Census worker came to our door. We answered them again over the telephone. Please stop counting us, I said.

But it was as if she wasn't even listening, just reading the script. We had to answer the questions, she said.

"Sic the Census police on me," I snarled as I hung up.

The next day I called the 2010 Census and started asking questions of my own. Of course I had to be persistent and listen to myriad recorded messages before I was able to get a live Census worker in Norwich. She was polite. She listened. She took a message. And surprisingly, I got a call back from Maureen, who commiserated with me - even said it was households like ours that helped keep her in a job - but offered no reasonable explanation for why my family was repeatedly being counted, and harassed, by the 2010 Census.

I asked Maureen to have her supervisor call me and several days later was still waiting for that call when - yes, they did it again - the 2010 Census called to count us one more time. My husband had picked up the phone and was beside himself. "My wife writes for a newspaper," he said. "She's going to write a column and say you people are idiots."

Well, I'm not calling anyone an idiot, but I do have my doubts about this 2010 Census now. So I called the Norwich office back again and spoke to Howard this time. He couldn't have been any nicer as he explained that our family's original form may have been lost and that likely triggered the visit and repeated calls. But Howard couldn't tell me why someone somewhere at the U.S. Census doesn't know that the department has repeatedly counted us.

"I guess it's possible that everything possible has gone wrong in your case," he said.

Now that's the first sane thing I've heard from the Census people since this count began.

Confronting The Obstinate Ms. Gretchen

By Ann Baldelli The Day New London June 21, 2009

Litigious Gretchen Chipperini told me to call her lawyer when I spoke to her Thursday and asked about her failure to comply with a town order to demolish her fire-ravaged property at 23 Library St. in Mystic.

And she wasn't friendly about it.

Chipperini has been anything but hospitable to her Library Street neighbors and Groton officials since September 1989 when her family acquired the house that became her 20-year-work-in-progress. So it is no surprise to anyone who has followed the case of the eyesore property that Chipperini is defying the town order issued 11 months ago that she raze the charred remains.

It is unfair that Chipperini has gotten away with such behavior for two decades. A town government with backbone would have ended her antics years ago and leveled her hazardous, fire-ruined property months ago. But once again, Chipperini is thumbing her nose at authority.

In Gretchen's world, the rules apply to other people, but never to Gretchen. And apparently she's right, because she's successfully ignored town orders and neighbors' pleas for 20 years. An examination of the file for 23 Library St. at the town's zoning office suggests Chipperini has two favorite tactics: return official correspondence unopened or have a lawyer respond and blame whatever the issue is on the town or someone else.

It's never Chipperini's fault.

The first indication of trouble at 23 Library St. came in February 1990, five months after the Chipperini family acquired the historic property once considered a treasure in the neighborhood. That first complaint - concerning her choice of exterior improvements - was followed by many, many more: about the paint job, skylights, mountains of earth in the yard, perimeter wall, jack hammering, and allegations of a dangerous, dirty construction site.

Others in the historic district have had their disagreements with buildings officials, but ultimately comply with regulations, but not the defiant Chipperini.

Neighbors still talk about the backhoe she would ride in her small yard - the one rusted on the property now - driving it back and forth as the Noank-Mystic Community Band played on the library lawn across the street. When someone would look at her askew, Chipperini would readily raise her middle finger to them.

And that's what she's figuratively done to the town. Nine years ago more than 500 neighbors signed a petition "demanding relief from this protracted assault on the life of a residential neighborhood," complaining "the intolerable situation" had gone on for a decade. They presented it to then-town council and town manager, and to date, they've gotten no satisfaction.

Other property owners are required to get permits and abide by land-use rules and health and safety codes, but not the owner of 23 Library St. And in fact, she is just the owner, because by all accounts Chipperini has never actually lived in the house, and abandoned work on it several years before the arson fire last July 25.

Four days later the building official issued a demolition order, saying the structure was in imminent danger of collapse. Predictably, Chipperini ignored the order and the town is now trying to force her to comply in court. Meanwhile, neighbors continue to suffer the indignity of having property near Chipperini's.

What compels a person to be so hostile? And what benefit has Chipperini gained in her battle with the Mystic neighbors and town of Groton? Answers defy sensible people.

Chipperini declined to answer my questions last week, but she did comment to a Day reporter the day of the devastating fire.

"It's a big loss for Mystic, and personally it's devastating," she said.

Ms. Chipperini, the big loss for Mystic occurred 20 years ago when you bought the property.

GINA BARRECA

Gina Barreca has been hailed as "smart and funny" by People magazine and "Very, very funny. For a woman," by Dave Barry. Barreca was deemed a "feminist humor maven" by Ms. Magazine. Novelist Wally Lamb said, "Barreca's prose, in equal measures, is hilarious and humane." Her weekly columns for The Hartford Courant are now distributed internationally by the Tribune Co. and her work has appeared in most major publications, including The New York Times, The Independent of London, The Chronicle of Higher Education, Cosmopolitan, and The Harvard Business Review.

Gina, who is a Professor of English at the University of Connecticut and winner of UConn's highest award for excellence in teaching, has recently joined the Mark Twain House & Museum Board of Trustees, is a member of the Friars Club and an honoree of the Connecticut Women's Hall of Fame. She is the author most recently of "If You Lean In, Will Men Just Look Down Your Blouse?" which was an ELLE Reader's Prize selection. Her earlier books include "It's Not That I'm Bitter, Or How I Learned to Stop Worrying About Visible Panty Lines and Conquered the World," the bestselling "They Used to Call Me Snow White But I Drifted: Women's Strategic Use of Humor" and "Babes in Boyland: A Personal History of Coeducation in the Ivy League."

Why I'll Never Give Students 'Trigger Warnings'

By Gina Barreca The Hartford Courant June 9, 2016

The day I'm forced to offer "trigger warnings" before teaching is the day I stop teaching. To insist that I, or any other teacher, warn students that the material in a class might upset them defeats the purpose of education. Colleges and universities must remain institutions that inflame curiosity and, by their very existence, disturb those who enter their gates.

But if trigger warnings become a perfunctory, sanctioned and unopposed knee-jerk reaction — however well-meaning — to precisely the kind of discomfort, dissatisfaction, disruption and disturbance of the peace that is the mission of authentic education, then I'll call it quits. If that day arrives, I'll be done with classrooms and will hold lessons in my house, or in the woods or on the city streets. Education is not designed to reassure; its job is not to soothe but to disturb — otherwise intellect and emotion both remain inert and unmoved. If you protect the unexplored intellectual and psychological landscapes within yourself, you end up with a wilderness.

In his poem "Andrea del Sarto," Victorian poet Robert Browning wrote, "Ah, but a man's reach should exceed his grasp, or else what's a heaven for?" But instead, are we encouraging today's students to insist that everything be modified in order to be in reach? If somebody can't get it, it should be taken off the shelves?

Put it this way: If you're afraid of cats and you're assigned "Winnie-the-Pooh," do you need a Tigger warning?

I believe it's a sign not of fragility but of immaturity to stick your fingers in your ears and say "nyah nyah nyah" if you're hearing something you don't like. If you spend your life putting your fingers across your eyes and looking between them because you worry about something disturbing, you're going to miss most of what's going on.

Like shutting the window to the sound of distant thunder or shutting your eyes to the sight of a beggar on the street, trigger warnings encourage you to interrupt or suppress responses before you encounter any representation, action, idea or emotion you suspect might make you uncomfortable. By doing so, trigger warnings inhibit a reaction to the essential ingredient of any great work of art — or any moment of human connection, for that matter — that might arouse pity, empathy, sympathy or connection.

The New Yorker's May 30 article, "The Big Uneasy," quoted a student from Oberlin who wanted "Antigone" to come with a trigger warning because, he argued, trigger warnings are "like ingredient lists on food." The Oberlin student went on to explain, "People should have the right to know and consent to what they are putting into their minds, just as they have the right to know and consent what they are putting into their bodies."

Greek drama is not Greek yogurt; college professors are not food tasters. Such a comparison reduces university students to the ultimate consumers.

Trigger warnings are the intellectual equivalent of refusing vaccinations: They are misguidedly seen as a way of protecting the young. As my colleague Kristina Dolce argues, the anti-vaccine crowd and the trigger-warning crowd both employ "fear of exposure" rhetoric, believing that exposure leads to contamination. But as Kristina argues, "Vaccines, like great works of art, make one more resilient, not less."

Here's a personal example: My mother died of a miserable illness when I was a kid. Had I spent my life avoiding dying female protagonists, I'd have stayed away from the Bible, Bambi and all the Brontes.

In trying to protect myself, I would have missed out on what I would now call "my life."

You can cry out about what you don't know, but you can't argue against it. Only those who understand something and have experience with it can wrestle with it, grapple with it, and if appropriate, undermine the authority of it. Trigger warnings are a version of a kind of intellectual eugenics. There's something sterile, unproductive, and grossly contorted about the process. Their fiercest advocates are poorly equipped not only because they are dealing with their own intolerance but also because what they're learning to cherish is ignorance.

You can't lead if you don't know what's in front of you or what's behind you. You can't lead if you're afraid to look around.

Conductor's Kindness Eased My Broken Heart

By Gina Barreca The Hartford Courant March 30, 2017

It was the kind of crying nobody should see, especially in a public place. I was on the late afternoon train out of London to Cambridge, heartbroken because my first real relationship was ending. ("I can't do this anymore," the medical student told me as we walked to King's Cross. "When you lived here it was one thing, but this is impossible.")

Taking a seat in the last row of the almost-empty last carriage, I shoved myself as close as possible to the window. I could feel that my face was raw and red from acidic tears and now looking at myself in the train's window, I could see that my eyes were crimson-rimmed with eyelids as white, puffy and thin as the skin on a mushroom.

What I couldn't understand was that it was simply an ordinary Sunday for everybody else in all the towns and villages we were passing. People would be reading the last of the newspapers, doing laundry or washing up after a big meal, but for me the world changed.

I kept my head turned to the window so that nobody could witness my shame and panic, but when the conductor came by to take my ticket and saw my expression, he sat down.

I was 22; he was probably 65, or 50, or maybe just 45. All I knew was that he was clearly a man whose days of crying in public, or even sitting next to girls who cried in public, seemed long past. Efficient, professional, courteous, at first glance you wouldn't have thought he was the type who'd check on an unhappy, bedraggled girl.

But that's precisely what he did. In a way that was not typical for many of the English people who I'd met, he took the seat next to mine and asked, in a straightforward manner as if merely seeking information: "Dear miss, are you quite all right?" I swear it was the word "dear" that got me. I looked up and because of his kindness — although the tears came to my eyes again — for the first time in hours I stopped crying.

Once I started talking, I kept talking. I explained how the most important relationship in my life was unraveling. I told him about how I'd bought a one-way plane ticket to England the year before, expecting never to return to the states because I'd found a boy out of a fairy tale. I told him that I'd learned to stop believing in love after my mother died years ago but that I had believed in it again, and now it was being taken away.

Finally, when I stopped to blow my nose in a tattered piece of tissue, he spoke. "You've got your life in front of you and plenty of time to make it a good one," he said in businesslike manner. "Better to learn what can't be fixed than hold onto useless bits and bobs."Then he rose, accepted my ticket and resumed doing his official job.

In the 38 years since that Sunday afternoon, I have indeed made a good life, although it hasn't always been an easy one. I found true and lasting love, discovered the work I was meant to do and created a community of friends more comforting and wise than I could have imagined when I was a girl.

But there's one thing I wish I could have done, and that's to thank the conductor on that train. His patient, sincere and yet disinterested concern for another human being who was clearly in pain made a irrevocable imprint on my life and changed it for the better.

I felt alone and hopeless before our brief conversation. Afterward, I felt as if the future might not be as miserable as I thought. It didn't take nearly as much as I thought it would to give me hope.

I still owe that man a debt of gratitude. I bet you owe someone that kind of debt too. If it can't be repaid personally, it must be dispersed outward. Every gesture toward someone in pain, lost or who needs help, is a way to pass those thanks along.

Making Sauce, Chasing Chickens Is My Destiny

By Gina Barreca The Hartford Courant August 17, 2016

Destiny: Those parts of your life you can't escape no matter how hard you've worked to avoid them.

I was making tomato sauce the other afternoon just as my Sicilian grandmother taught me: searing the sausage and the chopped meat in separate frying pans while getting the olive oil, garlic, parsley and the oregano ready in other small pots.

In Brooklyn, where I grew up, we always had sauce — or as my family referred to it "gravy" — simmering on a back burner. The original version had been there since 1948. It was stirred constantly by my Aunt Josephina, who had an arm like a longshoreman. Just one. The only time she left that spot was to go to Mass.

The women in my family used no recipes. They used a small handful of salt, fistfuls of fresh basil and olive oil (from somebody who had a connection to the good stuff) that they measured in a cup. A real cup, not a measuring cup. That's how we learned to cook. The only way I can teach somebody how to replicate a dish is by having them watch me. I can't explain it.

For Italians, cooking is more choreography than culinary.

My Sicilian family had the traditional kitchen arrangement: The upstairs kitchen was immaculate, perfectly equipped and too good for cooking.

No meal was prepared in that kitchen. The only people who would have been allowed to eat there would have been the people who could have sat in the living room that nobody ever used. That room had three pieces of matching brocade furniture covered in industrial grade vinyl and the lampshades still had the original cellophane protecting them.

I once asked my grandmother if it was safe to keep cellophane so close to a light bulb. She grabbed me by the ear. "You turned the light on in the good living room?" I realized we were in no danger from anything incendiary: Nobody would dare even switch on a light.

So, now, picture me in my Connecticut kitchen, which is as different from the basement kitchen as it is possible to be. It's airy, big, and looks directly into our nice backyard.

Yet there are echoes of my childhood: the hiss of the meat, the garlic on the chopping board, the scent of basil on my fingers before I drop it in the pot. I'm cooking because we have a big group of friends coming over for dinner.

It's quiet and I'm happy.

My husband, not Italian, but originally from New Jersey, so it's almost the same thing, has gone to buy wine to accompany the meal.

Then, I see the chickens.

Our new neighbors' chickens decided, like characters out of an old war movie, to make a break for it. A dozen of them scramble over the stone wall and invade our yard. They're eating birdseed and scratching up the mulch.

Suddenly, the ancient strands of my DNA awaken. I run outside, slamming the screen door behind me, and scream, "Get outta my yard, you lousy birds!"

I chase them around the yard while flapping my apron as if brandishing a weapon. The graying bun at the top of my head is coming loose, with strands of hair covering my face. I look like a cartoon of peasant life.

Everything I'd ever done in my life I'd done precisely to avoid this moment. I got my Ph.D., wrote a bunch of books and lectured around the world about women's leadership, and yet here I am, running after livestock and cursing. I am, in other words, doing exactly what my ancestors in Castelbuono did to protect their hovel from the neighbor's goats.

Without my realizing it, Michael had returned home and was witnessing this scene. When I saw him standing on the deck, I made a futile attempt to collect myself by tucking some strands of hair back into the bun. In a cheerful, slow voice containing a small tinge of horror, he asked, "And exactly what are you doing?"

I replied, "I'm finally becoming the woman I've been meant to be. It's destiny."

Michael did not look reassured. Still, we ate well that night. And no, we did not have chicken.

MARY ELIZABETH BARRETT

Mary Elizabeth "Betty" Barrett was one of those rare exceptions at The Courant in those days, a woman who not only had a secure writing job as the paper's women's editor but acted as though she owned the place. And she did, along with other family members and co-workers who took advantage of the opportunities to buy Courant stock, wrote Joe Nunes, retired Courant newsman and unofficial historian for the paper. Her brother, longtime personnel director Thomas R. Barrett -- who would rise to Courant treasurer, vice president and director -- for years was the go-to person for employees looking to buy shares as they became available. Betty Barrett started at The Courant in 1935 and became for many years a one-woman show in producing the so-called society pages. During her 42-year era, she became a pioneer in helping the "society pages" and "World of Women" evolve into a modern lifestyle section. She introduced innovations in first-person writing on topics that were usually kept private.

She was a lifelong Hartford area resident, a graduate of Weaver High School and attended The College of St. Elizabeth, Convent Station, NJ. She began as a part-time research assistant in the news library. She was active as a volunteer in numerous organizations including St. Thomas the Apostle Women's Club, The Noah Webster House, The Women's Committee of the Wadsworth Atheneum, The Auxiliary of The Hartford Symphony, Friends of Merciknoll, St. Agnes Home. She retired in February 1978 and died at 86 in 2000.

Wigs Go To Her Head

By Betty Barrett Women's Editor The Hartford Courant, Dec. 6, 1964

When you look like this – you just flip your wig.

You can keep the world in complete turmoil. "Doubting Thomases end up with your head of hair in their hands when they grab your silver tresses (they just can't seem to resist)."

Gentlemen do prefer blondes. They love to run their hands through blonde hair. And if you're a woman's editor, they do it.

Conclusions reached: Wig-wearers get plenty of attention. I got so much that I hardly found time to get any work done. And then you get into a mood that is awaiting the attention. It's quite a shock passing the mirror seeing a blue-eyed blonde that looks like you staring back.

Just the idea, when your own hair is drooping from its roots, that there is a wig, all carefully coiffured, all fitted to your own little head, ready to be whisked on, makes one feel so secure and sophisticated. You do a bit of pondering on what the mood is. Is it the suave, elegant look of ageless beauty in silver, or the delectable, gorgeous blonde, giddy and youthful.

It's wash and wear. You wash it like fine lingerie with a mild detergent. It dries in minutes, never loses its curl. It's simple to brush back into the original style, or even into a new style. It weighs two ounces. The molded cap expands to fit any head securely. Completely waterproof, the style does not wilt in humid, damp climate nor even in the rain. (I wore it on a rainy day to protect my own new hairdo the other day!)

The "brain-child" is the invention of engineer Bruce Reid, son of Rose Marie Reid, famous bathing suit designer, who with partner Garry Meredith and Union Carbide, developed this D-40 fibre in "hair" that behaves better than hair and feels like coarse hair sprayed. It can be rolled into a ball and tucked into a case and with a bit of brushing slipped onto your head. Permanently curly, it can be combed smooth without teasing, fingered into waves, or shaped into curls in a few minutes with hair clips.

Trained specialists are on hand to style these durable wigs of chignons to the individual.

Another wig is real hair. Soft, lovely, silken, golden blonde. All women dream about being blondes. And there a few that are born that way, and quite a few more that aren't. Then there are a few that like to be blondes intermittently (like me). So there's the wig.

Real hair wigs come in all prices. Like they look, blondes are more expensive. Silvery tones are just as expensive, too. Darker hair is easier to come by, and the prices are lower. Real hair wigs react to the outside world much the same as your own head of hair. The hairdo lasts quite a bit longer (about three months) for it doesn't get the hard wear of sleeping on it. Most probably you wouldn't dash out in the rain with it on. If you're clever you can set and style it yourself. It does need to be dry cleaned occasionally. There are multiple styles to choose from and shades galore. Just be sure when you decide on one that it really blends with your skin tones and doesn't look "wiggy." A trained specialist will guide you.

Ohh, She's Driving Her Pipe Around The Block

By Betty Barrett Woman's Editor The Hartford Courant Feb. 27, 1964

I've quit smoking. I really have. It may not look it, but I really don't smoke a pipe, or cigars, or cigarettes. I do have to admit, I've tried all three.

The latest, of course, is the pipe as you can see. I had to try it in as much as it arrived as a present from "The Peck Boys," the Messrs. Peck of Peck and Peck, New York. It's a ladies pipe…for daytime and Tweeds.

I'll have to initiate you into the ritual. You may not realize it, but the boys really go through great rigmarole to smoke a pipe.

I called in a veteran pipe smoker, the chief photographer, Philip Acquaviva, to find out how to pack in the tobacco. You don't just pack in the tobacco and smoke away.

First of all, you have to "break in " your pipe. You make up a syrup of water and sugar…or you may use honey or maple syrup…(and a bit of spit, of which I rebelled)…and you rub it into the bowl. You rub and rub and rub and rub. And when you've rubbed enough, you fill the bowl half full of tobacco, get into your car, light your pipe and go for a drive...with the pipe smoking and blowing in the breeze...

Then, and only then are you ready for your first puff. Naturally, I had to reload...restuff the bowl. The tobacco was rather sweet smelling. I carefully packed the tobacco in. Then came the lighting. I just can't decide whether I was smoking a pipe full of tobacco or just matches. You have to keep lighting, and lighting and lighting. The bowl gets pretty hot too.

Then the swarms arrived...all the pipe smokers in The Courant...all eager for me to try his special brand. I tried them all. To tell the truth, at the end of the day, I was completely warn out from lighting and puffing and trying to hold the pipe between my teeth...trying to find a comfortable spot for the pipe in the ashtray so it wouldn't burn up the copy on the desk.

Then, in a complete rush to get out, I stashed the pipe and tobacco in my pocketbook. That's fatal to do unless you're sure the bowl has cooled off. If you think you carry hot money around anyway, well I've got news for you. What little I have nearly burned up. The designers will have to add a few asbestos pockets to your skirt, maybe? Possibly the outer pocket of your bag?

Later, looking for my pen, I was completely flabbergasted...at the browned papers in my bag...tobacco spilled all over the bottom...and let me warn you, fellow...I guess I must mean lady pipe-smokers. The stem of your pipe looks absolutely ghastly with dried-up lipstick edging it.

No, really, I don't smoke a thing...and strangely enough, I don't even miss it...and I don't think I have turned into one of those righteous reformers, have I?

Social Tradition Retired By Bachelors

By Betty Barrett The Hartford Courant Dec. 14, 1958

This year of 1958 marks the ending of an era, socially in Hartford. The Bachelors of Hartford didn't hold their Thanksgiving frolic! For tradition has it, and it really dates back for more years than I care to mention – the

Bachelors of Hartford must launch the holiday social season!

Thanksgiving Eve was the night of rollicking smart humor all entwined with gay dancing, for these scintillating young men staged the most fascinating costumed affairs of the year! The themes were always unique, and the guests, in homage to such originality, arrived bedecked in dishabille, suited to the event.

There were plenty of rocky roads in the path of the robust young Bachelors. For by Thanksgiving Day they were looked upon with askance by their families, as they lounged in bed while the appetizing aroma of the turkey wafted through the house! In fact there was many a young wife of a benedict-bachelor member, who must hie herself up early after a late-late evening of fun, to care for that young baby or better, still get the turkey into the oven for she was staging the family Thanksgiving for the first time! In fact, the repercussions became so great that several years ago, the Bachelors transferred their gay-gay affair to Saturday evening following Thanksgiving (receiving their parental blessing as well as those of these same little hausfraus).

Too, for all these years we have borne with the chap who was designated to handle the publicity. It was natural that he came in with his fabulous ideas and with his intriguing invitations after the Sunday deadline. We trusted him gently, impressed, of course, by the ingenuity of these Bachelors.

We were proud of them when they branched out in the springtime with a picnic affair to supplement the year's social activities.

But this year it just isn't the same socially in Hartford without Our Bachelors of Hartford entertaining at their festive costumed ball at Thanksgiving Time, launching the tremendous series of holiday parties.

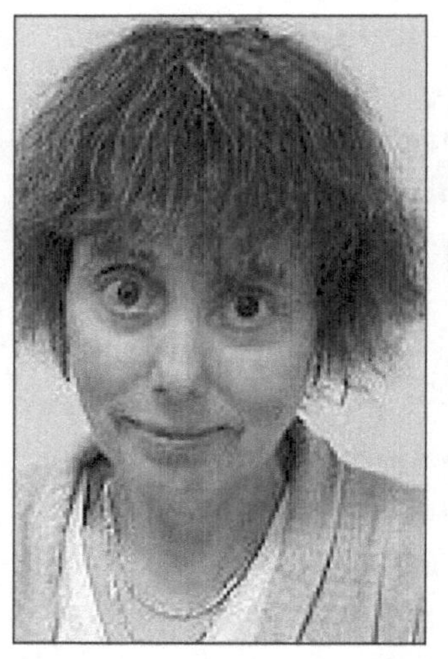

LYNN UHLFELDER BERMAN

Lynn Uhlfelder Berman was among the first women sports editor in the country, appointed to the position by Greenwich Time Editor Joseph Pisani. She graduated from the University of Missouri School of Journalism in 1981. Lynn is a diehard New York Mets and Jets fan, though she does remember listening to Yankees games with her father in the mid-1960s. After leaving the Greenwich Time, she worked for The New York Times News Service from 1990-1998, launching TimeFax, a summary of The New York Times in Japan, major resorts, cruise ships and the U.S. Navy and Army. Lynn spent nearly 20 years as Media Relations Manager at YAI, a not-for-profit serving people with intellectual and developmental disabilities (I/DD) securing placements in major outlets, including The New York Times, The Associated Press, The New York Daily News and Parents Magazine. She served as Public Relations Chair for the American Network of Community Options and Resources. She is working as a media consultant with AHRC New York City, the largest agency serving children and adults with I/DD.

---

6 Fouls, 4 Strikes, 5 Downs

By Lynn Uhlfelder Berman Greenwich Time Aug. 13, 1981

Sometimes I just don't understand why we bother making rules.

Sure there are those who believe rules are made to be broken. I'm not among them, but it seems as if this philosophy has made its way into the NCAA.

In walks the Big East Conference with its request to the NCAA to allow players to accumulate six fouls, rather than five, before they are forced to leave a basketball game.

What's the point? The five-foul rule has been used for years. Why fix it if it isn't broken? The college game is already too physical. So physical, in fact, that when it gets to overtime in the NCAA tournament, officials let the teams play the game. So what if players slap around each other while battling for a rebound? What's a little punch when there are less than 10 seconds to go?

But hey, if that's the way we're going to play the game, why stop with college basketball?

I can see it now, baseball decides it wants to switch to a four-out rule. Instead of three-plus hour games, we could look forward to more five-hour thrillers like last Sunday's Mets marathon. Just imagine one of those innings where no one hits into the fourth out – Howard Johnson could come up to bat two times at least. After all, baseball fans love to see batters hit, so let's cater the game to the batter.

And just imagine a grand slam play, opposed to the triple play. That's right. Brown to Tinker to Evers to Chance. Now that's really what the fans want to see.

Better yet, why not make four strikes a strikeout? Let the count go to 3-3 and then see what happens.

This six-foul rule makes about as much sense as allowing five downs in football. Just think of the scores we could see if we made the switch from four downs. I can hear it now, "it's fifth down and one." Or what about having five chances to score on a goal-line stand?

College basketball coaches such as Providence's Rick Barnes claim the six-foul rule will allow more aggressive teams to continue that style of play. "With our style of play, I obviously like that," Barnes said.

Of course he's going to like it.

Some say the rule will allow so-called stars to stay in the game longer. I don't buy that.

College basketball should not be catering to superstars who commit more than five fouls. Sure, the fans come to watch certain players. But hey, if the stars foul out, that's life. It's not as if there are no other players sitting on the bench.

Boston College coach Jim O'Brien voted against the proposal.

It's just another case of the rich getting richer," he said earlier this week. "The lesser teams work hard trying to get the other team's big men out of the game and now this just increases the better team's chances."

This proposed rule is not for the betterment of college basketball. It's merely a move to help a few hefty teams keep their big men in the game longer, which should lead to more wins, which in turn leads to more fans coming to games, which means more money for the schools and so on and so forth. Eventually, it means a better possibility of reaching the pot of gold at the Final Four. And everyone knows what that means – more money for the school and conference.

But the proposal doesn't stop there. The NCAA, in its wisdom, has decided to give individual conferences the option to adopt the rule. If you're going to change a rule, why not apply it to everyone? No, the NCAA insists the rule would apply to only conference games and the Big East tournament. Ah yes, it could be used in non-conference games involving Big East teams, provided both coaches agree to use it. The rule, however, would not apply to the NCAA tournament.

There's a method, if you want to call it that, to the NCAA's madness. Officials want to test the waters. But why not just let all the conferences try it and then get a national reading on this rule? Or, better yet, just let the five-foul-you're-out rule stand.

Can't you see players on a Big East team prepare for a six-foul game, then they go to a non-conference game, which uses five fouls, before heading into the conference tournament, six fouls. If by chance the team reaches the NCAA tournament, it's back to five fouls. I'm getting confused just thinking about it.

While we're at it, why not make boxing rounds four minutes? After all, we all want to see more blood, right? Then we could implement the Tyson Clause, which would require all Mike Tyson's fights to have 30-second rounds. That way fans could get more for their money. I bet they'd see at least two or three rounds.

Makes as much sense as allowing a six-foul rule.

Just One Look Is All It Took

By Lynn Uhlfelder Berman Greenwich Time Jan. 31, 1988

Nancy Leamy could tell by the eyes.

Karen Burkhardt could tell by the perseverance.

Does she have what it takes to be an Olympic figure skater?

Absolutely.

For those of us who have worked with and watched Riverside figure skater Gillian Wachsman over the years, her trip to the upcoming Olympic Winter Games in Calgary comes as little surprise. The ability was always there.

"She was the one who I couldn't pull off the ice," said Burkhardt, an ice skating instructor who worked with Wachsman between the ages of 10 and 11.

"The Zambino would come to clear off the ice and she just didn't want to come off. It was awful. I'd tell her she'd be able to get back on the ice after clearing (which wasn't always the case) and her mother would say, 'Come on I'll get you a treat.' She was definitely a skating lover."

That's obvious to anyone who has watched Wachsman and her partner, Todd Waggoner, compete in pairs competition. The duo charmed a crowd of nearly 900 with their twists, turns and jumps last week at Dorothy Hamill Skating Rink.

Leamy, head professional at the rink and the Greenwich Skating School, worked with Wachsman in the Greenwich Skating School for about a year. The young Riverside resident was about 9-years-old.

"She was a very quiet, very hard working little girl," Leamy said. "She didn't say too much."

But Leamy could tell that Wachsman was not your average pupil.

"You could tell by her eyes," Leamy said. "Whenever a good skater came on ice, she would watch very carefully."

For Wachsman it all started when her family took a vacation to Lake Placid when she was five. She saw an ice dance competition and knew that this was something for her.

Gillian described her feelings back in July of 1986.

"It was just a magnetism," she said. "I wanted to do that. I begged for four years and then they let me start skating when I was nine."

Skating instructors are always on the lookout for potential Olympians. And once they find them, the skater and his or her family must be prepared to make the commitment.

"There are no signs," Leamy said. "You really can't tell until they're 12 or 13 when the bones set."

Once a young skater has been pinpointed, that's when the fun begins.

"There are a lot of sacrifices," Burkhardt said. The skater must be prepared to endure endless hours of early-morning training.

"There are no Friday nights out and no sleepovers."

Under Burkhardt, Wachsman showed the drive required to become a champion.

"She was a very aggressive and tenacious skater," Burkhardt recalled. "She had a lot of spunk. She'd never quit."

Wachsman was not too fond of doing school figures – figure eights and other figures used to qualify for singles' competition. After passing her second and third figure school test, Wachsman realized pairs was the perfect place for her.

That's when she headed to Wisconsin to train with Mark Militano.

"Very few youngsters get involved in pairs at that age," Burkhardt said. "There's a lot of risk involved. The kids have to be real daredevils the way they're flipped over and thrown around on the ice.

"It was unusual but she had an eye for it."

Wachsman perfected her singles' training, working on jumps and spins, and developed her strength for the pairs competition.

Waggoner and Wachsman both have experience in singles and that can only help them at the Olympics.

"They've competed alone out on ice in front of an audience," Burkhardt said. "That helps when performing in pairs. They know how to relax and are having fun.

"If you're not enjoying what you're doing, you shouldn't be performing."

GA Coach Speaks Players' Language

By Lynn Uhlfelder Berman Greenwich Time Jan. 17, 1987

Greenwich Academy coach Angela Tammaro was talking to her basketball team about defense during halftime the other day.

Judging by her remarks, she may as well have been talking to her field hockey or lacrosse teams. After all, most of her basketball players play those sports.

"You've got to push them out to the sidelines, like in lacrosse,"Tammaro told her team during halftime Tuesday in GA's game against New York School for the Deaf.

Force them to take the outside shot. Close down the middle. The principles apply to all three sports.

The academy took the floor and proceeded to hold NYSD to seven points in the third quarter and eight in the final stanza. GA went on to win, 43-32.

Lacrosse and field hockey, as Tammaro knows, are her players' language. That's understandable, judging by the success those squads have enjoyed in the Fairchester Athletic Association in recent years.

Just look at the starting five for the basketball team – Katy Finch, Suzanne Rand, Katie Thurlow, Meredith McLean and Georgette Summers – also play lacrosse and field hockey.

Tammaro, who claims she is one of the few coaches "crazy enough to coach three sports," said she uses the similarities in sports to explain concepts.

"In teaching lacrosse, we use basketball," Tammaro said. "Lacrosse is just a bigger field. You can still run certain types of plays."

The cutting patterns in basketball are similar to those used in lacrosse, she said. Both sports require players to cut through zones and man-to-man coverage. The same principles are used to break down those zones.

"Some of the learning is transferable," Tammaro said. "All three sports make them aware of space and being able to run without the ball."

Basketball has never been as popular as field hockey or lacrosse at

Greenwich Academy. While the other sports offer a jayvee, varsity and third team, the basketball program only has a varsity and jayvee squad.

"Basketball is not a favorite sport here; some girls find it much too physical. It's not that they are faint-hearted, it's just that some kids don't like that much contact."

Cathy Roberts is the only basketball player from GA to continue the sport in college. She is the starting center at Princeton University.

"Others over the years have been capable of it, but they choose not to play," Tammaro said, referring to Phyl Fogarty, who played varsity field hockey this fall at Princeton University, and Sandra Lewis, who plays field hockey and lacrosse at the University of Richmond.

Then look at the number of graduates who have passed through Tammaro's field hockey and lacrosse teams and decided to continue in college.

At Princeton, Phyl Fogarty, Liz Fogarty and Emily Wilson all play field hockey; Yvonne Dobblemann plays hockey at Dickinson College in Pennsylvania. Suzanne Sammis is playing at the University of Vermont, while Kathy O'Domirok is the starting goalie at Smith College.

Roberts plays lacrosse at Princeton; Beth Pegg plays the sport at Harvard University, while Hilary Longstreth plays for University of Pennsylvania squad.

The list goes on. Those were the players Tammaro could come up with off the top of her head.

Tommaro said the school's basketball program is doing quite well for a community which doesn't emphasize the sport.

"I don't think there's a kid that touches a basketball in our community from the end of basketball season until the beginning of the season," she said. "They're not just sitting around. They're doing other things."

JUDITH WELD BROWN

Judith Weld Brown was editor and publisher of the New Britain Herald, a newspaper held by her family for more than a century. An employee at the newspaper since 1951, Brown was named editor of the Herald in 1969, succeeding her mother, Agnes Vance Weld. In 1975 she was named publisher, following the death of her father, Gardner C. Weld. The newspaper had been owned by Brown's family since 1880. The New Britain Chamber of Commerce honored her in 1990 with its Distinguished Community Service Award. In 1982, she was named Woman of the Year by the New Britain Business and Professional Women's Club. Brown served on the nominating committee for the Pulitzer Prizes seven times. She was the recipient of the Yankee Quill Award in 1979 by the New England chapter of the Society of Professional Journalists. The award is given annually to journalists for outstanding contributions to the advancement of the profession. Brown was elected to the board of directors for the American Society of Newspaper Editors in 1978, the first woman to be elected. She was founder of the New England Family Newspaper Conference. A member of The Associated Press board of directors since 1994, she was the first woman president of the New England Society of Newspaper Editors, which, after her death in 2001, established the Judith Brown Spirit of Journalism Award given to a New England woman journalist annually. As a reporter, Brown considered her most important story the New Britain museum's purchase of four Thomas Hart Benton murals in 1953. She also regularly reviewed the city's symphony orchestra performances, usually signed with her initials J.V.W.B. Among her numerous community ties, she was a director of the New Britain Chamber of Commerce, New Britain General Hospital and the New Britain Museum of American Art. She sold the newspaper to the Journal Register Co. in 1995. Brown was a graduate of Mount Holyoke College, past president and fellow of the Rotary Club of New Britain and a trustee of the Moreland Hill School.

Benny Goodman Delights Full House

Herald Review Dec. 17, 1979

It was nostalgia time for the 40 and over crowd, which even included some who seldom go to symphony concerts.

The occasion was the appearance of Benny Goodman with the New Britain Symphony Orchestra under the direction of Jerome Laszloffy. The famed clarinetist drew a packed house at New Britain High School auditorium yesterday afternoon for the season's second concert.

Tone and total mastery of his instrument are still main ingredients of Goodman's art, whether performing Von Weber's Concertino for Clarinet and Orchestra with the backing of the full orchestra, or the Rodgers and Hart favorite "Bewitched, Bothered and Bewildered" as a solo encore.

In the Weber, Goodman's clarinet glided like a pure and persuasive flash of light through the texture of the work. He accomplished the more melodic passages with warmth and achieved the allegro section with fluidity. He appeared perfectly at home with the work, and performed it with a jauntiness and ease that helped to keep it bright and lovely.

It was the familiar jazz songs, however, that Goodman's expert musicianship and sophistication with the clarinet became most apparent and endearing. This was also tremendously appealing to those who remember Benny Goodman as a now legendary symbol for the Big Band era. As Goodman, backed by the orchestra, went from the haunting "Here Comes that Rainy Day" to "Honeysuckle Rose," the creativity and totality of his playing were eloquent, indeed.

Of course, at times, the orchestra just didn't move fast enough for the jazz band conductor in Goodman, so he tried to hurry the musicians along with a few encouraging waves of the hand to the obvious enjoyment of the audience.

What he played, the familiar and the well-loved gracefulness with which he played, his association with great musicians and musicianship of the past, all contributed to the warmth which greeted Benny Goodman's performance yesterday and generated the standing ovation which was accorded him.

Conductor Laszloffy wisely chose short selections for the other works on the program, selecting Two Conzoni by Gabrieli, with a orchestra transcription by J. Laszloffy; Gluck's Dance of the Furies and Dance of the Blessed Spirits from Orpheus and Eurydice; Bach's Toccata and Fugue in D minor, orchestra transcription by Leopold Stoskowski; and Scherzo Capriccioso by Dvorak.

The afternoon got off to a dramatic beginning with the Gabrieli, which, with its antiphonal work between the brass choirs, produced some deep, bronze, tonal depths. As performed by the orchestra, the work was like a Renaissance painting, heavy with chiaroscuro and rich in resonance. The Gluck performance was characterized by some very lovely and delicate flute work, while the ethereal elements of the Spirits were well emphasized by strings.

Also highly dramatic and seeming appropriate to the Christmas season, the Toccata was full of ringing passages, brightened by brasses and the classical Bach harmonies. The Dvorak, the longest work played by the orchestra, was full of lively melodies and bright, spritely passages, well articulated by the orchestra.

Conductor Laszloffy led the New Britain Symphony Orchestra through the afternoon performance with authority and precision, achieving some fine depth from all sections. The addition of Benny Goodman as guest artist added another completely different dimension to the program, but all elements complemented each other splendidly, making a very pleasant afternoon for symphony goers.

J.V.W.B

Symphony Offers A Double-bass Delight

By Judith Brown Herald Editor Nov. 3, 1998

The New Britain Symphony launched its 50th anniversary season Sunday with a concert that had its large audience cheering the performance of guest artist Gary Karr mid-way through the afternoon at Welte Hall.

A dapper, lively individual who obviously considers his Double Bass his best friend, Karr, in addition to being a world-renown soloist and teacher on the instrument, could well be called a Victor Borge of stringed instruments, as he proved in his entertaining encores. Whether playing or taking a moment's rest with his free hand patting the double bass, Karr moved in rhythm to the music, obviously enjoying every aspect and conveying to audience members by body language as well as performance that they should find delight in it as well.

Karr's scheduled works with the orchestra began with a haunting rendition of Rachmaninoff's "Vocalise," in which the lovely melody line was smoothly and elegantly expressed by Karr's playing. The Grieg Concerto for Double Bass in A Minor provided an opportunity for the soloist to show off the versatility of his instrument, as well as the glorious tonalities he could evoke from the depths. These ranged from bronze sounds to lithe in the first movement, while Karr's superb technique was apparent in his solo section, as well as throughout the whole work. Under the baton of Dr. Jerome Laszloffy, the orchestra supported Karr's performance, never overwhelming but always enriching it.

Karr pointed out that when Florence Henderson introduced him to a television audience as playing the Paganini Fantasy Variations, which concluded the formal part of his presentation Sunday, she remarked that the amazing thing about him was that "he did it all on his G-string!" Although the piece was originally written for the violin, Karr soon made it the property of the double bass, emphasizing the sometimes stately, sometimes seductive work with style, grace and good humor.

He received a standing ovation, as much for the joyousness he shared in performing as for the impeccable performance itself.

With encores, Karr proved himself as charming as his music. Inviting concertmaster Sefan Tieszen to join him (without his bow), the two plucked their way through a delighted pizzicato by Paul Nero. He then moved to the celli where he pointed out that it was indeed unusual to have a cellist play second fiddle to a double bass, then handed over a melody by Rossini and played accompaniment himself. Then out of the symphony's double bass section came Joe Messina to help Karr in a scherzo by an "unpronounceable Dutchman." It was all great fun.

After intermission, Dr. Laszloffy led the orchestra adroitly and passionately through Tchaikovsky's Symphony No. 6 in B Minor, Opus 74. (Pathetique) the composer's final symphony work, ending in this instance not with a "whimper" but "with a bang."The emotions or themes which color this work play through the whole gamut of human experience, varying from sad and gloomy, to one of the most romantic melodies in a symphonic work, and including intimations of death and destiny. Expressing these moods, the orchestra performed with good attention to tonal colors, the opening bassoon solo played with sweet melancholy, setting one of he moods. The strings played with sweeping openness throughout, sometimes with a cheery, playful touch, while the woodwinds also performed with clarity. It was a handsome performance, with the orchestra under Dr. Laszloffy's direction playing with a sense of drama, excitement and intensity.

The place that the New Britain Symphony has held in New Britain's cultural heart is well deserved and should be regarded with pride by residents here. Its conductor, its musicians, and the guest soloists it attracts, as well as the dedication of the members of the Symphony Society, should all be applauded for their parts in the growth and stature of this cultural jewel as it celebrates 50 years.

SUSAN CAMPBELL

Susan Campbell teaches courses in journalism and mass communication at the University of New Haven. She is excited to introduce the next generation of serious journalists to an ever-changing and never-dull field. She is a columnist for The Hartford Courant, and the website, Connecticut Health Investigative Team, and an award-winning author of "Dating Jesus: Fundamentalism, Feminism, and the American Girl," and the biography, "Tempest-Tossed: The Spirit of Isabella Beecher Hooker." She was born in Kentucky and raised in southwest Missouri. For more than a quarter-century, she was a staff columnist at the Hartford Courant, where her work has been recognized by the National Women's Political Caucus, New England Associated Press News Executives Association, the Society for Professional Journalists, the American Association of Sunday and Feature Editors, the National Society of Newspaper Columnists, and the Sunday Magazine Editors Association. Her column about the shootings at lottery headquarters in March 1998 was part of The Courant's Pulitzer Prize-winning coverage. The mother of two adult sons, and the grandmother of seven, she has a bachelor's degree from University of Maryland, and a master's degree from Hartford Seminary.

After #MeToo, We Must Help With Pain

By Susan Campbell The Hartford Courant Feb. 4, 2018

We are at the cusp of a revolution, and we need to get ready.

An army of men and women is coming forward to speak publicly about the most personal of pain in the #MeToo movement. They are risking everything, but still they type, talk, tweet out acres of collective pain.

Some of the stories are decades old. All are difficult to hear.

We haven't yet talked about what happens next. As people come forward to talk about sexual misconduct, therapy may be their next step. It is what survivors do. They uncover the pain, and then they seek to understand it.

Recently, Christine Andersen added up the years she's been in therapy: 17, with something like 15 different people, including a Freudian who injected her with truth serum. (That didn't help.)

She hasn't added up the weight of the books she's read, or the dollars she spent to work her way through a horrific, 8-year bout of childhood sexual abuse that started when she was 31/2.

Her perpetrators were a father and his daughter known to her family where she grew up in New Jersey. She doesn't remember everything that happened, and maybe she never will. Though she held down a job, and raised two children, she wonders, sometimes, if she will ever be 100 percent. She tries not to think about what her life would have been, without the abuse.

(That's a losing game, as is asking who you would be if you had different parents. That's how deeply ingrained is childhood sexual abuse. You fold it in to your bones and your blood and your teeth and your soul.)

It took Andersen years to start to get the picture of what happened to her, and she's still building the picture. She waited until her son and daughter were grown before she told them. She created years of art, which she later burned. As she sought therapy, she too often found indifference, or a lack of understanding as to how long healing might take.

In an attempt to turn those bullets into butterflies, in 2015, Andersen and clinical psychologist Leslie Matlen established a fund with the UConn Foundation to provide training for doctoral students in the treatment of clients who have experienced trauma. Since then, the fund has reached about 54 therapists, said Marianne Barton, clinical director of the school's department of psychological sciences' psychological services clinic. Eight of those students recently attended a training this week on urban trauma, thanks to the fund.

The movement will need those therapists. Back in October, according to CBS, the #MeToo movement had grown to 85 countries and 1.7 million tweets. Started in 2006 by civil rights activist Tarana Burke, the movement went viral when the actress Alyssa Milano suggested everyone who had been sexually harassed, assaulted or abused use the hashtag on Twitter.

And so, in real time, as men and women are coming forward with their painful stories, titans of media, industry, entertainment have stepped down.

And now what? Well, one would hope the perpetrators will be brought to court, but equally important is appropriate therapy for the victims. And the field of mental health counseling isn't necessarily ready for everyone who has come forward.

Matlen has been in the field for years, during which she said she has encountered "institutional amnesia," or a "general unwillingness to acknowledge the validity, prevalence and impact of mental and physical abuse in the histories of patients." She was an elementary school teacher in New Haven, and a marriage and family counselor in San Francisco, and "It is only fairly recently that the psychological community is waking up to the psychological impact of trauma and trying to address it," she said.

Studies from the 1980s said that the incidence of childhood physical and sexual abuse is higher than originally thought, and it's is extremely high among people who seek treatment, said Barton.

"The #MeToo movement suggests to me that we are only learning about the frequency of these experiences," said Barton. "We know that most trauma victims, especially victims of sexual assault, do not seek treatment."

That most likely will change, the more we talk about these crimes in public. But there needs to be credible, well-trained therapists waiting to do the painful work of healing, along with them.

There Is A War On Spirit Of Christmas

By Susan Campbell The Hartford Courant Dec. 8, 2017

President Donald J. Trump recently told a Missouri crowd, "I told you that we would be saying 'Merry Christmas' again, right?" as if we'd stopped, as if that was something novel.

In the absence of Bill O'Reilly, fake general in the fake War on Christmas, we are reduced to having yuletide's ramparts guarded by Trump and fake Lt. Jim Bakker, who last month claimed that saying "Merry Christmas" had been outlawed, though his claim was light on details.

Can one actually outlaw "Merry Christmas?"

No matter. We who cling to the cross have reached a sad point when we rely on the Trump, O'Reilly, and Bakker, each one a bigger theological lightweight than the last, to defend Christendom's holy day.

In fact, the real War on Christmas started centuries ago, and for a while, Connecticut was ground zero, and the charge was lead by the Rev. Lyman Beecher.

Now there was a champion in the War on Christmas — though he fought for the other side.

Beecher was an 18th century Calvinist preacher who thought — as did so many of his contemporaries — the devil literally walked the earth, and that Christmas was from the devil — or Rome, which by his way of thinking was the exact same thing.

(Don't know what is a Calvinist? A Calvinist will stand at the top of the stairs, throw him or herself down, pick him or herself up, and say, "Phew, glad that's over.")

(Only another Calvinist can tell that joke.)

Beecher more or less launched his public career in the hills of Litchfield. The reverend, who is buried in New Haven, could hold a crowd enthralled for hours. He preached until he was wrung out, and once took a year off to plow a field, having spent every last ounce of energy from the pulpit. His antipathy toward Christmas was not weird for his time. Many Protestants looked askance at Christmas as a papal holiday to be avoided. If they celebrated at all, it was with a piece of candy solemnly handed to the nearest child on Christmas morning. No tree. No lights. No carols.

For all his seeming severity, Beecher raised an incredible family of social movers and shakers (Harriet Beecher Stowe, Henry Ward Beecher, and my favorite, Isabella Beecher Hooker), each of whom moved away from the Calvinistic teachings of their father toward a more gentle gospel that included a celebration Christmas.

These days, if we're so inclined, we're free to hang lights from every hook. There is no war on saying "Merry Christmas," though there is a war on the spirit of the holiday. The major skirmishes include, (but are not limited to):

—A tax plan that will shovel money into the pockets of wealthy people at the expense of the poor. Jesus would not approve, and that's not just me talking. The U.S. Conference of Catholic Bishops says so, too. Late last month, they called on the U.S. Senate to reconsider their "large tax cut to the wealthy."

— Repeated (and failed) attempts to repeal a health care system that has given insurance to millions. The National Association of Evangelicals, a group of 45,000 churches from 40 different denominations, has cried foul, and suggested that providing health insurance to people who need it is a good thing, even a Christian thing.

—A shocking disregard for the environment. In June, when President Trump backed out of the Paris climate agreement, the Anglican Communion Environmental Network was among multiple religious organizations that reminded us that part of our charge is to care for the Earth. The network released a statement that said, in part, "Our faith calls us to feed the hungry. Today, this means halting those actions which are causing hunger and starvation."

—An un-American drive to shut the door on immigrants and refugees that runs counter to Jesus' Beatitudes. In November, the pope chastised those who, he said, "for what may be political reasons, foment fear of migrants instead of building peace are sowing violence, racial discrimination and xenophobia, which are matters of great concern for all those concerned for the safety of every human being."

We've come to this: Say "Merry Christmas. Say "Happy Holidays." Say whatever you want, because in the end? They're just words. God judges actions. Even a fake Christian knows that.

It's Time To Fund Gun Violence Research

By Susan Campbell CT Health I-Team October 3, 2017

After a white terrorist (can we just start calling these people what they are?) shot and killed at least 59 people and injured another 527 at an outdoor country music contest in Las Vegas this week, Nelba Márquez-Greene took to Twitter:

"Guess what folks? Gun violence and grief hurt in EVERY zip code. In every color. Grieving mothers need your help."

Who can forget Márquez-Greene and her family? After her 6-year-old daughter Ana was shot and killed in the 2012 Newtown school massacre, Márquez-Greene and husband Jimmy Greene, the award-winning musician, have continually reminded this country that we can do more than offer thoughts-and-prayers over gun violence.

We could start with devoting some research into gun violence, but with little fanfare, the federal National Institutes of Health, which touts itself as one of the leading medical research centers, has allowed to lapse a funding program that supported research into the prevention of firearm violence.

That's because when it comes to gun violence research, money talks. And for the past 20-some years, the money has come from the gun-rights folks, most particularly, the National Rifle Association, which has thrown its fevered support to candidates who prefer to be Know-Nothings when it comes to gun violence—to the point that they're frightened of research that might help us figure out why we are shooting one another with such frequency. If you are against research and science, the NRA has some money for you.

This decades-long ban on funding for gun violence research has all but destroyed the field. Research for what one Stanford University researcher called the least-researched cause of death in the country, mostly happens in private, if at all. This despite physicians asking that gun violence be considered a public health issue.

"My understanding from people who are doing the research is that there are such limited funds, people don't even go into the field," said

Ron Pinciaro, executive director of Connecticut Against Gun Violence, an advocacy organization started in 1993.

In fact, the Centers for Disease Control and Prevention is left only to count the dead: 33,594 in 2014, the most recent statistics available. That's nearly the same amount of people who die in motor vehicle accidents, and you can bet the research dollars are available to study the latter.

The NIH program has funded 22 projects for $18 million since 2014. After the Newtown shootings, President Obama signed a series of executive orders meant to add a little common sense to the way we look at guns. It didn't work very well, particularly at the CDC, the organization most equal to the task.

This most recent defunding is not a surprise. Last April, President Donald J. Trump played to the crowd and told the NRA that "the eight-year assault on your Second Amendment freedoms has come to a crashing end." That's an unfortunate choice of words, but that's come to be expected as well. Precisely what assault he was referring to is unclear. Precisely why these right-wing snowflakes don't trust science is unclear as well.

This willful ignorance on the part of policymakers dates back to the Clinton-era Dickey Amendment, when then-U.S. Rep. Jay Dickey of Arkansas authored a bill that was inserted into an omnibus appropriations bill. His amendment didn't explicitly ban gun violence research, but it banned funding gun control advocacy. And that's when the NRA pounced. That industry lobbying organization began to stuff cash into the pockets of all the right (wrong) politicians. And boom! Just like that. No one was funding gun violence research.

That Dickey, a Republican, came to regret his amendment is a nice coda, but his mea culpas matter about as much as spitting into the wind. What speaks loudest in this realm is not dead children and teachers in a Connecticut school, or countless people shot dead by loved ones, or violence in the streets, or lives cut off or altered forever by a gun. What speaks loudest is money. Pinciaro's budget is roughly $400,000. He said the combined budget of all state and national organizations in the gun violence prevention field is roughly $80 million.

The NRA has an annual operating budget of nearly a quarter of a billion.

In 2016, the NRA pumped cash into the coffers of mostly Republican politicians. Their top recipient was the Republican National Committee. They also spent millions campaigning against Democratic candidates.

If there's a silver lining in this cloud, it's that Connecticut continues to set the standard for sensible gun legislation. "The good part for us is that in Connecticut, we have the second strongest gun laws in the nation," said Pinciaro. "We feel we've accomplished a lot during this time."

Immigrants' Lives Woven In Closing Church

Susan Campbell The Hartford Courant June 23, 2017

On June 29, the Archdiocese of Hartford plans to close the doors of several Roman Catholic churches including Hartford's Sacred Heart (Sagrado Corazón). Parishioners there will move to St. Peter's on Main Street.

This isn't a surprise. In May, the archdiocese announced it would close and merge parishes after several years' study of declining membership, a shortage of priests and aging buildings. The move shrinks 212 parishes to 127, with more cuts to come. A spokesman said the church hopes the mergers will energize new parishes.

Maybe that will happen, but the storied Sagrado Corazón has been home to generations of families who moved to Hartford — from Bonn, Germany, to Caguas, Puerto Rico — to try their hand at the American dream. Is it wise to close the doors on that?

Ground was broken for Sacred Heart in the 1890s. The church was dedicated in 1917 and quickly filled with German immigrants. This was just a few years after Emma Lazarus' poem, "The New Colossus," was engraved on the Statue of Liberty.

You could say Hartford was a different place then, but you'd be wrong. It was then, as it is now, a springboard for families eager to try their hand at the American Dream. When the church was young, Hartford's immigrants were mostly European. They came for Hartford's manufacturing jobs. The Germans were mostly better-educated than their Irish counterparts and for them, Hartford was a boon.

Over time, manufacturing jobs dried up or moved to the suburbs, and the newest residents in the capital city no longer spoke German (or Italian, or French), but Spanish. Post-World War II programs meant to create jobs for Puerto Ricans and abundant (but low-paying) work in the tobacco fields brought people from the island — U.S. citizens since 1917 — north. Before fanning out across the city and state, many settled in the Clay-Arsenal neighborhood and found their way to Sacred Heart.

In 1955, to answer the needs of the growing Boricua population, a priest at St. Peter's formed what became the San Juan Center and moved into the basement of Sacred Heart. There, a group of dedicated activists and teachers transformed a generation, as well as Hartford. This was the church of Maria C. Sanchez, la madrina (godmother) of the city's Puerto Rican community until her death in 1989, former Hartford Mayor Eddie Perez, and others. Upstairs, priests said Spanish Mass at what came to be known as Sagrado Corazón. Downstairs, the San Juan Center was a powerful incubator for a new kind of city leadership. Conversations rarely strayed from politics, said Luis Cotto, a former Hartford city councilor who is now executive director of Egleston Square Main Street in Massachusetts — and a former Sagrado Corazón altar boy.

"It was all politics — not local politics, mind you," said Cotto. "The Sacred Heart priests at the time — particularly Father Thomas Goeckler — were of the liberation theology branch so we went along that ride with them." When Father Goeckler died in 2010, he was ministering in Guatemala.

"We knew more about what was happening in Central America than any kids, anywhere," Cotto said. "We attended protest rallies regularly at the Groton submarine base, protesting nuclear submarines and our major 'retreat' was to D.C. every year for one rally or another."

But the center — and the church — went beyond building political awareness, said Cotto's sister, Carmen.

"We didn't know what college was," she said. "We were first generation, born in Hartford. What did our parents — tobacco workers — know about sending us off to college? I was told 'You are not college material' by my high school guidance counselor."

Fortunately, the center included a tutorial program. At the end of her sophomore year of high school, a priest there tested Carmen Cotto and found she was dyslexic. "That's when my whole mindset of education started changing, I started learning how to learn," she said. "Hartford schools never tested me. It was the church who tested me." The archdiocese says some buildings will be sold, and some may serve as sites for weddings, christenings and the like. Given its role in the creation of Hartford, Sagrado Corazón would make a fantastic museum for political activism, don't you think?

ANGELA CARELLA

After graduating Westhill High School in Stamford and Southern Connecticut State University in New Haven, she taught in an elementary school for a couple of years then landed a job at Satellite News Channel, an early competitor to CNN. But she wanted to be in "print journalism," applied for a spot in a work-study program at New York University's graduate school of journalism, newspaper concentration. With a master's degree in journalism, she moved back to Stamford with a job as an overnight copy editor at The Advocate. She learned layout and design and page paste-up in the composing room, and watched the press roll each night. She wrote headlines and edited live copy on deadline. She became Page One editor, a features desk editor, an assignment editor on the city desk, but aspired to be a reporter. She got the job writing profiles, covering cops and courts and city hall, and delving into investigations — her favorite. She earned first place from the New York City Deadline Club, New England Society of Newspaper Editors, AP, New England AP News Executives Association and Connecticut Society of Professional Journalists. All of it led to becoming a columnist — her ultimate, a column with an edge, a way to get to the heart of issues by putting facts into context and the powerful on the hot seat.

Scrap Metal Up, But What About Accountability?

By Angela Carella Stamford Advocate March 5, 2014

Last year the city sold more scrap metal than it has in recent memory -- 663 tons.

It was the fourth year in a row that the tonnage increased.

In Stamford the number is about more than filling city coffers with revenue earned from the sale of old light poles, snowplows, manhole covers, Dumpsters and traffic signs.

It's about justice and the integrity of government.

It's because in 2009, the year before a handful of officials acted on a tip that scrap metal in Stamford was vanishing, the city sold only 268 tons.

But in 2010 the number doubled.

It's because in April 2010 an official asked what had happened to some snowplows and, the next day, an Office of Operations supervisor showed up in the purchaser's office with $3,149, saying he'd just scrapped them.

Scrap metal sold:

2013: 663 tons

2012: 599 tons

2011: 595 tons

2010: 565 tons

2009: 268 tons

2008: 350 tons

2007: 350 tons

The purchaser called police.

There were investigations. One by an outside auditor cost taxpayers $150,000. The auditor, Kroll Associates, checked with the city's contracted Stamford scrap dealer, Rubino Brothers, and learned of 206 cash payments to city workers. But City Hall had receipts for only three transactions.

A Rubino's employee told Kroll that city workers sometimes asked to be paid in cash.

Kroll investigators interviewed city workers who told them they sometimes scrapped metal during their lunch hours for their own side businesses. Others said they were given cash when they scrapped city metals but they always put it on their supervisor's desk.

One worker reported that a scrap dealer handed him an envelope full of cash. Other workers said their supervisors spent the cash from scrap sales on pizza or lunchtime birthday parties.

Because it had found possible evidence of criminality, Kroll Associates turned over its findings to the city attorney.

Who handed it to the state's attorney.

Who gave it to Stamford police.

Who said they found no evidence that anyone had stolen anything.

The case ended up back in the hands of the state's attorney, David Cohen, who concluded that it was unlikely that city workers had "intended" to commit larceny because selling city metal for cash had been "the norm" in Stamford for 35 years. Cohen determined that the cash amounted to no more than $3,000 a year from 2006 to 2010.

Cohen dropped it there, even though the former police chief, Robert Nivakoff, said that theft from a municipality, even if it's $1, is a felony.

Note that in January 2010, the city sold 16.7 tons of scrap metal. In February it sold 3.3 tons and in March it sold 19.5 tons.

But in April 2010, the month the investigations began, the tonnage skyrocketed to 58.6 tons.

For all of 2010, in fact, the amount was 565 tons, twice the 2009 amount. And it kept going up.

In 2011 the city sold 595 tons.

In 2012 it was 599 tons.

And last year it was 663 tons.

Before the investigation, the city could expect to earn an average of about $50,000 a year in scrap metal revenue. Since the investigation, the city has earned an average of about $115,000 a year.

So the city has earned about $260,000 more since the investigation than it could have expected to earn had there been no investigation.

The city officials who launched the investigations say it was about more than money. It was about mindset.

They paid personally, professionally, politically and financially for raising the scrap flap. They were caught in a volley of ethics charges and legal wrangles that cost the law department -- that is, taxpayers -- hundreds of thousands of dollars. All the charges were withdrawn or dismissed.

"The civil servants involved didn't like the oversight, and they attacked us," said Bob Kolenberg, who was a member of the Board of Finance when the flap began. "We were dragged through the mud. Obviously we were correct, because the city is collecting more scrap metal. For those who were involved, shame on them. They went after the accusers to deflect attention from their wrongdoings."

Kolenberg remembers asking Rubino Brothers about whether the contractor had received any of the more valuable non-ferrous metals, such as copper, from the city. The answer was zero.

"So in 10 years the city did not collect one ounce of non-ferrous metal?" Kolenberg said. "Was it stolen? I think it's pretty obvious."

Elected officials have to call out wrongdoing, he said.

"We made an issue of this. If no one is there to make an issue of it, it will happen again," he said. "I hope the new mayor, David Martin, understands the sacrifices we made to uncover the corruption and I hope he will keep an eye on these things."

Sal Gabriele was a member of the Board of Representatives when he asked about the snowplows in 2010.

"The sense I got from some members of the board was that they were afraid to get involved," said Gabriele, now a member of the Board of Finance. "After the Kroll investigation, some reps said the city spent $150,000 just to uncover that $15,000 was stolen. Now we know it was much more, but that's not the point. It was wrong. If you look the other way, you allow it, and it will spread like a cancer."

Gabriele said he thinks the mindset is changing but the city "still has a lot of work to do."

Joe Tarzia fears the mindset remains. He was a member of the Board of Finance when he began asking questions.

"I think Martin is doing some things that will be good for the city, so maybe it will improve, but the people who did this are still there, still protecting their friends, still doing them favors. They got away with it," Tarzia said. "The Board of Representatives at the time was mostly silent. A lot of people went and hid, and they survived. The message to other elected officials is that if anyone has an inkling of having a backbone, you'd better mind your own business."

Joe Sargent, the Stamford attorney who defended Tarzia and Gabriele against ethics charges, often at his own expense, said the scrap metal case was about city officials protecting each other.

"All they had to do was arrest one person, and he would have squealed on everyone. It would have gone to the highest levels of city government," Sargent said. "In not going after the people involved in the initial thefts, city leaders lost their moral authority. The people who did it are still there. It says that those who steal can do what they want."

He fears that "the mindset hasn't changed at all," Sargent said.

This is why.

"The Operations Committee of the Board of Representatives has never called these guys before them to ask why the scrap metal keeps going up year after year," Sargent said. "Only in Stamford do they let people who do this stick around."

In Sprint for Stamford Betting Parlor, Public Trust Finished Last

By Angela Carella Stamford Advocate December 1, 2015

A year and a half ago, city officials raced to approve an off-track betting parlor for downtown Stamford.

It had to be among the fastest proposals ever set on a Board of Representatives track.

May 12, 2014: The board's Steering Committee places it on the agenda for the following month.

May 27, 2014: The Land Use Committee hears the proposal, holds a public hearing and passes it in one night.

June 2, 2014: The full board OK's it.

So, in three short weeks, a plan for Stamford's first OTB venue crossed the finish line.

Mayor David Martin, Downtown Special Services District President Sandra Goldstein, entrepreneur Bobby Valentine and his partner, Sportech, and some city representatives said the reason for the rush was that a betting parlor would be good for Stamford, and they wanted it to open before the running of the 2015 Kentucky Derby.

The Derby took place May 2. American Pharoah, ridden by Victor Espinoza, won before a record 170,513 fans at Churchill Downs. The television audience, at 16 million viewers, beat previous years. And the race set a new high for the amount of money wagered, $137.9 million.

But the OTB parlor in what was to be Bobby V's Restaurant & Sports Bar, planned for the building at 268 Atlantic St. that once housed the Rack 'n' Roll pool hall, wasn't open.

It wasn't open, either, two weeks later, when American Pharoah won the Preakness Stakes, or on June 3, when he won the Belmont Stakes and became the first horse to claim the Triple Crown since Affirmed did it in 1978.

The OTB parlor still wasn't open in October, when American Pharoah won the Breeder's Cup Classic, becoming the first in history to take the Grand Slam of American horse racing.

Valentine, a Stamford native and former Major League Baseball player and manager, said last week that plans for the restaurant and betting venue were delayed.

It's because Sportech, which has the state contract to run OTB venues - Connecticut has 15 - is in the middle of a takeover. But the Canadian company involved, Contagious Gaming, has not agreed to terms, Sportech President Ted Taylor said last week.

Because of that, he cannot get the $8 million needed to renovate the downtown Stamford building, Taylor told The Advocate. He said he hoped to have more information this week.

So city officials hurried up only to wait.

It came at a cost.

Goldstein and the DSSD, a group that promotes the downtown, had six months to ask questions about the OTB proposal. But city representatives had almost no time at all.

It came to the Steering Committee with minimal information. It quickly passed to the Land Use Committee with a little more definition but no time for members to research it, run it by constituents or amend it, because Steering had scheduled the public hearing and vote for the same night.

Usually a committee gets a proposal and talks it over, then schedules a hearing and vote for the following month or later, depending on representatives' concerns.

Instead, the OTB proposal went to the Board of Representatives with many unanswered questions: Does crime, such as loitering and mugging, increase in neighborhoods with OTB parlors? Do cities that approve them have to step up police patrols, and at what cost? How much revenue can the city expect?

Representatives might have learned, for example, that the OTB parlor in Bridgeport led the state with $27.4 million in bets in 2013. But that total was far from the $41.9 million Bridgeport drew five years earlier, before the recession took hold.

During their meeting, the Stamford representatives found out that the pastor of a church near the proposed OTB venue had negotiated conditions with Valentine and Sportech. The pastor was concerned about hours of operation, public disturbances, drunkenness and whether there would be pole dancing.

But many representatives had not seen the conditions. They had to call a recess, make copies of the conditions and distribute them during the meeting. That gave rise to another question - does Connecticut law allow cities to impose conditions when voting on state-sanctioned OTB venues? No one knew.

Representatives from both parties then retreated to separate rooms to caucus privately, which the law allows.

When Democrats appeared to be leaning toward delaying the vote on the OTB plan, party leaders called in the Democratic mayor and their party chairman, who are not members of the Board of Representatives. As soon as those two entered, the caucus reverted to a public meeting. But the public discussion continued in a private room.

Despite that, and all the unanswered questions, representatives voted 25-8, with four abstentions, to allow betting on horses, greyhounds and jai alai in downtown Stamford.

City Republicans later filed a complaint with the state Freedom of Information Commission, saying Martin and two Democratic board leaders, President Randall Skigen and Majority Leader Elaine Mitchell, violated laws governing open meetings. Board members then had to undergo FOI training.

So the public's trust in open government, in government for all, not just for people who know people, took another hit.

Now American Pharoah, after a year of electrifying the racing world, has come and gone, and post time for OTB in Stamford is anybody's bet.

For Vietnam Veterans, The 'Gesture' of March 30

By Angela Carella Stamford Advocate March 30, 2010

Born down in a dead man's town,
The first kick I took was when I hit the ground.
You end up like a dog that's been beat too much,
Till you spend half your life just covering up
From the lyrics to "Born in the USA"
Bruce Springsteen

Jimmy Sparrow grew up in downtown Stamford, in a neighborhood that isn't there anymore.

Then it was called the East Side; now it's a perpetual construction site known as The Hole in the Ground.

Sparrow's family didn't have a lot of money. He says he was a street kid with not much going for him, except an idea in his head about being a U.S. Marine.

In March 1965, Sparrow was sitting in English class at Stamford High School when someone handed him a copy of the New York Daily News. It had a big headline: "Marines Land in Vietnam."

Sparrow got up and walked out. "Where are you going?" the teacher asked. "I'm going to Vietnam," Sparrow said. It was three months before graduation.

At the Marine Corps station in the Federal Street post office, the recruiter told him to go back and finish high school. Sparrow graduated June 26, 1965. On June 29, he was in boot camp at Parris Island, S.C. He was 18.

"We were all working-class kids, some farm boys, some city kids,"

Sparrow said. "We weren't going to college because we couldn't afford it. It wasn't in the cards.

"That's who always goes to war."

Got in a little hometown jam,
So they put a rifle in my hand.
Sent me off to a foreign land,
To go and kill the yellow man.

Boot camp was tough, physically and mentally, Sparrow said.

"Imagine getting yelled at constantly and being told that you're in a chain, and the chain is only as strong as the weakest link," he said. "The peer pressure is incredible. But I was a tough street kid, a dead-end kid.

"I loved it."

He became a rifleman in the infantry, serving with several units, including one that resupplied missions and another that trained the South Vietnamese to defend themselves against the invading communist North Vietnamese and Viet Cong.

"They were all young kids or old men, because everyone else was in the Army," Sparrow said. "We taught them to patrol the villages, just like we do now in Afghanistan. We'd go in with medics, with something as simple as a Band-Aid and iodine, and they'd look at us like we were gods. Helping them was very rewarding work."

He remembers the day he accompanied his sergeant to meet a South Vietnamese man who was providing them with information. The man brought his daughter, and to pass the time, Sparrow showed her a photograph of him and some Stamford buddies standing around his 1956 Oldsmobile.

"I bought it for $150. She couldn't get over that I owned a car. She thought I was a rich person. I told her, `No, no, I come from a poor family. We live in an apartment house,' " Sparrow said. "Then it hit me what poor really is, and how we got it made in the United States, and how little we know about the rest of the world."

He doesn't have anything to say about combat.

I had a brother at Khe Sanh, fighting off the Viet Cong.
They're still there, he's all gone.

Sparrow became aware of the controversy surrounding the war on his way home after a year in Vietnam. On the plane from Okinawa, Japan, to Oakland, Calif., a first sergeant lectured the returning Marines.

"He said, 'You will see strange things when you get home -- men with long hair, these people called hippies who are nothing but drug addicts. They will spit on you and call you baby killer and wave Viet Cong flags,'" said Sparrow, who was 20 at the time. "I never heard of a hippie. We started laughing. We said, here we are, combat-hardened Marines, who the hell's gonna mess with us? We'll kill 'em."

When they landed in Oakland, the Marines "grouped up, four and five together. We said if one goes into the men's room, we'll all go, in case one of these hippies wants to get into it with us. But it was very uneventful. After that, I was looking for someone to spit on me, just to get in a confrontation with them."

The country went to war because it was thought that if South Vietnam fell to a communist country, communism would spread throughout southeast Asia. War protesters were alarmed by the number of casualties among the U.S. military and Vietnamese civilians. They thought the war had little purpose and could not be won.

Sparrow was never spit on or called a baby killer, though he would learn later that it happened to other veterans. The reason may be that he returned to the Marines to serve a couple more years in Central and South America. When he returned home for good in 1969, he came face to face with some of the assumptions people had about Vietnam veterans.

"We used to get together at a VFW post on Cove Road, and one day the Stamford Police Department raided us. They came at us like gangbusters. Somebody told them we were making bombs to blow up City Hall," Sparrow said. "It was because we had a reputation as dope addicts and baby killers. It turned out that the guy who called the cops was a deserter from the Navy."

There were drugs in Vietnam, but he saw much more when he returned to Stamford, Sparrow said.

"If you listen to some people, you'd think the drug culture in the United States came from Vietnam. That's a crock," he said. "I was shocked when I came home and met all these guys from high school who were dope fiends."

A month after he came home, Sparrow got married.

"Then I got a job working on I-95 by exit 9," he said. "I went from being a sergeant in the Marine Corps, responsible for 15 to 30 guys, to pumping gas. It was like, what's wrong with this picture? After that, I had a series of meaningless jobs. A lot of vets couldn't even find jobs."

Come back home to the refinery,
Hiring man says, "Son, if it was up to me."
Went down to see my VA man,
He said, "Son, don't you understand?"

For a while, he "went a little crazy," Sparrow said.

"I got so cold. A friend of mine from Stamford was killed in Vietnam, and my cousin came over dressed all neat and said to me, 'Aren't you going to the wake?" Sparrow said. "I said no, I didn't go to anybody's wake when I was over there. That was my bitter cold attitude at the time."

He was headed down a dark path.

"I got arrested in Stamford for hitting a cop. The court jammed me up at first, but in the end, they didn't go too hard on me because he was a problem cop and they were trying to force him out. After that, I said the hell with Stamford. I lived in Puerto Rico for three years, then I lived in Florida for three years."

Down in the shadow of the penitentiary,
Out by the gas fires of the refinery.
I'm ten years burning down the road,
Nowhere to run, ain't got nowhere to go.

He returned to Stamford in 1977. The VFW hall on Cove Road had become a place of solace for Vietnam veterans. A year or so after Sparrow was back, a call came in to the pay phone at the hall.

Paul Reutershan, a Vietnam veteran from Stamford in his mid-20s, was calling from Norwalk Hospital, where he was dying of cancer.

"Back then, if you were a Vietnam vet, anybody who wasn't, wasn't worth talking to. I took the phone," Sparrow said. "It changed my life. It gave me a very big purpose."

Reutershan, a health nut, couldn't understand how he had cancer. He began to wonder whether it could be linked to his time in Vietnam, where he was a door gunner on a Huey helicopter, flying support missions for the big C-130 cargo planes that were spraying Agent Orange, a chemical the military used to defoliate the forests where Viet Cong were hiding.

"He flew right through the spray, again and again," Sparrow said.

There was almost no environmental law at the time, and people were just beginning to question the unintended effects of chemicals. From his deathbed, Reutershan was insistent. He began to get some press.

"Other veterans heard what he was saying and linked up with him. Besides cancer and other diseases, a lot of them talked about birth defects in their children," Sparrow said.

When he died in 1978, Reutershan was 28. He made his sister, Jane, and Sparrow, then 30, and other veterans promise they would continue the fight.

Stamford became the center of the Agent Orange battle. They traveled the country, camped out at the offices of lawyers and judges, even grabbed President Jimmy Carter at a hearing, to tell them what was happening to veterans.

"I got such an education, I'd go speak at places and they'd think I was a doctor. Me," Sparrow said.

The veterans sued the huge chemical companies that made Agent Orange. It became the largest class-action suit in the nation, representing 250,000 veterans. In 1982, against all odds, the veterans won. The chemical companies immediately appealed but lost two years later, when a federal judge in New York awarded the veterans $240 million.

The court administered the money to veterans groups all over the country, including the one started by Reutershan in Stamford. One of Sparrow's prized possessions is a big book, "The Legacy of Vietnam Veterans and Their Families," a summary of all that was done with the money.

"Back in the 1980s, a lot of these guys had either no insurance or not enough," Sparrow said. "Their kids were being born with cleft palates or no eyelids, but the insurance companies would not pay for treatment because they considered it cosmetic."

About 3 million Americans served in Vietnam; 300,000 were wounded and 58,000 were killed -- 10 times more than have died in Iraq and Afghanistan so far.

Congress recently passed a resolution designating March 30 as Welcome

Home Vietnam Veterans Day, and states slowly are signing on. The goal is to honor those "who served bravely and faithfully during the Vietnam War, and were caught upon their return home in the crossfire of public debate," it reads.

Connecticut's resolution is before the House of Representatives. March 30 was chosen because on that date in 1973, the last of the U.S. troops left Vietnam.

"It's a nice gesture, but that's all it is," Sparrow said. "If they really want to honor veterans, they'll hire more VA doctors. I'm at the federal veterans' hospital in West Haven every week, visiting guys and helping them with what they need. It's so undermanned, it's awful."

He has come to understand the war protesters, Sparrow said.

"I think the anti-war movement was populated mostly by people who wanted to get high and evade the draft, but there were some who were opposed to the war because they opposed violence and killing," Sparrow said. "They were righteous people. The older I get, the more I feel like they do.

"Now I see that war is old men with money sending young kids without money to go die to make the old men more money. It's how it's always been."

JACQUELINE S. CARLSEN

Jacqueline S. Carlsen is the editor of The National Beauty School Journal. She was a fashion writer for the New Haven Register. Carlsen also has been an account manager for Calvin Klein and a coordinator for Estee Lauder and a copy writer at Conair. She studied journalism at the University of Bridgeport and English and theater at C.W. Post College. A Rippowam of Stamford High School graduate, she lives in Norwalk.

Come On, Baby, Let's Do the French Twist

By Jacqueline S. Carlsen New Haven Register April 26, 1990

GET OUT your love beads. Dust off your Nehru jacket. Dig up your go-go boots.

The '60s have returned in all fashion arenas, including hairstyles. Taking a fond look back at the age of Aquarius is as easy as flipping through the pages of any fashion magazine of today.

Even Ivana Trump has jumped on the bandwagon (or the Volkswagen as the case may be). During Fall Fashion Week in New York City earlier this month, Trump appeared Monday morning with a tres '60s Brigitte Bardot French twist. By Wednesday, this hairdo graced the heads of any runway model who still has long hair.

But will these retro hairdos catch on in New Haven? That all depends on your age group, says Alex Marnel, manager of Panache, a hair salon on College Street.

"Women 25 years old and up are going with this '60s feeling," she says. They like the sleekness and simplicity.

"Yalies are still going for the traditional bob, and girls from 18 to 24 still like the `big' hair look," Marnel says.

But if the word "groovy" gives you the creeps and you have never called anyone, male or female, "man," don't despair. Even if you aren't enamored of this particular decade, keep an open mind. If you're old enough, you might remember stiff, sprayed, helmet-like hairdos, but the '90s versions will be more free flowing.

"The '60s bob is back," says Maggie Cantarella, a hair stylist at V. Farricielli Hair and Skin Studio in Hamden. "It is called the swing bob, and it is short, blunt and straight, but there isn't a lot of hairspray like there was back then," she says, "there is movement and the hair is soft to the touch."

The word bob has been tossed around a lot lately, so you might ask yourself what a '60s bob looks like.

"It is rounder," says Eric Fischer of Wichita, KS, a member of the Joico International hair design team. (Joico is a California-based hair products company). "There is a lot of graduation in the back. Picture the way Barbra Streisand used to wear her hair," he says. And these kind of styles require good, technical hair cutting and styling.

Desiree Coleman, of West Haven, has adopted a '60s style, at least for occasional wear. "My hair is very straight, and comes right below the ear - the bangs are above the eyebrow. It is smooth and straight, like the Sassoon bob of the '60s," she says.

Coleman likes the movement of the style and thinks it will catch on with younger people. "These are nice hairdos, done in modified versions."

Coleman's modified bob can be styled in other ways - ask your stylist for a '60s cut that presents other options.

Fashion is catering to individual tastes, and personal style is now more important than trendiness. So it is logical that stylists would look back two decades, when people were encouraged to "do their own thing," for inspiration.

"The '60s was the height of styling in the hair world. Every head was like a work of art. It was much more personal - not carbon copy hair like the '70s," says Catherine Frangie, a former salon owner and president of Creative Communications, a consulting firm to the beauty industry in New Rochelle, N.Y.

The '60s styles in the '90s will use less teasing and less harsh colors, but will call on old techniques such as finger waving, setting and hot rollers, Frangie says.

Michael Christopher Hemphill of the Zotos Artistic Council says that in the beginning of the '60s, there was a lot of height at the crown of the hair, a look which was achieved by the dreaded backcombing and teasing.

"We are putting height back in the crown in a much softer way," Hemphill says. The height will now be achieved by area perming, (giving a permanent wave to a specific area of the hair for lift instead of an all-over perm).

The other hot look will be hair done in an upstyle. "But not like it was in the early '60s," Hemphill says. "Those hairdos looked like furniture," he says. Look for soft and simple twists instead.

The one drawback to this trend is that it requires another pair of hands to create. Unless you can train a friend or family member to dress your hair, this could mean more trips to the salon.

And believe it or not, wigs and clip-on hairpieces are making a comeback as well, Cantarella says.

"Women with short hair are buying add-on hair pieces and falls to get length, while women with long hair are buying wigs to have the option of a bob," Cantarella says.

See you at the love-in.

Glitter Guru Trump Led A Parade Of Fashion Disaster In 1988

By Jacqueline S. Carlsen New Haven Register Dec. 29, 1988

Associated Press - Ivana Trump appears to be the guru of glitter.

This year will be remembered as a year of fashion rebellion. Women - tired of being dictated to - made their feelings known by refusing to buy what they didn't like.

And what didn't they like?

Just about everything. The leg-baring skirts and body-hugging clothing of spring hung on the racks, unsold.

The good news for fans of more conservative fashion was that by fall, the excesses of the previous season had all but faded away, leaving behind only painful deficits for retailers.

There were a few standouts over the course of the year - people and fads that were better left unseen - at least from a fashion standpoint.

Here's a sampling:

Ivana Trump - Someone should clue Ivana into the fact that less is more when it comes to style. Trump's overdone clothing, jewelry and hair are enough to make Mr. Blackwell cringe. And speaking of hair, we all know that most blondes over the age of 20 usually need a little help maintaining their status, but Trump's rather unnatural hue can only lead us to believe that perhaps she feels all that glitters is gold.

Nancy Reagan - The first lady is supposed to represent our nation, and as such should be well-dressed and exhibit good taste. However, not at the cost of her integrity. The aforementioned dress-borrowing incident, in which some of the dresses were "borrowed" and not returned is questionable, to say the least.

Barbara Bush - After Nancy Reagan's dress-borrowing scandal, perhaps we should be relieved that our new first lady will not be caught with her hand in that cookie jar. However, it would be nice to have a first lady with some fashion savvy - Barbara Bush's style (or lack thereof) harks back to the days of Mamie Eisenhower, nobody's nomination for the "10 best-dressed" list. Kind of makes one long for the days of Jackie's pillbox.

But for all of Barbara Bush's fashion blunders, it will be encouraging to have a first lady who appears to be comfortable with herself - who isn't a size four fashion plate and doesn't feel the need to lose weight or dye her hair.

The mini-skirt - Baby boomers who gladly donned the mini during its first time around in the '60s gave its return appearance a resounding thumbs down. Retailers panicked as sales sank and consumers exercised their right to fight back against fashion tyranny. But the mini isn't totally dead - it is still available for those who like it.

The pursuit of perfection - plastic surgery is on the rise at an alarming rate as more people are getting nipped, tucked, suctioned, and implanted. One of the most popular games played at the fashion shows in New York this fall was "Guess Who's Had Implants?" as formerly flat-chested models bounced down the runways with obvious new bounty.

Whatever happened to the good old days when if a style didn't suit you, you just didn't wear it? Isn't that the reason that a variety of styles are offered?

Why, when styles include low-cut or tight fitting tops must a woman rush out to fill them? Or, when skirts climb, must a woman have her knees liposuctioned in order to look good in a mini?

One of the purposes of fashion is to find a personal style - to accent assets and hide flaws.

Shouldn't we find a style to suit ourselves, rather than change ourselves to suit the style?

The pouf - the pouf pooped out, especially on women who pop out in the wrong places. While those in fashionable circles in New York took to the pouf, fashion mavens in the hinterlands preferred their hindquarters to appear of normal size.

There were a few other jarring notes this year, including palazzo pants and garish floral prints that were better suited for curtains. But just think what we have to look forward to in 1989! Stay tuned.

Large And Lovely

By Jacqueline S. Carlsen New Haven Register Oct. 13, 1988

Big women are big business.

One-third of the women in the United States wear a size 14 or larger, say industry experts, and their fashion needs must be addressed.

The Plus-Size Expo, held earlier this month at the Jacob K. Javits Center in New York City, showed just how far the fashion industry has come in serving the needs of larger-sized women.

A mere 10 years ago, polyester pantsuits were the norm and a fashion-conscious woman who wasn't a size 8 had to comb the racks for stylish clothing.

Not any more. Large women are no longer ignored by designers or the fashion media - fashion magazines geared toward plus-size women are Radiance and BBW (Big Beautiful Woman). The industry also has a business magazine - Earnshaw's Plus Sizes.

Everything from plus-size exercise attire to wedding gowns are now available for women who are "ample, not sample" - a perfect size 8 - as guest speaker Virginia Graham, author and former television hostess, put it.

Well-known designers including Dennis Goldsmith, Givenchy, Kenar and Regina Porter have jumped onto the plus-size bandwagon and are giving the women what they want - color, style, flash and glamour.

"Large-sized women are treated like they have a handicap - they want to wear exciting prints and exciting clothes like everyone else," says Robyn Kramer of K Co. Bodywear of New York, a line of high-fashion exercise clothes that provides vibrant, patterned bodywear for larger women.

Anne Sheehy, of Robby Len swimwear, in New York, points to the new use of color for large-sized women.

"Everybody used to do black, brown and navy. Now there are bright color accents and pizazz. There is a lot less fear of wearing bright colors. Big women are not afraid to be big," she says.

The large-sized apparel business is booming because large women are speaking out. "Large-women are fashionable and if you don't cater to them, they'll let you know," Sheehy says.

"Younger large-sized women are being brought up to feel that big is beautiful and to feel good about themselves," she says.

Beverly King's company, Large Corporate Structure, of San Francisco, was born out of her frustration trying to find business clothes for herself, a size 20.

"We go to work everyday like everyone else, and we are hard to fit," she says.

Large Corporate Structure features business suits and separates in fine fabrics, and because King feels she has a special understanding of large-sized women, they are designed especially with the customer in mind.

"Manufacturers had a tendency to do small, medium and large. But the structure has to be there to get a clean business look," King says.

Accessories are another area that require special consideration for heavier women. Jewelry designer Jeff Lieb of Chicago is the large-sized woman's dream.

"I don't like little things," he says. His costume jewelry, created on a large scale, is the perfect accent for a bigger woman, on whom small pieces tend to get lost.

One of the high points of Plus-Size Expo was the fashion show. Guest speakers Jane Russell and Virginia Graham offered humor and advice.

Russell, who says she has been a size 14 since she was in high school, says that there are tricks for the "full-figured gal."

She suggests that large-sized women use a one-color scheme, avoid horizontal stripes and not wear belts, which break up their silhouettes.

She favors large accessories that show up, as opposed to small ones that, as Lieb explained, can get lost on a large woman.

Graham talked about how large-sized women are made to feel like outcasts.

"One of the most sensual pleasures in the world is eating," she says. "And look at stars like Faye Emerson and Ava Gardner - once they were released from bondage, they ate."

Graham says that large-sized women are going from "shame to fame," thanks to clothing and accessory manufacturers who are now paying attention to their needs.

"They are bringing style to people who deserve fashion and deserve style."

MAURA CASEY

Over a 34-year journalism career, Maura Casey wrote columns and editorials for four newspapers: The Lawrence (Mass.) Eagle Tribune, The Day of New London, The Hartford Courant and The New York Times. She has won more than 45 national and regional awards for journalism, including a shared Pulitzer Prize for reporting, the Scripps Howard Walker Stone Award for outstanding editorial writing, and the Sigma Delta Chi Award for editorial writing. In 2016, the New England Society of News Editors gave Casey the Yankee Quill Award based on lifetime achievement in journalism.

Casey, a Buffalo, NY native, holds a BA in Political Science, magna cum laude, from Buffalo State College and a master's degree in Journalism and Public Affairs from the American University.

She has been married for 35 years to Peter J. Panzarella. They have two adult children, Anna and Tim.

Catholic Women Must Speak Out

By Maura Casey The Hartford Courant Feb. 19, 2012

My mother, a devout Catholic, had heart trouble before having six children in seven years during the 1950s. Exhaustion, combined with her weak heart, contributed to bouts of pneumonia and the removal of a lung.

Afterward, she tried to talk to my equally devout father about using birth control. It upset him.

"We'll go to hell," he said.

"I'm in hell now," she replied, and took a bus 75 miles to Rochester, N.Y., to obtain contraceptives. My parents had no more children. My mother made certain her four daughters had no qualms about using birth control. Still, I wonder whether having such a large family so quickly contributed to her death in her 50s.

Now I am in my 50s with two children of my own. Recently, American Catholic bishops ordered priests to read a letter at Mass denouncing as a violation of religious liberty a proposed federal birth control mandate. Although parish churches are exempt, religious institutions that accept federal funds (and employ many non-Catholics) would have had to make available free contraceptives through health coverage. The controversy forced compromise; the Obama administration passed the mandate onto insurance companies.

Yet the bishops remain unsatisfied. The use of birth control is against Catholic teaching, a sin and part of "a culture of death," as New York's Archbishop Timothy M. Dolan has said.

But the majority of Roman Catholic women — 98 percent according to one poll — have used birth control. Like me, many such women have received periodic fundraising letters from the church usually addressed to the woman of the house. They've enrolled their children in Catholic schools and watched their children participate in the sacraments.

Like me, many would consider themselves irresponsible mothers if they did not tell their children to ignore the church's teaching on birth control — particularly when using birth control makes abortions far less likely.

Of 100 Catholic women friends and acquaintances I could name, 99 use artificial birth control. But have we spoken out? No. Instead, we have spoken to each other,

The church has made us Galileo, who, legend says, whispered, "But still it moves!" when theologians forced him to recant his discovery that the Earth revolves around the sun.

Ladies, whispering is no longer good enough. We Catholic women need to raise our voices, acknowledge the vast disconnect between Catholic teaching and the reality of our lives, and we need to do it now.

We need to support the availability of birth control in letters to the editor. We need to write to the White House and Congress. And, we need to say, with respect, "I disagree, Father. I use birth control, and I've told my children to use it, too."

Otherwise, the priests, bishops, Republican presidential candidates and scores of male commentators will get away with the pretense that they are speaking for us.

They aren't.

Speaking out is uncomfortable. We don't want the hierarchy to accuse us of being "cafeteria Catholics" or denounce us in other ways. We don't want to debate canon law. We don't feel like experts.

Yet we are: On being women.

Men who denounce birth control in the name of religious liberty will never feel labor pains. They will never understand what we know about being a woman, a wife or a mother.

We are the authorities on the importance of birth control to our health and freedom. We understand pregnancy as far more than a nine-month inconvenience.

One-third of all U.S. pregnancies have medical complications. The maternal death rate is higher here than in 40 other countries. Why? A lack of birth control and poor availability of health care, two factors that the Obama administration is trying to change against vehement right-wing opposition — and their allies in the clergy.

Republican presidential candidate Rick Santorum has advocated allowing states to decide the legality of birth control. Newt Gingrich has spoken in favor of declaring fertilized eggs persons, making some birth control illegal. Mitt Romney pledged to end a federal law that provides family planning to millions of women.

We need to hear from the great, as yet untapped voices of sanity on these issues: the legions of Catholic women who disagree.

Like my mother, they are strong, smart, they use birth control — and they vote.

Silence is a luxury we can no longer afford.

The Joy Of Not Drinking

By Maura J. Casey The Hartford Courant Dec. 29, 2010

Even after all this time, I can still sense the occasional awkwardness when people discover I don't drink, particularly around the holidays. I can see it in their eyes as they start to discuss with me the wine list at a restaurant, only to stop, or when they laugh while relating a boozy escapade and then cut the story short.

I understand their discomfort. They believe this: Maura cannot drink. The statement is correct, but, 25 years after the December night when I last had one too many, the emphasis is all wrong.

It's true that when anyone decides to quit, he or she starts by saying, "I cannot drink." But year after sober year, the statement changes to a living affirmation: I can not drink. There's no deprivation involved, and certainly no sympathy necessary.

Indeed, the personal growth needed for sobriety, as opposed to the white-knuckled and resentful abstention of alcohol, is neither negative nor the equivalent of a closed door. Instead, it is a series of yeses.

Yes to savoring a sunset without reaching for anything to enhance its beauty.

Yes to raising a glass of sparkling cider during the wedding toast — or when the clock strikes midnight on New Year's Eve.

Yes to greeting the arrival of a baby or celebrating a graduation without needing or even wanting anything more to accompany unvarnished joy.

It sounds Pollyannaish, I suppose, to those who haven't lived it, but it is possible to enjoy not drinking as much as drinking. Of course, that takes a certain maturity, a quality sorely lacking in media portrayal of alcohol. Instead, that portrayal has a comic-strip feel, as a recent article in The New York Times pointed out; on television, alcohol is either a rollicking good time or "a life destroying scourge." Neither deals with either the complexities or contradictions involved.

What rarely is shown is the simple joy of sobriety. Yet it is as real and as rich as all the well-publicized extremes.

Few can quit entirely alone, and recovery is famous for relying upon support of others in words and meetings. But overlooked is the silent power of personal example. While still a committed drinker, I became friends with an accomplished journalist. Joanna had it all: a big job at a major daily, a Pulitzer prize and, to my surprise, a refusal to imbibe. "I like life to move at its own pace," is the most she would say, smiling, and I envied her sense of balance. Her example, more powerful than words, helped me stop later on. A year after I stopped, my sister Ellen did, too.

Not drinking has provided unexpected humor, like the time I asked someone to drink for me. At a whiskey taste at Ireland's Shannon Airport, I asked a stranger to sample and evaluate some morning shots so I could buy a bottle for my husband. He gallantly agreed.

Sobriety has given me a season of gratitude. It has made me a better wife, mother and writer. And, yes, it entails doing without sometimes. Fine wines at restaurants never held much attraction, and now I don't have to pay for them. I miss the occasional cold beer, but I am grateful in the knowledge I need never play beer pong, a pointless amusement not yet invented when I finished my last brew. And the airport whiskey? I have to admit, when the bottles were opened and I got a whiff of that still-familiar scent, I salivated.

It's OK. By now, I, too, like life to move at its own pace.

Memories Of A Friend Named Anne Frank

By Maura Casey The Day, New London March 29, 1992

"Anti-Semitism never dies," said Hilde Goldberg when I described recent incidents that occurred at Kelly Junior High School in Norwich.

Mrs. Goldberg is a gracious, dignified woman who lives in Teaneck, N.J. She has lived through far more than seeing swastikas carved on student desks, as has happened in Kelly; she knows more about prejudice than enduring the insult of having a young man say, "Hitler didn't go far enough," as has also occurred at the junior high school.

Yet she is better qualified than most to reflect upon religious bigotry. After the Nazis arrested her parents and sent them to their deaths in Auschwitz, she joined the underground. She risked her own life fighting against Adolf Hitler's brutality. She smuggled Jewish children out of Amsterdam in the night, snatching them from the claws of the Gestapo. Any of those experiences would make her perspective worth heeding.

But Mrs. Goldberg's childhood friendships give her a truly unique frame of reference. One of her best friends in the years preceding the war was Margot Frank, whose birthday, Feb. 16, was just two days before Hilde's own. They looked enough alike that their teachers confused their identities.

Margot had a scrawny, pesky little sister who used to hang around the two more than they cared for, yet they forgave her, for she was funny and kind. Her name was pronounced Anna, but we remember her as Anne – Anne Frank.

Mrs. Goldberg became acquainted with the Franks when they moved from Frankfort, Germany to a house three blocks from her Amsterdam home in 1933. The Franks attended the same synagogue with her family. Hitler was a still-distant menace.

The invasion of Czechoslovakia years later, then Poland, shattered the serenity. Within weeks German troops stormed into Holland.

"When the invasion came," said Mrs. Goldberg, "First we Jews were not allowed to keep our cars, then we were not allowed to ride bicycles, then we were forced to wear the Jewish star. Then we couldn't have radios, then we were barred from public schools or universities, then we were restricted to a few hours and stores to do our shopping."

The Dutch people were sympathetic. Dock workers went on strike. Non-Jewish college students wore the yellow star. The German occupiers executed 15 of the students in the town center for their show of solidarity.

"Suddenly the Franks just disappeared. We heard a rumor that they had gotten away through Belgium to Switzerland. We were very pleased, of course, that they had escaped. Nobody knew that they were in hiding."

One day, Mrs. Goldberg said, her parents sent her to the country to check out a possible hiding place. When she returned, her parents were gone, their home ransacked. Soldiers had taken them away.

She went to the house of her father's accountant, a Christian. She was determined to follow her parents and help them escape, but her father's friend locked her in a room to keep her from such a foolhardy mission.

Then a piece of paper arrived with a note in her mother's handwriting. It had no stamp. She had thrown it out of the train bearing her to the concentration camp in a desperate attempt to get a message to her daughter, hoping that some kind person would find the scrap and deliver it. "Whatever you do, don't follow us," the note said. Mrs. Goldberg entered the resistance instead. It was August 1943.

The Frank family remained in hiding until the Nazis arrested them in 1944. The family was sent to Auschwitz, then Margot and Anne were transferred to the concentration camp at Bergen-Belsen.

Mrs. Goldberg fought in the resistance in Belgium until Allied troops liberated the country in 1944. She joined the British Red Cross as a nurse and interpreter, and later the organization asked her to help nurse the ill and dying at "Belsen Camp" – Bergen-Belsen. German guards had surrendered there and 60,000 emaciated prisoners and thousands of unburied corpses were mute testimony to what had happened.

Dutch inmates of the camp told Mrs. Goldberg that the Frank girls' mother had died at Auschwitz. The Frank sisters, emaciated and covered with lice, tried to hang on.

But Margot, who was always nearsighted and had no glasses, fell out of her top bunk one day and died of a concussion. Anne tried to survive without her sister, clinging to the hope of seeing her beloved father again.

A fellow inmate shattered that dream. Otto Frank was dead, the inmate said. The girl despaired. Anne Frank, whose diary would make her an icon, the symbol of 6 million murdered people, died just a few weeks before Allied troops liberated the camp April 15, 1945. The official cause of her death was typhus, but she may just as easily have died of a broken heart.

But Anne's father wasn't dead. Mrs. Goldberg soon returned to Holland and met Otto Frank on the street. "We realized the two of us had survived. It was then that he told me about the diary," tossed aside after Nazis ransacked the Frank home, but kept safe by friends. "He said he needed to publish the diary. He felt it should be the mission of his life. It was heart-rending for him." Otto lived to the age of 92.

And what would she say to the student in Norwich who told a Jewish girl, "Hitler didn't go far enough"?

"I would ask him to read the diary, and make a report in front of an entire assembly, and make amends," Mrs. Goldberg said. "It isn't a matter of punishing children, but informing them."

And what would she say to the 12-year-old victim who didn't suffer the harassment in silence, but who spoke out?

"I admire her," Mrs. Goldberg said. "You know, Anne was just about that age when anti-Semitism happened to her. Discrimination never dies," she sighed.

"You have to be brave…and understand."

LISA CHEDEKEL

To her colleagues, Lisa Chedekel didn't just write stories. She chased kernels of truth, weaving together beautiful, almost lyrical pieces on subjects that were anything but, her colleague Vinny Vella wrote in her obituary Jan. 13, 2018. Chedekel, who helped form the grant-driven, nonprofit Connecticut Health investigative Team health-news website, died from cancer. She was 57. She leaves two children, Bernard and Evelyn, and her wife, Isabel Morais. Chedekel grew up in Andover, Mass., attending Phillips Academy. She graduated from Wesleyan University in 1982, with a degree in English. She worked first at the New Haven Advocate, then the New Haven Register, covering city hall and writing a metro column. She moved to The Hartford Courant where she and other Courant reporters won the Pulitzer Prize for breaking news coverage of the deadly shooting rampage at the Connecticut Lottery Corp. One of her most championed pieces was "Mentally Unfit, Forced to Fight," a 2006 investigative series with Courant Staff Writer Matthew Kauffman exposing that the military, in violation of its own rules, was sending mentally ill men and women to war in Iraq and Afghanistan. The series won numerous awards, and was a finalist for the Pulitzer Prize in Investigative Reporting. Chedekel left The Courant in 2008 and began writing for the Boston University School of Public Health and teaching journalism at Northeastern University.

Disaster in Bridgeport: 'Pontes' mourn colleagues' deaths Small Italian town grieves with immigrants

By Lisa Chedekel New Haven Register April 28, 1987

In the past 25 years, Antonio Petta, an Italian immigrant, has turned a small concrete company into one of the busiest subcontractors in the state.

He has done so with the help of a group of immigrants from Pontelandolfo, Italy - Pontes, as they are known - who took jobs, one by one, at the Waterbury Foundation Co.

Just months ago, Petta's employees gathered to celebrate the firm's quarter-century in business.

But on Monday, company officials and workers mourned the deaths of seven colleagues in Thursday's collapse of the L'Ambiance Plaza project in Bridgeport. Four other workers are missing and presumed dead. A 12th worker is hospitalized, while four others escaped injury.

The 16-man crew from Waterbury Foundation was pouring and finishing concrete on the L'Ambiance project when the building dropped from the skyline, company general manager Anthony Pelosi said Monday. Most of the 16 workers were Pontes.

At the time of the accident, the crew was "just getting through pouring one of the garage slabs," Pelosi said. "Most of them had gone up to the fourth floor to do miscellaneous patching work."

William Pelkey of Prospect, one of the workers at the site who escaped injury, said he was on the ground running a concrete pump when he heard a loud noise and saw the concrete slabs falling.

"When I looked up, I could see six of our guys standing there under it on the fourth floor," said an emotional Pelkey. "There was nothing I could do."

Pelkey said concrete for the floors being hoisted on the day of the collapse was poured in December. He said he believes the accident may have stemmed from a problem with the lifting mechanism.

Pelosi said Waterbury Foundation specializes in pouring and finishing concrete, and "has nothing to do with testing it, purchasing it or jacking up the floors."

He said the company has worked on projects with the same lift-slab construction technique in recent years, among them the Bridgeport Plaza Hotel and Atlantic Condominiums.

Pelosi and others said Petta has been inconsolable since the accident. He knew most of the dead and missing workers personally, they said.

The majority of the 30 employees who work year-round for Waterbury Foundation are Pontes, Pelosi said. In peak periods, the firm employs about 100 workers.

At the Pontelandolfo Community Club on the north side of town, a group of Pontes talked Monday about the deaths of their friends and colleagues.

"There were about 14 of us Pontes working for the Waterbury Foundation," said Mennato Guerrera, a company employee. "Now half the group is dead."

The men said the 600 club members meet after work to socialize, drink and play cards. The club was built "stone by stone" by the members in 1967. Outside stands a replica of a fountain built in Pontelandolfo in 840 A.D., erected by club members two years ago.

Four members of the club have been confirmed dead in the L'Ambiance collapse; three are missing.

"This is felt very, very bad by every member of the club," said Guerrera. "These are people who all grew up together in Italy."

The first Ponte immigrant came to Waterbury in 1885, said Sal Perugini, former club vice-president. The Ponte population here now numbers more than 10,000 - more than double the number of Pontes remaining in Italy.

"The majority of us are here," said Donato Polletta, who came here two years ago. "Most of the ones left in Italy are the old ones, retired." He said immigrants are "still coming, one or two at a time, every year."

The Pontes pride themselves on their skills in carpentry, masonry, and bricklaying. They are known for working long hours in physically demanding jobs.

"When Pontes work, we work together as a team," said Guerrera. "That company (Waterbury Foundation) started as a nothing. Then the owner takes us in and they're a million dollar company now ....

"It wasn't a job - it was one family," he added.

At a noon meeting Monday in the Bridgeport's mayor's office, Pelosi, local Pontes, and Board of Aldermen president Paul Vitarelli shared information about the tragedy with Massimo Roscigno, vice consul of Italy from New York, and Concetta DiLoreto, vice consul of Italy from Hartford.

"We want to convey our grief for this tragedy from the Italian government," Roscigno said. "The people of this city have been struck by tragedy."

A delegation from Pontelandolfo is expected to arrive in Waterbury this week to aid victims' families and offer support to compatriots here.

Funerals for two Waterbury Foundation workers, Rocco Mancini, 61, of Waterbury, and William D'Addona, 30, of Prospect, are scheduled for today.

After 49 Years, It's Last Call For P.J. Strawhince

By Lisa Chedekel New Haven Register May 20, 1987

Who are they kidding? They don't want him to go. It's as certain as the change in seasons. "You're gonna miss me," Paul Strawhince says from behind the bar with a wink of a sparkling blue eye.

"I ain't gonna miss you," C.P. replies from a barstool, motioning for a refill of beer.

"I swear Norman Lear walked in here, saw Paul, and started 'All in the Family'," Rita says, shaking her head.

Strawhince shrugs.

"Everybody's a comedian," he sighs.

There are no tears on this rainy morning at P.J.'s Cafe as Paul Strawhince and his employees - bartenders Rita and C.P. - prepare to part ways.

There is only laughter and the clinking of glass on glass, the creak of a stool and the sporadic static from the video machine - the sounds Strawhince has come to know and love in his 49 years of tending bar.

After running the Howe Street bar that bears his name (the "P.J." stands for Paul Joseph) for two-thirds of his life, Strawhince, at 74, is packing it in. One by one, he's taking down the photos above the bar - yellowed black-and-whites of his days as president of the Lions Club, coaching wrestling, a visit from the Clydesdale horses.

On his last day before selling the bar and retiring, this burly, white-haired bartender is ever the storyteller, the philosopher, the kidder - showing off that warm blend of qualities that kept him in business so long.

Today, he wants to tell the story about his dead dog.

When he was a kid, he explains, his dog had to be put to sleep after it attacked a drunk staggering out of a saloon. OK, so it was 70 years ago - but Strawhince can still taste the bitterness it left behind.

"I was so angry, I said to myself, 'When I get older, I'm going to beat up on every drunk on the street'," he says. "And I've maintained that. I have no tolerance for people who over-indulge."

Strange words from a guy who may be New Haven's longest-standing permittee?

Not really. You can run a successful saloon and still hold true to your values, Strawhince says.

"It's had its trials and tribulations," he says. "I've always been active and I love the people. But I've just about exhausted my perseverance."

Much has changed since Strawhince opened up shop on Howe Street in 1938. In its early years, P.J.'s was a sports bar that attracted a white, middle-class crowd from the immediate neighborhood, with "regulars" like Albie Booth and Yale football coach Mal Stevens.

In the last decade, the bar gained a diversity of patrons but lost what Strawhince calls its "neighborhood" feeling. Still, he's rolled with the changes, never suppressing the part of him that loves to chat, play to the crowd, draw out a stranger.

"This business has given me a lot of good things. I have no qualms about it," he says simply.

It's not going to be easy for Strawhince to break his routine. He got to P.J.'s by 6 a.m. every day, opened up at 9. At noon, he would hand over the bar to his "adopted kids," C.P. and Rita.

"The one thing I've emphasized with them is to give me a fair game," Strawhince says. "I'm strict and demanding."

Rita and C.P. would agree. They don't have to remember the days when a shot of whiskey was 15 cents to understand one man's dedication to his business. They don't have to recognize the faces in old photographs to appreciate his way of sharing laughter.

"You're gonna miss me," Strawhince says.

And it's as certain as the change in seasons that they will.

Spring Sparks Memories of Very Special Trainer

By Lisa Chedekel New Haven Register March 21, 1990

The Huskies. Volvo. World Cup soccer. It's the season of sports in Greater New Haven.

Spring. Walt. The years go by, but I still connect those two things in my mind.

I got to know Walter Grockowski in the spring of 1979, when I was a freshman at Wesleyan and I twisted my back out of whack while running for a long, looping pass in lacrosse practice. I had only played in two varsity games then - and I had played lousy, to boot - and the last thing I wanted was to end up injured, unable to prove to my coach that I really was, deep down, the hotshot she had recruited.

Walt had seen every variety of bruise, blister and sprain in his thirty-something years as Wesleyan's athletic trainer, so he didn't exactly pour on the compassion when I came wincing in to see him. Instead, he acted like . . . well . . . like Walt.

"You did a job on yourself," he told me, slapping an ice pack against my spine with a calloused hand. "You gotta sit out for a week or so."

My spirits sank. "But there's a game tomorrow," I whined.

"Hey, Chedekel," Walt replied, looking me straight in the eye through his black-rimmed glasses, "Don't worry. You'll get your chance." That was it.

That was Walt.

In my four years at Wesleyan, Walt taught me a lot about sports. Not how to play them - (supposedly, I knew that already) - but what they were really about.

He made me understand that sports are ultimately a test of character, an exercise in willpower and perseverance that lets you examine your limitations up close and gives you that once-in-a-blue-moon chance to break them.

He helped me see that sports mirror life, and that's why we appreciate them so much: The thrill isn't really in the victory, it's in the awesome resolve to break free of the stuff that makes us only human.

Walt saw life in sports, and he wanted young athletes to see it, too. To him, there was a lesson in every game you played, in every long, looping pass you missed or caught.

With me, Walt was pretty tough. My back got better in a few weeks, but my playing didn't. I was in a slump, intimidated by older teammates, and I ended up spending most of my freshman year on the bench. I was discouraged enough to think about quitting when Walt called me into the training room one day.

"What's going on?" he said. "You feeling sorry for yourself?"

I shrugged and leaned against the training table. As usual, the room smelled strongly of adhesive tape and BenGay.

"She put me on the bench," I said. "I blew it. She thinks I can't catch a ball to save my life." I paused. "She's right."

Walt shook his head. "You know how to play this game," he said. "You don't have to prove that to anyone. Play jayvee (junior varsity) for a while. Get your confidence back. You wanna play better, you gotta go play. Be patient. It'll come."

Walt was right. I played jayvee for a while, and sure enough, near the end of my sophomore year, it came. I was back as a varsity starter, playing lacrosse the way it's supposed to be played. With confidence. With resolve. My senior year, I was an All-New England player.

Walt had taught me not to quit.

I had learned the first lesson of sports.

Walt will be 70 on Friday. I haven't seen him in four years - not since his retirement dinner at Wesleyan - but I called him a few days ago, just on an impulse. He's still living in Middletown, not far from the campus, and he works part-time as a trainer at the local high school. When he asked what made me call him, I said it must've been the start of spring.

He laughed.

"That bit of advice I once gave you - about being patient - did it ever come in handy?" he wanted to know. But before I could answer, he finished for me.

"Yeah," he said - and it was just like he was looking me straight in the eye - "I figured it would."

MAUREEN E. CROTEAU

Maureen E. Croteau is a professor and head of the Department of Journalism at the University of Connecticut. Her first job was as a reporter at The Hartford Times. She also worked as an editor and reporter at The Hartford Courant and The Providence Journal. Her freelance work has appeared in newspapers throughout the United States. She is co-author of two books: Shipwrecked in the Tunnel of Love and The Essential Researcher. She is a member of the Board of Directors of The Day of New London and of the Connecticut Journalism Hall of Fame. In 2014, she was named New England Journalism Educator of the Year. She is a graduate of the University of Connecticut and the Columbia University Graduate School of Journalism.

Neighbors, But Not Even Close

By Maureen Croteau The Day New London Sept. 20, 1987

The people who lived across the street were odd, as far as I could determine.

A variety of cars would come and go at odd hours. Their trash bags could be stacked at the curb days before the regular pickup. They never came out into the yard. In fact, in the two years that I had lived across the street from the little Cape Cod house with the faded red paint and the unruly shrubs, I had never seen any of the occupants.

They were quite unlike the rest of us. The other owners of the other Cape Cod houses on the other quarter-acre lots on the street have adopted an informal code of neighborhood decorum. We all work in our yards. We all keep our driveways swept. We all nod to each other, although we do not, for the most part, know each other's names. The names, after all, don't really matter. We are only neighbors.

That is why I did not notice the obituary at first.

I wouldn't have noticed it at all, except that lately I have started reading the obituary page. Really reading it. Looking for people I know. The habit would be ghoulish if it were not so horribly productive. The fact is, lately there have been a lot of names there that I know. Some close, but some so far from in distance or time that I would not know about their deaths if I did not look for them. So I look. And often I find. And my world gets much smaller.

I noticed my neighbor's obituary because of the address. He was 83, a retired policeman, and been living across the street from me with his wife, which had explained why they did not follow the neighborhood code. Age kept them inside, and brought people to them in cars at odd hours, and those people carried the trash to the curb when they left.

My neighbors were not odd. They were old. Now one was dead, and surely that called for something.

I was raised to do the right thing, but that was in another time.

When my father needed to locate water, the elderly man who lived next door would appear with a forked cherry branch, and he would hold the ends tight and level, and walk our property slowly and purposefully, and wait until the divining rod shook and twisted straight down. My father would dig there, and another neighbor would help, and there would be water. And when our neighbors needed help from my father, there would be that, too. Being neighbors had a dowsing force to it then, a natural pull that drew you to do the right thing.

Now though, it is hard to know what is right where neighbors are concerned.

It is even hard to know what neighbors are. I think, sometimes, that people on my street are not my neighbors at all. We move too often. We have too little in common. In the two years I have lived there, I have watched the two houses closest to mine empty and fill. Eight people have lived in those houses. I have known one last name and four first names. I have known what two of them did for a living. We have all agreed on the weather.

I think sometimes that we are no more neighbors than people who stand next to each other on a bus. We are just there until the next stop. Still, when one of us dies, that demands some kind of notice.

I had imagined that I knew something about my neighbor's from reading her husband's obituary. I envisioned her suddenly alone in the home where she had cared for her husband in his final days. I imagined her setting the table for one, watching television alone, dependent on her grandchildren for errands and their company.

I thought, perhaps, that she could use a neighbor.

Flowers, I decided would seem like too much. I didn't even know the man. A mass card would be all right, but nobody would recognize my name. So I bought a dozen doughnuts. I didn't have time to make a cake. I bought a dozen doughnuts. At least it was something. And I wrote a note on a card and I rang the doorbell and waited.

"Come in," a woman called.

The kitchen was like my kitchen, except that the appliances were old and the linoleum was worn. One of the secrets of aging is that everything around you grows old too.

"I'm in here," the voice called.

I followed the voice to the bathroom where a young woman was fixing her skirt.

"Oh, I'm sorry," she said. "I thought you were my relief nurse. I'm the 7-to-3 nurse, and I'm getting relief for an hour and a half so I can go to the funeral."

My neighbor was in the next room, in a hospital bed, with the covers pulled up to her chin. Someone had set her hair in foam curlers.

"This is one of your neighbors, Jenny," the nurse said. "She's come to offer her condolences for Ray."

Her head moved back and forth on the pillow. She made sounds. Perhaps she understood.

"I'm sorry for your loss," I said and patted her on the shoulder. "I brought you some doughnuts."

Her head moved again. Perhaps she was trying to say thank you. Perhaps she was trying to do the right thing.

"That was very nice of you," the nurse said.

It was nothing. Really.

Bureau Botch A bad Dream For Motorist

By Maureen Croteau The Hartford Times March 22, 1972

This is the story of how David McNeil spent more than $100 to confess to a motor vehicle violation he did not commit in a car he did not own in a city he has visited only once in the last six years.

It is also the story of why David McNeil is not on the best of terms with the state Motor Vehicle Department.

It began last April when McNeil, a sales engineer from Somers, went to New York for a design show and found that someone had designs on his wallet.

He reached into his pocket one day, expecting to find the reassuring feeling of leather padded with $125 in small bills and found, instead, only a heartbreaking void.

That was his first problem.

He told the New York City police about his misfortune, wrote off the $125 as irretrievable, cancelled his credit cards and got a duplicate drivers license from the Connecticut Motor Vehicles Department.

He thought everything was settled. It wasn't.

Because somewhere in New York a man was driving around with McNeil's license. And that man wasn't a careful driver. And early in June he was stopped and given a $15 ticket by a policeman. And in return he gave the policeman McNeil's name, address and date of birth.

This was McNeil's second problem. And it was the beginning of others.

New York sent the information to Connecticut, which honored it as an out-of-state violation, even though McNeil had informed the Motor Vehicle Department of the theft.

McNeil received a summons. The honor of his presence was requested in a New York City court. He declined the invitation, explaining his circumstances.

In September he received a second summons. Again he declined, this time by phone. He called the police department and just about anyone else he could think of, including New York Mayor John Lindsay's office. In total he made more than 20 calls, running up more than $100 in toll charges.

Again he thought it was cleared up.

But last month he received another official letter, this time from the state Motor Vehicle Department saying that his license would be suspended in a couple of days.

"It was just unbelievable," McNeil said. "The people at the Motor Vehicle Department were understanding, but they just kept telling me there was nothing they could do. I'd have to fight it out myself. It was like a bad dream."

He received a three-week extension of his license and tried again. This time he changed his tactics, though. He sent the $15.

But last Thursday he got a certified letter from the Motor Vehicle Department saying his license would be suspended March 20.

"This was too much," McNeil said. "This had been going on for the better part of a year and now they were going to take my license away after I had paid a fine I didn't owe." The department was never notified of his payment.

He tried the Motor Vehicle Department again Monday, and when that didn't work, he called Gov. Thomas J. Meskill's office. A secretary there listened to him and had an official with the state Motor Vehicle Department call him. His license was reinstated immediately.

"I'll say this," McNeil said, "once I called Meskill's office it was all cleared up in an hour – but I've been getting the run-around since June. The Motor Vehicle Department didn't want to help me at all. They kept telling me I was on my own, that it was between me and New York – but then they wanted to take my license away."

Now, however, McNeil just wants to forget the whole thing.

"If I could blank this whole episode out of my mind, it would be fine with me," McNeil said. "I'm told now that it's finally settled, and I hope it is. I didn't see how there could be any foul ups this time, but it wouldn't surprise me. Nothing would surprise me anymore."

We Are Professionals, Not Bounty Hunters

By Maureen Croteau The Hartford Courant Sept. 7, 1997

When Diana, princess of Wales, and Dodi Fayed left the Ritz Hotel in Paris and stepped into their armored Mercedes-Benz on Saturday, Aug. 30, they were followed by a pack of bounty hunters.

In Hartford, as in other cities and towns across the country, journalists were working. It was the long Labor Day weekend, but journalists are used to working on holidays. There was news to cover. In Manchester, residents were recovering from a flash flood. Elsewhere in town, a supermarket was closed because of a bomb scare. In Rocky Hill, the residue in an oil tank caught fire.

In Paris, the bounty hunters swarmed around the Mercedes as it sped from the hotel. The strobe lights from their cameras flashed. A tourist who saw the spectacle said there were so many motorcycles that he thought he was watching an official cortege. Then there was a horrible crash. And the bounty hunters trained their sights on their prey and shot them with their cameras as they lay dead and dying.

In the past few days, I have heard these bounty hunters called journalists. I am a journalist. The people who spent that Saturday writing and editing the newspaper that arrived on my doorstep that Sunday morning are journalists. And we are as good and as bad as most people, with as many failings. But the only things we have in common with the mercenaries who circled that smoldering car is that we are all human. And even that is a disturbing similarity.

There are elements of the human spirit of which no one of us should be too proud.

When a police officer waves us past an accident on the highway, we stare with unhealthy curiosity. We are fascinated with the extremes of human behavior. We like our film stars larger than life, and we are transfixed by their transgressions. We are captivated by television talk shows that show us the worst side of our nature. We want to know things, to see and hear things, that are really none of our business. Things that do not elevate us or inform us. Things that titillate. Things that – from a paparazzo's point of view – sell.

I am, as a human being, as guilty as anyone. The Hartford Courant has not been supplying enough information about the JonBenet Ramsey murder case for my tastes. I check the Web site of the Denver Post, where the story is local and is told in greater depth. The people in Colorado have a legitimate interest in the details of the investigation of that awful crime. I do not. I have read the entire medical examiner's report.

I am not proud of this. But I know that I am not alone.

What keeps the paparazzi in business – what made a blurry photo of Princess Diana kissing Fayed worth hundreds of thousands of dollars several weeks ago – is an all too human lust for sensation. It is enough to fuel an international market, and to sell millions of copies of scandal sheets that masquerade as newspapers. What they sell is not news. What they sell was old when Romans in togas cheered the bloody entertainments in the Colosseum. What they sell is as old as sin itself.

In the years that I worked as a reporter, I covered many tragic stories. A child burned to death. Lives lost to drugs and violence. Mental patients abused and left to die. I did not write those stories because they would make me rich. They did not. I did not write those stories because the job was glamorous. It was not. I wrote those stories because they mattered. To the people involved. To readers who needed – not lusted – to know. I wrote them because the fundamental duty of a journalist is to inform. That is what we do.

The fundamental job of a bounty hunter is to stalk prey for money. That is what they do. There is no sense of duty. There is only greed. We are not in the same business.

We journalists are a long way from perfection. Even mainstream publications and television networks get caught in the undertow of celebrity and gossip.

People magazine ran Princess Diana's picture on its cover 43 times.

Respectable newspapers and newscasts that would never have stooped to report on her private life themselves did report on what the scandal sheets were saying.

Now, print and broadcast journalists have been so swept into the maelstrom of grief resulting from Princess Diana's death that no amount of coverage seems too much. Experts are interviewed about how her sons will react. We hear that they will be devastated. This passes for news. We are wrong in this, as in other things, but not by intention.

As the final chapters of Princess Diana's tragic story are being written, we are all learning lessons. We are learning that humans can be as base as the paparazzi, as irresponsible as a drunken driver, as noble as a doctor who stops his car in a tunnel in the middle of the night to help a woman he does not know. We are learning that we can care deeply about someone we have never met, and that we can, as humans, be united worldwide by a common grief. These are important lessons. And they are being brought to us by journalists.

BETTY CURREN

From The New York Times a decade before her death in 2011:

THE voice on the answering machine is as lilting and aristocratic as Daisy Buchanan's, only with a hint of urgency.

"It's Betty, sweetie. Give me a little jing-a-ling, will you, dear?"

The message is from Elizabeth G. Curren and she is working the phone; on deadline, again. For more than 37 years, Mrs. Curren has been the chronicler of high society in the New Haven area, home to Yale University and all of its prestigious trappings. She has hobnobbed with princes and presidents, philanthropists and playwrights.

Curren was born in New Haven in 1922 and lived there her whole life. She worked at the New Haven Register from 1960 to 2006. Betty was a graduate of Hillhouse High School, and the University of New Haven where she later received The Distinguished Alumni Award of the University. She also attended New York University. She was a member of the New Haven Library Associates and was treasurer of the National Kidney Foundation.

August's Arrival Has White Barn Theatre Buzzing

By Elizabeth G. Curren New Haven Register Aug. 9, 1998

There's nothing quite like a night at Lucille Lortel's tiny White Barn Theatre in Westport, where during the month of August for the past 47 summers, everyone who is anyone in theater is either in the audience applauding like mad or on stage acting up a storm.

That was the case over the Aug. 1 weekend when Carmen de LaVallade and her husband, Geoffrey Holder, appeared in their own "Two for Tonight" revue.

De LaVallade opened with "The Creation," her signature piece according to the program notes, and closed with "Willie's Ladies," starring an old favorite Lady MacBeth, who is always easy to spot in a crowd.

"I loved Carmen's explanation that God was lonely and that's what moved him to create the world," observed the White Barn Theatre's official photographer Tina Tippet Brown.

Holder reflected on his arrival in New York from his native Trinidad in the early '50s to audition for "House of Flowers," landing in the chorus and quickly rising to principal dancer and lasting fame.

"I was 6-foot-6 and wasn't a basketball player and very shy, although I tried to cover it up by acting aloof," chuckled Holder as he recalled his trepidation about auditioning.

"Agnes de Mille was the choreographer and sensed my nervousness and tried to put me at ease. I thanked her over and over again for that.

"Lucille Lortel was at the opening of 'House of Flowers' and invited me to join her at her table after the show . . . and I remember I wore my wonderful tuxedo made in Trinidad, which I was very proud of because it fit well and that's because we have wonderful tailors in Trinidad," Holder earnestly announced from the footlights of the stage. He bowed deeply to Lortel when the spotlight landed on her smiling face in the audience, the nostalgia building.

Holder and de LaVallade were married on Lortel's estate in 1956.

"The excitement was building and the guest list was growing. And I had $750 to my name and I began to wonder how I was going to pay for it," said Holder, meekly advising Lortel of his predicament.

Quickly Lortel put him at ease. "You don't have to worry about anything like that; I'm paying for everything." That was 42 years ago and they're still living happily ever after.

Here 'N' There: Carousel Ball a Nostalgia Trip

By Elizabeth G. Curren New Haven Register June 1, 1986

From the way things are shaping up, that merry-go-round celebration at Lighthouse Point Park on June 21 should be a great nostalgia trip - judging from the enthusiasm of the 70-year-old carousel's many supporters.

"The purity of the building and the whole mechanical workings of this thing are just astounding," said Nancy Stiner, who looked straight out of yesterday in her genuine antique summer white finery (complete with pantaloons!) at Wednesday's photo call to promote the ball. She's an estate appraiser and naturally has an appreciation for fine old things.

E.J. Shumway's view of the restored flying horses at Lighthouse took another tack. "They remind me of childhood and family and the good old summertime," she said wistfully.

Carousels (you'll be happy to hear) are Roland A. Hoover's middle name. "That A stands for Armitage," Hoover said, carefully spelling his name out for me. His family manufactured merry-go-rounds under the Armitage-Herschel label in Buffalo, N.Y., in the old days. That alone's enough to give a carousel buff a pleasant hormonal rush.

As to ball attire, we're talking 1916. "Try to get as close to the turn of the century as possible," a member of the Friends of the Lighthouse Park Carousel earnestly suggested when the subject came up. She's researching the family album for clues. Authenticity's the name of the game with these folks.

Which is why this party'll be up there with June's "best fetes." Bud Finch's playing for dancing, Cathy Connorton's preparing a scrumptious late-night supper (She recently got a spread in Connecticut Magazine.) of lobster salad on the half shell and the man we love to love, Andy Rubenoff, whipping up appropriate decorations. Need we say more?

And forget the carousel - the star of the evening?

Not on your life! Not with those lavishly carved ponies prancing by, four abreast, and "Sweet Rosie O'Grady" playing on the band organ and those glitzy lights and those happy riders twirling round and round on the flying horses by the sea on a moonlit night in June.

So much for nostalgia.

And now for the now. Just learned that the Federal Republic of Germany's former president Walter Scheel plans a stopover in New Haven June 12.

But it'll be business as usual - in this case, the perfume business for the man who led West Germany from 1974 to 1979. Scheel's a member of the board of the House of 4711 in Cologne - a perfume that's as old and as famous as Napoleon - and gave us the word cologne. Which is rather sweet.

What's interesting is that 4711's American plant, Colonia, Inc., is sitting out in Orange, practically under our nose, manufacturing a whole line of fashionable scents besides golden oldie 4711. There also are Gucci, Lanvan, Pavlova, Kanon, Payot, Tabac, Amun and Camp Beverly Hills.

"That's the hottest scent on the market right now," said Colonia's New York publicist, Audrey Wertheim, referring of course to Camp Beverly Hills, which has all but taken over the young, upscale audience that advertisers drool over.

Wertheim did the New York promotion for Camp Beverly Hills last June, launching it at a party to benefit the Actor's Fund of America at the Josh Logans' penthouse overlooking the East River. Scheel, who couldn't make it, missed hearing Logan sing a little ditty from "Knickerbocker Holiday."

"We haven't met, but I understand he's very handsome ... has a great nose ... and, of course, is very charming," Wertheim said.

We'll soon find out. Scheel, 68, is scheduled to land at Tweed-New Haven Airport about 2 p.m. Word has it he's flying down from Canada in a private jet and will take off that evening - but not before high tea. We have Wertheim's word.

When called for, high tea is very high at the American home of 4711.

Tally-ho and ho-ho-ho. The Yale Golf Course recently experienced an invasion of English tastes - thanks to the presence of the English Speaking Union.

"Basically, we wanted to see this beautiful new Yale Golf Club," said Marie Weltzien, a member of the English Speaking Union and a proper Brit in her own right. Their host was Yale's golf pro David Paterson, a Scotsman.

The crowd sipped high tea and nibbled on dainty little sandwiches and soaked up the gorgeous view, then got down to business - the awarding of two summer travel study scholarships to New Haven inner-city schoolteachers.

Norine Polio, a teacher of English for speakers of other languages at Robert Clemente School on Columbus Avenue, and William Coden, who teaches language arts and humanities at Conte Arts Magnet School, take off for the University of London July 7, each with a $2,700 stipend to study English theater, literature and culture.

The bottom line is that the experience will rub off on their students. "Previous recipients have been very enthusiastic, not only about the overall experience, but of the ways it has improved their teaching," said ESU scholarship chairman Margaret Cannon, who did the honors in presenting the awards for the fourth year in a row.

Bully for the ESU - and for chintz, and coziness and marmalade, too.

Bully, too, for the American Shakespeare Theatre Guild on its 30th birthday. Bully also for keeping appearances up when the theater needs it most.

Congressman Bruce Morrison, one of the guests at the organization's recent Elizabethan Tea, came toting a framed citation and a promise that he'd say more nice things about them in the Congressional Record. He's so sincere.

"Our purpose is to enhance the image of the theater," declared Dorothy Gamble, the chairwoman of the tea. The problem is - at least dramatically speaking - there isn't an image to enhance these days. The theater is dark except for its student season.

To its credit, the AST Guild keeps the gardens and costume museum up and gives guided tours when called upon. It even keeps the flags that fly outside in good shape. Members dig into their own coffers to replace them when they get tattered beyond repair.

It takes money and dedication and the AST Guild is there with both, throwing teas, luncheons and an annual antique show. Yesterday's showcased 75 exhibitors on the banks of the Housatonic River in Stratford and raised a tidy sum.

Let's hear it for the AST Guild. Bless them, they refuse to roll over and play dead.

DONNA DOHERTY

Donna Doherty retired as Arts Editor at the New Haven Register in 2013. Previously she rose from assistant editor in 1979 to editor from 1990-98 of Tennis Magazine, *the only female editor of a major sports publication at the time. Her sports writing career began in 1974 as the first woman sportswriter at the New Haven Register, where she covered football, basketball, hockey on all levels, including the New Haven Nighthawks. She was named arts editor in 2005. She earned a bachelors degree in English at Northeastern/ Syracuse universities.*

When Our Arts Editor Isn't At The Shubert Or NHSO

By Donna Doherty Arts Editor New Haven Register Jan. 12, 2012

Some people make New Year's Resolutions. I've decided to come clean and make a New Year's Revelation.

I admit it, and I'm certainly not alone: My guilty pleasure is reality TV, but I'm a snob. My viewing has vicarious implications. No "Jersey Shore" for me. Just too declasse, and besides, who wants to live like Snookie, et al?

There's a trend to my affliction. I won't call it an obsession, though I did tune out of "The Good Wife" Sunday night to watch "The Beginning of the End" with the Kardashians.

While the Kardashian drama queens are my train wrecks of choice, to me it's more about seeing how the other half lives. No different than the old "Lifestyles of the Rich and Famous," right? Mondays, it's "The Bachelor," which is rife with cringe-worthy drama queens, but how about those exotic date locales?

Does it make us feel better to see that money doesn't always buy happiness? Or that we're smarter than most of these folks? Are we, if we watch this drek? I swear I watch it to understand why, too. Why they and an empty Chanel suit like Paris Hilton are famous. Is it the sex tapes?

I sit there smugly thinking I've never married/dated a "box of rocks" as my friend Mike at the gym calls Kris Humphries, the soon-to-be ex-husband of Kim Kardashian. Never had to go to Dubai to discover I'd rather be in the Mideast than with my new husband.

We make fun of these twits and their appalling lack of taste in men -- Kourtney is about to have baby No. 2 with that simpering cuckold Scott Disick, who is still struggling with his addictions, from what I can see.

I've never flown in a private jet. I obviously don't have a hair and makeup person coming to the house every day to do my hair and attach four pairs of fake eyelashes. I won't be renting the penthouse suite at the Gansevoort Park Avenue hotel any time soon. There won't be any gazillion-dollar wedding.

While the Kardashian women are very polite to those who aid them, like limo drivers, the pilot of those planes and hotel personnel, there are moments when I hear my mother's voice remind me that money doesn't buy class. An oil enema??? But even with that ever-present camera, they've been known to act out, and that's why we watch.

Why no shame? Because I know -- and I'm sure you do, too -- these aren't really reality shows. They're cleverly scripted -- well, maybe clever is too strong a word -- shows cast with people we either love or hate who are placed in "real" situations that make for as much entertainment as a bad sitcom. And who among us can say we aren't watching bad sitcoms these days?

Did you really think that Bruce Jenner -- who never does anything but play golf and eat on the show, while wife, Kris Jenner, oversees the lucrative brand she's created -- really came up with the idea of going to Bora Bora to celebrate their 20th wedding anniversary?

Did you really think that the clan all thought it would be a great idea to have two of the Kardashian sisters and their significant others -- and kid -- move in together, fresh from the honeymoon of one of them?

Or have a naked yoga session in the same suite? Or that Disick came up with the notion of buying a Steinway baby grand on a lark while window shopping? Or that the younger Jenner/Kardashian sisters thought they should pop downtown and visit a homeless shelter in L.A.?

As the guys on ESPN's "Sunday NFL Countdown" -- football being my other guilty pleasure -- would say, "C'mon, man!"

All I can say is Hump, as he's called, said to be dismayed that he is being portrayed on the show as the bad guy in the break-up of the 72-day marriage, comes off as the only real person on it.

And he should be Tebowing everyday that he's out of that quagmire.

Poor Hump, he never had a chance. He's obviously just a big, immature kid, a bit arrogant as professional jocks can be, and clueless about the Rules of Kardashian House: Never upstage the ladies. And never do anything on your own without dragging the clan along or without their approval beforehand.

His own reality is a stint in college, a Minnesota upbringing without servants cooking for him and cleaning up his messes that make "wifey" go bananas and ultimately decide she's not good at sharing her world with this lug.

"Cake Boss" is fun, and its artistry appeals to the arty side of me; ditto "Project Runway" and "Design Star," where creativity abounds. "What Not To Wear" is kind of like a fashion Dr. Phil.

"Dancing with the Stars" is as nerve-wracking to watch as a skating competition, but there's skill involved. Live TV. Anything can go wrong, from the dancing to a wardrobe malfunction.

"Toddlers and Tiaras" is all about acting out, but count me out of that one. The ones enjoying vicarious experiences should be viewers, not the pathetic mothers coaching these brats from the audience.

"Dance Moms"? This "teacher" should be reported to DCF. But one does have to check in to these before knowing to check out, right?

The tattoo people are too weird, the Little People as boring as the rest of us.

But the Kardashians are the perfect blend of "reality," fantasy, soap opera, glam and faux celebrity. Can't wait for the new season of Khloe and Lamar on Feb. 19 to see if Dallas is big enough for a Kardashian influx.

Ex-Strad-inary Quartet

By Donna Doherty New Haven Register July 24, 2005

Tokyo String Quartet returns to Norfolk with its priceless Stradivari instruments The cello has its own seat on flights. The viola and violins are stowed carefully in the overhead bins - the equivalent of popping a Van Gogh up among the tote bags and laptops.

The Tokyo String Quartet is world renowned, but even they admit that their celebrity is eclipsed by their Paganini Quartet, the famous Stradivarius instruments they play with dazzling virtuosity all over the world, in residence at the Yale School of Music and the 92nd Street Y in New York City, and, starting Friday, in their season-closing stint at the Norfolk Chamber Music Festival.

The Paganinis - two violins, a viola and a cello made by the master Antonio Stradivari, range in age from 269 to 325 years old. These musical masterpieces are named after the famed Italian virtuoso and composer Niccolo Paganini, who owned them until his death in 1840.

It's nearly impossible to put their value into perspective. Last April, "The Lady Tennant" Strad, made in 1699, was sold at auction to an American collector for a record $2,032,000.

But, while most masterpieces hang on museum walls protected by high-tech security, these instruments are working pieces of art, lovingly played and appreciated by their "guardians" who are well aware of their place in history.

They are the rock stars of classical instruments. The Paganini violin, made in 1680, even has its own biography, "Stradivari's Genius: Five Violins, One Cello and Three Centuries of Enduring Perfection" by Toby Faber (Random House), which follows six Strads from their beginnings in the Cremona, Italy, workshop to the present.

"You have to know how to get the best out of them," said cellist Clive Greensmith, speaking from Tokyo on the last leg of the *Quartet's* Japan tour prior to heading to Norfolk. "The great thing is, the more you play them, the more you get to know them and the more they give in return.

"If you're not skillful enough to get the instrument to ring out its overtones or get the colors and nuances out, you're not operating as you should," he said.

It's hard not to speak of them anthropomorphically, because they are made of living materials and they respond to touch, feel, the weather and overuse as mortals do.

After six weeks on the road, Greensmith notes, the musicians loosen their strings and literally put them down for a rest.

The "Strads," have been through a series of collectors, but since 1995 have been owned by the Nippon Corp., which loans them to the *Quartet* and takes care of the undisclosed insurance premium on them.

The only caveat is that they are always played together, which ensures, as Greensmith puts it, "a unanimity of sound ... a kind of shared sonic beauty..."

He could be talking about his own group. *The Quartet* is often touted as one of the best *string quartets* in the world, but they are anxious to get to Norfolk and indulge in another passion - teaching young artists about technique and the history of their Strads.

Kikuei Ikeda plays the oldest Stradivari violin, the famed 1680 Paganini, crafted specifically for Paganini, who was so fond of the instrument that he vowed never to part with it for as long as he lived, and did not.

Greensmith's cello is, by most documentation, the last cello made by Stradivari the year before he died in 1737 at the age of 93.

"Stradivari can be credited with the development of the modern cello," says Greensmith, noting that its smaller, now traditional, size gave musicians more virtuosic possibilities for solo roles.

First violinist Martin Beaver, the quartet's newest member (2002), plays the Strad dated 1727, and the founding member of the quartet, Kazuhide Isomura, plays the Strad viola dated 1731.

What makes the Strads so special? Some feel the sound comes from a combination of craftsmanship, the wood and the varnish. According to Faber, Stradivari kept no work records, though Paganini has said that the wood came from "trees on which nightingales sang." This lack of data only adds to the mystique.

Certification papers describe the cello as having a poplar back with maple scroll and sides and a top "of choice spruce of wide grain." The violins and viola are maple and spruce in varying hues of brown described as "soft golden orange" to "dark red," a physical beauty that matches their tonal quality.

"I would say Strad instruments have the best of all worlds," says Greensmith, "with a translucent clarity of sound and great brilliance along with a rich patina and broad sounds."

They can be as demanding as divas, requiring that those who play them have skills befitting their reputation, and magnifying the mistakes of those who don't.

"They demand a certain kind of control from the performer, because they have such a purity of sound," says Greensmith. "If there's something imperfect in my play, I notice it - the way you draw the sound and the intonation - when it's not quite true, you'll hear it."

Day-to-day maintenance requires only careful wiping with a cloth, sans artificial polish, to keep perspiration and rosin from damaging the precious natural varnish, which could not be replicated today. "On hot nights, if you don't wipe the sweat off immediately, it can definitely permeate the varnish," says Greensmith.

Periodically, a seam will split from the humidity, requiring an expert's repair.

Traveling is the hardest thing the Strads do. Stradivari certainly never envisioned his instruments flying at 35,000 feet, skipping through weather vagaries of high humidity or dry desert.

"In July when we travel from New York or Boston to Colorado, the instrument literally goes into shock for a few hours. It might adjust eventually, but it can be very difficult to deal with," says Greensmith.

Most people, though not all, are dazzled to be in their presence. Once an overzealous pilot relegated the cello to the cargo hold, despite its seat ticket. Greensmith still sounds shaken when recalling the incident, which ended in a refund - but no apology.

Conversely, on a flight to Brussels one year, he and his cello sat in business class. A well-dressed man in front of him gave the cello a bemused look and said, "If your cello is flying business class, I hope it's a Strad."

Greensmith sheepishly said, "Well, yes, it is."

The man waited for him at baggage claim, and said, "You're kidding, right?" Greensmith gave him a ticket to that night's concert.

This Fan Admires Tom Brady For His Pocket Presence

By Donna Doherty Arts Editor New Haven Register Jan. 19, 2012

If you didn't know last week that football is within striking distance of the end line, certainly you know it this weekend with the New York Football Giants and the New England Patriots in the mix to gain a spot in the Super Bowl Feb. 5.

As a diehard Patriots fan, this weekend presents a very scary deja vu possibility: the Giants and the Patriots heading to a rematch of the 2008 Big Game, when the Giants upset the undefeated Patriots and ruined their record-setting dream season.

The march these past few weeks is eerily similar to that run, the Giants coming out of a swoon to knock off some big guns on the road en route to and in the playoffs, notably the defending Super Bowl champ Green Bay Packers last week.

As in the 2007 season, the Patriots are on a roll, racking up records in nine straight wins en route to Sunday's divisional championship against the Baltimore Ravens. Their last loss was to, gulp, the Giants in the regular season (30-34).

And why do I know this or care? Because I am part of the demographics of the NFL's successful marketing outreach campaign to attract women viewers.

According to the Nielsen Ratings company, more American women watch the NFL than any of the other team sports. In fact, 2010 statistics show that one-third of NFL viewers were female, and the numbers keep growing.

A lot of us are selective viewers. An artist friend of mine told me she hated the brutal hitting, but loved the artistry of the pass, and how receivers sprinted down the field to get on the other end of those passes, and the athleticism involved in making those catches.

I totally agree. I almost turn away when there's a bone-crushing hit, but watching my favorite Cardinal Larry Fitzgerald separate himself and go vertical for the snag is balletic and entrancing. And watching Tom Brady is always entrancing. But I digress.

A couple of things can ruin a game for me: histrionics in the end zone -- Pats' wide receiver Aaron Hernandez, who went to Bristol Central High School here, could cool the dramatics after a catch; and the analysts' over-the-top explanations of things that most of us don't care about or understand.

I am willing to bet when they start talking about a "fire zone blitz from the 4-3," "loading the box," a "cover 2 defense" that a lot of the men watching don't know what the heck all that means. I think it just gives the old football player/analysts a chance to feel like they're still playing. And, just as men will never stop and ask directions, doubtful they'll admit pigskin jargon is beyond their ken.

It's one extreme or the other, too. Saturday, I was yelling at the television when an announcer said for, I kid you not, the eighth time, that the Saints just couldn't find a rhythm. Duh! Don't insult my intelligence. Tell me something that I can't see for myself.

But find a happy medium of explanation that gives those of us who never played football a little more insight without making our brains hurt.

I know the game is far more complex today than when I was covering football for the Register (yes, in another life), but there's just so much we need to know to enjoy a game. I think of that scene in "Bull Durham," where the coach tells his lousy baseball team that baseball is a simple game. To paraphrase, "You catch the ball, you throw the ball and you hit the ball."

If you want more, however, there's a cool book out now, complete with DVD, which can help both male and female viewers, (though I still think it could also be simpler): "Take Your Eye Off the Ball, Playbook Edition," by Pat Kirwan of NFL.com, Triumph Books, $24.95.

It's subtitled "How to Watch Football by Knowing Where to Look."

Most of us, including the cameramen, are watching the ball, where it's going and what happens to it. Kirwan wants us to notice the guys on the other side of the ball, too, and understand how defenders respond to those complex offenses -- something we don't really think about.

It's both illuminating and confusing. The football vocabulary list is fun. It's really up to date, and the breakdown of an NFL work week is interesting. Unless you're a coach, the play-by-play charts and play diagrams are over the top.

The fun part are the simple question-and-answer boxes which answer things casual fans would ask: "Do offensive linemen have to be smarter than defensive linemen?" (in a word, yes). "All things being equal, what kind of defense would a quarterback prefer to face?" (veterans prefer the blitz, rookies, not so much). Or how can you tell if a college quarterback has potential to make it in the NFL? (pocket presence).

And if you don't know what pocket presence is, maybe we can watch the game together. I may go back to the days of the single wing, but I know one thing: Tom Brady has fearsome pocket presence.

And who takes their eyes off Brady in the pocket anyway?

PHYLLIS DONOVAN

Phyllis Donovan had her first written piece published when she was 11 years old on the Springfield (MA) Daily News weekly children's page. She has been writing ever since. A graduate of the University of Massachusetts with a BA degree in English, she has spent her entire career writing feature stories, mostly for newspapers. Her features have appeared in The New York Times, New Haven Register, The Hartford Times and Connecticut magazine, among others. As Features/Lifestyle editor at the Record-Journal in Meriden for 25 years, she specialized in travel features and theater reviews and also wrote a weekly column long into retirement.

Stone Walls Tribute To Times Past

By Phyllis S. Donovan Record-Journal Meriden Sept. 11, 2016

I love the stone walls of New England. They can be the old and disintegrating remnants marking long abandoned farmlands stretching back into woods grown up in long ago pasture lands. Or they might be brand new, sturdily constructed barriers outlining wealthy new properties. I admire any and all walls I see in the towns and along the back roads of Connecticut.

Walls were part of my upbringing. We lived just down the street from my grandfather's property, which extended up the side of one of our Berkshire hills. He came here as a young man from the Dolomite region of Northern Italy and the hills reminded him of home.

In the process of single-handedly clearing his stony land, he removed thousands of rocks and boulders which he used to create stone walls. By the time I came on the scene, my grandfather was an elderly man and we didn't give a second thought to the stone walls surrounding the pastures and orchards on his land where we played.

His two cows still grazed in the pasture and he didn't mind our playing up there on the mountain but cautioned us to always close the gate between the pasture and the apple orchard. He claimed the cows would get drunk if they ate the fallen apples under the trees. I don't know if that was true but whenever we went through the "gate" which was two poles set across an opening in the stone wall, we made sure the poles were back in place.

Sometimes he let us bring the cows back down from the pasture to the barn at the end of the day. No problem. They were usually standing at the gate eagerly waiting to walk down the wall enclosed lane to the barn to be milked.

In the opening line of his poem, "Mending Wall" Robert Frost says, "Something there is that doesn't love a wall." He goes on to say that natural weathering, hunters passing through and time in general take their toll on stone walls which have to be tended regularly as the stones topple off them.

Our grandfather also had a host of grandchildren sitting on, climbing over and walking along the tops of his walls. I admit, more than once we dislodged boulders that were too heavy for us to replace.

Building a stone wall is more than just piling up a bunch of rocks. There is a real science to the art. I recall Homer Babbidge, one time president of the University of Connecticut, was a master stonewall builder and shared his art with others.

Traveling around Connecticut, we see examples of good stone wall builders' art. In Windham county in northeastern Connecticut, there are several towns where we've seen beautifully constructed walls, clearly all created by the same wall builder.

Likewise in Northwestern Connecticut, we've admired sturdy, natural looking walls which are obviously the work of another great wall builder. They have the look of old walls but are done with the precision of a practiced hand.

We don't like some new walls where the stones are all mortared in, giving a flat, artificial look to the surface. They will probably stand up to time, but we prefer the look of old fashioned free standing walls whose boulders will inevitably roll off with time.

But hopefully they will have owners or caretakers who will take the time to replace those stones, because, as Robert Frost points out, "Good fences make good neighbors."

Cursive Writing vs Printed Word

By Phyllis S. Donovan Record-Journal Meriden March 12, 2017

For many years now, I have been bemoaning the fact that cursive writing wasn't being taught in the public schools. Our own children grew up using mostly the printed word to communicate in writing. Then our grandchildren came along and they too basically learned only to print. What with using the computer and texting, they pretty much never had to learn how to use cursive writing in their day to day routines.

But what about writing their signatures or reading letters or thank you notes sent by the older generation? As far as I can see, these children, left totally unacquainted with the cursive style of writing, have to be at a certain disadvantage translating what to them must seem like a foreign language.

That's why I was happily surprised to read a recent newspaper item headlined: "Cursive sees revival in school instruction." The story explained that Alabama and Louisiana passed laws in 2016 mandating cursive proficiency in public schools bringing the number of states that require it to 14. And more recently the New York City schools are also encouraging the teaching of cursive writing to students in third grade.

It couldn't come soon enough in my opinion. When I was in grade school, I remember having the Palmer Method of writing drilled into us. I recall filling sheets with ranks of ovals and push-pulls in an effort to develop the flowing style of cursive writing. In fact, the class was called "penmanship" and even the sloppiest writers among us had to strive for legible handwriting that would make us proud.

Being left handed, I had my problems with practicing the Palmer Method.

My series of ovals ranged from having a serious back-hand slant to nearly lying down with a forward slant. My mother helped to solve the problem somewhat. She asked the teacher to make sure my paper was slanted just the opposite of right-handers, lined up, as it were, with my writing arm and elbow. That saved me from the awkward position of having my hand smearing my work when we were using ink. A simple but effective solution.

I worked very hard to develop a reasonably readable script I could be proud of. All those years for naught. Somewhere along the line the practice of cursive writing fell by the wayside and "writing" no longer evolved past the printing stage.

Not too long ago, however, I was encouraged when I received a thank you note from a granddaughter who attended parochial school in another town. The note was neatly written in a very readable cursive script which, I later learned, was being taught in her school. What a relief it is not to have to print notes to her and her brother now they have not only learned to write but read cursive script.

Actually, I should think it would be easier and quicker to write in the logically connected cursive style instead of printing each letter separately whether taking notes or writing letters.

I have noticed that most of the younger folks in our family have developed their own method of connecting some of their printed letters in a sort of hybrid style which combines the two in a pseudo manner of writing.

The result is mostly legible but, until a new generation learns to write properly from scratch, it's a far cry from what we once proudly described as "Penmanship."

Passwords Thwart Her Facebook Use

By Phyllis S. Donovan Record-Journal Meriden Feb. 4, 2018

I don't use Facebook that much, preferring to keep in touch with family and friends by personal texts. So I was surprised last week when a former neighbor now living in Florida, texted me.

"I received a message from you on Messenger (Facebook)," she said, "I'm wondering if it's really from you because it's a rather odd message. "You may want to change your password … it appears your account was hacked."

Soon after, another friend texted me that she had received the same strange message and said she also suspected my account had been hacked.

My first friend offered to report it for me so I could change my password to make my account more secure. She did, and I soon got a perky message from Facebook prompting me to change passwords after they had checked the files in my account.

The problem was, the first thing they asked for was my old password. Now you must know how many passwords or pin numbers we all use in our daily lives. Many we scribble down on bits of paper "just for the time being" until we can make a more permanent record of them. Some soon get lost in the shuffle. But under "special notes" in my iPhone, I keep a list of many of our most recent passwords.

I had no qualms about plugging in the last Facebook password I had listed there and going on to the next step, entering a new password. The first one I came up with, I got a curt message saying "weak." Since when do computers judge the strength of a person's password? Probably because we use the same variations of names and special days that are easy for us to remember…plus rather simple for any hacker to figure out, I suppose.

My next try was more creative and when repeated was accepted. But the original password I gave was refused so they wouldn't let me in any further. Try as I might, and I used every password on my list which included several of my husband's computer and iPhone accounts, I couldn't get a new password. Absolutely nothing worked!

So now every time I want to browse new posts on Facebook, that help page keeps popping up. It's very annoying that they're trying so hard to help me and I can't come up with that old elusive password which is the key to making the change.

Frustrated as I am, I still have an ace in the hole. Our granddaughter at UConn has a campus job as an IT troubleshooter helping professors and teachers having problems with their technical equipment. She will be coming here to visit this weekend. I know she'll figure out how I can bypass my problem in no time.

Meanwhile, I think I'd better recheck the rest of the passwords on my list. Who knows. by now maybe a lot of them are also obsolete. I guess I'd better do that before our granddaughter visits. Maybe she can help us set up a whole new set of passwords for everything so I can record them all in the same place with the date on which we put them there.

Yes, we live an orderly life but sometimes, in this complicated electronic age, we just don't keep track of things as efficiently as we once did. There's truth in the old saying: "Keep up or fall behind." And we've no intention of being left in the dust.

IRENE DRISCOLL

Irene Driscoll, a 1968 UConn honors grad, was The Hartford Courant's *first woman State Capitol Bureau chief, covering governors Thomas Meskill and Ella Grasso and supervising statehouse coverage. She was later appointed assistant managing editor, at the time the ranking woman in The Courant newsroom, where she worked for 15 years. She later held posts in Massachusetts, as the city editor of The Patriot Ledger in Quincy, MA, where she worked for six years, and assistant metro editor at The Boston Globe for 10 years.*

Her Sex Still A Quiet Issue

By Irene Driscoll The Hartford Courant Oct. 27, 1974

Although she downplays its significance, it has not gone unnoticed that Ella Grasso, Democratic candidate for governor, is a woman.

At first, at least, it added jokes to the repertoire of countless male politicians, including Gov. Meskill, who often accused Mrs. Grasso of "skirting" the issues. Such puns have mainly passed into the netherworld where they belong, but the prospect of the first woman governor elected in her own right has continued as at least a minor undercurrent of a somewhat dreary campaign.

It brought to Mrs. Grasso an unusual amount of national attention, perhaps to the disadvantage of her Republican opponent, Robert Steele. As the possibility that Mrs. Grasso will be elected governor next week turns more into probability, a new wave of attention may develop.

Over the weeks, feminist groups and publications have taken extensive note of Ella Grasso, who dismisses questions about her liberation with such statements as "I was liberated 20 years ago."

Throughout the campaign, some state Republicans continued to cling to the issue of sex, still asking in bumper stickers if Connecticut really wants a "governess" and applying more subtle tactics to remind voters that Mrs. Grasso is not a Mr.

Many national publications wrote Ella Grasso stories, always noting that she would be the first woman elected governor of a state apart from the political achievements of her husband.

Among state Democrats, there has been some modest concern that in the most traditional families, private sentiments about a woman's place might be reflected in the voting booth, something impossible to gauge.

Much mention has been made of Mrs. Grasso's casual style of sometimes mis-matched plaids, pant suits and practical walking shoes could be a drawback. It has been said that other women might be turned off by her careless costumes.

At lest one political columnist thought it was politically significant that Mrs. Grasso wore an "orange tee-shirt" to a big parade.

But other observers contend that Mrs. Grasso's lack of conventional glamor takes the edge off the entire issue of sex.

One way or the other, it was debated.

No similar critique of Steele's style of dress has cropped up. His polyester suits and white shoes escaped all but the most fleeting commentary. Recently, a woman television reporter questioned Steele about his newspaper advertisement depicting Mrs. Grasso as "screaming" in her battle against the Public Utilities Commission. The word, not usually applied to men and carrying a hint of "female" emotionalism, struck an unpleasant note in some quarters as a subtle, sexist slur.

The novelty of having a woman running for governor has worn off somewhat in the state since the initial rush of stories of Mrs. Grasso's "first." It will probably end up a footnote in election history.

But some people, feminists and antifeminists alike, are watching. And if Mrs. Grasso becomes governor, they will continue to watch with special scrutiny.

Early in the campaign, one woman's group with a strong pro-abortion stand showed it felt a personal stake in Mrs. Grasso's success when it endorsed her despite her philosophy, which rules out abortion.

On the other side, there are certain to be at least a few looking for the weak, vulnerable spots in a Grasso administration. They'll be watching not only to make a political case against her, but also to back up their skeptical forecasts of how a woman would fare in high office.

BETHE DUFRESNE

Bethe Dufresne is a former editor, reporter and columnist for The Day of New London. Her work has appeared in many publications, including The Hartford Courant, New York Times, Commonweal, Newsday, Connecticut magazine, and The Christian Science Monitor. She has won numerous regional awards for her columns and reporting, and in 2007 she received the "Spirit of Journalism" award for career achievement from the New England Society of Newspaper Editors. As a journalist, she has reported from multiple countries, including Cuba, Kenya, Russia, the People's Republic of China and Israel/Palestine. Now a freelance writer living in Old Mystic, throughout her career she has specialized in reporting on culture, religion, and race. She is a graduate of Dickinson College in Carlisle, PA, and holds a master's degree in English from Trinity College in Hartford.

Unsavory Times At Academy

By Bethe Dufresne The Day New London July 7, 2006

So the U.S. Coast Guard Academy is marking its 30th year of admitting women. The first-ever cadet to be court-martialed is off to jail for extorting sexual favors. And the commandant of cadets has pledged to make it easier to report sexual infractions.

As a citizen and – especially -- as a woman, I suppose I should be happy that female peers of one Webster M. Smith forced him to face responsibility for his shameful conduct. Yet after repeated testimony by his accusers that they were either too drunk or too timid to stand up to him, it seems a fragile victory.

Late last month Smith was convicted of sodomy – which includes oral sex in the military definition – extortion and indecent assault. He was acquitted of rape, a charge made by an on-again, off-again girlfriend who testified that she couldn't recall because she had guzzled three liters of wine, vomited and passed out.

After the incident, which left her pregnant and led to an abortion, she had sex -- admittedly consensual – with Smith again.

The extortion charge stemmed from another cadet's claim that after she told Smith about an act that could have brought her dismissal from the academy, he requested "motivation" to keep her secret. This led her to pose naked with him, she said, which they had joked about doing before, and to exchange oral sex with him.

Startling testimony that Smith deleted the nude photo because its existence made the woman nervous revealed at least a modicum of decency on his part.

There are so many sad things about this trial but the saddest of all, to me, is that it seemed to send a message that women want the freedom to act as recklessly as men, yet at the same time be protected from our own unique consequences.

Don't get me wrong: We women have every right, or at least the same right, to get drunk, have casual sex or make complete fools of ourselves, and none of this entitles men to do with us as they please.

But here's the thing: men are usually stronger physically, and don't get pregnant. So equal opportunity to control the situation or escape the consequences of alcoholic stupor remains something of an ideal.

The young women in this case were rightfully not on trial, including in the media. That's progress. But I know I wasn't the only woman wondering, day after day, what did they think might happen if they put themselves in such a vulnerable position, and why were they so ill-equipped to deal with it?

Virtually all of us have slipped up, and you have to give the women credit for coming forth when their own part in all this was so embarrassing.

Maybe I've seen too many pictures of sloshed college women allowing themselves to be slobbered over and pawed at during spring break, but I found myself concerned that maybe they weren't embarrassed.

Then I had to ask myself, as a member of the generation that brought you the sexual revolution: what hath we wrought?

Capt. Judith Keene, the first woman named commandant of cadets, wants to ensure that cadets feel free to report sexual harassment, and confident they'll be taken seriously. But if that's all the academy does, it's shirking its duty.

Although you can argue that the trial of Webster M. Smith didn't prove he was a criminal, it showed him to be untrustworthy, arrogant, and certainly no gentleman. According to the rules, that makes him unfit to be an officer in the U.S. Coast Guard.

The unspoken question, which only the academy can answer, is this: what does it mean, if it means anything at all, for a future U.S. military officer to act like a lady?

Prisoners Could Be A Swing Block In Elections

By Bethe Dufresne The Day New London Jan. 20, 2006

Last week's flap about the failure to remove a jailed former governor and mayor from the active voting rolls reminds me of how it feels to be riding on an airplane when the reading light malfunctions or the arm-rest falls off.

In the grand scheme of things, it's really pretty inconsequential. But it makes you wonder. What else in the way of maintenance or monitoring has fallen through the cracks?

Former Gov. John G. Rowland, due for release Feb. 12 after serving a brief sentence for corruption, and former Waterbury Mayor Phillip A. Giordano, serving 37 years for sexually abusing two young girls, were apparently never removed from the "active voter" lists in their hometowns.

State law prohibits convicted felons from voting while in jail, and – just to be sure, I guess – also requires they be stricken from the voting rolls.

They are allowed to vote while on probation, and can apply for reinstatement on the rolls once their probation is completed.

While there's no evidence that either Rowland or Giordano somehow managed to vote in last fall's elections, and no harm done if they did, politicians are racing to make sure such an egregious oversight never occurs again.

Unlike Canada, where the Supreme Court ruled in 2002 that prisoners could not be denied the right to vote, we as a nation exhibit little sympathy for convicts. This despite the fact that so many of us are or have been in prison.

The U.S. Justice Department Bureau of Statistics reported in 2003 that one in every 37 U.S. adults had "prison experience," meaning they were either in jail or had served time. At the end of 2004, there were more than 2 million in federal, state, and local jails, or 486 inmates for every 100,000 U.S. residents.

This is a huge shame, and a huge potential political resource.

According to The Sentencing Project, a national nonprofit lobbying group for prisoner rights, only Maine and Vermont allow those in jail to vote, 36 states restrict voting rights for those on parole, and 11 states allow convicted felons to be barred from voting for life.

I have to wonder why some people are so scared of prisoners voting, unless perhaps it's because half the Americans eligible to vote can't be bothered to do so. The Federal Election Commission recorded nationwide voter turnout for federal elections as 51 percent in 2000, 37 percent in 2002, and 55 percent in 2004.

Given our voter apathy, if inmates had the right to vote and exercised it, they could (pardon the pun) become a swing block. Personally, I'd love to watch the campaign stops.

The Canadian Broadcasting Corp. reported that only 9,250 out of a total of 36,378 eligible prisoners cast ballots in their 2004 federal election, the first time all inmates could vote. However, if the same percentage voted here, we're talking roughly half a million votes, about what separated Bush from Gore in 2000.

All I've done today is play with numbers. But I submit that, instead of looking for ways to keep people from voting, we should be looking for ways to keep people voting. Given the percentage who go to jail, what better place to develop the habit?

As for Rowland and Giordano, I'm far less worried about giving them the vote than about how we ever gave them power.

No Fooling, We're Doing The Best We Can

By Bethe Dufresne The Day New London May 23, 2003

Jayson Blair would never have made it here.

In the wake of the affair of Blair, the ex-New York Times reporter now negotiating a book deal about his suspicious rise to stardom and his firing for fabricating stories, reporters and editors across the country are pausing for reflection.

Not pausing very long, mind you, because most of us are on deadline. But one thing in particular about this sorry case has made me decide that all newspaper readers deserve an explanation.

I happen to think The Day is an exceptionally well written paper, but I'm sure I speak for all my colleagues when I say that we could do better. A lot better.

Our prose could be edgier, juicier, naughtier. The news itself could be more shocking and enthralling.

Take, for example, our coverage of this week's visit by President George W. Bush. We could have told you how the president looked out from Air Force One flying over his birth state Wednesday morning and said, "You know, boys, my Texas ranch could eat this 'burb for breakfast."

We could have told you how Homeland Security czar Tom Ridge shuddered when he caught sight of the Millstone nuclear plant and realized he'd forgotten to pack his potassium iodide pills.

We could have told you all this, and much more.

But we didn't, because it didn't happen.

The more I hear about the Blair case, the more I realize that the vast majority of reporters are working under a big handicap. Worse yet, some readers may not even know it.

In a report this week from Florida's Poynter Institute, which is dedicated to making journalism better, readers surveyed nationwide about the Blair affair said one reason they don't report more errors in the newspaper is that they believe reporters deliberately embellish or fabricate to make their stories more interesting.

This, to me, was a horrifying revelation.

If readers assume that we are making this stuff up, then they must think *this is the best we can do.*

Blair, in an interview with the New York Observer, reportedly said his "favorite" story was about the West Virginia family of rescued POW Jessica Lynch. In it he wrote, without ever leaving Brooklyn, N.Y., how Pvt. Lynch's father "choked up as he stood on the porch here overlooking the tobacco fields and cattle pastures."

First, let me say, that if this is the best Blair could do with free reign of imagination, his bosses really were hoodwinked. It would take a lot more to impress my editors.

That Blair had been promoted as an African-American star caused Times editors to ignore mounds of evidence that they had picked the wrong guy and he was messing up big time. Elsewhere in the Observer interview, Blair brags about fooling "some of the most brilliant people in journalism."

He also gets irate that Stephen Glass, the white self-promoter fired for making up stuff in the New Republic and now hawking a novel based on his deception, is called brilliant while he's dismissed as an aberration of affirmative action.

I could care less whether Blair or Glass is the better fiction writer. I only care about the fall-out for all of us, black and white, whose reporting may be judged as fiction.

Pvt. Lynch's family, negotiating their own book-and/or-movie deal, apparently didn't make a fuss over Blair's creative writing. Maybe they liked his view from the porch better than their own.

All I want to say is, if you think we're dull, please don't blame us. We're doing the best we can with the facts here. Honest.

MARYELLEN FILLO

MaryEllen Fillo is an award-winning reporter, beginning her journalism career in 1971 at The Hartford Courant where she covered education, business, and politics. She started as a reporter covering her hometown of Plainville. For nearly 10 years she was the Courant's Java columnist and also wrote the newspaper's A La Carte column and a column on education. She also wrote for Hartford Magazine, hosted a weekly segment on Fox 61 and could be heard on WDRC. Fillo attended Hartford College for Women and CCSU, having earned degrees in communication, graphic arts and marketing. She has worked as an English-As-A-Second language tutor and adjunct professor at University of Hartford and CCSU. She retired from the Courant in 2016 but continues as a freelance writer for The Courant, Hearst publications and Connecticut Health Investigative Team, and continues to teach.

A Good-Faith Effort To Save A School

By Mary Ellen Fillo The Hartford Courant March 26, 2001

Each school day begins with the "Prayer to Save Our School," informing God that the school "is currently in the state of financial difficulty" and imploring him "to restore it to its former state so that our students may receive a good education."

And although the 56-year-old Mary Immaculate Academy was established as a faith-based school, parents, staff and students are hedging the hope of divine intervention with a fund-raising blitz and accounting overhaul. In an effort to stay open, the financially strapped private Catholic high school is pulling out all the stops: intensive recruitment efforts, a host of fund-raisers, the establishment of a new athletic booster club, a development drive, an increase in tuition and the promise of an anonymous bequest.

"We have probably visited 10 to 12 parochial middle schools in the area to let students know about our school and encourage them to come here," said Amelia Barbagallo, the 16-year-old junior class president. She and fellow students have become the school's unofficial "salesmen."

"Tuition here is a lot less than some of the other area parochial high schools and it's a good school," said Christine Thibeault, a senior. "This is a school that offers a lot," the student council president said. "This is a school that is meant to be here and stay here!"

The school, which is run by the Congregation of the Daughters of Mary of the Immaculate Conception, is considered a landmark in New Britain, where it sits on 200 acres off Osgood Avenue. It was one of a host of religious-affiliated facilities built under the direction of the late Monsignor Lucian Bojnowski, who founded Sacred Heart Church and the Daughters of Mary. The school has 149 students.

In recent years the coeducational school has become increasingly dependent on subsidies from the order. The deficits began mounting, prompting officials to announce in February that the school was in danger of closing unless changes were made.

Within days, the school announced that tuition would increase from $3,500 to $5,300 a year. Lay teachers agreed to pay cuts, with some of the salary savings earmarked for tuition assistance for students with financial need.

A development drive aimed at parents, alumni and the business community will begin in a few weeks. Parents have also established the school's first athletic booster club, which will try to end the financial reliance on the general school budget for athletic programs.

"It is amazing how hard the parents and everyone are fighting to keep this school from closing," said Sally Carlson, an alumna who has two children who graduated from the school and a third who is now a student there. Carlson was one of many parents who lamented any closing as "a great loss."

"The school emphasizes moral values, a good academic education and fosters a sense of community. Those are old-fashioned but solid ideals," she said, adding that she wishes the financial troubles had been explained earlier so even more could have been done.

The closing scare is of particular concern because the city's other parochial high school, St. Thomas Aquinas, closed less than two years ago. Many students from that school transferred to Mary Immaculate. "Those are the kids I feel sorry for," said Barbagallo. A recent open house attracted about 30 new families to the spic-and- span building that was spruced up for visitors. Balloons and a welcome sign marked the entrance. Inside, display boards graced the hallways, featuring dozens of pictures of happy students involved in classroom and extracurricular activities. Students provided tours and an upbeat narrative about the school. Entrance exams were held over the weekend and by March 30, the school must know if it has the 140 students, and the tuition money, it needs to open in September.

"I pray every day for success," said Sister Mary Jennifer, school principal.

The crisis has a positive side, she said. There is better attendance at school activities, more participation by parents and a mood that is optimistic, focused and intense. "If all these things can happen in the next several weeks, we feel comfortable that anyone coming into [the school] as a freshman will graduate from this school."

No one understands the drive the school is experiencing more than a school that has faced the possibility of closing.

"I certainly understand their passion, I think it's a sense of community that developed in a Catholic school," said Joseph Bischof, principal at St. Paul Catholic High School in Bristol.

St. Paul considered closing twice in the last several years and both times, parents and supporters were able to come up with the enrollment and funds to keep the doors open.

"In any situation like this at one of our schools, there is a tremendous allegiance," Bischof said. "We all feel the pain when any of our schools are faced with closing and are pulling and praying for them."

Fireplaces On The Menu

By Mary Ellen Fillo The Hartford Courant Jan. 19, 2006

"I weathered some merry snowstorms, and spent some cheerful winter evenings by my fireside, while the snow whirled wildly without."

--Henry David Thoreau

When it comes to eating out, there is one thing New England restaurants can serve up better than anyone on those gray, cold, bone-biting, shivering days of winter.

Fireside dining.

While most of us have had it with snow, ice, the dark and cabin fever, winter does bring the chance to settle down and savor the welcome warmth and ambience of a roaring fire. Fortunately, for those of us who refuse to let winter weather keep us in, there are dozens of restaurants that offer one of the season's nicest pleasures.

Places to fine-dine fireside range from the exclusive, such as the Copper Beech Inn in Ivoryton, to the traditional, such as the Old Riverton Inn in Riverton or the Stone House in Guilford. Looking for something a little less formal? Try the Saybrook Fish House in Canton, where you can find some winter solace in front of one of two of their recently refurbished fireplaces. Maybe just drinks? Head to the Silo in Farmington, where you can curl up on a couch in front of a cozy fire. Interested in eating without having to get too gussied up? Pettibone's Tavern in Simsbury, with its assorted fireplaces, offers lighter tavern menus that can also be comfortably enjoyed in front of a cozy fire.

The bottom line is that, when it comes to winter dining in Connecticut, there are lots of places that offer the kind of flickering flames and welcome warmth that will surely take the sting out of the coldest season of the year -- no matter what you are eating.

Here are a few other places where diners can be served up some warmth, New England-style.

Sharpe Hill Vineyard, 108 Wade Road, Pomfret

The back-road drive to this expansive vineyard in the state's northeast corner may seem a bit challenging if the weather is especially frightful. But once you step inside this two-story restored colonial house, you know it was well worth the ride. Guests are immediately welcomed by a wine-tasting bar and the wafting warmth and fragrance from the fire in the 4- by 5-foot wood-burning fireplace near the first-floor entrance. Climb up the staircase to the second-floor restaurant, where you are greeted by two more fireplaces that provide flattering, flickering light and cozy warmth to diners at strategically placed clusters of tables that all have a view of flames. If you are lucky, grab one of the tables directly in front of the fireplaces, tables made even nicer thanks to the comfortable upholstered chairs that are the perfect companion to a winter fire.

"People adore fireplaces because of the history and the romantic thoughts that go with them, New England and winter sleigh rides," explains Catharine Vollweiler, who owns the vineyard and restaurant with her husband, Steven. Noting the fireplaces have set the mood for many a marriage proposal or as a backdrop for weddings held at the site, Vollweiler says the fireplaces aren't just for decoration. Soups and stews served as part of the menu are cooked on the first floor fireplace. Apple and cherry wood-fired grills in the kitchen are used to cook many of the entrees.

"I think a fireplace serves as the center of things, reminiscent of when the fireplace provided the heat in a home and everyone gathered there," she says. "People are still drawn to a fireplace."

J. Timothy's, 143 New Britain Avenue, Plainville

J. Timothy's, known for many years as Cooke's Tavern, has been serving up fireside dining for as long as anyone can remember. Five of the six brick fireplaces, all original to the 217-year-old building, set the mood in this local landmark.

"We've switched the five fireplaces we use from wood to gas over the years mostly because they were old and all the years of burning wood took its toll on the mortar inside," explains Tim Adams, who, with Jim Welch, has owned the place for more than 20 years.

As with most any restaurant with a fireplace, seats around the fire are the most coveted.

"We try to accommodate everyone's request to sit near the fireplace," says Adams. "It's easier with the people who get here early in the evening, but others who come in to eat later are willing to wait just to sit near the fire."

The restaurant, which serves tavern fare and full meals, has fireplaces in the lobby, two dining rooms, another in the pub and one in the old forge. The fireplaces have also been featured in a book on architecturally historic fireplaces, Adams says. While local lore says George Washington once slept at the tavern, Adams says there has never been any real proof that the country's first president ever warmed himself in front of any of the tavern's fireplaces. "But we have heard that Thomas Jefferson may have slept here," Adams says.

Simmer, The Shoppes at Farmington Valley, 110 Albany Turnpike

If you enjoy a contemporary setting try Simmer, one of Canton's newer restaurants, which has taken the idea of fireside dining to new heights, literally.

Unlike the brick or stone fireplaces that are firmly planted at floor level, Simmer's fireplaces are sharp, mod, and eye-catching, thanks in part because they are mounted on the walls. A kind of flame-fueled art, if you will.

"There is a magical element to fire and we wanted the warmth and coziness but not in the traditional sense," explains co-owner Randy McNamara.

Diners are greeted by a large black glass fireplace in the lobby, and another hung on a wall in the intimate lounge. The dining room features a kind of tower of fire made possible through some creative stacking of the flat screened "fire pits" that are fitted with special burners.

"This time of year people love the fireplaces," says McNamara noting that because the dining room fireplace is higher than diners' heads, everyone can enjoy the view from the dancing flames.

The Griswold Inn, 36 Main St., Essex

The "Gris," as The Griswold Inn is best known by locals, is the epitome of fireside dining in winter.

"It's just where we go when the first snow arrives," says Jane Stillman, a Middletown resident whose winter always includes at least one trip to the Essex landmark.

Built in 1777, the inn has three fire sources including fireplaces in the lobby, and the Covered Bridge room, where wood is still used for fuel. The Tap Room has a potbellied stove that has its own following especially among those who like to settle in, enjoy the warmth and entertainment.

"We keep the stove and fireplaces running all the time this time of year," says owner Joan Paul. Everybody likes a good fireplace," she explains, noting that even in California and Florida, there are restaurants that will use fireplaces when there is a little chill. "A fireplace adds to the atmosphere and is a link to the past." Add a dining choice from the inn's extensive lunch, tavern or dinner menu, the new wine bar, the signature maritime art, mood lighting and a seat by the fire, and you'll have the makings for a winter memory.

Here are other Connecticut restaurants with fireside dining.

Old Riverton Inn, Barkhamsted; Stone House Restaurant, Guilford; Cugino's, Hartland; Curtis House, Woodbury; Randall's Ordinary, North Stonington; Bantam Inn, Litchfield; Pettibone's Tavern, Simsbury; Saybrook Fish House, Canton; Silo, Farmington; Copper Beech Inn, Essex; Union League Café, New Haven.

No Debating It, Team Is Enjoying Its Success

By Mary Ellen Fillo The Hartford Courant Dec. 4, 2000

Lauren Forstbauer has always considered herself a pretty outspoken person with a strong personality.

Several weeks ago, the aggressive personality traits of the New Britain High School senior also caught the eye of one of her teachers, David Messina. He knew she was the kind of person he wanted on the school's debate team.

So, as team coach, he signed her up.

And with that she became one of several new people in the school's mostly female debate club, which, despite its relatively novice status this year, has already won seven trophies.

"We're doing real well considering we practically have a brand new team," said Messina, who, along with fellow teacher Jeff Prokop, coaches the team. "Having so many new members is very unusual."

The two popular teachers have brought a new kind of attitude to the team, which, at most schools, is often considered the place for the "brainy students." Messina, who took over the team last year, said he not only waited for students to come to him about the club, but also alerted teachers to watch for students who appeared to have the traits and interest that could be parlayed into debate team material.

"It was my history teacher from last year who suggested joining the team," said Amber Smith, a sophomore and one of the two veteran members of the team. Although she hasn't won any awards yet, Smith said the debate club has not only taught her how to be more aggressive and work with a partner, but also helped her develop a more effective public speaking style.

"I really have a soft voice," she said. "Debating has helped me a lot in learning how to make a good oral presentation. I want to be a lawyer so this is a really good way to work toward that."

The team practices every Tuesday for competitions that are held two or three times a month among teams from all over the state. Students debate as two-member teams and as individuals. Each debate contest includes several exercises, including one where team members know ahead of time what they will be debating. There is also a surprise or extemporaneous topic portion in which competitors are given a short time immediately before the match to prepare, not knowing what side of the argument they will be taking. There are individual and team debates as part of the competition.

Debaters are scored, by judges, in a variety of categories during the competitive arguments. Areas include quality of argument, preparation and oral presentation.

"You definitely learn a lot from all this," said Kathy Rutkowski, another sophomore member of the team.

Rutkowski, who belonged to the Sacred Heart School debate club when she attended middle school there, said she wants to be a lawyer and a politician. Being a member of the club will help her get there, she says.

"It makes you stay up to date on current events and it makes you not only listen to both sides but weigh them, because in the competition you have to be prepared to take either side of an issue."

For school Principal Paul Salina, the accomplishments of the debate team may not be as well known as the band or the football team, but are as important to the school community.

"School spirit is a positive thing," said Salina, who regularly announces the debate team match results as part of the school's morning announcements.

"Students who work for the school in a variety of ways, like sports or the band, usually get more attention," he said. "The fact that we have students working in a different capacity but still are going to a competition and bringing back awards is wonderful."

JENIFER FRANK

Jenifer Frank is a writer and a former editor at The Hartford Courant, where her positions included politics editor, Page 1 editor and editor of Northeast, the former Sunday magazine. One of the first women to be graduated from Trinity College, she is editor and coauthor of "Complicity - How the North Promoted, Prolonged, and Profited from Slavery" (Ballantine Books). She is now a mother and grandmother, a freelance writer and editor, and teaches writing to middle school and high school students. She lives in Hartford.

Home In Hartford's South End: A City Neighborhood

By Jenifer Frank The Hartford Courant Jan. 8, 2017

It's great news that more people are moving to downtown Hartford. I can see the appeal of being a pioneer, living in a cool new space in a sharp edgy area.

But if you have Hartford on the brain, here's another thought, especially if those downtown prices are intimidating: What about the South End?

After owning a home for more than 25 years in West Hartford, I moved into a three-family home off Franklin Avenue a year and a half ago. My first floor apartment has three bedrooms, two porches, an eat-in kitchen and built-in shelves in the living room. The shelving and doorways are framed with elegant molding, as are my 13 tall windows, which fill my rooms with light.

I first discovered the South End as a Trinity College student in the '70s.

Driving through its crazy quilt of streets in search of Italian food, passing its rows of tidy homes, fences exploding with roses, gardens teeming with tomatoes and eggplants, I fell in love.

Several years ago, divorced and working in Hartford, I thought about buying a condo, but shuddered at the thought of owning again. I considered the West End, but saw it as too similar to West Hartford and a little too pricey. I wanted a change, I realized. I wanted to live in a city and know I was living in a city. I also wanted a neighborhood.

I began obsessively checking crime reports on the police department's website. I studied U.S. Census data. I followed news about the city more closely. I drove around areas that were less familiar to me. The South End was in the back of my mind, but I wanted facts, not nostalgia, to dictate my decision.

Two neighborhoods — South End and South West — felt right. South West, which borders Wethersfield, is lovely, more exclusively residential, and I now take walks through its streets.

But the South End won out, as perhaps it had to.

I found my home through Craigslist, and my landlords are precisely what I was looking for.

They're a late-20s/early 30s couple from South America who bought this 1905 house two years ago and live on the second floor. In addition to full-time jobs, both are working on advanced degrees, and they consider the house an investment.

One of my neighbors stood in my kitchen recently and gawked. "You can't believe what this used to look like," she said.

In addition to a floor-to-ceiling rehab, which they'd begun months before, the owners reconfigured the plumbing for my washer/dryer, and painted my bedroom the shade of lavender I wanted. Last summer, after replacing the garage roof and rebuilding the back steps, they replaced every window and the front door with energy-efficient models. A text from me with a question or a problem gets a response within hours.

I realize my new environment would not suit everyone, however. Let me talk about being "the other."

I appear to be the only non-Latino white person in my immediate area of multifamily homes and small apartment buildings. Until my dog, Henry, died several months ago, I used to walk him daily around streets more accustomed to muscle dogs than a tall white poodle.

Henry always attracted goofy smiles and outstretched hands, but I felt self-conscious and still do on occasion. I tend to be fairly outgoing and will talk to just about anyone, but I'm feeling my way here.

One thing in particular has made a seismic difference in my sense of belonging. Soon after I moved in, a boy from next door, a charming, gregarious 12-year-old, asked permission to pet Henry. One thing led to another, and I've been tutoring him twice a week for almost a year.

I've gotten to know his mom and his older sister a little. I've met a few of his friends, and communicate regularly with his teachers at Bellizzi, the middle school up the street.

It may be predictable: Invest in something, and there are returns. But I am staggered at what this gives me, at the difference this has made in how I feel about where I live.

When I walk to the library's Campfield branch or to Modern Bakery for a coffee or up South Street to Goodwin Park, the jewel of the South End, I see the challenges that every city faces. I see broken glass on the street, a home not cared for, a sketchy pedestrian.

But I also pass my neighbors hurrying to work, kids in school uniforms waiting for crossing guards, trucks unloading at Carbone's restaurant. There are social clubs and storefronts denoting a dozen nationalities.

And, in the spring, summer and fall, there are gardens bursting with flowers.

Living here makes sense to me and although I haven't been here that long, it seems to have waited for me to claim it as home.

The State That Slavery Built: An Introduction

By Jenifer Frank The Hartford Courant Northeast Magazine Sept. 29, 2002

Connecticut was a slave state. Does that sound wrong? Does it feel wrong? It shouldn't. Connecticut has a history to confront as much as any Southern state.

This reconsideration of Connecticut and its complicity in the institution of slavery is not an academic one. It is driven by the growing, clamorous debate across our country over reparations.

Connecticut is one of the richest states in the richest country, but much of that wealth is stained with the blood of slaves.

That may shock many in Connecticut, who know their state was a force in the abolition of slavery, and that it sent thousands of its young men to die in the war to free the enslaved and end an inhuman, ungodly institution.

But the fact is that politically and socially and economically, Connecticut was as much a slave state as Virginia or Mississippi. It even had that most iconic of slave institutions: the plantation.

The big difference is that we hid most of our involvement because, well, we could. In large part, the slavery that Connecticut benefited from happened somewhere else.

Consider:

Connecticut became an economic powerhouse in the 18th century, far out of proportion to its tiny size, because we grew and shipped food to help feed millions of slaves, in the West Indies.

The rivers and streams of Connecticut in the 19th century were crowded with more than a hundred textile mills that relied on cotton grown by hundreds of thousands of slaves, in the South.

Up to the edge of the 20th century, two towns on the Connecticut River were a national center for ivory production, milling hundreds of thousands of tons of elephant tusks procured through the enslavement or death of more than a million people, in Africa.

Harriet Beecher Stowe, Hartford's most famous abolitionist, said this was slavery the way Northerners like it:

All of the benefits and none of the screams.

It wasn't just about commerce.

Through the 17th and 18th centuries, thousands of enslaved people lived in Connecticut. They were nearly all of African origin, although we began by enslaving Indians. At the height of slavery in Connecticut, half of all ministers, lawyers and public officials owned slaves.

Slaves were bought and sold and traded, often between friends. They lived under laws designed to control and terrify them.

Connecticut was the last state in New England to free its slaves. When a policy on gradual emancipation was adopted, the law was so loose it was easily ignored.

At the Constitutional Convention, Connecticut delegates brokered a fatal agreement to extend the importation of Africans by 20 years.

A few years ago, Connecticut anointed Canterbury resident Prudence Crandall the state heroine for opening New England's first school for black girls. Posthumous honors are fine. But here's what actually happened to Prudence Crandall:

Her neighbors ostracized her, tried to destroy her school, passed laws to shut it down, put her on trial and put her in jail. She fled the state.

The first time a black person's name appears in a public record in Connecticut was in 1639, when a man named Louis Berbice was murdered by his owner in Hartford.

But by the late 19th century, the view of life under slavery in Connecticut had been neatly sanitized, and summarized, by the historian who declared that Connecticut "had little to be ashamed of in her treatment of the Negroes."

He must have missed James Mars' hair-raising account, published in Hartford in 1868, of his childhood as the slave of a Litchfield County minister. Mars' story is laced with whippings, threats, fear and the punishing uncertainties of life as human chattel.

In Connecticut, as in the South, slaves were property, no matter how we have deceived ourselves, perhaps, into thinking that those Southerners were the bad guys, and we Northerners were the good guys.

And that concealment continues. If Connecticut schools even approach slavery, they generally focus on topics that show the state in a positive light, such as the Amistad episode, or the Underground Railroad.

This is understandable. Our role in slavery is hard to talk about. It's hard to know that Connecticut flourished because human beings, most of whom did not even live here, suffered and died as slaves.

But it is important to know this, and important to talk about it.

The story of slavery is not over. The reparations movement is compelling the nation to re-examine its past, to reconsider how we think of ourselves. But, more than that, as a state, as a people, we should know where we come from.

Flora, the young woman on our cover, is as much a part of Connecticut's story as Nathan Hale or Mark Twain.

Flora, and thousands of people like her.

Just look at her.

King OF The Hill; An Aerial Look At What The High And Mighty Are Up To

By Jenifer Frank and Daniela Altimari The Hartford Courant Nov. 18, 2001

If you're from Colorado Springs or Seattle, you no doubt laugh at us, who dare call it a mountain.

It's not Pikes Peak or Mount Rainier (both of which exceed 14,000 feet). But 800-foot-high Avon Mountain is still an important point of reference to many of us, especially, perhaps, to the 26,000 commuters who scale it via Route 44 every day. In short, it ain't much of a mountain, but it's one of the few we got.

And now look at it! Shorn and shaved, looking a tad ... chastened.

Or, more accurately, Chased, as in Arnold, developer and telecommunications magnate. The Chase family, headed by influential Hartford businessman David Chase, has owned numerous radio and television properties in the U.S. and Poland.

Arnold Chase owns the top 123 acres of Avon Mountain, and he is planning a ... well, we're not really sure of the details because neither he nor his attorney will talk.

This is what is known:

Chase bought at least 34 acres of the site in 1990 from stockbroker Graham Jones for $1.73 million. Today the entire property, which straddles West Hartford and Avon, could be worth as much as $10 million, according to one Avon appraiser.

Building lots on nearby Deercliff Road that lack a view go for roughly $250,000. With a view, the price rises to $500,000. And that's just the raw land: house not included.

Of course, Chez Chase will make those homes look like garden sheds.

West Hartford zoning rules permit Chase to erect one house every 2 acres. For this 123 acres, his preliminary plans indicate a single large house. Town planner Don Foster estimates it could be as big as 20,000 square feet. "One lovely home with beautiful views. Who wouldn't want to live there?" Construction is to start in 2002.

Ron Van Winkle, West Hartford director of community services, has walked the summit. "The site itself was awful. Rocky, the trees were scrubby." Since the clearing began, the land "has a surface of the moon feel."

"When I looked at it," Van Winkle says, "I thought, 'How's he going to do this?'" Since then, Chase has been hauling in truckloads of topsoil to create the lush grounds that will ultimately surround his home.

Even the driveway is big: A 28-foot-wide private street will snake from Route 44 to Deercliff.

The view? That's Ely Pond to the west, which is part of the estate. And on a clear day, the Chase famille and guests will have a clear line to Massachusetts.

How big is 123 acres?

The site is almost as large as Westfarms mall (92 acres) and Adriaen's Landing (33 acres) combined.

The incomparable Elizabeth Park is 102 acres.

The only possibly comparable house in the area may be the Farmington white elephant built by real-estate swindler Ben Sisti and eventually bought by fighter Mike Tyson in 1996 for $2.8 million. That 52-room, 48,500-square-foot monstrosity has a potential buyer, but the deal has not yet closed. The asking price is $5 million, down from the $22 million Tyson originally sought. But that house is on just 17 acres and lacks a spectacular view.

Which brings up an issue for which there is no easy answer:

Is it right that in this super-densely populated region, such extraordinary real estate be inaccessible to the public? The easy truth, of course, is that

that's capitalism. A more philosophically grounded truth is that we're pretty lucky that all of that land south of Route 44 is owned by the MDC and is open to all, as is much of the Talcott Mountain Range, of which Avon Mountain is a part.

Nonetheless, it gives one pause.

ROBIN GLASSMAN

During Robin Glassman's 50-year career in journalism, she served as reporter, writer and editor for numerous newspapers including the New Haven Register and the New Orleans Times-Picayune. She also wrote for The Atlantic Monthly, Harpers, and Life magazines and United Press International wire service. She earned a BA in journalism at Tulane University in 1945 and an MA in Psychology from Yale University in 1950. She founded the Journalism Department in 1979 at Southern Connecticut State University and was named Teacher of the Year at SCSU in 1986. She received the Distinguished Teacher of Journalism award from the national Society of Professional Journalists (SPJ) in 1989. SPJ also named their Lifetime Achievement Award after her. Robin is a member of the Connecticut Journalism Hall of Fame. At age 70 she started writing a column for the Connecticut Post in Bridgeport. She died in 2009.

Education Owes Much To Lois King

By Robin Glassman New Haven Register March 21, 2001

Since the death last month of one of my oldest and dearest friends, I've been reviewing her life and thinking about its meaning. Lois King, who made her home in West Haven most of her life, passed away in her sleep on Feb. 13 at 98.

King's career as a public school teacher, teacher of teachers and college administrator spanned four generations. When a retired school principal heard of her death, he said, "She was my teacher in the sixth grade!"

In fact, she was responsible for the education of almost every teacher and school administrator in the area for almost half a century. She was the first dean of professional studies and then dean of the School of Education, which she helped develop at Southern Connecticut State University.

As we grow older, sometimes we feel close to death. The concern is not necessarily about the end of our own lives, but as family members and friends die, we feel diminished. Thinking about their lives and the qualities that nourished friendships and accomplishments, we can come closer to terms with the loss.

Obituaries are cold announcements. But the people who knew her remember King's contributions to their lives and to education in Connecticut.

In recent years, I've written several articles about Lois, but at her request I've never used her name. She said she couldn't imagine what would be worth writing about a woman in her 90s who spends her days in a wheelchair in a nursing home. She was losing vision and hearing, and most days she had lunch with three women who could barely communicate because of language differences and memory problems. She said her only activity was bingo — adding with a grin, "I hate bingo!"

In one sense she was trapped in a small space, but her spirit soared with ideas, memories, generosity and love for friends and 28 grand- and great-grand nieces and nephews. I'm fortunate to have shared her life for almost half of her years.

During our biannual visits in Pennsylvania, where she had moved to be close to her family, we would talk as best we could and remember and laugh — and eat cookies. One Christmas Eve we laughed and shared memories over a platter of shrimp and a bottle of her favorite wine. I saw her in November, as cordial and lovely as ever. How did she feel about being 98? She said simply, "It's fine as long as I feel all right."

I also see her contributions to education spanning nearly 47 years. She earned her teacher certification in 1925 at New Haven Normal School. When the demand for teachers outgrew that school, she worked on its expansion to become New Haven State Teachers College, Southern Connecticut State College and then Southern Connecticut State University.

After teaching in the West Haven school she had attended as a child, she was appointed to the Normal School faculty in 1927. When she completed her doctorate, she was named the first dean of professional studies, which would become SCSU's School of Education.

During her career, she participated in many organizations and served on the boards of the West Haven Public Library and the Congregational Church in West Haven, which will honor her with a memorial service at 1 p.m. March 31.

In 1942, she organized the nation's first day care center for the children of parents employed in the defense industry. We met in 1950 when I was a Yale doctoral student with my first full-time faculty appointment at the Normal School. She was always ready to talk about anything, and she soon became part of my family and I part of hers. After my children were born, I became involved with a nursery school in Westport, where we lived. When I asked her to join our board, she agreed without hesitation.

Lois King's experience was only one of her priceless gifts. To all the generations she has touched, she leaves the legacy of an appreciation for learning and an eagerness to share that gift with others.

She was delighted to hear that both my daughters, now in their 40s, are going back to school for more advanced degrees to change their careers from teaching and counseling adults to teaching and student counseling in the public schools.

My children, who have always called her "auntie," join me in mourning, but our sorrow is tempered with the belief that her influence lives. For as long as she was able, she shared herself with the rest of us. Lois King's life was complete.

BARBARA GRADY

Barbara Grady is communications manager of the California Program at Ceres. She writes blogs, press releases and articles, and develops and manages press strategies for promoting Ceres work on climate and water in California. She spent many years as a journalist, reporting most recently for GreenBiz as a senior writer and earlier for The New York Times, the Oakland Tribune, Reuters the New Haven Register and other news outlets. She has won national and regional journalism awards. She lives outside San Francisco with her family.

The Drug Culture: Everyone Pays

By Barbara Grady New Haven Register Dec. 17, 1989

Every night, victims of drug overdose, drug-related violence and accidents arrive at the city's two hospital emergency rooms.

Their care may cost anywhere from hundreds to thousands of dollars.

Since half of these people have no health insurance, the cost to treat them is passed on to patients who do have insurance.

As a result, insurers are cutting back what they will pay for; companies are asking insurers to hold down costs; and drug-treatment centers are looking for ways to treat patients less expensively.

Earlier this month, New Haven's only residential drug-treatment program became a victim of the cycle. The Shirley Frank Foundation, faced with a growing reluctance from insurers to pay for its 28-day inpatient program, decided to close it.

Drug abuse may seem a faraway problem to many people - a problem others grapple with or one that's concentrated in inner cities.

But its price hits everyone. One way is through rising health insurance costs.

Some 3,115 people came toYale-New Haven Hospital's emergency room so far this year with drug or alcohol overdose as their primary diagnosis. It cost $210 to treat each overdose victim in the emergency room. Some are later admitted to the hospital if their problems are complicated, and the hospitalization costs could run to the thousands.

Claims for substance abuse treatment paid by Blue Cross and Blue Shield of Connecticut reached $2.1 million in the first nine months of 1989 - already matching 1988's total. Those rising claims costs are responsible for higher insurance premiums the following year.

About half the overdose victims who arrive at emergency rooms have no insurance, and the costs of treating them are incorporated into the rates charged to insured patients, hospital officials said. At Yale-New Haven Hospital, that amounted to $327,000 last year for 1,558 uninsured overdose victims.

Treatment of drug dependence and illnesses brought on by drug use is "definitely a big part of the increase in health-insurance costs," said Harry J. Torello, executive vice president of Blue Cross and Blue Shield of Connecticut.

Blue Cross reports that the number of visits to substance abuse treatment centers and psychological counseling by people it insures have skyrocketed 152 percent in two years.

The number of hospital admissions for drug and alcohol abuse doubled in the past three years for Community Health Care Plan of Connecticut. Treatment for substance abuse now accounts for 4.5 percent of hospital admissions among CHCP subscribers and 12.5 percent of the days its clients spend in a hospital.

In the average group health insurance plan, treatment of nervous and mental disorders account for 15 percent to 25 percent of the cost of the plan. As much as 75 percent of those claims are related to drug and alcohol abuse, said Otto Jones, director of an Aetna Life & Casualty Co. subsidiary that operates employee-assistance programs.

"But there's a lot more that a company pays for when an employee is a drug abuser. It's paying for excessive absenteeism, accidents, pilferage and poor work performance," Jones said. Those costs can make that employee 300 times more expensive than the regular employee of average health, he said.

Drug rehabilitation alone averages $9,000 per visit in New England, said Francis Rizzolo, director of the Shirley Frank Foundation.

Rehabilitation usually involves a few days of detoxification and then 28 days of residential counseling, he said.

The high cost of rehabilitation comes as rising health-insurance costs generally have become the bane of business. As a result, insurers recently have cut back on what they will pay for in drug treatment and counseling.

Most insurers pay for a percentage - typically 50 percent or 60 percent - of outpatient psychological counseling, whether drug related or not. For those with substance abuse problems, insurers have imposed stricter criteria on the number of outpatient visits and what conditions merit residential treatment.

With inflation in psychological and substance abuse care running 25 percent to 30 percent a year, employers have told insurers to hold down these costs.

Insurers have responded by offering employers "managed care" - programs in which the insurer helps decide the type of treatment a person needs. Often it has meant approving shorter stays at treatment centers or outpatient treatment instead of residential treatment.

Blue Cross and Blue Shield began offering managed care in substance abuse and psychiatric care early this year. Travelers Insurance Co., Cigna and Aetna Life and Casualty also have managed care, as do most health maintenance organizations.

"As more and more employers became aware that their psych (psychiatric) and substance-abuse costs were exploding, they said to us 'do something,' " said Richard Kunnes, a psychiatrist and medical director of mental health benefits for Travelers.

Blue Cross reports that most employers who renew policies are asking for managed care.

Now, Blue Cross's own staff helps decide an individual's treatment and then monitors the patient's expenses, Torello said. In the past, a patient and doctor decided care, and the insurer paid whatever the bill was.

As a result of managed-care controls, the number of insured patients admitted to substance abuse treatment centers across Connecticut has dropped sharply in the past six months.

That's what happened at Shirley Frank. There were not enough insured patients to pay the costs of operating the 36-bed facility. Seventy employees will have to find work elsewhere.

Many of the eight other residential treatment centers in Connecticut are in similar straits, said Jacquelyn Coleman, executive director of the Connecticut Association of Chemical Dependency Treatment Programs.

"When you have empty beds it means less revenues," she said. Most centers have 20 percent fewer insured patients on any one day than a year ago, she said.

Treatment centers offer different types of care, including outpatient day visits, halfway houses and residential treatment. Residential treatment is by far the most expensive, said Coleman. Several insurers agreed.

Anticipating that more insurers will seek alternatives, Shirley Frank expanded its outpatient treatment programs before deciding to close the residential treatment center, Rizzolo, its director, said. The cost of outpatient treatment is half the cost of residential treatment, he said.

"Addiction doesn't always have to be treated on a residential basis," said Rizzolo. "We've been positioning ourselves to offer various levels of care." The industry generally is beginning to structure treatment programs that start with a few days of residential care and follow that up with daytime visits or outpatient treatment. He said a day visits for several months can be just as effective as one-month residential treatment.

However, at least some people worry that a complete turn away from residential treatment could leave some addicts unable to get adequate care.

"We are concerned that there are indeed some people that do require residential treatment and it is not being decided on a case-by-case basis,"

Coleman said.

Federal law requires that insurers and employers offer alcohol-abuse treatment and psychiatric counseling. But there are no requirements for drug-abuse treatment. The choice to offer it to employees as a benefit is up to the employer.

Southern New England Telecommunications Corp. in New Haven has among the most extensive programs. Its employee assistance program has a drug and alcohol rehabilitation program that has been a model for other companies. SNET spokeswoman Beverly Levy said that besides good employee relations, the program means bottom line gains for the company.

"An employee who is drug or alcohol dependent is not able to function at full capacity and this costs the company in lack of productivity. Statistically, these employees have higher accident rates, higher absenteeism and higher health care costs," Levy said.

DEBORAH HORNBLOW

Deborah Hornblow is an award-winning journalist and former staff writer and film critic for The Hartford Courant. Her work has appeared in newspapers around the country including the Los Angeles Times, the Chicago Tribune, and the Minneapolis Star-Tribune. In 2001, she received first place for arts criticism from both the American Association of Sunday and Features Editors and the New England Society of Newspaper Editors. She resigned from the Courant in 2007. She attended classes in landscape design at the New York Botanical Garden in Bronx, NY, and combines her love of writing and gardening by working as a full-time copywriter at White Flower Farm in Morris, CT. In her free time, she sings in a band, The Central Park Zoo, and designs gardens for friends.

Bonds Babes: The Evolution Of The Babe, From The Soaking Wet Ursula Andress To Halle Berry's Slinky Cia Operative

By Deborah Hornblow The Hartford Courant Nov. 22, 2002

Her name is Bond.

Bimbo Bond.

Judging by outward appearances, she has not changed much in four decades of 007 movies.

Since a soaking wet, bikini-clad Ursula Andress stepped out of the sea in the first James Bond movie, 1962's ``Dr. No," the Bond Bimbettes have physically corresponded to a particular type.

De rigueur is what my brother once admiringly called ``the body of death," a Mattel-like assemblage of parts composed of legs that should be licensed to kill, come-hither eyes that could paralyze her majesty's secret service, and curves that could outdo even 007's specially equipped Aston Martins. Also requisite are monikers that might better suit strippers or women working in what is tamely referred to as the "adult entertainment" trade: Honey Ryder, Lupe Lamora, May Day, Octopussy and Pussy Galore.

Bond's babes look equally fetching in silhouette, bathing suits and evening gowns. The object of every plot line (aside from putting Bond in very expensive trouble and watching him get out, unruffled), is as transparent as most lingerie: Sooner or later, the Bond babes will give it up for 007.

Bond's women are not virgins. In fact, their sexual experience and confidence are part of their allure. They are, to varying degrees, as randy and adventurous as he is. But the Bond babe's particular brand of adventurousness has heretofore largely been confined to the horizontal position.

This baseline (or shall we say bust line and waistline?) established, it can now be said that Bond's babes have evolved quite impressively in other areas. A recent review of the Bond oeuvre -- 20 films in all -- reveals a startling and wholly unanticipated fact: Bond women have come a long way, baby, keeping pace with women's lives off screen.

Bond's bombshells have evolved by increments since the film franchise spawned by Ian Fleming's novels was launched in the midst of the turbulent '60s -- a period of social change, civil rights protests and bra-burning women's-rights marches. Andress' conch diver, Honey Ryder in ``Dr. No," is a competent shell-picker, but in all other ways, she amounts to a symbol of female helplessness and passivity. In the critical climax of the first Bond film, 007 is left to his own devices to save himself and destroy the criminal opposition. Honey remains shackled (and quite fetchingly, too) in another room, helplessly awaiting rescue like the age-old damsel pinned to the railroad tracks.

Flash-forward to ``Die Another Day," and the span of 40 years finds Halle Berry's American CIA operative Jinx in the midst of her own mission, and matching 007 shot for shot, stunt for stunt. She emerges from the ocean, soaking wet and bikini-clad, in an homage to Andress' "Dr. No" hello. (The audience at a New York screening greeted this vision with applause.) But here the comparison to Andress' role ends. Jinx shows the same flare for cool-headed thinking and creative improvisation that her more experienced British counterpart does. She handles all kinds of munitions, sets explosive devices, rappels, punches, parachutes, fences with swords and daggers, flies jumbo aircraft and manages the ultimate special agent challenge: high-diving off a 12-story cliff and landing in the surf without losing her bikini bottom. (You go, girl!)

Before "Die Another Day" is over, Jinx has saved Bond almost as many times as he has saved her. Bond, a charter member of the Sistas Be Doin' It for Themselves Fan Club, is both admiring and appreciative. (Call it stirred, not shaken.) He manifests no symptoms of what Susan Faludi called the "stiffed" male, the one who feels emasculated by a woman's accomplishments. (Quite the opposite, in fact.)

If the leap from Andress' helpless Honey to Berry's high-jumping Jinx seems deceptively easy, the growth of the Bond babe has been gradual. Taken as a whole, the Bond franchise charts the changes in women's roles and the effects on male-female relationships the past 40 years. Besides offering various degrees of entertainment, the Bond movies exist as sociological artifact, an ongoing celluloid litmus of how women are defined by society and how men and women defined themselves in relationship to one another.

Andress' Honey yielded by degrees to Bond babes who were specially skilled -- and not just in the bedroom. From Barbara Bach's gun-toting Major Anya Amasova in 1977's "The Spy Who Loved Me" to Famke Janssen's kinky Xenia Onatopp in "Goldeneye" (she of the deadly gams) to Michelle Yeoh's martial arts expert in 1997's "Tomorrow Never Dies" and Maud Adams' dangerous "Octopussy," women were allowed to battle with Bond or back him up (almost always after bedding him, of course), but they never, ever got the upper hand

Except perhaps in 1969, when Bond met his match in ''On Her Majesty's Secret Service." In Diana Riggs' Teresa, Countess di Vincenzo, Bond was allied with a woman who proved as capable and courageous as Berry's Jinx. But the differences in the plot line, and the way the screenwriters handle Tracy, as Teresa is called, and Jinx, spell out the world of differences between women's lives then and now.

Riggs' Tracy is the spoiled daughter of a wealthy and powerful crime boss. She globetrots and cavorts -- but it is on her daddy's dime, not her own. If she goes on to demonstrate that she has everything it takes to be a secret agent -- she drives like Mario Andretti, skis like Jean-Claude Killy, fights fearlessly hand-to-hand, swills cocktails and tosses off witty retorts -- she does all of this for 007 because she is in love with him. She does not do it for herself or for an employer like Jinx's CIA.

It is no wonder Bond marries her.

It is also no wonder that Tracy is killed immediately after the wedding.

Tracy's death serves two purposes: It frees Bond to a lifetime as the perennial womanizing bachelor (he of the secret heartache and no faith in love), and in 1969, Tracy's demise reminded women everywhere that being too confident and too capable could be injurious to their health.

Riggs' matchless, bravura performance was all the more remarkable because she played opposite George Lazenby, the least credible Bond in a line that began with Sean Connery and has included Roger Moore, the underrated Timothy Dalton and now Pierce Brosnan (who is delightful when he is not being subdued by digitized special effects, Bond's most potent enemy, to judge from the new film). The only good news is that after "Her Majesty's Secret Service," the evolution of Bond women has continued apace.

Take Miss Moneypenny, the selfless, loyal secretary at the British intelligence offices. In early Bond films, she was confined to the role of the silent sufferer, the one who loves from afar and waits her turn to be the chosen one.

"Moneypenny, what would I do without you?" Bond asks in ``Her Majesty's Secret Service."

"My problem is you never do anything with me," she replies.

Moneypenny would do whatever she could to help Bond, even when he was AWOL. But all the while she pined for him without hope of his serious attentions. (If you can call his casual dalliances serious.) But by degrees, Ms. Moneypenny has come into her own. As the Bond cycle progresses, Moneypenny in a little black dress lets Bond know she is dating other men and not waiting around for a global crisis to bring him into proximity. In

"Goldeneye," she warns 007 that his double entendre office-talk might be construed as sexual harrassment. And in "Die Another Day," Moneypenny is allowed a moment of virtual sexual fantasy. A hot and bothered Miss Moneypenny? It's about time.

Then, too, there is the matter of Bond's boss. In the first 007 pictures, the character known as M is an eminence gris embodied by paternal-looking actors including Bernard Lee and Robert Brown. But in 1995's "Goldeneye," M is replaced by a woman played by the formidable Dame Judi Dench, who embodies the presiding authority as naturally as she has a host of queens in films, from "Shakespeare in Love" to "Her Majesty Mrs. Brown."

In Dench's first outing as M, she calls Bond a "sexist, misogynist dinosaur" before pouring both of them a bourbon. If their relationship seems even chillier in "Die Another Day," it appears to have more to do with M's pattern of making merciless but pragmatic decisions than it does any sexual politics.

Some will argue that Bond's womanizing, his tendency to seduce and abandon or sleep with several women per picture, makes him a cad par excellence. But until women are forced to bed Bond under threat of his license to kill, it seems hard to blame him for trying or having success at it.

Besides, he is not the only one.

Consider Miranda Frost, the British agent played by Rosamund Pike. Here is a young woman who knowingly uses her sexual allure as a weapon, dropping her dress to achieve an ultimate victory. ("The coldest weapon," Bond admits.) Like Jinx, and other Bond women before them, Miranda is sure of her sexuality and knows how to use it, but it is only part of who and what she is.

In Bond films, a girl takes her chances, and she pays for them. That "Die Another Day" leaves nothing off limits to Jinx makes the franchise seem remarkably and surprisingly progressive.

In the area of ethnicity, the Bond pictures have also been way out front for decades. A chorus line of Bond babes would form a veritable rainbow coalition emblematic of 007's adaptability to different cultures and tastes. Special agent Bond has always been an equal-opportunity seducer, his tastes for the exotic underscored by the changing skin tones and native tongues of his consorts, who range, sometimes inside the same picture, from Caucasian to black to Asian.

So where does this leave the Bond babe? Can she evolve any further?

There is already industry talk suggesting that Berry may get her own action series as Jinx, the CIA operative. She is bound to become a franchise of her own alongside 007 and Vin Diesel's XXX.

Before starring in ''Her Majesty's Secret Service," Diana Rigg had also appeared in an action series. But hers was television's ''The Avengers," the beloved 1960s series. But ''The Avengers" featured a male British agent, John Steed, and his variety of female cohorts, of whom Rigg became the defining icon when she joined the show in 1966.

Berry's Jinx will doubtless be her own girl -- perhaps with a Q support mate and a Moneypenny-style secretary.

Her name is Jacinta.

''Jinx" for short.

Does Celebration, Or Condemnation, Await Kazan At Oscars?

By Deborah Hornblow The Hartford Courant March 21, 1999

Amid the pomp and celebrity of tonight's Academy Awards program, one moment promises to be the dramatic high point. It is the instant the curtain will go up on 89-year-old director Elia Kazan, who will accept an Oscar for lifetime achievement.

Will audience members applaud in an "Oprah"-like moment of catharsis and forgiveness? Or will they, as some are urging them to do, "sit on their hands" in silent condemnation of Kazan's decision (on April 10, 1952) to name names before the House Committee on Un-American Activities.

"I can't imagine that happening," says Robert Rehme, president of the Academy of Motion Pictures Arts and Sciences. ''I think when the presenters -- and I won't reveal who they are, but they are major artists -- when they present the award and talk about his impact on directors and actors for generations and we run those films clips ... then this frail old man walks out, it will be a very special moment."

But not by everyone's estimation.

For some whose careers were destroyed by the blacklist, their surviving relatives and opponents of Sen. Joseph McCarthy's infamous anti-Communist "witch hunt," honoring Kazan constitutes an outrage. Almost 50 years after his "friendly" testimony before HUAC, Kazan remains a Judas, a celebrated director who could have used his professional stature to defy the committee but instead made a decision to cooperate when others did not.

The drama surrounding Kazan's award pivots on a moral question: Can -- should -- the work of an artist be separated from objectionable behavior?

Rehme says academy bylaws eliminate the issue of whether Kazan should be denied the award. The academy is defined as "an organization of established prestige that is expressly prohibited from concerning itself with economic, political or labor issues," he quotes. Kazan's nomination was uncontested -- "No debate, no demure," Rehme says.

But outside the confines of the academy offices, the debate rages on.

Emily Mann, artistic director of the McCarter Theatre in Princeton, N.J., and director of Hartford Stage's 1984 production of Jeffrey Sweet's McCarthy-era drama ''The Value of Names," compares Kazan to Pete Rose, whose induction into the Baseball Hall of Fame has thus far been prohibited by a history of gambling but whose career is unquestionably legendary.

"I think Kazan's character will be judged by history and by God, not necessarily by the academy. When it comes to awards of merit, I don't think you can mix in character questions with artistic achievement."

Even among Kazan's fiercest detractors, there is no doubt that his artistic achievements are extraordinary. As director of such films as "On the Waterfront," "A Streetcar Named Desire," "East of Eden," "Gentleman's Agreement" and "Splendor in the Grass," Kazan's contribution to film is significant, lasting and irrefutable. His theater credits are also the stuff of legend. During a period of critical change on the American stage, Kazan was the man of the moment -- the first-choice director to interpret the works of many of the country's greatest playwrights, including Arthur Miller and Tennessee Williams. Kazan brought both Miller's ''Death of a Salesman" and Williams' ''A Streetcar Named Desire" to Broadway.

Kazan "was probably the key figure of the 1950s," says Jeanine Basinger, head of film studies at Middletown's Wesleyan University and curator of the school's film archives, where Kazan's personal and professional effects are housed. "He had a dominant influence on styles of acting and directing for both theater and film. He took us out of a repressed era into the next decade. His work in the 1950s, primarily a repressed era, was not repressed. It was overtly emotional and brought to the surface things that lay hidden -- sex, anger, politics."

As Kazan wrote in his raw, often self-flagellating 1988 autobiography, "Elia Kazan, A Life" (Knopf, $24.95), he does not regret his decision to name names, but his is not a proud but a Pyrrhic stance.

In a diary entry the day after his testimony, Kazan wrote, "Miserably depressed. Can't get my mind off it. I know I've done something wrong. Still convinced I would have done something worse if I'd done the opposite."

What Kazan did was admit his own membership in the Communist Party -- which he joined for two years in 1933 -- and the names of eight fellow party members, including playwright Clifford Odets (who, by prearrangement, named Kazan in his own testimony), actress Paula Strasberg (wife of acting guru Lee Strasberg), actor Morris Carnovsky and his wife, actress Phoebe Brand.

In recently released interviews conducted by Jeff Young in 1973 and '74 -- more than 20 years after the testimony -- Kazan regretted ``the human cost" of his action. (Young's interviews are to be published in spring by Newmarket Press under the title "Kazan: The Master Discusses His Film.")

"Anybody who informs on other people is doing something disturbing and even disgusting," Kazan told Young. "It doesn't sit well on anybody's conscience. But at the same time, I felt a certain way, and I think it has to be judged from the perspective of 1952."

In 1952, the blacklist already had been a political and social force for five years, a byproduct of the "Red Scare" and fear of Communism that was sweeping the country. In headline-grabbing attempts to prevent the spread of Communism and its tenets, past and present members of the Communist Party and those thought sympathetic to the cause were publicly identified and subpoenaed to testify before the government committee led by McCarthy.

The trials were immediately decried by liberals as a witch hunt, and McCarthy was branded an ambitious zealot (his name recently has been linked to that of White House special prosecutor Kenneth Starr).

Those named faced dire social and economic consequences. In Hollywood, being blacklisted was tantamount to career death.

Kazan's decision to name names actually marked his second appearance before the intimidating, sometimes threatening House committee. In his first, a closed session held on Jan. 14, 1952, he refused to name names. (Meanwhile, individuals including Budd Schulberg, who would later write "On the Waterfront" for Kazan, and Broadway director Jerome Robbins had, among others, "sang" before the committee.)

The pressures that came to bear on Kazan between Jan. 14 and April 10 were considerable. As one of -- if not the most -- visible and successful celebrities called before the committee, Kazan represented a prize for either side; a pawn whose defiance or cooperation would be played in the press.

At the time, HUAC was pointing fingers at Hollywood and calling it the "financial angel of the Communist Party." Nervous, image-conscious studio execs, including Kazan's sometime angel Darryl Zanuck at 20th Century Fox, were urging Kazan to testify "friendly." Kazan was aware that refusing to cooperate would cost him his film career. At intervals, Kazan also believed a refusal to cooperate could bring jail time.

More important by his own account, Kazan had begun to believe that by not cooperating, he was helping to perpetuate the secrecy and "stealth" of the Communist Party. To some, this logic appears a convenient, conscience-salving justification. Others say Kazan had already had enough dealings with the party to loathe their tactics and fear their power.

Kazan had joined as an alienated, angry young intellectual -- the eldest son of an Anatolian carpet dealer -- and a new member of the radical, fledgling Group Theatre. But two years after firsthand exposure to some of the party's tactics -- and the sheep-like obeisance of some of his fellow members -- "I quit in disgust," he wrote.

He was now an affluent, successful director with a debt to the American way of life.

Also weighing on Kazan at the time were his experiences with

Communist Party leaders in Mexico who had tried to influence the script of "Viva Zapata!" and the reservations of his wife, Molly, whose job at New Theatre magazine was being threatened by Communist Party leaders, and his therapist.

As Kazan's probable course of action began to shift, he sought out his friends and colleagues. In his autobiography, he recollects conversations with Miller, Odets, the Strasbergs and Lillian Hellman. He and Odets agreed to name each other; Miller, according to Kazan, told him to follow his heart; the Strasbergs voiced no objection to Kazan's plan to name Paula; and Hellman, Kazan says, abruptly ended the conversation. (Some of Kazan's harshest invective is reserved for Hellman, whom he accuses of manipulating circumstances in the aftermath to cast herself as a cultural hero.)

In the end, Kazan did what he did because, as he writes, "I believed it was the duty of the government to investigate the Communist movement in our country. I couldn't behave as if my old 'comrades' didn't exist and didn't have an active political program. ... I knew very well what [the Communist Party] was, a thoroughly organized, worldwide conspiracy."

Following his testimony in a public hearing, Molly Kazan was inspired to write a defense of her husband's action, which the Kazans ran as an ad in The New York Times.

"Secrecy serves the Communists," it explained. "At the other pole, it serves those who are interested in silencing liberal voices."

But Kazan had named names, effectively damning former colleagues to economic peril and ostracism from Hollywood.

This act and the ad that followed outraged many.

Overnight, the most celebrated theater and film director of the time became a pariah. Subsequent to his "friendly" testimony, Kazan found himself the scourge of liberals, and many friendships and professional alliances -- including the important alliance he shared with Miller -- were compromised. (He and Miller worked together 10 years later, but their close friendship was never the same. Miller, who lives in Connecticut and is currently enjoying the successful Broadway revival of "Death of a Salesman," politely refused through a publicist to answer questions pertaining to Kazan's award.)

In a haunting anecdote in his autobiography, Kazan describes meeting actor Zero Mostel (who was blacklisted) on the street in New York City years after the HUAC testimony. The two went to a bar and sat, with little conversation, over a few drinks. Mostel finally put his arm around Kazan's neck. "Why did you do that?," he asked. "You shouldn't have done that."

"You can only know if you're there, if you're faced with that decision yourself," Rehme says. "[Blacklisted writer Dalton] Trumbo's words are really the best. He said, 'There were no winners. There were no losers. Only victims.' [Kazan] was a victim, too."

"Unless you've been through what he's been through, it's hard to judge," says Mann. "He's said he acted on his conscience. Let's hope so. The older you get, you realize one can be put in a very difficult position on a moral and ethical level. You pray you're not put in one of those, and if you are, you pray you do the right thing."

Kazan's defenders attempt to lessen his offense by saying he gave up only names already known to the committee. But others chastize him for naming those he may have held grudges against -- with the exception of Odets. (Kazan's autobiography makes clear that he disliked Carnovsky and had reasons to hold a grudge against Paula Strasberg, who revealed to Molly Kazan that her husband was having an affair.)

Americans love a hero -- especially the man who stands alone against powerful opposition.

Cinema has a long history of celebrating such individuals -- Eliot Ness, Gary Cooper's sheriff in "High Noon" and, of course, Brando's boxer and dock worker Terry in the Oscar-sweeping ''On the Waterfront." (Released in 1954, it is a film Kazan calls "my reply to the beating I'd taken.")

But history has shown -- and Kazan has, too -- that not everyone can be a hero. Kazan's work has been consistent in showing us that most of us are merely human.

One of the hallmarks of Kazan's work -- especially his legendary Broadway production of "A Streetcar Named Desire" -- is what Williams first called "fidelity to life" and Kazan's refusal to paint issues in a morally comfortable black and white.

This intellectual stubbornness is typified in Kazan's legendary Broadway debut of Williams' "Streetcar." Although other directors went on to render

Stanley as the "black-dyed villian" Williams feared, and ennobled the ruined Blanche Du Bois, Kazan refused. Guided by Williams' entreaties, Kazan created a production far more complex and far more human.

It is one of the ironies of Kazan's lifetime achievement award that it has instigated his second trial by public opinion and by the press.

Throughout the controversy, he has remained silent.

But how he has made the rest of us talk.

MARGE HOSKIN

Marge Hoskin has been writing her weekly "Quiet Corner Whispers" column for The Bulletin in Norwich since October 2000. She grew up in Connecticut's Quiet Corner (Northeastern Connecticut), graduated from UCONN (an English major), then joined the U.S. Navy where she served for 20 years retiring with the rank of Commander. Marge and her husband, a retired naval officer, returned to northeastern Connecticut where she has been an active volunteer with numerous nonprofit organizations with a penchant for nature and/or local history. She is one of the founders of The Last Green Valley National Heritage Corridor, an area covering 35 towns in Northeastern Connecticut and Central Massachusetts. Its mission: "to ensure a natural and cultural legacy for generations to come."

She says her columns have brought her new friends, and have been great exercise for her head.

Quiet Corner Whispers: Tailwind Was A High-flying Groundhog

By Marge Hoskin The Bulletin Norwich Jan. 29, 2018

Friday is Groundhog Day. Through the years, my family always called groundhogs "woodchucks," while others know them as "whistle-pigs" because of that little whistle they make to warn their buddies when we gardeners give chase.

And chase them I have, for I have found them to be some of the most enthusiastic vegetarians I have had the displeasure to meet.

They are cute when they are young and lay flat on their tummies on my sun-heated stone walls, but unfortunately, like the rest of us, they become adults too soon.

Recently, a friend offered to share his recipe for cooking (and eating) a groundhog, but I explained that I am not as adventurous a cook or eater as I once was.

At the Smithsonian's National Air and Space Museum (Archives Division), I recently discovered a photograph with a story about a flying groundhog named Tailwind.

Tailwind belonged to Edna Newcomer, a nurse and licensed pilot, and the Smithsonian's newspaper photo pictures them both in the window of the cockpit of a Bellanca Skyrocket named "The American Nurse" at Floyd Bennett Field, New York, in September of 1932.

Dr. Leon Pisculli is also seen in the photo. He was the organizer of the non-stop New York-Rome flight to study "the effects of long-distance flight on humans" (and, perhaps, on groundhogs?)

According to newspapers of the day, Edna Newcomer had planned to bail out in Rome dressed in white riding clothes and descend by parachute. (It was said she had also brought along a dress just in case she was presented to King Victor Emmanuel III.)

The last time the Skyrocket and its passengers were seen was by the S.S. France some 400 miles from the plane's European destination. Edna, Leon, their pilot and Tailwind the groundhog were never seen again.

For a photo of the aircraft complete with groundhog, visit the website airandspace.si.edu/stories.

"Groundhog Day" is one of my favorite movies, but if I had to keep repeating the same winter day like its hero did, I would prefer that it be in warmer weather when I would listen for a "whistle pig" warning its colony that they were about to meet a human being with an anti-groundhog attitude.

Work Done By Civilian Conservation Corps Remains A Treasure Today

By Marge Hoskin The Bulletin Norwich June 24, 2008

Think we're facing tough economic times? Chat with someone who lived during the Great Depression of the 1930s to discover what the word "adversity" really means.

In 1933, President Franklin D. Roosevelt established the Civilian Conservation Corps — the CCC. One of the "alphabet agencies," it was part of his New Deal program to bring immediate economic relief as well as long-term reforms.

For nine years, the corps were supervised by the U.S. Army and provided work and vocational training for unemployed, single young men. By 1935, more than 500,000 men in 2,600 camps were working on projects to conserve and develop the country's natural resources.

Walter Sekula Sr. of Norwich reminded me that 2008 is the corps' 75th anniversary. He joined the corps in 1938 "when the feds were looking for volunteers to go west of the Mississippi," he said.

After orientation at Fort Devens in Massachusetts, Sekula spent two years in Meeker, Colo., building "drift fences, watering holes and sheep dips," he said. In 1940, he joined the U.S. Army.

Several corps camps were located in northeastern Connecticut. Camp Fernow was in Natchaug State Forest in Eastford and Camp Lonergan in Pachaug State Forest in Voluntown.

In recent years, corps alumni established the Northeast States Civilian Conservation Corps Museum at the former corps Camp Conner in Shenipsit State Forest in Stafford Springs. The museum has photographs, documents and memorabilia from many of the camps. Call 684-3430 for information.

Crews at Camp Conner worked on a myriad of conservation projects and provided disaster relief after the 1936 Flood and the Hurricane of 1938. The beautiful mountain laurel sanctuary in Nipmuck State Forest in Union was a corps project.

Marty Podskoch, who spoke recently at the Mansfield Historical

Society, collects corps alumni stories. His Web site, www.CCCstories.com, has a link to the 1933 newsreel of Roosevelt lunching with workers at the first corps camp to be established, Camp Roosevelt in Virginia's George Washington Forest.

Whether it's a mountain laurel sanctuary in the Quiet Corner or Skyline Drive along the spine of Virginia's Shenandoah Mountains, corps workers have left us a remarkable legacy.

Quiet Corner Whispers: I Can't Forgive Scientist Who Loosed Tree-killing Pests

By Marge Hoskin The Bulletin Norwich June 26, 2017

On the whole, scientists are great people who work to improve the lives of mankind including me; however, I do have a bone — or wing — to pick with amateur scientist, lepidopterist Leopold Trouvelot.

It was Trouvelot according to most sources who let several individual adult gypsy moths, part of an experiment he was conducting at his Medford, Massachusetts, home, escape to the outside world in 1868-69.

He was trying to find a new species of silk-producing moths resistant to the diseases of the silkworm moth. Instead, we now have a forest pest that has defoliated millions of acres in our area of the United States as well as Virginia, North Carolina, Michigan and even a number of Pacific Coast states.

Rocky Mountain locusts in the 1800s are said to have been even worse than our gypsy moths. There were "flying hordes" of the locust that destroyed acres of crops in fields from California east to Minnesota and south to Texas.

"They were easy to please," Carol Yoon wrote in the science section of The New York Times in 2002. The locusts ate "barley, buckwheat, melons, tobacco, strawberry, spruce, apple trees — even fence posts, laundry hung out to dry and each other."

We humans can be equally dangerous. In the Windham County Transcript newspaper a century ago, Feb. 28, 1901, the editor complained about "the wholesale slaughter of forests" in northeastern Connecticut being caused by "greedy human beings." The wood was primarily used for charcoal fuel.

"Keen speculators … have been buying the wooded hills of Connecticut and stripping them of all vegetation, while manufacturers and the public have suffered thereby from the drying up of neighboring streams," he wrote. "Forests not only conserve the rainfall, but they help to create it and to regulate the climate in general. Now a heavy rainfall will be carried off by the streams in a few days instead of feeding the springs and reservoirs gradually. This winter, for the first time in man's memory, the reservoirs are dry."

I can understand the Rocky Mountain locusts and even the "greedy human beings," but have yet to forgive Leopold Trouvelot and his gypsy moth escapees who this month have made my life so darn miserable.

KAREN HUNTER

Karen Hunter is a writer, editor, and associate director of communications at Hartford Hospital. Working in Fund Development, she produces and manages communications about the hospital's philanthropic community. Before joining Hartford Hospital in 2013, she served as assistant director of marketing communication at the University of Hartford. Formally trained in journalism at Howard University in Washington, D.C., Karen spent more than 30 years working in the news industry as a reporter, copy editor, copy desk chief, columnist and ombudsman before joining the University of Hartford. In addition to The Hartford Courant, she has worked for The Baltimore Sun, The Wall Street Journal, Dow Jones and Co., and CNN. She served two years as a Pulitzer Prize jurist. She lives in Middletown. During her free time, she volunteers at Hartford Hospital and tends to her backyard garden. She also produces social media marketing campaigns and creates and manages websites for small businesses and social organizations.

Where's Spirit Of Christimas?

By Karen Hunter The Hartford Courant Dec. 31, 2006

The news staff and I have come to expect the e-mails and calls that arrive on Dec. 25 from readers perturbed that The Courant's front page is not dressed with "Merry Christmas" or reindeer leading Santa across the nameplate.

The disagreement is so ingrained that the newsroom bulletin board is decorated with the "Merry Christmas" that the Journal Inquirer sent to its readers on Christmas Day.

As the inevitable letter to the editor from a Bristol reader said, "When we retrieved our issue ofThe Courant this morning, what came immediately to our attention was not what was on the front page, but what was missing. Just in case all of you have forgotten, today is December 25th, a day millions throughout the world celebrate, CHRISTMAS.

"In your infinite wisdom to remain 'politically correct,' and an attempt not to 'offend' anyone, you have certainly offended many. So to all of you at The Courant, MERRY CHRISTMAS. If that is offensive, you have our deepest sympathy, for you have missed the true spirit of the season...PEACE and GOODWILL to ALL."

The complaint has come up every year since I've been reader representative and probably since the holiday greetings disappeared from the front page in 1997. For Managing Editor Barbara Roessner, the explanation of the decision is simple.

"The nameplate 'greeting' is inappropriate in an increasingly diverse culture, and among a readership that includes many non-Christians. I think it's fine if the editorial pages want to offer a direct message, but very rarely does the institution of The Courant speak directly to readers on the news pages. The role of the journalist is to be an astute and engaged observer. The mission of the news pages is to chronicle what's happening in our communities with stories and photos and interesting graphics. We did that amply before, during and after Christmas, as we do with other holidays, whether they're religious or secular. In fact, there was a very eye-catching image of a Christmas tree on the front page on Christmas Day, and plenty of holiday-related coverage throughout the paper."

As I have said in the past, if it were my decision, I would provide readers with the obvious acknowledgment of the holiday that some desire. However, those so quick to criticize the newspaper's lack of holiday spirit should take a moment to reflect on the story "A Long Road Home." They would find within it the true spirit of the season.

In telling the story of Navy veteran Roger Slight's struggle to find a home in Middletown for himself and his dog, reporter Alaine Griffin and photographer Cloe Poisson touched some readers in a way that the mere words "Merry Christmas" could not. It did what any editor hopes a newspaper does best: reach readers with stories about people who make a difference.

The dozens of readers who contacted the newspaper looking for ways to help Mr. Slight found the story to be "the perfect holiday gift," as a Hartford reader wrote.

A Willimantic reader understood.

"Bless you and thank you for the wonderful, riveting photographs of Roger Slight and Malachi on Christmas. It takes only modest insight to appreciate their value, their good lessons, and the angels seen and unseen. For the record, I do not know any of those referred to above.

"I hope this sort of thing reminds ... that being jaded about publishing a newspaper might be the wrong attitude. My hat is off to the photographer and to whoever had the powerful idea that the photographer captured.

"I wish Mr. Slight, Malachi and everyone at your newspaper a fortunate and happy New Year."

Yes, if you looked at the superficial on Christmas morning, you might have seen a Courant that didn't send a personal holiday greeting. But we all know that Christmas is more than red letters and glitter.

The Courant's front-page story captured that fact on Dec. 25.

Happy New Year.

Why Not Take 'Man' Out Of Titles?

By Karen Hunter The Hartford Courant Dec. 4, 2005

The request from a Bristol reader seemed fair enough, especially in this day and age.

"I would like to see The Courant move toward gender-neutral titles in all articles," Mary Rydingsward wrote in an e-mail last month. Her point being that "language sends an important message that is not only immediately received by the readers, but also resonates in the reader's subconscious."

Rydingsward suggested referring to town council representatives as "councilors." She noted that "other local newspapers have taken this path to eliminate gender bias." It would be a small change, she said, that would "have a huge, long-lasting affect."

The Courant has a style committee -- made up mostly of men, by the way -- whose charge it is to mull over and decide the newspaper's "particular manner of dealing with spelling, punctuation, word division, etc." -- to borrow a definition from Webster's New World Dictionary, Fourth Edition.

The chairman of the committee, Harvey Remer, also happens to be the chief of the news copy desk. (Notice the mixture of gender-designating and gender-neutral titles.) I presented Rydingsward's request to Remer, who said, "I appreciate the reader's concern for gender-neutral language. We have moved toward this with terms such as firefighter, police officer, but we're stymied by women who insist on being called first selectman."

Indeed, The Courant's stylebook advises, "Don't use sex-designating words or phrases when an alternative is available: examples are business executive for businessman; firefighter for fireman; mail carrier for mailman; members of Congress, representatives, lawmakers or legislators for congressmen ... police officer for policeman or policewoman; salespeople for salesmen; and supervisor for foreman."

The stylebook even offers a suitable alternative to councilman/ councilwoman in "council member."

Still, Remer presented the reader's request to the style committee, which gave a thumbs-down to using "councilor." The reason: "The most common argument against 'councilor' was confusion with 'counselor,'" Remer said.

So, the "councilor" argument was lost, but Rydingsward point applies to some other titles frequently found in the newspaper. The Courant's stylebook adheres to gender designations when referring to chairman/ chairwoman and selectman/selectwoman. The stylebook says: "When a woman is running for chairman, selectman, etc., leave the designation as -man until she wins the position, then call her chairwoman or selectwoman as appropriate."

As Rydingsward noted after hearing the "councilor" verdict, "I see that there is work to do in the realm of communicating gender equality through the written media."

Why Polls Didn't Get Races Right

By Karen Hunter The Hartford Courant Feb. 17, 2008

With pre-primary polls taking a beating lately, it's only logical to wonder what the problem is.

As a reader asked days before Super Tuesday, "What is going on with political polling in Connecticut, and specifically the Connecticut Poll?"

What caught his attention was a poll released Jan. 20 showing Sen. Barack Obama trailing Sen. Hillary Clinton by 14 percentage points. The idea that Obama "surprised" The Courant with his Feb. 5 primary victory made the reader's questions even more interesting.

He wanted to know the methods used in the Jan. 9-17 survey, sponsored by The Courant and the Center for Survey Research and Analysis at the University of Connecticut.

Were minorities left out of Hartford Courant polling? he asked. Did the UConn survey center use voter registration lists matched to unreliable resources and databases?

"Connecticut phone matching is notoriously poor," he said. "Cities like Hartford, Bridgeport and New Haven, which are home to most of Connecticut's minority voters, have historically poor list presence.

"Connecticut has seen a surge of new voter registration, particularly on the Democratic side. The list-based method excludes these new and motivated voters who are the most likely to vote in a primary. Another huge flaw. It would be well if we could analyze the impact of this fault, but CSRA's press release specifically omits the demographic profile of respondents."

Obviously, this was someone who pays a lot of attention to polls and wanted much more than the margin-of-error disclaimer.

Research director Monika McDermott of the UConn survey center said much of the details about the organization's polling methods and the demographics of respondents are available to anyone who contacts her organization. She admitted, however, that the poll did not predict the type of momentum that is defining this primary season. It wasn't meant to, she said.

"It was released two weeks before the primary. It was meant to be a snapshot, to capture the state of mind of voters at that particular time. The media says, 'Here's where things stand right now.' So comparing the poll to the election results is an invalid criticism," she said.

"Pollsters try to be responsible vehicles of learning and provide useful information. What the media gives is a horse race....I send out a 15-page press release with detailed questions and the media focuses on two numbers. But that's understandable. That's what sells newspapers. Everyone likes a contest."

McDermott was emphatic that minorities were not left out of the poll, but she conceded that any telephone polling underrepresents certain segments of the population.

"It's an admitted industry-wide problem. You miss a certain portion of the population when you do telephone polling because of the times the calls are made. You miss people who work at night. You may miss people who have two jobs...This race is a tough one for that reason. In a race like this where young voters and minority voters are important, it could be an issue," she said.

Pollsters agree that this race has been particularly difficult. As Jay H. Leve, CEO of the research firm SurveyUSA, said, "It's a perfect storm. A black man and a white woman running for president is unprecedented. Then you have very passionate voters. Passion is difficult to pick up in a poll."

Given the fascination factor and the learning opportunities this historic race provides, The Courant and the survey center would do well to answer the polling industry's request for more transparent polls by detailing the methodology on their websites - if only to satisfy the serious poll-watchers.

MICHELE JACKLIN

Michele Jacklin was a journalist for 30 years, 28 of them with The Hartford Courant where she was a town news reporter, bureau chief, legislative reporter, chief political reporter, editorial writer and political columnist.

Over the course of her career, she covered the Connecticut General Assembly; state, local and national politics; public policy; Connecticut's congressional delegation; and the administrations of Govs. William A. O'Neill, Lowell P. Weicker, Jr., John G. Rowland and M. Jodi Rell. She attended seven presidential conventions, beginning in 1988 through 2000. She has won numerous awards, among them the Allan B. Rogers Editorial Award from the New England Newspaper Association; the Harriet Tubman Award for Social Justice from the Connecticut chapter of the National Organization for Women; a Woman of Excellence Award from the National Foundation of Women Legislators; First Place Awards for Excellence in Journalism from the Society of Professional Journalists; the President's Award from the Connecticut Public Health Association; and the Champion of Open Government Award from the Connecticut Council on Freedom of Information. Jacklin continues to be active in politics and public policy. She serves on the boards of Common Cause Connecticut, the Connecticut Foundation for Open Government, the Connecticut Council on Freedom of Information, the Connecticut Medical Examining Board and 1000 Friends of Connecticut. She lives in Glastonbury, CT, with her husband, James Estrada.

What's At Stake: The Right To Privacy

By Michele Jacklin The Hartford Courant Nov. 9, 2005

Connecticut is where it started. It was here that a group of courageous individuals made a stand, staking their claim to a constitutional right to privacy that was later affirmed by the U.S. Supreme Court. This year marks the 40th anniversary of that landmark case, Griswold v. Connecticut. Also this year, Dr. Hilda Crosby Standish, a hero in that legal drama and in the fight for reproductive rights, died at the age of 102.

But 2005 could be notable for another reason: It could turn out to be the year that President George W. Bush shifted the balance of power on the high court and snuffed out Americans' right to privacy. With John Roberts Jr. having been confirmed as chief justice and Samuel Alito Jr. having been nominated by Bush to the fill the vacancy created by Sandra Day O'Connor's retirement, the privacy right that Connecticut was so instrumental in guaranteeing could be in jeopardy.

Because of the central role that Connecticut played, state residents have a lot riding on the outcome of the Alito vote and -- assuming that he is confirmed -- on his and Roberts' willingness to abide by court precedent or stare decisis, the legal principle that courts should generally avoid undoing their past rulings.

Some historical perspective: Back in 1879, the Connecticut General Assembly passed a law criminalizing the discussion and distribution of materials related to reproduction and contraception. Attempts to repeal the law were repeatedly turned back. The state said it had a legitimate interest in encouraging procreation.

Not until 1935 was the anti-contraception law openly flouted. That year, the Maternal Health Center in Hartford was started by birth-control advocates under the direction of Standish, who had recently graduated from Cornell Medical College. With the Hartford clinic serving as a model and demand for contraceptive services growing, 10 centers sprang up around Connecticut.

But a raid of the Waterbury clinic brought a swift halt to operations. The clinic's staff was arrested and its supplies were confiscated. The courts refused to step in, and by 1940, all of the centers had closed. More court appeals followed, all in vain, until the U.S. Supreme Court decreed that a person would have to be arrested for a valid case to be brought.

And so it happened. In 1961, Estelle Griswold, director of Planned Parenthood of Connecticut, defied state law by opening a clinic in New Haven. Shortly thereafter, police arrested Griswold and medical director C. Lee Buxton, charging them with "aiding and abetting" the provision of contraception. They were convicted and fined $100. Their appeal was argued before the high court by Thomas Emerson, then the dean of the Yale Law School.

In June 1965, the court struck down Connecticut's anti-birth control law, finding a "right to privacy" in the U.S. Constitution. Writing for the 7-2 majority, Justice William O. Douglas asserted: "We deal with a right of privacy older than our Bill of Rights, older than our political parties, older than our school systems."

In 1972 that same right to privacy was extended to unmarried women, and in 1973, the doctrine was applied to abortion in the now- famous Roe vs. Wade case. Whether these fundamental rights will continue to be upheld by a new Bush court is uncertain. Pro-choice groups and civil libertarians say Alito's record on privacy rights is cause for concern. As a student at Princeton, he offered a strong defense of privacy, declaring that "no private sexual act between consenting adults should be forbidden." But he's written troubling appellate court decisions, among them a 1991 opinion that states can require women seeking abortions to notify their spouses. The Supreme Court disagreed with Alito.

Connecticut Sen. Christopher J. Dodd has expressed disappointment over Alito's nomination, while Sen. Joseph I. Lieberman, one of a pivotal group of 14 centrists, has held his fire. Lieberman said his support could hinge on whether Alito's judicial philosophy is so extreme as to be "outside the mainstream of American jurisprudence."

But in deciding how to vote, Dodd and Lieberman have an additional burden to bear. They aren't just two of 100; they carry the weight of Connecticut history. Standish, Griswold and Buxton stood up for Connecticut women in the face of long odds and at personal peril. That our senators show similar courage is the least we should demand.

Leave UConn Out Of Budget Games

By Michele Jacklin The Hartford Courant March 11, 2001

Like every other constituency in this year of state budget cutbacks, the University of Connecticut wants more money.

The idealist in me says give 'em the money if for no other reason than the Huskies' brilliant, inspiring win over top-ranked Notre Dame in last week's Big East championship game. Give 'em the money for bringing gobs of attention to the university and, almost single-handedly, thrusting women's collegiate basketball into the nation's sports consciousness. And for restoring the meaning of scholar to scholar-athlete, the concept of teamwork to what ought to be a team sport and for showing Connecticut and the nation what selflessness, dedication and hard work can accomplish.

Give 'em the money in the name of Abrosimova and Ralph and Bird and Cash and Rizzotti and Lobo and all the female athletes who came before and played in cold gyms in front of empty bleachers and laid the groundwork for the Huskies' success.

But the pragmatist in me knows that a university's budget shouldn't be predicated on the success of its sports teams no matter how many victories they pile up or how proud they make us. There are other, more persuasive reasons to give Connecticut's premier public university enough money to fulfill its mission.

(In the interest of full disclosure and because I have been asked this question by readers, let me say I have no ties whatsoever to UConn. I have not, nor has anyone in my family, so much as taken a course there. My husband worked for UConn at one time but left several years ago.)

In the mid-'90s, after years of budget neglect, programmatic drift and lackluster leadership, UConn was told to get its academic act together. It was given several goals to meet, chief among them to catapult the school into the top rank of public universities. It was also directed to upgrade the Storrs and regional campuses, raise academic standards and beef up private-sector fund-raising and its endowment.

Today, UConn is well on its way to achieving those goals, in part because of the financial support given by the Rowland administration and the legislature, particularly the $1 billion for campus improvements.

Student applications are up (as they are at most schools), SAT scores have risen, enrollment is growing and research money is flowing. In the all-important fund-raising department, the endowment's assets have climbed from $50 million to $221 million over the past five years, private gifts have increased by 44 percent and the number of donors has grown by 32 percent.

Indeed, the picture is so bright, says the governor, that "the school is running a surplus of more than $33 million." What's more, the governor asserts, the state's investment has been "extraordinary," as reflected in budget increases of more than $60 million over eight years.

But the governor is playing fast and loose with both his nomenclature and his numbers. What he calls a surplus is, in actuality, a reserve fund that has already been depleted by $3.5 million to offset retroactive budget cuts made by Rowland's budget czar. Of the $30 million balance, $15 million is committed to various projects, such as furnishing and equipping new dorms and dining halls. The rest of the reserve fund -- which university officials insist is more like a checking than a savings account -- will pay for utility overruns, books and wage hikes, and a portion is needed to back the integrity of the UConn 2000 bond issuances.

As a result, if the university's budget for 2001-03 isn't increased by more than the governor has recommended, the reserve fund will dwindle to virtually nothing in two years.

Ironically, Rowland is asking UConn to do what he claims he is not doing with the state budget -- that is, using "surplus" funds to pay for ongoing expenses. Moreover, the governor is playing a shell game. By requiring UConn to dip into its off-budget reserves, it allows him to create more room under the spending cap, thus freeing up state money for other programs.

So perhaps you can begin to understand why UConn supporters are peeved. They're also unhappy with Rowland's characterization of the school's spending trend.

While it may be technically correct to say the university's budget will have risen by $60 million over eight years, it's also true that from 1991 to 2003, the state appropriation for UConn will have increased at only a

2.8 percent compounded annual rate. In inflation-adjusted dollars, it will have decreased. Plus, the decline is even steeper if you measure UConn's appropriation using the Higher Education Price Index instead of the Consumer Price Index.

To see just how far UConn has slipped vis-a-vis other state agencies, consider this: In 1991, the school accounted for 2.2 percent of the state budget. In 2003, it will account for only 1.6 percent if the governor's proposal is approved unchanged by the legislature.

Lastly, there's this item that sticks in the craw of university officials: the Waterbury branch. As proposed, nearly half of UConn's piddling budget increase would go for enhanced programs at the newly-relocated campus in the governor's hometown, a move that UConn hadn't sought.

So give 'em the money. Not because 13 wonderfully talented women can put a ball through a hoop. Give 'em the money so that the university-- its faculty and all of its students -- will have the tools and facilities they need to soar to the same heights as the women's basketball team.

Ethics Commission Devours One Of Its Own

By Michele Jacklin The Hartford Courant Sept. 15, 2004

The little agency that could just couldn't anymore.

After two decades of standing tall, the State Ethics Commission collapsed under the weight of the Rowland administration scandals.

For years, it had stood up to powerful interests, taking on political bigwigs, legislative leaders, lobbyists, state bureaucrats and even a sitting governor. Unlike other public watchdogs, the ethics commission didn't pull its punches.

But the pressure from external forces was withering, the attacks were relentless and last year's budget cuts were a shot across the bow. "Back off or else" was the message. The commission didn't back off, and for that Connecticut residents should be grateful. But the attacks took their toll. One former commission member suffered a career setback after he voted to impose a fine on an influential political figure. Word got out: The ethics commission was neither a launching pad to stardom nor a comfortable place to be. The atmosphere had become poisoned.

Executive Director Alan S. Plofsky and the staff attorneys walked around with bull's-eyes on their backs. But who would have thought it would be Plofsky's subordinates who would fire the fatal shots? It's still not clear why the three lawyers filed a whistle- blower complaint against their boss, a man who had led the commission for 16 years and had treated them with kindness and respect. Plofsky was fired last week as a result of those complaints at a hearing that was perfunctory at best and a witch hunt at worst.

The man who had long served as the firewall between lawfulness and government misconduct was reduced to begging for his job. "My entire life has been devoted to public service," he told members of the commission before they dropped the guillotine. "I have never engaged in substantive misconduct in my life. I don't deserve this. My job is at risk, and my reputation has been destroyed."

Having contributed to Plofsky getting the boot, the three lawyers who filed the complaint -- Brenda Bergeron, Alice Sexton and Maureen Regula -- might have at least answered a few questions. But no, they clammed up, deferring to their attorney.

Plofsky's lawyer, Gregg Adler, attributed his firing to "animosity" on the part of commission members, who were publicly embarrassed by the release of a letter from Attorney General Richard Blumenthal. That letter, in effect, scolded the commissioners for improperly disciplining Plofsky, failing to comply with the Freedom of Information law and violating personnel policy.

All told, Plofsky stood accused of four transgressions -- that he told a subordinate to lie if she were forced to appear before a grand jury; that he directed the same person to destroy the tape of a February commission meeting; that he didn't tell the commission of his role in the release of the letter; and that he abused his compensatory time. Even though Plofsky wasn't given detailed information about the charges prior to the hearing, he forcefully and, to my mind, convincingly refuted each of them. For example, not only was the tape not destroyed, Plofsky turned it over to Alan Mazzola, the personnel officer who investigated the allegations. What's more, it appeared that the meeting, conducted by speakerphone, had been taped illegally. Thus, even if the tape had been destroyed, what of it?

If Plofsky is guilty of anything, it is gross tactlessness for calling former Gov. John G. Rowland a liar in a public forum. But lack of diplomacy is not cause for termination. And besides, he was right. Plofsky also was known to leave his office early on occasion. That, too, was dumb, especially for the director of an agency that holds public officials' feet to the fire. But Plofsky, who spurns computers in favor of writing briefs and opinions in longhand, claims he would go home and burn the midnight oil. He says he would walk in first thing in the morning with documents ready to be typed.

The clerk of the ethics commission would be able to confirm that, but she, like the others, wasn't talking.

I wanted to ask the three whistle-blowers if they thought justice was served by Plofsky's firing. I hope I will someday have that chance. In the meantime, Connecticut has lost one of its most dedicated public servants. A kangaroo court saw to that.

Kate F. Jennings did not use a photo with her columns

KATE F. JENNINGS

Kate F. Jennings wrote an arts column for The New Haven Register. She has a degree in Art History from Columbia University. She is the author of many books on renown American artists including "Remington & Russell and the Art of the American West" (1995)," Ansel Adams" (1998), "N.C. Wyeth" 2004, "Grant Wood" 2005; and "Winslow Homer" 2008. On Good Reads her books are "highly recommended."

Artists Reveal Varied Styles At Silvermine

By Kate F. Jennings New Haven Register Oct. 23, 1988

Three very different artists reveal their styles at the current exhibit at the Silvermine Guild in New Canaan.

Beth Moffitt of North Haven finds new meaning for the late impressionist manner of Georges Seurat, Robert Loebell of Farmington builds unusual, polymorphic sculptures, and Anthony Krauss of Woodstock, N.Y., paints clean, technical paintings.

Moffitt, a professor at the University of New Haven, explores a pointillist technique in pastel landscapes. The small, dot-shaped morsels of paint become fields of confetti dancing in gentle harmony.

It takes a bit of time to adjust one's eye to the blurred and fragmented effect of these paintings - afterward, real trees and pastoral venues are distilled through this special lens.

"Winter Wood" is a particularly successful work - the contrast in lights and darks is stronger than in other paintings. Shimmering pine trees project and recede in a lime green setting.

Their forms are pleasing conical shapes arranged in an undulating rhythm - we sense a quiet mystery about this forest.

"Great Goddess" is a wave of pale yellow, lavender and rose rising and ebbing over a series of canvases. The panels are each pretty and complete - together, the float of light and delicate vibration of dots is mesmerizing.

The fresh, spring green fuzziness of "New England Triptych" is like a rock garden on a distant hill. The large scale of this work requires that one step back to appreciate its content. Moffitt's control of so many small pieces engineered into accord is remarkable.

Krauss favors hard-edge geometric forms and he has a strong predilection for diagonal stripes. He employs for the most part a minor-key palette - rusts, grey, mulberry, tan. The canvases look stripped of emotional content and painterly texture - they appear more as symbols, corporate logos, industrial designs.

The works are called photosculptures, using carefully clipped prints, neatly planed, painted pieces of wood and evenly brushstroked passages. Fitted together, they look like pop-art paintings.

The gleamy steel segments add to the cool, rational impression. One half of "V-Diptych" is a pattern of slim blue and silver parallelograms - a beautiful swath of sleek wrapping paper.

Krauss' "Third Rail" is a particularly striking image - two lean copper-colored diagonal strips are the identifying three-dimensional elements. We don't sense any danger or electricity here, yet somehow the real focus and objective reference makes the work stronger.

"Carevesterol" has the bright primary colors of a seascape silkscreen. Combinations of circles and lines have the gaiety and clean-cut design of windsurfing sails. One is reminded of James Rosenquist's paintings where he synthesizes American popular culture.

"A Lexmosphere" looks like a piece from a domino game - a white circle is sliced by two black stripes and placed on a rectangular background. This is the basic form of Krauss' punctuation before he adds color and complexity in the larger works.

Loebell's sculpture is wild and woolly. These wooden constructions are remnants of journeys, each with a story to tell and all with personality.

"Walden Store" is a large, floor scaled piece with six points like a star. The separate segments have idiosyncratic carvings - wineglasses, knives and forks, personal hieroglyphics that look like usable objects but may just be decorative. It doesn't matter - the collective effect is mythical and encourages different readings by the viewer.

The pleasure of Loebell's work is his invitation to consider its inner mechanisms. We wander around these tribal, primitive assemblages trying to uncode the calligraphy. Even when it eludes us, the sculpture itself is physically interesting.

"Murder Mystery" is a large, three-totem extravaganza with neoexpressionist schemata yet a less doctrinaire sense of humor. Charred plaques stretch out on the floor like a tableaux of tabloids with loud headlines: "What Happened," "Marriage Announced" and "Dog Accused of Outrage". This is a playful, ambitious drama.

"Picasso Bull" is an elegant wall sculpture. One curved tusk forms the backbone and auxiliary trangles and appendages hammered together have the cubist instinct and wit for a proper homage.

The exhibit at the Silvermine Guild continues through Nov. 13. The Silvermine Guild is off Exit 38 of the Merritt Parkway in New Canaan.

A Pinball Machine Designed By Edgar Allan Poe

By Kate F. Jennings New Haven Register July 16, 1989

Twenty-two artists representing an eclectic, individual spirit in the arts are on display at the Bruce Museum in Greenwich in its first Connecticut biennial exhibit.

In the museum courtyard is "Quicksilver," by Greenwich artist Robert Perless. This tall, sleek, technical totem suits its location amid pine trees. A slim, black tapering column intersects with a polished stainless steel stylus. Three sets of six metal rods project from this beam like tailfeathers. The sculpture benefits from the space surrounding it; several of the works inside are a bit crowded for their environs.

In the entrance gallery is "Unfinished Sympathy" by Deborah Cooper-Sidlin of New Haven, wife of conductor Murry Sidlin. Her oil on paper painting is an amalgam of personal symbols, organic forms and flourishes of paint, which seem at times to embellish and at times to obscure them. Yin- and yang-styled objects are the central focus in orange. These are painted over with a target and bordered with blue, fuzzy tendrils like a jellyfish. The strength of the shapes has sculptural dimension. There is a sense of a struggle in the dynamics of this work which is underscored by the ironic, punning title.

Nearby is a work by Werner Pfeiffer of Cornwall Bridge. His "Multispacial 1987," is a delightful construction in bright primary colors that conveys a sense of flight and sailing with sea breezes. Triangular pieces of wood painted pink, yellow, rose, orange and blue cascade about the interstices of a white trellis frame. Birds, wings, kites and serendipity come to mind. This piece is carefully composed, yet seems effortless for the viewer.

In the corner of the first gallery, "Exactitude is not the Truth" by Michael Steiner of Bridgewater waits like a large, metal black widow spider. Circles and cylinders of ebony-painted bronze are welded together and perch on two sturdy legs. Segments of grating and vents add surface detail and the whole sculpture looks concise and comfortable in its lair.

Wisely placed on the far wall is Woodbridge artist Richard Lytle's "Siren Fold." This large, colorful canvas fills the eye like a movie studio set. Sweeping, sensuous flowers blossom forth from a backdrop of lavender-blue mountain ridges, cloud formations and pools of water. The paint is thickly applied in smooth strokes and the curls and colors of Hawaii beckon the visitor.

In the second gallery, beyond the museum store, is a group of sculpture, paintings and combinations of the two media. Here is New Haven painter, Miklos Pogany's "Between Us," resplendent with playful forms and bright colors. The freedom and loose brushstrokes of this abstract oil on paper suggest finger painting; its simple, vibrant strategies recall Joan Miro. A large red mass dotted with blue and black notations enfolds a green, reclining figure. The schematic plan resembles Henri Rousseau's primitive painting "the Sleeping Gypsy." The tones are quite different, though, and create a tension of contrasts.

"Circuits," a triptych in oilstick on paper by Kitty Sweet Winslow of East Hampton, has the childlike appeal of crayon drawings. Projections like whale snouts emerge from deep, ocean blue vistas. These panels remind one of chalk on blackboards, and their elementary nature is pleasing.

Quietly inhabiting one alcove is "Samos Sanctuary" by Carol Anthony of Bridgewater. This is a kind of diorama painting on a small scale - inspired perhaps by the romantic, personal boxes of the late Joseph Cornell. Soft, mottled pastel tones recall the marble in Greek temples. A tiny table in the lower half of the image and the altar arrangement above in raised relief lend a feeling of peace and contemplation.

Upstairs the show continues with "8 Ball/Target" by Maureen McCabe of Quaker Hill. This could be a pinball machine designed by Edgar Allan Poe. Inside a case, a black crow diagrammed with numbers is connected to a black rabbit and miscellaneous paraphernalia with red string. These creatures are surrounded by black fake fur and feathers and set against a black velveteen swath studded with rhinestone constellations. A dangling fishhook, cryptic "X" and several pool balls complete this three-dimensional mystery. A visitor is tempted to deposit a quarter and start the game in motion.

Peter Poskas of Washington is the sole realist in the show working in a careful, deliberate style reminiscent of the Hudson River School of painters. His sensitive rendering of "Sunset, Lake Waramaug" reveals the soft, delicate virtues of the pastel medium. It is a lovely Connecticut vista.

A large canvas by Cleve Gray of Cornwall Bridge, "Devil Take the Hindmost," appears like a great, huge bug outlined in black and white. It harkens back to Franz Kline's powerful abstract expressionist works and its lyrical, descriptive contours are engaging. The image could be a grasshopper under a magnifying lens or a diagonal group of boulders. There is a nice balance between the pink and white horizon and the turbulent black foreground separated by these spheres.

This selective sampling of Connecticut artists includes some intriguing work. The new wing at the Bruce Museum will be appreciated, especially for variegated displays of modern art.

The show will be up through Sept. 3. Gallery hours are 10 a.m.-5 p.m. Tuesday-Saturday and 2-5 p.m. Sunday. Take Exit 3 off Interstate 95.

TERESE CAROL ARONOFF KARMEL WITH FORMER YANKEE JOHN ELLIS

Terese Carol Aronoff Karmel known as "T.C." to her friends and family was a prominent writer, journalist and educator in Connecticut for almost half a century. She was a news reporter and sports writer for The Hartford Courant, columnist and features editor for the Willimantic Chronicle, and covered UConn womens' basketball for the Record-Journal of Meriden. She also wrote for Connecticut magazine and has free-lanced her columns across the state. She is the author of "Hoop Dreams: UConn Huskies Women's Basketball (2005)". T.C. also wrote and published many articles and pieces about horse racing in national publications such as "Blood-Horse". She was born in Washington D.C. and earned a B.A. in journalism from George Washington University. Later, she earned an M.A. in English Literature from the University of Connecticut. T.C. started work as a reporter with The Courant covering local news out of the Mansfield bureau in the early 1970s. A decade later she joined the sports department covering everything from Double A minor league baseball to boxing. She also taught English at Eastern Connecticut State University and sports reporting at UConn.

She has presented her literary work at the Major League Baseball Hall of Fame in Cooperstown, New York. Its symposia provides academics and researchers with a platform to present and discuss a variety of topics concerning the game of baseball and how it relates to our culture and society. She last presented in May 2017, "Racing Presidents: Baseball's Most Ingenious Marketing Campaign." She was still teaching and writing when she died from heart failure and cancer in December 2017 at the age of 79.

Love Affair: Baseball, My Radio And Me

By Terese Karmel The Hartford Courant Aug. 21, 1983

That annual sense of loss is flowing over me again. I know there are a couple of great pennant races going on in the major leagues, but October will be here too soon and it will be time for my yearly separation from my summer companion: my radio.

This is a love affair that began years ago as I sat with my grandmother, her sight failing, and listened to the tiny brown plastic radio that put her in touch with the world of baseball she adored.

This is the love affair that gave my brother, Marty, his start in the unique occupation of sports statistics. With his childish penmanship of scrawling numbers and the radio stuffed under the sheet, he would spend the better part of most evenings keeping a makeshift scorecard of his beloved Washington Senators. His bedroom was a mini-ballpark and old scorecards were piled everywhere.

Baseball put us in touch with cities and ballparks we'd only read or dreamed about. Much of the excitement came from flipping the dial to pick up out-of-town games from places called Comiskey or Sportsmen's Park. The cities of Chicago and St. Louis were the Far West. No matter what the geography books told us, the country ended at the Mississippi.

The radio greats of the past gave us colorful additions to our vocabularies with phrases like: "Hi neighbor, have a Gansett," the familiar greeting of Curt Gowdy when he was with the Red Sox; "He's heading for the barn," Washington Senators announcer Arch MacDonald's (himself as big as one) way of describing a homerun hitter's trot; Mel Allen's "Ballentine Blasts," and "White Owl Wallops" when the Yankees hit them out of the park; old Red Barber's "Ducks on the Pond" when men were on base and "Can of Corn" to describe an easy fly ball.

And still I'm a slave to the talking box.

Baseball commentators have been the summer chorus that accompanies me to the beach, remains vigilant during Saturday afternoon naps, keeps me alert on long drives to an from vacation spots. The sound of the crowd, the occasional cry of "beer here," the announcer's starts and stops fill large dusky living rooms where humming fans and buzzing mosquitoes compete for attention.

"Happy to have you with us along the Red Sox network," Ken Coleman's chirpy voice greeted me from a radio planted among the tall weeds in my yard one hot afternoon this past May.

"Happy to be with you Ken," I answered back, as I turned over the earth to begin spring planting. In the past few years, the Red Sox network has become my warm weather friend, replacing the voices of MacDonald and Vin Scully, whose comfortable voice seduced me into a fling with the Dodgers during a brief stint in the Los Angeles area, and the various other flirtations that have caught my fancy during my relationship with baseball and radio.

That Saturday afternoon, through a sudden summer shower that caught me by surprise, Coleman's voice gave the day continuity and balance, as it does most nights.

The Red Sox have accompanied me to the edges of New England as I've left the area for vacations and upon return, the information on the car radio that Yaz was at bat or that Eckersley gave up a game-winning RBI has signaled that I was nearing home.

Once crossing the Bourne Bridge over the Cape Cod Canal, Ricky Henderson danced off first base and the radio blacked out. When sound returned seconds later, he had scored. On a recent trip to Canada, begun at the inauspicious hours of 4:30 one Sunday afternoon, the Sox were just getting things started in Seattle and stayed with me through Brattleboro, Keene, White River Junction and the green Vermont meadows whizzing by like so many infields.

More often than not, I don't attune to every pitch, every swing. The commentary, like the game itself, is full of ellipses, pauses, small graceful phrases. (Once during the height of late spring hay-fever season, I sneezed a couple of dozen times between pitches). The rat-a-tat-tat of hockey commentary that shouts from my car radio on winter drives home from work sets a frantic pace that I sometimes wonder whether I need at day's end.

But baseball is, indeed, suited for evening when the body starts to lag and the thoughts run free.

Through hot, sleepless summer nights, a twist of my wrist transports me to Texas, where it's hotter still, and Coleman is complaining about an overly spicy tamale. Through the dark, I'm whisked to another coast, where the night is still young and the fans alert. In my mind's eye, I envision thousands of waving arms at men in white uniforms running around a floodlit stadium. Even the letters of Yankees' chatterbox Phil Rizzuto from friends in New Jersey or his golf game accounts or complaints about the Lincoln Tunnel have become part of the August ambiance of my home.

I doze off in the second inning, a dog barks, the phone rings, someone calls my name, I wake. "The throw to first, the runner is out..." drones the voice. The star of the game is interviewed. And then the familiar, comforting reminder, "We'll be back tomorrow..." In early October, when I hear, "thank you for joining us this season," then and only then will I peer out at my TV in preparation for those cold Sunday afternoons in pigskin land.

Five Decades Of Creating Journalists

By Terese Karmel The Connecticut Post April 16, 2016

A half century ago, a tough World War II veteran, after some coaxing by University of Connecticut President Homer D. Babbidge Jr., agreed to start a journalism department in Storrs.

It was Babbidge's contention that the flagship state university owed its constituency the responsibility to train students to become members of the Fourth Estate, a term said to be originated by 18th century Irish statesman Edmund Burke, who elevated the press to the level of the three divisions of Parliament: the spiritual Lords, the temporal Lords and the Commons.

For 50 years, thanks to the persistence and persuasive talents of the late Evan Hill and others who followed, the UConn journalism department has been turning out hundreds of members of the Fourth Estate although never in Burke's wildest imagination would he have envisioned these young journalists, for example, following a group of migrants fleeing Syria, translating World Cup Spanish commentary for ESPN, recording the behavior of the alligators in the Florida Everglades and Katrina survivors of the Louisiana Bayou, managing a national website about Broadway shows, or covering planning commissions in small towns across Connecticut.

The department has trained students to observe and record these varying exploits as well as helped them find jobs in the profession, many of whom are giving back to the state, which gave the opportunity to them.

This weekend the department celebrates its golden anniversary with receptions, panel discussions about the past, present and future of journalism and reunions of dozens of alumni who will return to their alma mater.

Since Evan Hill retired some 33 years ago, the department has been led by Maureen Croteau, a witty, highly professional chairman, who knows the university inside and out and has worked her tail off to bring the department into the new world of journalism. That work has paid off with accreditation by a prestigious national journalism review board, making us the only journalism department at a New England public university to achieve the designation.

Some of the alums may be surprised by the department's new digs: Three and a half years ago, we moved from one of those large brick lake-front L-shaped buildings, with its leaky roof, crumbling staircases and creaky old elevator (you walk four flights of stairs several times a day) to Oak Hall, the campus' newest academic building where we are once again on the fourth floor only a high speed elevator takes us to the editing suite for projects, a video studio, offices and, most importantly, two state-of-the-art computer labs where 90 percent of the classes are taught with 16-student limits.

In these labs, the 250 or so majors learn their trade in all of its forms: blogs, written stories, movies, online posts, radio and television broadcasts. They specialize in public affairs, photography, the environment, sports, investigations — all of the areas of any modern media outlet.

But though we're about as up to date as the latest social media trend, we do not overlook the basics: reporting, writing — getting to the heart of the matter fairly and accurately.

Each year we give away thousands of dollars to the students who have demonstrated an understanding of these principles. The awards are a recognition of some of the most prominent former state and national journalists, whose families and friends have created memorial funds in their names: Solomon, Litsky, Sheehan, Whalen, Breen.

In my dual role as an instructor and academic adviser, I meet regularly with first and second year majors. "Will I get a job?" is their most common question. And you know what: The answer is by and large "yes," whether at a major newspaper, or a Connecticut television station or a large organization seeking representation to the media.

My own mentors were not in the classroom, but in the newsroom — hands-on, head-over-my-shoulder "instructors" who told me when a lead sucked or when I needed more confirmation on a tip. I had one journalism teacher in high school — Dr. Regis Boyle — who told me I should develop the little talent I had, although I majored in English lit in college. (Nothing wrong with reading the best writers if you aspire to be a writer, I figured.)

But when I see what we provide our students — not just the digital system du jour, but the basics of reporting and writing news stories — I wish I were back in those classrooms and I were my teacher!

Confessions Of A Book Hoarder

By Terese Karmel The News-Times Danbury Sept. 5, 2017

This commentary was inspired by one written by Richard Brookheiser, who was told to get rid of his paper (including a massive book collection) because his firm was going all digital.

After I read and laughed through it, I cast my eyes around my six-room first floor and realized my home was overrun by books — shredded, dusty, coverless hardbacks dating back decades to college, stacks of paperbacks making it hard to move around, Fantasy baseball magazines in the days when the late Tony Gwynn was a first-round pick.

So taking Brookheiser's lead, I started sorting through my books to see which could be pitched.

Tossing books (or somehow trucking them to a library — which would and should reject my shabby offerings) was for me like throwing away my life. Books pile up like memories — I've probably only read (or thumbed through) 50 percent of the hundreds that are driving me out of house and home, but it's time to settle accounts.

It wasn't as easy as just finding a massive trash barrel and pitching them like batting practice.

How do you throw out Homer? George Lyman Kittredge's "The Complete Works of Shakespeare," (published 1936) de rigueur for every English major. My copy has tissue-thin pages, many torn or crushed beyond reading, but I got a kick out of some of my adolescent observations of the Bard's words.

"Isn't this an example of a mixed metaphor?" I scrawled in the margin of the Duke Orsino's "If music be the food of love, play on…" speech in the opening lines of "Twelfth Night."

"Does he really mean this?" another notation, this next to Marc Anthony's funeral oration in "Julius Caesar," suggesting Brutus is an "honourable man."

Many of the books were freebies, from years of teaching literature at Eastern Connecticut State University to a group of dozing students at 8 a.m.

I have every Norton Anthology in their catalog: short fiction, poetry, general lit, world lit — the list is endless, anthologies provided gratis (under that freeloading faculty ruse of "desk copy") from years Norton has been making millions by changing, for example, one or two stories and billing the collection as the 129th edition. But for the most part, the same short story authors have remained and for good reason: Raymond Carver, Flannery O'Connor, James Baldwin and Ernest Hemingway (winner of the 1954 Nobel Prize when political correctness wasn't a determinant). Yes that old sexist pig is still considered worth reading.

The 2016 Nobel Prize winner for literature, Bob Dylan, a great choice, is also represented in many of the poetry anthologies collecting dust — like him — on my shelf and shall remain there.

Piles of mysteries I never read or figured out by the second chapter make it difficult to walk around my bedroom, piled on graduate school cinderblock and wood plank shelves, and computer room. And don't ever let your friends and family know of your passion: I have every book on horse racing ever written.

Some books have been put to other use: My son's gift of a collection of Monty Python's humour, reflecting that phase of my life, now holds a window open in summer.

I guess I could technically be considered a hoarder, after all, I lived with one for much of my early life when my brother, Marty, kept piles of Sporting News, baseball scorecards, Washington Post articles and other sports stuff in his bedroom. I lived in fear the fire marshal would invade our home and put yellow emergency tape across his door.

I guess one solution is to do books digitally, then the "delete" button solves all your problems, but well, as you may have guessed already, I'm of a generation that prefers to hold books in their hands or stuff them on a shelf.

Anyhow here's the saving grace: Decades from now at least someone will discover them and turn to their friend, with a moldy "Medieval Epics: Beowulf, The Song of Roland, The Nibelungenlied, and El Cid," in one hand and their hand holding their nose with the other, and ask "what's this?"

But basically, I've given up. I may have found at most a dozen books I could part with, so like one of those agonized images of German printmaker Käthe Kollwitz, in the not-too-distant future, I picture myself huddled in my backyard, fear in my eyes as the books take over my house completely.

Now to tackle my vinyl LPs.

Can I really throw out Cat Stevens?

Wayne Norman Is A 'Yes' Kind Of Guy

By T. C. Karmel The Chronicle Willimantic July 3, 2000

People who know him -- and if you count the 50,000-watt, 38-state University of Connecticut sports network, that figure probably numbers in the millions -- have a habit of calling him Way-No. The name was even once on his license plate.

But a better name would be Way-Yes, the Molly Bloom kind of "yes" of affirmation for life and all of its imponderables and complexities that Joyce's character was speaking of in her soliloquy at the end of "Ulysses."

For Wayne Norman, whose voice area residents have woken up to for the past 30 years on WILI radio, is a "yes" kind of guy: yes to the countless listeners who have asked that their or a family member's name be added to the morning Birthday Club; yes to the dozen or so weathermen who have set him straight or who he has set straight about historic storms or heat waves; yes to broadcast partner Joe D'Ambrosio during play-by-play of UConn basketball games; yes to my request to watch and listen to him on a so-called "typical" morning drive; yes to the variety of civic and official organizations that count on his services to make their functions memorable -- as will happen Tuesday, of course, when he assumes his rightful spot as grand marshal of the city's 14th annual Boom Box Parade.

The marshal's job is one of the many he relishes each year; for the rest of us, it's a chance to attach a face (long, thin, shock of graying brown hair), and 6-foot-3-inch frame beginning to show its 50-ish years, to the voice that catches the airwaves and drifts through eastern Connecticut each day.

A transplanted Californian, Wayne Norman moved to Connecticut as a boy when Westinghouse transferred his father to Bridgeport. He went to UConn and there, after becoming involved with WHUS, found his passion.

This morning, four days before he struts down Main Street in whatever get-up -- secret until the big event -- he's selected for this parade (past choices: a UConn basketball player in Jake Voskuhl's uniform, riding a spooked horse, trying to keep his balance a la lookalike Dick Van Dyke on roller blades, in a fire department cherry picker), that passion is manifesting itself in a plea to Ray from South Windham to call the studio again so Norman can get his full name and phone number for that evening's drawing of the "which came first?" contest.

After answering correctly that paper money (1862) came before Chanel No. 5 (1921), Ray hung up and the vital information was lost in that dead air between downtown Willimantic, dawning lazily on Main Street, and the sleepy little borough to the south of us.

As I watch his perpetual motion, it occurs to me that in an earlier-life Wayne Norman was probably an octopus. At any one time during his show, his long arms are reaching in a dozen directions: to carts with pre-recorded ads, to a file scribbled with bits of Willimantic history (this day is the 17th anniversary of the Windham-Willimantic consolidation), to the phone ringing in front of his red and green sound board, to notes propped up in front of him, to a CD or a tape on shelves behind him.

His is a life that is measured in nanoseconds: a 30-second ad cut, a three-minute Beatles song, a five-minute chat with the weatherman du jour, Ron Anderson, a one-minute synopsis of the previous night's baseball scores, given with the authority of someone who has been creating and reading box scores for nearly half a century.

A jungle of microphones separates an elevated Norman from a semi-circular table for guests, from his swivel chair where he presides each day from 6 to 10 a.m., the Weather Channel announcers emoting silently from a mute television overhead. (Norman's lively chatter and knowledge of weather would put that crew to shame). This morning, Buddy Holly's "Peggy Sue" is jerking its way through the string of rooms that is the underground bunker of WILI-AM and FM because it is "Forgotten Oldie Friday," that morning each week, Norman tells me, "when we bring back the good stuff."

For Wayne Norman, the good stuff includes the Red Sox, the Beatles, UConn basketball and football, the Willi-Mac softball league (he's a designated hitter now that the years are setting in) and Willimantic, with which he has had a 30-year love affair. One would be hard-pressed to determine who gives who the most in this arrangement, although the balance may be tipped in favor of the radio man who was Romantic Willimantic's first ever Cupid, back in 1982, when the tables were turned and possibly for the first time in his life he was left speechless, when surprised in his own studio with the honor.

As I drive down Main Street, which four days hence will be filled with the rousing sounds of John Phillip Sousa and the UConn fight song, Wayne Norman's familiar voice is with me on the boom box that is my car radio.

And in one long, winding sentence, that voice is putting its history, its loves and losses, on the line for its listeners.

Having just played Peter and Gordon's 1964 recording of "A World Without Love," Wayne Norman is sharing an experience: "I have the original 45 of that," he tells us with the intimacy of a close friend and the universality of a music historian.

"I bought it on Sunset and Vine in Hol--ly--wood ...," he continues, launching into the fact that it was one of the few songs by Lennon and McCartney that the Beatles did not record.

Later, he tells me of riding on his bike, delivering papers in Glendale, Calif., with the Peter and Gordon tune floating out of the portable radio in his back pocket, perhaps at the exact moment -- who knows? -- when the dream of filling homes with his music and stories made its way through the airwaves into the heart and soul of Wayne Norman.

LINDA TUCCIO-KOONZ

Linda Tuccio-Koonz followed her father into journalism. As a cub reporter in Maine in 1984, she helped the FBI solve a coed's murder. In 2013, she was part of the writing team that captured a national award for a narrative on the day of the Sandy Hook Elementary School shootings. Much of her career was at The News-Times in Danbury where she was features editor. She now writes entertainment features for Hearst Connecticut Media based in Norwalk. Her writing also has appeared in The New York Times, The Philadelphia Inquirer and Newsday, as well as in "Chicken Soup for the Working Woman's Soul." She and her husband, Brian Koonz, have two sons. She feels lucky to have had the chance to record and reflect on some of their early shenanigans in a series of parenting columns.

Thanks Mom. Wish I'd Said It Sooner

By Linda Tuccio-Koonz The News-Times Danbury Mother's Day May 14, 2000

My dad didn't know the rules. Dads are supposed to be old when they die, not in their 40s. The night my father died changed everything. I was 16. Decades later I still feel cheated.

At first, all I could think about was myself. I cried until my whole body ached. How could life go on? Then I cried some more for my sister. She was only 13. She hadn't even gotten to know him as well as I had. It was so unfair.

I didn't really think about how my mother was feeling at the time. After all, she was an adult, and she always seemed so capable. But now that I'm a mother myself, I realize it was probably the hardest on her. And she never let us know.

Mom was always there, doing all those mom things. She cooked and cleaned and made sure we always looked presentable, even if we were just going out to play kickball. She pulled our hair into ponytails and fussed with the ribbons until we wanted to scream.

Each week she quizzed us for our Friday spelling tests until there was no doubt we would score 100, plus extra credit for the bonus words. She also drove us everywhere from ballet to bowling. And during those rare breaks between activities, she harped on us to practice piano, even though we were more interested in our teacher's motorcycle than his lessons on Mozart.

Mom did her thing – which was everything – and we did ours. We hung out with our friends, tied up the phone lines of suburban Long Island, and took Mom for granted.

If I did think about her, it was in a fleeting way. When the ice cream man came we'd hit her up for money and then, halfway out the screen door, yell "Whaddya want?" before racing back to the street. "Surprise me," she'd say.

I always thought it was strange she didn't have a favorite treat, like the vanilla ice cream bar with the big chunk of chocolate inside. She'd say, "I like everything, so it doesn't matter."

It didn't matter to her, so it certainly didn't matter to me and my sister. Sometimes we even let the ice cream man pick her dessert. Was Mom having a rough day? Did she need a pick-me-up? Or was she happy in her life? We had no idea.

Mom worked as a nurse on weekends when she wasn't catering to us. That's when we spent time with Dad – hero of the household.

It wasn't that he did anything miraculous. It was just that we didn't see him around all the time like Mom. He worked all day as the education editor at Newsday, and when he came home for dinner, his attention wasn't scattered, it was on us.

This was back in the '70s. We'd watch "Star Trek" with Dad while Mom finished dinner preparations. Then we all shared the events of the day at the table. After baths it was time to finish homework or relax again with Dad. Mom was still busy, washing dishes, vacuuming or folding clothes.

Saturday was Dad's day with us, since Mom was working. We'd do errands, like taking clothes to the cleaners, and always wind up at this one luncheonette. I don't remember what it was called, but we had our own name for it – "The Favorite Place."

They made great burgers and egg creams at "The Favorite Place." At the long counter there were plenty of stools to spin. I always got an Archie comic book and a 1-cent piece of Bazooka. We'd talk about school or how we were going to change the world when we grew up.

Whenever we left the luncheonette, it seemed there was always someone who wanted to chat with Dad. He knew a lot of people because of his newspaper column. He wrote about school budget battles and the need for desegregation. Sometimes racist readers would send death threats in the mail, but Dad never wavered. He believed in education, that life was a blessing, and there was hope for the future.

My sister and I – the two princesses – waited patiently when strangers stopped Dad to discuss their views. To me, it was like being with a celebrity, only I didn't mind sharing him because I knew we'd soon have his full attention again.

At home he watched us do tricks on our bikes in the driveway, or graciously fawned over the half-inch thin cakes we made in our Easy Bake Oven. Sometimes he'd use a pencil and paper to make up board games for us, or take us to the ice rink, where he'd sit on the cold, wood bleachers while we chased each other on skates.

He also spent a lot of special time with Mom. They'd get a sitter for us and go out at night, like teens on a date. Mom always smelled so good — Chanel No. 5. She'd blot her lipstick on a tissue and then kiss us before leaving.

The night Dad died was after one of those special evenings in February 1976. They'd gone to the wedding of a neighbor's son. It was after midnight when I awoke to my mother's frantic screams. Straddling my father, she was performing CPR and yelling at him to breathe. But he just lay there.

An ambulance arrived and my father was carried out. Mom went, too, and a neighbor came over to watch us so we wouldn't be alone.

It was Feb. 9. Dad suffered a massive heart attack. He never came home. He was only 45.

The next days were a blur of tears. Flowers and fruit baskets arrived as neighbors and relatives wandered in and out. I didn't want to go anywhere or do anything. I was consumed by my grief.

In the fog of that pain, something struck me. My sister and I had lost our father, but we would go on to college and probably marry and have families of our own. My mother was only 41, the same age I am today, and she had lost her lifelong partner and best friend. She would have to raise us alone, bearing all of the responsibility herself.

From that moment, I began to see my mother differently, and to appreciate her. She wasn't just this person who made us drink milk at every meal. She was a woman who worked hard to make sure we had everything we needed to succeed on our own.

She had never managed money before – my father had just given her whatever she needed. She had never written a check before he died. And she could barely drive anywhere beyond our hometown, because he had always done the driving.

Seeing what she has gone through since that time has made me a stronger person. I've watched her struggle and learn. Her checkbook is always balanced to the penny and she has driven to many places she never ventured before.

Mom once threw a compass out her car window because she was so frustrated with it, but the point is that she hasn't given up. It's hard to be on your own, and she's managed all these years.

My sister, who is married with two children, lives near Mom. I had my second child last year, and of course it was bittersweet. Mom and I often talk about how my father would have loved to see all these grandchildren.

My dad didn't know the rules. He left too soon, and without saying good-bye. All these years later, I still dream about him. We're talking or walking… or playing chess. I ask him questions: Where are you? Can you come back? But somehow he's never able to answer. I wake up feeling blue and call Mom.

Mom is always home these days, or so it seems. She enjoys her grandchildren, but I wish she'd get out more and enjoy herself. She doesn't seem to want to.

My husband and I bought her a plane ticket to Florida to visit relatives, but she wouldn't go. I was pregnant then and she wanted to stay home. In case I needed her, she said. It turned out I had a horrible case of the flu that week and my husband was away on business. She came and nursed me back to health.

Always the mother. That's how she is. I just wish it hadn't taken me so long to appreciate her.

Welcome To The World of Parenthood

By Linda Tuccio-Koonz The News-Times Danbury 2001

Sitting at my desk one morning, I was deeply engrossed in an important project – trying to rebutton my shirt so each button lined up with the right hole. One side of my blouse was definitely hanging at an odd angle and I wanted to fix it before most of my co-workers arrived.

Making sure I'm dressed properly is something I normally do at home in front of a toothpaste speckled mirror, but this morning there'd been no time. This morning I had played the home version of Army boot camp. My goal: to leave the house and drive to work. The obstacles: a toddler and a 9-year-old boy.

Every time I tried to make a strategic move like tying my shoes or finding my keys, there was a child at my feet who desperately needed something. My 9-year-old claimed he needed to have a sandwich for school because the cafeteria was serving the wrong kind of pizza.

He likes "personal pizza," which was round, but this day it was square. Apparently, the round pizza tastes like it just came from the oven of Italy's finest bistro, while the square pizza is inedible. "It's too tomato-y," he explained.

Then my two-year-old sneezed just after I placed a heaping spoonful of oatmeal in his mouth. This necessitated a change of my clothes, but there was no time, no time to be choosy. It was my turn to drive my 9-year-old and his friend to the bus.

I grabbed a clean blouse from the dryer, threw it on, and ran out the door with the whole gang. We made the bus, and I dropped my toddler at the sitter's before racing to work. Is it any surprise my shirt was buttoned wrong? I'm just glad it was buttoned.

As I contemplated what I could have done to ease the morning mayhem, several colleagues arrived in the office, including my boss. He had a funny expression on his face, like he was trying to hold in a sneeze, it was a grin.

"I have good news and bad news," he said. All present opted for the good news first. It turns out he and his wife are expecting a baby this summer – thrilling news.

My colleagues and I, many of whom have children, told him we knew he'd be a great dad. He and his wife, a schoolteacher, have been married several years and have big hearts. Their house is already filled with the playful chaos of five formerly homeless cats.

After a round of congratulations, his early words. "What's the bad news?" I asked.

"The bad news is the same as the good news," he said. He'll take a block of time off when the baby's born – good news for him, but bad news, i.e. a tougher workload, for the rest of us.

I didn't see it as bad news. Like they say, what goes around comes around. When I gave birth to my younger son, I took a four-month maternity leave. My boss covered for me, and I'm more than happy to do the same for him. Besides, when he's a father he'll have a better understanding of what it's like to juggle work and childcare.

The announcement that he will soon be crib shopping meant we had a new person to initiate into the ranks of parenthood. We began giving him a preview of how his life will change.

"You won't be going to the movies any more because you'll need to buy diapers – lots and lots of diapers," one colleague intoned.

Yeah, and then when the baby is out of diapers you'll be able to go to the movies again, but they'll all be cartoons," warned another. "Your whole life will be rated G."

My boss laughed and said that's why he stores rented videos. He pointed out that he and his wife can still enjoy the pleasures of dining out.

"For now," said a female co-worker. "But once the baby is older you won't be asking about the soup du jour any more. You'll be reading the

'Happy Meal' menu and trying to get through a dinner without someone spilling their drink all over you."

"So let me get this straight," my boss said. "I'll spend all my money on diapers and I won't ever go to the theater or eat out? Well, I can still ride my bicycle this summer."

A male co-worker, an experienced father, slowly shook his head. "Nope, you won't be doing any of that. No more bike trips."

My boss gave him a smug look and announced he could always get a buggy that attaches to his bicycle.

"Sure you could do that but it will be a waste of money," said the dad. "My son didn't sleep through the night for months. His sleep cycles were reversed. When's your baby due? June? Trust me, you'll be too tired to go biking."

At this point a female co-worker. The mother of two teen-age daughters, walked over to put her two cents in. "Actually, you should go home and go to sleep right now. That way, you might have a chance at getting through this whole fatherhood thing," she advised.

"And don't worry if you come to work with your shirt buttoned wrong," I added. "We'll understand."

Quite Happy Here On Earth

By Linda Tuccio-Koonz The News-Times Danbury Sept. 6, 2002

If men are from Mars and women are from Venus, where are children from? It must be some mysterious uncharted universe, because they certainly have some strange ideas.

My 3-year-old son, Taylor, insists babies come out of your bellybutton, and that he's having one. He's also under the impression I have intimate knowledge of all police activity on the roads we travel. Every time we see a police car with its lights flashing, his little pumpkin face turns deeply serious.

"What happened?" he asks, wrinkling his brow and holding his hands palms up with his fingers spread.

"Who-body in that car?" he says, if the police car is parked next to another vehicle.

"Who-body?" What kind of word is that? That's not English. I'm guessing he got it from the strange planet he came from. Apparently, it's a planet of nosey rubberneckers. Why else would he ask about every police car we see?

I usually tell him the police officer has pulled over to help a driver whose car broke down, or to give someone a ticket for speeding. Either way, his response is always the same.

"Why?" he says.

If there's no police activity on the road, Taylor still assumes I have mind-reading powers that I should use to answer all the other important questions running through his head. Being from the rubberneckers' planet, he's especially interested in large trucks on the road.

We saw many of these on a trip last month to Sesame Place, an amusement park in Pennsylvania. My husband, who clearly IS from Mars (he'd rather poke his eyes out with flaming shish kebab skewers than stop to ask for directions) was our driver. As Dad gallantly battled traffic and heavy rains, Taylor studied the huge trucks that kept blocking our view of the road signs.

At one point a huge 18-wheeler was right in front of us. "What's in that tuck, Mommy?" asked Taylor, who has an aversion to the letter "r."

I thought about making up an answer, but there were no letters on the truck to give me a hint, so I decided to just be honest.

"I don't know," I said.

Apparently, he didn't believe me, so he switched to his super loud "I-want-it-now" voice.

"WHAT'S IN THERE?" he demanded. "OPEN IT UP!"

The awful traffic was at such a standstill then, I probably could have complied, but I didn't. I didn't want him to think he was in charge, not just yet. Anyway, his older brother, Michael, is still under the impression that's he's in charge.

Michael, 10, was born at Danbury Hospital, just as Taylor was, but I don't think that necessarily means they're from Earth. Judging from the questions Michael asks, he's from a planet of creatures who are obsessed with the "Guinness Book of World Records."

This wasn't so apparent when he was younger, but by the time he was 8, it was hard to hide. That's when he began asking things like, "If you put your hair up in a bun right now and never took it out for the rest of your life, could you get into the "Guinness Book of World Records?"'

I tried to make sure he was busy a lot to keep his mind off such odd pursuits, but nothing worked. Even in winter, when he was outside all day building tunnels in the snow by our house, he couldn't keep his mind off setting a world record.

"Do you think the 'Guinness Book of World Records' has a category for most tunnels in an igloo? Because I think I would win," he said. "Oh, but they would have to come over today, do you think they would?"

Hmmm. That was a tough one. I didn't know quite how to answer; I think I got out of it by offering him a hot chocolate.

Another day he asked me how many times he would have to say "great" before "great-grandmother" to get back to where she would be a cavewoman. There was no mention of the "Guinness" book in that question -- but I suspect he was wondering in the deep recesses of his mind, if there was some related category. (Grandma with the longest title?)

Michael usually seems quite happy here on Earth, but once in a while I get the feeling he's thinking about how it would be to go home to the "Guinness" fanatics' planet. He once asked me, "Is there a place in the air where you could cut a hole and stick your head through and there would be no air?"

That one I knew how to answer. I told him the air thins gradually.

No doubt there will be more unusual questions from my children as they grow. My friend, Karen, a mother of three, has already warned me the questions won't be getting any easier. She tells me her 16-year-old daughter came up with a real doozy recently.

"Mom," said the teen, "When I have sex for the first time, do you want me to tell you?"

Not that she was thinking about doing it any time soon, Karen said, but that's what she asked. "I never talked to my mother about things like that when I was 16," Karen said. "Did you?"

"No," I told her. And I certainly wasn't thinking about sex. I was still contemplating my first real kiss.

I must say I'm not quite ready for that sort of question from my children, but I guess I'd better get ready. Michael has already received a love letter from a girl, and that was last year in fourth grade.

Maybe it's time to start developing some of those mind-reading powers Taylor thinks I already possess. Then I'll know who's doing what, and whether it's worthy of a world record. For now, there's only one thing I'm sure of: if Taylor's correct (that babies come through your bellybutton and he's having one), the folks at "Guinness" will want to know when it happens.

Heck, they might even come out that very day.

KATHLEEN V. KUDLINSKI

Kathleen V. Kudlinski is an author, a former columnist for the New Haven Register, and has also worked as an elementary school teacher. She makes frequent visits to classrooms to talk about writing. She was presented with the "Master Teaching Artist" citation from the Connecticut Commission for the Arts; The "notable children's book in the field of science" citation from the National Science Teachers Association – Children's Book Council, for Dandelions; Learning Magazine, and the Teacher's Choice Awards for It's Not Easy Being Green and Food for Life. Born 1950, she has a B.S. from the University of Maine. She is a prolific author of historical fiction, biographies, and science books that reflect her passionate interest in the natural world and preserving its treasures. She has contributed to the series, "Once upon America" and "Girlhood Journeys," which introduce middle grade readers to real events in American history through the first-person adventures of fictitious heroes and heroines. Her more than 20 books include, Rachel Carson: Pioneer of Ecology; Pearl Harbor Is Burning: A Story of World War II; Animal Tracks and Traces; Night Bird: A Story of the Seminole Indians; Facing West: A Story of the Oregon Trail; Rosa Parks, Young Rebel; Harriet Tubman, Freedom's Trailblazer; Sojourner Truth, Voice of Freedom; and The Spirit Catchers.

Columnist Kathleen Kudlinski Wraps Up 34 Years of Nature Writing

By Kathleen Kudlinski New Haven Register July 4, 2014

We have seen wonderful things together, haven't we, Dear Reader? This is my last nature column after 34 years in newspapers. I'm done. But, oh, the places you and I have been.

Remember the night back in '04 when we went out to the pond and pointed a flashlight down into the dark water? We saw fish sleeping soundly near the bottom wrapped in their protective slime blankets. Snapping turtles, too, slept peacefully while leeches swam their magical zero-gravity dance in the shallows. We've hiked at night ('94), stood in the rain ('07) and watched our oak tree die ('99).

How about that day in '91 when we went out to Hammonasset and caught sight of a weasel standing tall on his hind legs, spying on us? It is just luck that gives us fleeting glimpses of nature like that — and rewards those who stay alert. Other wonders are predictable. We found the dependable drifts of slipper shells at the high tide line back in '90 and marveled at how the snails had clustered piggyback, changing sexes as needed to produce another generation.

For most of the '80s and '90s, I wrote about seeing nature through the eyes of my own kids, school classrooms and scout troops. Kids notice and ask and challenge more than the rest of us do. Want a new view of the world? Tag along with someone for whom everything is new! Remember in '89 when one of my scouts stood on the beach trying to hold her breath as long as a loon did on a dive? I was frantic watching the girl turn purple-faced. Finally she gave up and gasped long before the bird came up for air.

What columns do you remember? I'd love to know so I can savor those memories with you. Let me know at kathkud@aol.com. I haven't given up writing: I'm busy rewriting old columns to submit as a book this year, and I have three more children's books coming out next year. But I won't be meeting you weekly in the newspaper.

I will miss you, Dear Reader, for you were always there in the back of my mind, driving me to find something fresh and new and fascinating in nature to share with you on Sunday mornings. Much to my wonderful editor, Rick Sandella's, dismay, I never wrote a week ahead or kept a pile of back-up essays to submit. I only pointed out things you could see for yourself the very day you read them.

Then I researched each column idea to add a further sparkle of "Gee whiz!," facts that even I hadn't known. So I've learned a lot about nature, thanks to you. Now it is your turn. When you see something, Google it. Takes but a few seconds now, compared with all the book research I did back when I launched the column in the Springfield Republican a lifetime ago.

Now it is up to you. Get yourself out there. Visit the natural places you've been with me and others that only you know about. Take a kid or a spouse along. Take a sketchbook or go empty-handed. Keep your eyes and your mind open to wonder.

Please keep abreast of political actions that affect the environment when I'm not there to nag you about them. Become a pest, writing both fan and protest letters (or emails or phone calls), attend town hearings, join local land trusts and conservancies, and back candidates who treasure nature as much as we do.

I don't want to lose track of you. When you see something fabulous or just curious, I'd love to hear about it or see your photos at my Facebook page "Kathleen Kudlinski Author and Naturalist." I'll post short nature notes for you there, too, several times a week and on www.kathleenkudlinski.com. Let's keep our friendship going as we continue exploring the natural world together. But even if we never connect again, I want to thank you, Dear Reader, for enriching my life.

Guilford naturalist Kathleen Kudlinski is the author of "Boy, Were We Wrong About Dinosaurs," and 40 other children's books.

Outdoor Baths Are Strictly For The Birds

By Kathleen Kudlinski New Haven Register June 30, 1988

Neither of my kids complained about taking their baths during the winter months.

Why should they? An every-other-day occurrence, bathing was mostly playtime. After all, how dirty can you get inside a snowsuit?

But baths are no fun anymore - they are daily, rigorous scrubbing sessions that barely manage to keep ahead of the grime. The kids are tired of the same old toy boats, ducks and bubblebaths. I need to inject some variety into the chore so the bathtub doesn't become a battlefield.

Perhaps I can take a hint from the birds: they take three different kinds of baths. The kids and I have watched sparrows scooping out holes in dry dirt and settling in for a "dusting." Every feather is fluttered into the fine, dry soil until the absorbent dust works down to the skin.

Then the sparrows, apparently in avian ecstasy, drowse in the sunshine. Then they rouse themselves, shake the dust out and fly off, fresh and clean, bird fashion. Sometimes my kids spend the entire day taking dust baths. They just get dustier, not cleaner, so that's no solution.

Many birds take ant baths, lying near an ant hill and spreading their feathers to invite the insects aboard. Some species pick up the ants with their bills and tuck them into feather clumps or smear them against their skin.

Interpretations on this "anting" behavior vary. Ants may eat parasites they find on the bird's skin. They may be mad enough to release formic acid, a bitter-tasting chemical that could repel feather mites or fleas. Or perhaps they just scratch the itchy places a bird can't reach for itself. I refuse to allow my children to try "anting." Even a naturalist/mother has limits.

Of course birds bathe in water, too. They splash with evident delight in shallow puddles, then preen their feathers until dry. They often reach down into the feathers on the top of their tails to squeeze a drop of oil out of a special gland there. That oil works like a moisture lotion on their feathers, keeping them glossy and supple. The kids would enjoy an outdoor bath, but I'm not sure how the neighbors would react to two sudsy children frolicking in the backyard, naked as, well, jaybirds.

Maybe I can set out a bird bath to remind the kids how much fun baths can be. It doesn't have to be an expensive cement ornament. It simply needs to hold a puddle of water no deeper than two inches, have a rough bottom so the birds won't slip, and be sheltered from predators.

An upturned garbage can lid lined with gravel and wired to a pipe would work just fine. I'd have to flush it out with a hose everyday or so, since the birds will use it as a "watering hole," too. That will also keep mosquitoes from breeding there.

Later this summer it could be a lifesaver for the birds if other water sources go dry, but I can imagine how practical it could be right now.

The kids and I would be standing at the window watching the birds splashing happily outside. As dusk falls, and the birds reluctantly abandon the bird bath, I'd lead the kids away and gently pop them into a waiting tub before they know it.

"You know, kids, baths aren't just for the birds." It might just work - once.

It's An Earth Day Garden Party

By Kathleen Kudlinski New Haven Register April 21, 2012

Happy Earth Day, you with your feet on this Earth! And especially to those of you who garden the earth. Here's some unlikely friends you can invite to your garden to make it greener, healthier and far more interesting. These all-natural critters do the work of artificial pesticides without poisoning your family, the neighbors or the water table below.

Welcome all the birds you can to your garden. A chickadee needs 200-500 insects a day to keep up his energy and feed his family. Sure they'll eat seed during the winter, but for baby food, nothing does it like a protein-rich bug. All birds switch to a carnivorous diet just about the time your plants come up and you want to reach for a pesticide.

Swallows, which eat 1,000 flying insects in a 12-hour shift, appreciate nesting boxes under the eaves. House wrens, towhees, phoebes, bluebirds and robins all have insatiable insect-appetites.

Many birds are lured in by standing dead wood. If that dead branch (or tree) isn't likely to fall on your house or a neighbor, leave it for a few seasons and watch the birds move in. Ninety species of birds and animals make their homes in dead trees. (Do I hear the Earth Day theme song swelling in the background?)

Birds are the day shift, working for you for free. Bats take up the same job in the dark. A single bat may eat 4,000 mosquitoes in one night, if you have that many to spare. They'll just as quickly snag up a winged aphid, thrip or other garden pests.

But aren't bats scary? Not if you know the facts: They do not fly into human hair or pose any danger to us at all unless somehow you manage to touch one. So don't touch. Bats are happy to move into trees, slide up behind shingles or the bark on a dead tree, or snooze the day away in a big ol' wood pile.

Another night-watchman who'll help in your garden is a toad. They'll eat any bug that comes within reach of their long sticky tongue. So you don't like the looks of toads? They aren't much fond of you either, and hide away under cover until dark. They do need shelter and a source of water to drink. An overturned flowerpot is a toad's castle, and the pot's drainage saucer nearby makes a lovely pond.

You can transplant any toad you see to this new kingdom (they don't give warts.) Offer a toad bounty to a young neighbor and you'll have all you want.

Earthworms do double duty in your garden and yard. They "lighten" the soil and "turn" it. As they tunnel, they eat tremendous amounts of dirt. It passes through their digestive system purified, milled to near dust and enriched.

Remember that young neighbor with the toads? Offer a dime a worm and see what happens. You can plant them right in your garden.

Garter snakes eat grubs, caterpillars, slugs and snails. If little snakes bother you more than slugs, skip to the next paragraph. To find snakes, look under fallen logs, flat stones, old tar paper, lumber, old plywood that has been lying around your property for a while. Or ask that intrepid young neighbor to find a small snake for you.

Since snakes don't dig burrows, they'll need a flat shelter in or near the garden they'll loyally patrol.

Praying mantises are the large green insects that eat any smaller bug they come upon. You can buy an egg case from a garden center, or find one and transplant it. (Young neighbors may have better eyes than yours and more time for the search, and as you've seen, they can be bought.) The mantids that hatch are teeny, but voracious and eat ever-larger pests as they grow throughout the summer. Ladybugs, too, eat aphids, and so do ladybug babies. You can buy their eggs through a garden center.

It is a generous thing to do, for some of the hundreds of ladybugs (or praying mantises) are likely to fly to neighboring gardens and set up pest-eating services there. Perhaps they'll land in that newly rich kid's garden, thanking his parents for letting him work for you for an afternoon or two around Earth Day.

DONNA LARCEN

Donna Larcen grew up in Philadelphia and at 15 knew she wanted to work in newspapers. She majored in journalism at Temple University, stayed on for a master's degree in education, moved to Connecticut, and was hired at The Hartford Courant, *where she worked as a reporter and editor from 1974 to 2013. During that time she wrote a children's news column, ran a statewide arts contest, covered real estate, consumer affairs, and wrote about fashion. She was the arts editor responsible for theater, music, books, fine arts, and movie coverage for a 32-page weekly Calendar section, Sunday Arts section and daily stories. Since leaving The Courant in 2013 she has worked in communications and events planning in the nonprofit world for the Charter Oak Cultural Center, Hartford Public Library, and now is at The Mark Twain House & Museum.*

Voice Strong, True, Baez Forever Young

By Donna Larcen The Hartford Courant April 03, 1998

At the end of the Joan Baez concert at Woolsey Hall in New Haven Thursday she sat in a chair at the lip of the stage with her Martin guitar and sang a heartfelt ballad by her longtime favorite songwriter. Bob Dylan's "Forever Young" is exactly where Baez is in her life, her career and her relationship with the audience. She has always been courageous, stood upright and been strong, as the lyrics say.

Her performance, a benefit for the New Haven Symphony Orchestra, showed the best of Baez. Surrounded by able side players and joined by guest Richard Shindell, she stepped out front, sang harmony when Shindell took the lead on his own songs and collaborated on drums while the band showcased its talents.

Baez spoke early of her guest spots with Pete Seeger and now the torch has passed to her. She's the elder, still leading the way, but bringing others like the talented Shindell and Northampton's Dar Williams with her. She opened with Williams' "If I Wrote You" from the "Gone From Danger" album released last year.

Baez promoted the disc asking Shindell to join her on his Civil War anthem "Reunion Hill" about a widow who comes back to the battlefield to remember her last meeting with her missing soldier husband. She dipped way back into her musical repertoire with "The Night They Drove Old Dixie Down," also about loss in war.

She sang two by Irish songwriter Sinead Lohan, "No Mermaid," a woman's independence tale, and "Who Do You Think I Am?" a look at communication in relationships.

Baez confronted the difficult subject of child abuse in Betty Elder's "Crack In The Mirror" and "Play Me Backwards" from her album by the same title.

She explained the choices of songs in her newest album as coming from younger songwriters "who write about the 90s in songs that I can sing."

Not all was deadly serious. She poked fun at her early somber song selection, explaining that when she was a coffeehouse performer early on she sang ballads about unrequited love, star-crossed love and deaths of the major players. "I was such a shrew then," she said. "If anybody dared to read a book when I emoted, I stopped the show."

She also talked about her new limited edition Joan Baez signature Martin guitars. There are 59 of them, marking her breakthrough at the Newport Folk Festival in 1959.

"When they took the old Martin apart, they found someone had left a message from an earlier repair that read 'Too bad you're a communist.' I had them put that message in every new Baez guitar."

With that story, she launched into the union anthem "Joe Hill" to great applause.

Baez sang "Swing Low Sweet Chariot" without benefit of amplification, harkening back to her days singing in black churches during the civil rights demonstrations with Dr. Martin Luther King. She, of course, sang her signature "Diamonds & Rust," and a lovely version of John Prine's lament to getting old and outliving your friends and children, "Hello In There."

Baez, who smiled at generous applause as she hit high notes strong and true said modestly, "I'm not responsible for this voice, I just do maintenance and delivery." Maybe so, but let's hope she stays forever young.

Seegers, Guthries In Grand Folk Tradition

By Donna Larcen The Hartford Courant August 11, 1995

It was a night of old masters and young apprentices Wednesday as Pete Seeger and Arlo Guthrie entertained alongside Tao Rodriguez Seeger (Pete's grandson) and Abe Guthrie (Arlo's son and Woody's grandson.)

Standing firmly on the slowly swirling stage at Oakdale Theatre in Wallingford, the Seegers and Guthries performed in the best folk tradition: acoustical guitar and banjo, with gently miked voices; ancient tunes with new lyrics; and wry stories.

"My purpose in life is not to put music in people's ears but on their lips," says Pete Seeger, 75, who can get a crowd singing "She"ll Be Coming Round the Mountain" with a wave of his hand.

The best test of any work of art is time. Does it hold up and have new meaning for years? Does it have universality?

"Where Have All The Flowers Gone?," Pete Seeger's classic antiwar song, seems as fresh today as it did in 1962, when the Kingston Trio made it a hit.

His union anthem about mine workers in Kentucky is applicable to modern office workers caught in downsizing:

"I don't want your millions mister,
I don't want your diamond rings,
All I want is the right to live mister,
Give me back my job."

Their job finished, the Seegers sat in modest chairs as Arlo and Abe Guthrie began their set. That pattern continued all evening as the two families shared the spotlight, sometimes backing each other, sometimes watching in obvious appreciation. And as Tao Seeger took center stage late in the concert for two Spanish language songs (he lived in Nicaragua for nine years), Pete, Arlo and Abe followed his clear tenor voice and his tempo.

Arlo and Abe, in matching pony tails, one frosty gray and the other chestnut brown, began with "Ukelele Lady," a nonsense tropical song dedicated to Arlo's brief television career on "Byrds of Paradise," a failed ABC drama shot in Hawaii. ("I played an aging hippie," he said. "Big stretch.")

In the middle, he stopped, explaining to the crowd, "This song has no social significance; it's just fun."

He dedicated a love song to his friend Jerry Garcia, read a children's poem about a moose ("Enough of these stories that make kids feel good. Let's scare them back under the covers") and explained how he writes his new songs shorter because "the old ones take too long to sing." (He refused requests for his legendary saga, "Alice's Restaurant.")

Folk tunes are passed from generation to generation, old tunes are freshened with new lyrics and ancient poems are interpreted with new music. And as the next generations of Guthries and Seegers make their way, they carry with them the strong voices and social awareness of their father figures.

A New Jersey Town And 9/11 "Trauma To Hope

Sheehy's Sobering Study Of Loss And Grief"

By Donna Larcen The Hartford Courant Nov. 09, 2003

MIDDLETOWN, AMERICA:
ONE TOWN'S PASSAGE FROM TRAUMA TO HOPE
By Gail Sheehy (Random House, 412 pp., $25.95)

Middletown, N.J., is a ferryboat ride away from the financial district of New York City, where the World Trade Center towers stood. The 41-square-mile township is a collection of quaint villages, historically home to farmers and fishermen. The newer residents, in their $400,000 homes, are husbands with high-paying jobs in lower Manhattan and wives who stay home to rear the kids and organize fund-raisers. Jon Bon Jovi calls it home, and Bruce Springsteen lives up the Navesink Road in nearby Rumson. Realtors would call the area a sweet, safe place to live the American dream.

On one late summer Tuesday, about 50 Middletown residents started their day commuting by train, by highway or by ferry to those good jobs in the shiny towers. It was the morning of Sept. 11, 2001. They never came back.

The people they left behind are the subjects of Gail Sheehy's latest book.

Sheehy has spent the past two years following the survivors -- widows, children, parents, siblings, rescue workers, cops, firefighters, counselors and clergy -- as they work their way through loss and grief.

Among the many lessons from the horrific events of 9/11 is the lesson about grief. Trauma affects the human psyche forever. Some heal; some hide; some hurt. All are changed.

This book is a thorough piece of reporting, detailed and authoritative. In the hands of a lesser writer it might be maudlin or muddy. Sheehy's prose is clear, though her task is hefty: juggling the stories of 50 people, yet keeping an understandable narrative.

It's a lesson in how a community tries to heal.

Not all of its members succeed. Sheehy tells of a 37-year-old sergeant from New Jersey assigned to the Port Authority. Co-workers told her about spending grueling months searching for bodies at Ground Zero. She didn't witness it herself, but even so, on March 1, 2002, Tracy Vetter carpooled to work, went into the ladies room and shot herself.

Her supervisor, who put in soul-crushing time sifting through rubble, begged for more counseling for his squad. He counts Vetter as one of the victims of 9/11.

Those in the helping fields concentrated on the psychological damage associated with an event so huge. Traditional trauma treatment uses a talking cure -- put the monstrous experience on the table and you can deal with it. But survivors and rescuers of 9/11 were often not ready to do that immediately. Some, like Vetter, never did. Sheehy pressed for more explanation.

She consulted Hilda Kessler, a psychologist from Berkeley, Calif., who explains that traditional counseling does not take into account the neurological aspect of trauma. The fear response overrides the thinking parts of the brain that separate real threats from false alarms. In trauma mode, a primitive part of the brain (the amygdala) floods the body with stress hormones that power the heart and muscles in anticipation of flight.

As Sheehy writes:

"It also burns into a substrate of memory every sensory cue attached to the trauma as vividly as burning a CD. Not surprisingly, then, it takes conscious effort and clever strategies to overwrite these memory cues."

Kessler says denial is often an appropriate initial response. Another psychologist explains it this way:

"You take it; you put it in the box; you put a lock on it. You put the box down in the basement, and you put a dragon down there to watch the box. Then you're free to go on about your business. … But you have to remember to feed the dragon." And that means repressing the bad memories.

That worked for some, but not all.

Bob Planer, a trader with Keefe Bruyette and Woods, worked on the 89th floor of the South Tower, the second one attacked. He had survived the bombing of the World Trade Center in 1993, but was trapped for five hours in an elevator. Moments after the North tower was attacked, he called his wife, who urged him to leave. He did, and was on a ferry in time to see his building fall. He spent the next several months going to funerals and trying to rebuild the company while looking out for the families of 68 dead workers. Sheehy observes that Planer was stuck in the trauma, never rebuilding his own psyche.

Others did share and share and share.

What Sheehy finds is that those who do tell their personal trauma stories and succeed in moving on must attach meaning to their stories. Some feel an urgency to tell what happened, over and over. Where they were when the planes hit the towers. Who died and was dear to them. But how to put this day into the context of a life shattered? How to get to what comes to be known as "the new normal"?

A bad omen appeared in the backyard of Kristen Breitweiser, 30, a former Jersey-girl surfer with a law degree, just before the tragic Tuesday. She saw a raven and took it as a sign that the tumor in her breast awaiting biopsy would be cancerous. The blond, stay-at-home mother of a 2 1/2-year-old said to Ron, her broker husband, that he should call his father and make peace.

"Life is short," she said on the afternoon of Sept. 9, 2001.

Shorter than they could predict. Breitweiser, who did not have cancer, had to take on another kind of battle: making sense of the death of her husband.

"No, I can't turn into this miserable depressed person. I'm only 30. And I'm a widow. I went to the library. Where is the book for a 30-year-old woman with a 2 1/2-year-old child whose husband was killed by terrorists and who watched it on TV? Where is the book for that?"

Breitweiser marshaled her rage and fear and energy and leads a group called Just Four Moms From New Jersey. They want to know why the authorities weren't better prepared for the attack. This becomes her mission. She leads the three other moms who push for a commission to investigate the poor planning.

Around the six-month mark after 9/11, New Jersey's caregivers reached out to their counterparts in Oklahoma City, where they learned that terrorist-caused psychological trauma is cumulative. And here's the sobering part: Three years after the bombing of the Murrah Building, survivors were entering the bleakest period of grief. Behavioral problems increased.

Doug Manning, a grief counselor from Oklahoma, says, "I think the only effective effort is through 'companioning.' I think people in grief usually need someone to walk with them."

Sheehy concludes that everyone she talked to was in some degree 18 months out from the horror, moving on.

"We're at a point where we've all decided we have a chance to live," says Karen Cangialosi, widow of a Cantor Fitzgerald trader and mother of two. "And we're choosing life."

DOLORES LASCHEVER

Dolores Laschever, as an assistant managing editor, started writing a weekly column for the Register-Citizen of Torrington in 1985. She was married for 65 years to Barnett Laschever, also a journalist and for many years director of tourism for the state of Connecticut. A decade later, under new corporate ownership the Register-Citizen launched a Sunday edition. The new Journal-Register Co. publisher was angered by a story that contained complaints from readers who had not received the paper. He fired the reporter who wrote it and then the editor resigned. When the publisher would not let Laschever run letters critical of new management, she resigned.

"This is a company that is primarily interested in business and does not care about journalistic ethics," Laschever said. She and the reporter sued the company. They eventually settled out of court.

The Laschevers raised four children. She worked for the weekly Lakeville Journal, editing her husband's columns and the opinion and viewpoint pages well into her 80s.

Legislators Ought To Legislate

By Dolores Laschever Register Citizen Torrington March 11, 1985

In the last two months, two Connecticut legislators have flaunted the law which is not only their responsibility to make but, it would seem, to uphold.

On Jan. 14, Connecticut's Lowell Weicker became the only U.S. senator to be arrested for protesting apartheid outside the South African embassy in Washington.

Last week State Rep. Christopher Shays, R-Stamford, was charged with contempt of court and jailed in the Bridgeport Correctional Center for refusing to leave the witness stand during a grievance hearing on the conduct of two Hartford area attorneys, Alexander A. Goldfarb and William W. Graulty.

Both Weicker and Shays have long been involved in the two issues in which they were trying to draw attention. Weicker has been for years an outspoken critic of the inequity of discrimination against and segregation of blacks and other minorities in South Arica. And Shays for two years has protested the delay in judicial action and sought severe disciplinary measures against Goldfarb and Graulty as well as Hartford lawyer Paul Aparo and Hartford Probate Judge James H. Kinsella. All have been charged with mishandling the $38 million estate of an elderly West Hartford woman, Ethel F. Donaghue.

This is not to say that the issues Weicker and Shays champion are wrong. But surely, as legislators they could have dealt a blow for the issues without breaking the laws which they have a hand in making and therefor a responsibility in upholding.

By getting arrested, both Weicker and Shays drew attention to themselves, thereby making the news and pushing the issues for which they were fighting into the background.

It has been argued that legislators are also citizens and have a right to publicly protest. But inherent in their decision to run for a legislative post -- and after they win the elections that give them those responsibilities – is the requirement to behave in a manner that is within the law. Breaking the law makes a mockery of the position and of the law.

Protesting may be one of the only recourses open to the ordinary citizen, but a legislator has other avenues open to him that enable him to accomplish his goal with greater ease and effectiveness. As a legislator he is a public figure and his word on an issue is significant. A press conference or speaking before appropriate organizations can be valuable in getting his opinion to the public. But even more useful is taking advantage of the functions of the forum of which he is a member. He can speak before that forum, and he can work with other legislators to make laws which can help to accomplish their goals.

Shays could continue to push for action on the Donaghue case within the legislature. And action within that case is only part of a larger problem on which Shays could use some of the tools at his command: to speed up action in the courts on cases that have been on the docket for years.

Shays has been chairman of an Appropriations subcommittee which oversees the judiciary and his contempt citation led to his being stripped of that post. His effectiveness there could have had greater impact than his refusing to leave the witness stand.

His actions and his arrest kept the state House of Representatives arguing Wednesday for over two hours – time that could have been spent on more crucial issues – until they decided to seek his release on a writ of error. Part of the discussion in the House dealt with whether his contempt citation was a civil or criminal offense and concern was expressed that pressing the issues would lead to a "constitutional confrontation" with the judicial branch of government.

Weicker and some of his fellow Connecticut legislators managed to do Thursday what should have been done in place of his protest two months ago – they proposed legislation that would impose economic sanctions, including bans on U.S. bank loans and investments, on South Africa.

That is one of the effective ways that a legislator can create change.

Maria Petroro Carries Through

By Dolores Laschever Register Citizen Torrington March 25, 1985

"This is Maria," the voice came over the phone when I answered it at the office on a recent Saturday.

Before I could ask "Maria who?" she continued.

"You only gave me 24 instead of 25 papers."

I began to realize who Maria was. "Can you sell the other paper?" I asked.

She was way ahead of me. "I'll borrow one from the gift shop, but you should replace it." I told her I'd leave a note for the circulation department, she said thank you and I heard the phone click off.

I sat for a moment thinking about Maria and decided I wanted to meet her.

Thursday I walked the floors with the small, compact woman with the quick smile who started delivering the Register Citizen to patients at Charlotte Hungerford Hospital at the end of February. Maria Petroro is the result of a happy arrangement among representatives of the hospital, the Litchfield County Association for Retarded Citizens (LARK) where Maria is a client, and our circulation department.

Maria, who is 37, has cropped, dark hair and wears blue jeans, sneakers and a blue smock with Register Citizen printed on the back. She pushes a cart with a change box and a pile of newspapers and she smiles a lot. She started out with 45 newspapers Thursday and by the time we had made the rounds she had sold all but one.

Maria started at 1:30 and it took about an hour to cover the 3rd, 4th and 5th floors. She stopped at the nurses' station to find out if there were any rooms she shouldn't go into and, avoiding those, she knocked on the doors, first on one side of the hall and then on the other. "Hello," she said to each patient, "Would you like to buy a paper today?"

The paper costs 25 cents and often Maria had to make change. Someone gave her 35 cents and she returned the dime. "No, it's only 25 cents."

"But it's for you," the patient answered.

"Oh, no, m'am," Maria said, "here, it's all right," and she gave it back.

Sometimes a patient asked her for a glass of water or for help getting out of bed. "I'm sorry," she replied, "I'm not a nurse."

Sometimes the nurses stopped to buy a paper from her. A few visitors did, too. She always peeked into a room before knocking. "When I see people sleeping or have nurses with them, I don't go in," she explained. Then she added with her quick smile, "Sometimes people are waiting for me to come."

When she finished the three floors, she took a break and went down to the cafeteria to have a cup of coffee. "I don't go up to the 6th floor until after

3," she said. That's the maternity floor and she must wait until the babies who have been visiting their mothers are returned to the nursery. "That floor's easy to do," she said.

Working with patients comes easily to Maria. She told me she also works Friday mornings at the Torrington Extend-a-Care where she serves coffee and tea to the residents and often uses the sign language she learned at LARK.

She used to work at the Edward E. Sullivan Senior Center office, at Dee's and Joanne's Restaurant and she also has had an assembly job doing piece work at LARK. Formerly a resident of Tunick House, Maria now lives in a supervised apartment where someone is available to offer advice and help her with her bills.

Before Maria started to deliver the papers, Carol Sprouse from LARK, Candace Lewis from the Register Citizen's circulation department and Cyril Skidmore from Charlotte Hungerford Hospital spent some time with her, showing her around the hospital and telling her how to communicate with the patients. Skidmore, hospital President Robert Summa, and Circulation Manager Jerald Devine worked out the original idea. They have only one minor problem.

"I'm not allowed to get sick," Maria laughed, "because there's nobody to take my place." Soon, however, she will train someone who can fill in for her if she's unable to come to work.

Maria likes delivering the paper to the patients. "They're all very nice people," she said.

She thought for a moment. "They taught me what to do and I'm doing great. They're pleased with me and I just like to make people happy, you know."

Yes, we know.

Compromise For Branch Way To Go?

By Dolores Laschever Register Citizen Torrington May 13, 1985

Something is wrong with the compromise agreement to save the Torrington campus of the University of Connecticut by turning it into the Northwest Connecticut Educational Center.

The compromise doesn't save the Torrington branch of the university – it makes of it an altogether different facility. If the compromise bill passes, the campus will no longer be a university. It may develop its own special qualities over a period of time, but it will be a mongrel lacking in importance in the education field, where snobbism – whether you like it or not – exists.

True, courses will be offered by UConn, but within two years the bill allows those courses to be cancelled if fewer than 10 students sign up for them. The core courses required for freshmen and sophomores should be exempt from that provision – if they cannot be guaranteed that they will find the necessary sequential courses at the center, good students will be unlikely to go there.

If the university insists on cancelling those core courses, will provision be made for students who in the past were guaranteed admission to Storrs if they received acceptable grades in the required courses? What about the other institutions which will participate in the education center and have different requirements for entry to the university? Surely a lot more thought and planning must go into the center before it becomes a reality.

Another concern is the staff, which, faced with closure of the branch has already been assigned to other UConn campuses. If reassigned to the Torrington center will staff members still honor those other assignments? If not, who will fill those other positions? Where will the money come from? One wonders whether a part-time staff here can provide a university program. Professors and instructors must be available to students.

The bill allotted $50,000 to establish the center. The UConn vice president in charge of the branches, Lewis Katz, questioned how so small a sum could be used effectively. In this day and age, $50,000 will barely scratch the educational surface.

The university has wanted to close the branch because of low enrollment, and one wonders if the above-mentioned problems might also keep students away. Although no minimum size of the student body was included in the legislative bill, one wonders if enrollment does not pick up, how long the university and the state will be willing to prolong the life of the education center.

At a time when the number of high school graduates is expected to drop quickly, as much as 43 percent in the next decade, UConn at Storrs will be competing with is own branches for students. One senses that Storrs, because of its past behavior concerning the branch system and recommendation of the compromise agreement by UConn President Don DiBiaggio, would have done anything to get rid of the Torrington campus. Does eliminating the Torrington campus as a branch of the university give administrators the go ahead to close other branch campuses as well?

The compromise worked out by State Rep. Otto Neumann, R-Granby, who never expressed interest – unless it was negative – in the branch, was based on an alternative proposal by Marvin Maskovsky, who heads the Litchfield County Committee on Higher Education, the area-wide organization formed to save the branch. The proposal, presented in March, did not go into detail but outlined cooperation by area educational institutions to offer diverse educational access and opportunities to all students.

Maskovsky should be commended for his and his fellow committee members' extraordinary efforts to save the higher education facility for Northwest Connecticut. They ultimately came to the conclusion because of lack of support in and political pressure from the legislature and the governor's office, that the compromise might be the only way to accomplish their goal.

If this is the agreement with which they have to work, then they have their work cut out for them. A lot of questions have to be answered and a lot of planning has to go into the Northwest Connecticut Educational Center.

WENDY LECKER

Wendy Lecker is an education columnist for the Stamford Advocate and Hearst CT Media Group, and is senior attorney at the Education Law Center, Newark, NJ. She was a staff attorney at the Campaign for Fiscal Equity (CFE) in New York. She has also worked as a consultant in education finance and policy for The Rural School and Community Trust and Connecticut Voices for Children. Before joining CFE, Wendy was a staff attorney at both the Legal Aid Society, Criminal Defense Division, in the Bronx, and at My Sister's Place, a domestic violence agency in White Plains. She also served as the Assistant Legal Director and House Counsel for the American Jewish Committee. Wendy has a B.A. from Cornell University and a J.D. from New York University. She is the former president of the Stamford Parent Teacher Council.

Fueling The Teacher Shortage

By Wendy Lecker Stamford Advocate September 9, 2017

A serious teacher shortage is plaguing school districts across the country. The Learning Policy Institute ("LPI") recently found that in addition to teachers leaving the profession, enrollment in teacher preparation programs has dropped 35 percent.

It is no wonder. Over the past decade, teachers have been subjected to a barrage of unproven mandates that hamper learning. They are judged by evaluation systems, based on student test scores, that experts and courts across this country have rejected as arbitrary and invalid. And, as one former teacher and current Colorado state senator remarked, "Teachers are constantly being bashed ... It's not the same job it used to be."

Connecticut is no exception to the teacher shortage, nor to its causes. Teachers have undergone a revolving door of evidence-free mandates, invalid evaluations and vilification from our governor who infamously declared that all teachers have to do for four years is "show up" to get tenure. Every year, hundreds of positions go unfilled in Connecticut classrooms.

LPI issued a report in 2016 on the causes of the teacher shortage, based on a review of an extensive body of research. Of particular note for Connecticut is the finding that inadequate preparation is a major factor in teacher attrition. Alternatively certified teachers have markedly higher turnover rates than traditionally certified teachers, with the largest disparities in high-minority schools. Teachers with comprehensive preparation were 2 1/2 times less likely to leave than those with weak preparation. Accordingly, LPI recommends providing scholarships and loan forgiveness for strong teacher preparation programs, and robust induction programs.

Some districts are making strides in identifying and addressing the root causes of teacher shortages. In Niagara Falls, New York, for example, the district embarked on a multipronged effort to cultivate teachers, particularly teachers of color. The district provides a scholarship for a graduate of its high school entering the teaching program at Niagara University. It also received an endowment at Niagara University for paraprofessionals who want to be trained as teachers; and provides financial assistance, reduced workloads and other supports to ensure success.

Niagara Falls public schools provide high school seniors with the opportunity to shadow teachers as an internship. Twelfth-grade teachers partner with Niagara University to ensure that students will not incur the expense of remedial education once they matriculate. They have also partnered with the local community college to establish academies such as the physical education academy. The superintendent reaches out to local African-American churches to request contact with graduates who have left the area in order to entice them to return. However, the superintendent does not favor lowering certification standards or weakening preparation. Those avenues would not only devalue the profession but also would harm the needy children in his district.

As featured in my previous column, Long Beach, California, also partners with its local university to train teachers, who student teach in the district's schools. The high-poverty district has a 92-percent retention rate and credits its partnership with the university for protecting it against teacher shortages.

Connecticut had promising programs for growing teachers. Last year, Bridgeport initiated a comprehensive minority recruitment program for paraprofessionals to become teachers. Hartford, Waterbury and CREC had similar programs. Just as this program was to expand, the state pulled the funding. The State Department of Education ("SDE") had a successful program, Teaching Opportunities for Paraprofessionals, however its funding was eliminated in 2002.

Connecticut also has high quality, university-based teacher preparation programs, which have made efforts to identify and address specific shortage areas and minority recruitment.

Rather than build on these successful efforts, SDE and the State Board of Education seek to weaken teaching. Last year, they approved an unproven fly-by-night outfit called Relay to provide alternative certification.

Now, they intend to lower teacher certification requirements. One idea they are considering is abandoning the requirement that bilingual teachers have content certification, as if English Language Learners do not deserve a teacher who knows the subject she teaches.

Weakening teacher preparation or certification will exacerbate the teacher shortage problem. As LPI found, poorly prepared teachers do not stay long. And schools serving our neediest kids are most at-risk of this disruption.

New York's Education Commissioner and Board of Regents' Chancellor just issued a forceful letter supporting strong teacher certification standards. As they point out "no parent wants their child to be assigned to a classroom teacher who has not had the best training."

Connecticut's most vulnerable students need and deserve a strong and stable teaching force. The state's current ill-conceived plans would undermine this vital goal.

The Segrenomics Of U.S. Education

By Wendy Lecker Stamford Advocate January 6, 2018

For children in Baltimore classrooms, 2018 opened with buildings where temperatures never topped 40 degrees. An incensed teacher wondered why persevering in abominable conditions is something "we only ask of black and brown children."

A new book by Cornell professor Noliwe Rooks, "Cutting School: Privatization, Segregation and the End of Public Education," traces the history of separate and unequal education in America.

White America's reaction to the prospect of educating children of color has ranged from outright and often violent opposition to promoting weak substitutes for adequately funded, integrated schools — substitutes that fail to ensure educational equity. Throughout U.S. history, these maneuvers have presented opportunities for hoarding resources for the white and affluent and even profiting at the expense of children of color — a phenomenon Rooks calls "segrenomics."

From the earliest days of tax-supported public education, states found ways to deny African-American communities equal educational opportunity. One method was to simply refuse to fund African-American schools.

In 1914, South Carolina spent on average $15 per pupil for white schools but fewer than $2 per pupil for black schools. Appalled at the conditions in which African-American children were forced to learn, that state's superintendent of education remarked: "It is not a wonder that they do not learn more, but the real wonder is that they learn as much as they do."

As Rooks chronicles, officials in the South outlawed integration, double-taxed African-Americans, refused to build African-American schools and engaged in violence. Public money, even if raised by African-Americans, almost exclusively benefited white students.

Some white philanthropists resolved to help African-Americans — on their terms. They required poor African-American communities to front money for schools that the philanthropists would match. Determined African-American communities all over the South expended herculean efforts to raise the required money.

The philanthropists had a constricted vision of education for African-Americans. To them, it was a means to provide effective and subservient laborers to ensure the South's economic health. As one organization put it, the goal was "to train these people as we find them to a perfectly ideal life where they are."

Rooks illustrates how officials and "reformers" have virtually ignored successful models for education, such as: adequate funding, integration, and community-initiated reforms.

As she demonstrates, inequality, hoarding and profiting off the backs of poor children of color continue today. Schools have resegregated. States persistently underfund schools serving predominately children of color. They offer false "solutions" that hurt more than help — like charter schools.

Charters, concentrated in poor communities of color, are no better than public schools, increase segregation and often result in or benefit from closing neighborhood schools.

As Rooks notes, charters are "cash cows" for many operators, whether in the form of tax incentives; public funding; or the billions of dollars stolen by charter employees and operators. Charter expansion is a credit negative for poor communities, weakening their ability to raise money for public works. Authorities exact little oversight over this theft of public dollars.

Many affluent white communities hoard educational resources. Wealthy districts invest in investigating and prosecuting non-resident parents of color who attempt to enroll their children there. Strict oversight of wealthy district boundaries starkly contrasts the lax regulation of charters in communities of color.

Segrenomics continues to benefit the privileged at the expense of communities of color.

The same narrow view of education for children of color continues in many charter schools. Professor Pedro Noguera once confronted John King, then a charter principal, later U.S. Education Secretary, over the harsh discipline in his school.

Noguera asked "Are you preparing these kids to be leaders or followers? Because leaders get to talk in the hall. They get to talk over lunch, they get to go to the bathroom, and people can trust them. They don't need surveillance and police officers in the bathroom." King's response was that "this is the model that our kids need.'"

Rooks draws hope from communities of color mobilizing to protect their schools. As scholar Sally Nuamah observed, schools were the first public institution to which African-Americans gained access. Public schools are community anchors and a path to the middle class, providing stable employment. They are also a forum for organizing and speaking out.

Rooks cites groups such as the Student Unions in Philadelphia and Newark, who staged walkouts and sit-ins to call attention to the lack of resources; and the Chicago community that conducted a hunger strike to protest school closures. Rooks predicts that these engaged and organized communities "may save us all."

History Repeats, And Repeats, And Repeats ...

By Wendy Lecker Stamford Advocate March 4, 2018

The satirical newspaper, The Onion, once had a headline that read: "Historians politely remind nation to check what's happened in past before making any big decisions." On the 50th anniversary of the publication of the Kerner Commission report, it is instructive to review what our nation has refused to learn about racism since the civil unrest of the 1960's.

President Lyndon Johnson convened the Kerner Commission, chaired by Illinois Gov. Otto Kerner, in July 1967, to understand the civil unrest that occurred that summer, in Detroit, Newark and neighboring communities; and to devise methods for preventing its recurrence.

After extensive investigation and study, the commission concluded that the primary reason for the unrest was "the racial attitude and behavior of white Americans toward black Americans." The report declared that segregation and poverty had created a destructive environment for African-Americans totally unknown to most whites, but "(w)hite institutions created it, white institutions maintain it, and white society condones it."

The report is a comprehensive assessment of all aspects of society, from its institutions to societal attitudes, to media coverage of race. The commission observed that African-Americans rightfully felt frustration at pervasive discrimination, exclusion from local government, officials condoning white terrorism against nonviolent protest, official resistance to desegregation, and inadequate investment in their communities.

The report emphasized that poverty and racism were intertwined and both must be addressed to move our country forward.

The commission concluded that the nation faced three choices: continuing current policies of inadequate investment in African-American communities and a failure to integrate; investing more in African-American communities and abandoning the goal of integration; or pursuing integration and enrichment of African-American communities.

The commission rejected the first and second options. While enrichment of African-American communities was a viable interim strategy, the commission declared that since power and resources reside among whites, only integration would create true equality.

Owing to the pervasiveness of racism and its effects, the Kerner Commission's prescription for preventing future unrest was as comprehensive as its investigation; covering employment, education, public assistance programs and housing. The report observed that the recommended programs would require "unprecedented levels of funding and performance." It concluded that "(t)here can be no higher priority for national action and no higher claim on the nation's conscience."

The commission declared that "education in a democratic society must equip children to develop their potential and to participate fully in American life." Integration was the commission's priority. However, recognizing that integration would not be immediate, the report also recommended methods to strengthen public education in African-American communities, including: early education, services for at-risk children, teacher training, class size reduction, and adult literacy; increased opportunities for higher education; improved vocational education; enlarged opportunities for parent and community participation in public education, including making schools community centers; and revising state funding formulas to ensure adequate and equitable funding.

President Johnson, unhappy with the projected cost and with the failure to credit his Great Society programs, ignored the report. Its recommendations lay unimplemented.

What progress have we made in 50 years?

Today, racism is as pervasive as it was in 1968. Not only are our schools more segregated than they were then, we have consistently refused to invest in schools serving predominantly children of color. Nor have our societal attitudes changed. Contrast the suspicion brave African-American youth protesting gun violence as part of the Black Lives Matters movement have endured with the praise showered upon the equally brave youth protesting gun violence in response to the horrific school shooting in Parkland, Fla.

Education reformers and politicians claim the mantle of advancing civil rights, but their "reforms" run counter to the ideas and ideals of the Kerner Commission. Leaders resist full funding of segregated and impoverished schools, declare those schools "failures," then disenfranchise parents and communities and replacing them with segregating charters run by unelected boards. Rather than provide disadvantaged students necessary support, in the form of early education, compensatory education and the rich curricula and activities white schools have, they establish false metrics such as standardized tests that force a narrow focus on math and reading.

Testifying before the commission, sociologist Kenneth Clark described prior investigations as "a kind of Alice in Wonderland — with the same moving picture re-shown over and over again, the same analysis, the same recommendations, and the same inaction."

After 50 years of inaction, and an increasingly divided nation, it is time to revive the Kerner Commission's focus on integration, full participation and investment in our communities of color.

SARAH WESLEY LEMIRE

Sarah Wesley Lemire is an award-winning journalist and humor columnist who writes for numerous publications, including Hartford Magazine and The Hartford Courant. An avid football fan, helicopter parent, couch film critic, and travel junkie, Sarah is originally from Minneapolis and has spent the last two decades trying unsuccessfully to lose her Midwestern accent, and figure out the difference between a hoagie and a sub and a grinder.

Slams The Door On Some Of Her Own Parenting Behavior The Day Mom Threatened To Kick Your Friends' Asses.

By Sarah Wesley Lemire The Hartford Courant July 30, 2016

When I was little, my mom accidentally shut my hand in the door of our tan, wood-paneled station wagon.

Back in the days of no seat belts or fancy automobile safety features of any kind, I had been hanging out of the car door waiting for her to finish putting groceries in the back, when she came around and pushed it closed.

I don't really remember much of what happened after that other than the emergency room doctor admonishing me for crying too much over what was obviously just a simple thumb amputation.

Nineteen stitches and a roll of gauze later, my mom brought me home. Riddled with guilt, she apologized, but not for having shut my hand in the door. Instead, she said she was sorry for having ruined my chances of ever being a hand model.

And she should have been. When I look at my stocky fingers, bleeding hangnails and the crescent-shaped scar on my right thumb, I mourn the loss of what could have been a lucrative career.

If it weren't for my mom's negligence, I could've been somebody, could've had fame and fortune as the Tyra Banks of hand models, draping pearls across my knuckles or gently rubbing lotion on age spots for magazine ads and commercials. I might have even had my own reality TV show where young hopefuls with tapered fingers and perfect cuticles compete against one another for a contract on "America's Next Top Hand Model."

I try not to hold it against her.

I also try to forgive the fact that of all the local pediatricians in my hometown, my parents settled on a German doctor named Mildred Schaffhausen, a woman who bore more than just a passing resemblance to her name. It didn't matter if I was there for pink eye or head lice, Dr. Schaffhausen always insisted on ending every appointment with at least one shot, if not more.

Once after receiving penicillin injections in each of my legs for an apparent case of strep throat, I gingerly made my way out into the waiting room. "Don't walk funny," my mom sharply reprimanded. "You'll scare the other children."

In hindsight, I should have pulled the fire alarm and implored them to run for their lives, ear infections, croupy coughs and all.

But, fearing repercussion, I remained silent and did my best to walk as if Frau Farbissina hadn't just plunged a couple of knitting needles into my upper thighs and then been ordered by my mom to pretend it never happened.

Of course, that was a long time ago and we can joke about it now. That's probably because after having kids of my own, I've come to realize that my mom didn't corner the market on what not to say or do as a parent.

When my oldest daughter was in 6th grade I volunteered to serve as a chaperone at one of her school events. Before long I noticed that a few of the girls were picking on her as girls sometimes do.

After she came to me in tears, I got down on my knees, tucked her hair behind her ears and told my daughter that everything would be all right and then proceeded to say that if the girls continued their bullying, I'd go over and kick their prepubescent classes, sans the "cl."

It was meant to be reassuring and maybe make her laugh a little, too.

Sometime later I noticed that the mean girls had turned their attention to me. Trying to understand why they were whispering and pointing in my direction, I called my daughter over and asked what was going on.

"I told them," she said.

"Told them what?" I asked.

"That you said you're going to kick their (cl)asses."

Even though this occurred a few years ago, I'm pretty sure that even back then, a playgroup mom threatening to beat up a bunch of 12-year-olds wasn't looked upon favorably by school officials or local law enforcement.

I spent the next week in a cold sweat waiting for flashing lights to appear in my rearview mirror, or the fuzz to show up at the front door and haul me off to the slammer in my capris and sensible sneakers.

Thankfully, however, I managed to avert serving an extended sentence in the state penitentiary for attempting to cheer up my kid. Then again, maybe it wouldn't have been so bad. I could have used the extra time to work on my manicure.

Dead Plants Society

By Sarah Wesley Lemire The Hartford Courant Aug 3, 2017

Me? I'm just happy the kids are still around considering my complete inability to grow anything requiring oxygen and water.

It's not from lack of trying. I really like plants, and have a decent collection of them scattered throughout the house. Of course most of them are plastic, but even those appear as though they haven't been watered in a while.

The few live ones are of the "hardy" variety, meaning that much like cockroaches, they're able to survive a nuclear winter - the requirement when I bring one home.

It's somewhat surprising since gardening is in my DNA. Growing up, my grandmother loved planting so much that she and my grandfather purchased an acre of land a short distance from their home and turned it into one, big garden they called The Ponderosa.

As a kid I loved going to The Ponderosa. There were massive flower beds, rows of lush vegetables, corn stalks, strawberries, raspberries and a big oak tree with a tire swing that hung from a long branch.

I spent a lot of summer days sitting beneath the shade of that oak. According to my grandmother, one afternoon when I was 4, I studied a caterpillar making its way up the side of the tree before asking her where she thought it was going.

She replied that it was probably going home to its family. I then wondered if the caterpillar had a mother and father, and she said yes.

I asked a couple more philosophical questions before the conversation took an awkward turn. If my grandmother is to be believed, I also apparently asked if, in name of science and discovery, I could pee on it to see what would happen. In her infinite wisdom, she simply asked if I wanted the caterpillar to pee on me, effectively ending the discussion, since I didn't.

Those were some happy memories, which is probably why, despite my botanic limitations, I attempt to put in my own garden every year. Each spring, like an emperor going into battle, I maneuver my oversized push cart with the single, squeaky wheel stuck to the left, up and down the aisles of The Home Depot garden center, looking for soldiers brave enough to join me in the fight.

Though I can't be sure, I sometimes get the feeling that some are playing dead or feigning a blight in hopes that I'll keep walking. I'm no fool, however. I still manage to spot the true warriors, the herbs and vegetables that look hydrated and ready to sacrifice their lives, all in the name of ancestry and horticulture.

Upon arriving home, I unload them from the trunk and judiciously set them near the rocky, clay-packed dirt patch they'll call home for the summer, before promptly forgetting that I ever went to the store. A week or two later, I remember while checking the mail, and by the sheer grace of God and natural selection, a handful survive, so I plant them just for trying.

Feeling guilty, I initially tend to my weakened, fledgling annuals like Martha Stewart. Wearing stylish gardening gloves and pastel pants, I breezily announce to everyone that I'm "going out to the garden," where, for a time, I fastidiously weed and water my plants, all while dreaming of the pesto I'll make with my bumper crop of basil and the salads that will benefit from my garden-fresh cucumbers.

But as with most things, I eventually run out of steam, complaining that it's just too much work, it's too hot outside, I'm too busy, I need a pedicure, whatever, and neglect settles in. By mid-August, anything that isn't dead is either crawling with Japanese beetles or deformed in some spindly way, as though it attempted to grow itself out of the garden and into a place where there might actually be sunlight or water.

It's around this time that I throw in the towel, swearing off gardening forever, before developing amnesia a year later, and doing it all again. Maybe one day I'll get it right, in honor of my grandmother and The Ponderosa. Then again, there's always Whole Foods, which, last I checked, has plenty of basil and cucumbers, and, as far as I know, no caterpillars

---

The War Of The Cats

By Sarah Wesley Lemire The Hartford Courant June 22, 2017

Most people like either dogs or cats. I'm a cat person.

That's probably because when I was growing up, our dog, Max, an amicable cockapoo, routinely gobbled feminine products out of the garbage and used the braided rug in our living room as a city park.

At least once a week I'd come running in, barefoot, to watch Half-Pint give Nellie Oleson a piece of her mind on TV, before feeling the unmistakable squish between my toes and gagging off to the bathroom.

Max was also a barker. He barked at the mailman, the neighbors, the septic tank. It was like he was rehearsing to cut one of those doggie Christmas albums in a single take, including "Jingle Bells" and "Good King Wenceslas."

It's no wonder that as an adult, I prefer the quiet, non-tampon eating, poop-in-a-box, sort of pet.

When our kids were little, we adopted Spooky, a sweet cat, whose only fault was frequent hairballs. One time she vomited directly into my open jewelry box, requiring a massive, Exxon-Valdez cleanup effort if I ever planned to wear my earrings again.

To keep Spooky company we added Daisy, a stray kitten. A few years after that came Buddy, a rescue cat, in a need of a home.

First of all, anyone who says that there's no difference between owning two cats and three is lying. Effective immediately, our relatively peaceful home was transformed into a 24-hour animal shelter, with multiple litter boxes, bowls of stinky food pebbles and hissing cats everywhere.

The new couches we'd saved years for, were repurposed into walnut-beige scratching posts, something I can only assume Pottery Barn didn't take into account when they upholstered them with delicate, special order linen.

And no one left the house without looking like they'd first pulled their coat out of a barbershop trash can.

The bigger problem, however, was that Buddy and Daisy didn't seem to get along. My first clue was discovering that over the course of a couple months, they had systematically peed on every rug, in every single room of our house.

For good measure, they also hit a few bookshelves, the front door, coffee table, shower curtain, bath towels, most radiators and a laundry basket full of my favorite clothes in some epic, feline territory war.

Though I knew something smelled off, my husband insisted that it was just his coffee, leading me to wonder if he was spooning in ammonia instead of Splenda, which, at least, would explain why he couldn't tell the difference.

It's been seven years since The War of the Cats began. Spooky has since retired to the great litter box in the sky, leaving Buddy and Daisy behind to continue their festering urine feud.

As a result, we've divided our house into two separate cat zones to ensure that we don't have to burn it down when we move out.

The upstairs belongs to Daisy, the more frequent urinator, and the downstairs, Buddy. Since cats don't really respect invisible boundaries, we've been forced to employ drastic measures to make it work.

Hours of searching the internet produced the Scat Mat solution. It apparently teaches your pet to "avoid areas that you want to protect," by using a "gentle," static impulse.

Though the cats have been largely unfazed by the introduction of electroshock therapy, the rest of us have stepped on it enough times to be terrified of going upstairs for anything other than an obvious emergency.

Because the mat wasn't effective, we also set up a tall, iron gate, creating an East-West Berlin situation in the middle of our hallway.

Simple things like doing laundry require strategizing, considering that the washer is across the border. And guests who want to come upstairs must first pass through Checkpoint Charlie, displaying proper credentials and agreeing not to pee in any of the bedrooms before being allowed in. Even so, the cats still fight through the slats of the gate. Short of installing a drawbridge and moat, there's not much else we can do besides wait it out.

Once they've used up what's left of their nine lives, it's unlikely that I will ever be convinced to get replacements, because come to think of it, I'm not a cat person after all.

SARAH DARER LITTMAN

Sarah Darer Littman has worked as a financial analyst (ask her about sexism on Wall Street) a farmer's wife (ask her about the lactation yield curve of a dairy cow), a political columnist (ask her about the hate mail) and a freelance business writer (ask her how expensive it is to get health insurance). Her favorite and most rewarding career is writing for young people. She is the critically acclaimed author of YA novels Anything But Okay, In Case You Missed It, Backlash; (winner of the Iowa Teen Book Award) Want to Go Private?; Life, After; and Purge; and humorous middle grade novels Fairest of Them All, Charmed I'm Sure, and Confessions of a Closet Catholic, winner of the 2006 Sydney Taylor Book Award.

With Iraq War Vets, Don't Repeat Mistakes

By Sarah Darer Littman Greenwich Time September 21, 2004

Unsurprisingly, my last column generated quite a bit of mail; a few were particularly vitriolic, but these were offset by a greater number of positive responses.

The letter that affected me most arrived by regular mail. It was hand-written on lined notebook paper, and read as follows, with the exception of parts I had to delete because they contained words that cannot be printed in a family newspaper:

Dear Miss Littman,

No one talks about the Vietnam veterans who were forced to go with threat of jail time if they didn't. It seems to me that no one cares about the damage it

has done to me and other vets. There's not a day that goes by that I don't think about Vietnam. Alcoholism, PTSD, depression, thoughts of hate are constant reminders of a war I did not deserve. Vietnam was wrong then and still is today. President Johnson sent me to Vietnam, (deleted expletives). If the U.S. government apologizes, pays off the vets, or if the government is overthrown, this will bring closure for me. While I'm waiting for this to happen, (expletive) this country and (expletive) God.
Vietnam Veteran

P.S. The military won't talk about the suicides committed during basic training. There was so much artificial stress, some of these people could not take it.

In its own way, this letter is as extreme as some of the other responses I received. It certainly contained some pretty graphic language. But having received it the same week as the death toll of U.S. soldiers in Iraq exceeded 1,000, it got me thinking about how this country failed its veterans after Vietnam and the danger that we will continue to do so today.

I tried to imagine how the war in Iraq will be perceived by the people who served there when they look back on it in 30 years time. There are differences between the two situations, it's true. Unlike my bitter correspondent, the soldiers serving in Iraq are not there as a result of a national draft. But as with Vietnam, some soldiers find their presence confusing. Are they risking their lives for a war, liberation, or an occupation?

"We never really knew what was going on," said an Army infantryman home on leave. "We were told, 'we're just here to do good, to help Iraqis. They want us here.' And we know that's just pep talk from politicians – a bunch of professional liars."

A National Guard sergeant commented "It's all a game over there. It's all about politics, oil — who the heck knows? I'm livid."

Much has been made of the 1,000 death toll, but what about the more than 7,000 severely disabled and injured soldiers, whose lives have been irrevocably changed as a result of their injuries? They are returning to a Department of Veterans Affairs already under strain, with costs increasing by 10 to 15 percent a year, and aging facilities.

And that's just the physically disabled. What of those suffering from post-traumatic stress disorder, one of the "hidden wounds of war"?

An Army survey published in the New England Journal of Medicine back in July said 15.6 to 17.1 percent returning from Iraq exhibited anxiety, major depression, or other mental health disorders. The study, which included interviews with about 6,200 soldiers, was significant because researchers were able to obtain pre-deployment data, allowing them to gauge how much of the psychiatric symptoms reported result from deployment to Iraq or Afghanistan.

Another study of 1,300 paratroopers of the 82nd Airborne who'd taken part in the Iraq invasion, done three months after they'd returned to Fort Bragg, found that 17.4 percent exhibited PTSD symptoms.

Will these soldiers get the help they need to return to civilian life? Not if the current surge in demand on the Veterans Administration system (the largest since Vietnam) continues.

"It's clear that veterans are not a national priority to this administration," said Alan W. Bowers of the Disabled American Veterans earlier this year, when criticizing the severe underfunding for VA medical care in the 2005 fiscal year budget. "It's utterly disgraceful to shortchange America's veterans at a time when this government has placed so many of our troops in harm's way in the War on Terror, considering that many of them will need VA medical care for decades to come."

I just hope they get better care than my correspondent, the Vietnam Vet, did.

Don't Shield Young Readers From 'Hunger Games'

By Sarah Darer Littman Greenwich Time April 12, 2012

In last Thursday's paper, local bookstore owner Diane Garrett of Diane's Books wrote an Op-Ed declaring that the popular series "The Hunger Games" is not a book for children due to the violent premise. Suzanne Collins' trilogy is a compelling dystopian vision of the United States in the future. Now called Panem, a wealthy centralized Capitol rules 12 impoverished districts with an iron fist. Every year, the districts are forced to contribute two child tributes, one male, one female, to compete in The Hunger Games, a televised gladiator competition to the death in which only one victor can survive.

According to an interview in School Library Journal, Collins said she conceived of the idea from imagining a cross between the war in Iraq and reality TV after flipping through the channels one night and observing the juxtaposition between coverage of the Iraq War and reality television shows.

The violence in the series isn't gratuitous. While the premise is shocking, it is, above all, a challenge to think deeply and carefully about a political and economic system that would not just allow but require children to fight to the death in televised games.

The Book Page blog asked Suzanne Collins what she hoped the books would encourage in readers. She answered: "I hope they encourage debate and questions. Katniss (the protagonist) is in a position where she has to question everything she sees. And like Katniss herself, young readers are coming of age politically."

Why would one want to hide a trilogy with such rich themes, books with which one could introduce teens to discussions of Theseus and the Minotaur, Juvenal's Satires, and questions about economics, politics and ethics?

Unfortunately there are many grownups like Mrs. Garrett who think one should build a white picket fence around childhood and pretend that it is a place of Little Princesses and Secret Gardens, of Wind in the Willows and Hugo Cabrets. All of these are wonderful books that I myself love. But limiting kids' range to books such as these is doing a disservice to our "beautiful children," because it is underestimating their capacity for learning and discussion, not to mention their resilience.

Mrs. Garrett questions if children are reading Orwell in middle school (yes, some certainly are) and thinks that "The Hunger Games" trilogy would make a "sumptuous university seminar." Unfortunately, like too many adults, she is not honoring young people with the respect they deserve.

Erica Beaton, a 10th grade humanities teacher at the Tech 21 Project-Based Service Learning Academy at Cedar Springs High School in Michigan, used an essay I wrote for the Hunger Games anthology "The Girl Who Was

On Fire," to highlight some of the deeper themes of the series with her students. She wrote about the result on http://nerdybookclub.wordpress.com and it was thrilling:

"After reading Sarah Darer Littman's 'The Politics of Mockingjay' with my whole class, students actually gave up their own lunchtime to independently research the international laws of torture that Gale and Beetee presumably violated in terms of weapon design. Never have I had a book that caused students to audibly exclaim "Ooh! Burn!' at intelligent literary argumentation until this one."

Violence and dark themes in childhood stories are nothing new. Read the original, non-Disneyfied tales of the Brothers Grimm.

It is denying that violence can be a part of childhood that is the mistake, not reading and discussing "The Hunger Games" with your "darlings." According to the Centers for Disease Control, about one in four teens reports verbal, physical, emotional, or sexual violence each year. Approximately one in five high school girls has been physically or sexually abused by a dating partner, and dating violence among their peers is reported by 54 percent of high school students. Books are some of the best vehicles we have for creating discussion. Let's not be afraid to use them.

Reps Betray Oath When They Defile Constitution

By Sarah Darer Littman Greenwich Time December 22, 2011

Back when Connecticut still employed voting booths with curtains and levers, I took my two kids to the polls so that the act of casting a ballot became a learning experience in democracy, civic responsibility and politics. I'd talk to them about the reasons I'd made my choices, and why it's so important to vote.

My son, now 18, has always been keenly engaged by history and politics. He counted the years until he could vote. Yet now that he finally has that long coveted ability, he is so disillusioned by the political process that when we discussed the 2012 elections this week he told me he wasn't even sure he wants to. He views both parties as "corporate shills" and identifies more with the Occupy Wall Street movement than either of the traditional parties.

After the last few years, I have a hard time arguing with him. The Citizens United decision, allowing corporate "personhood," one of the worst Supreme Court decisions in the history of our nation's highest bench, stacked the deck even further in favor of moneyed interests. The tax polices commenced under Reagan and exacerbated under George W. Bush have resulted in a massive concentration of wealth for the most fortunate Americans, and a relative decline in the fortunes of the rest. This isn't just a myth perpetrated by Occupy Wall Street. Congressional Budget Office figures bear it out.

It's not just economic factors that have made us disillusioned with government but issues that lie at the very core of our democracy - like trusting that those we elect will hold to the oath they take upon entering office: "I do solemnly swear that I will support and defend the Constitution of the United States against all enemies, foreign and domestic; that I will bear true faith and allegiance to the same."

Since 2001 when the Patriot Act, a draconian bill that gave sweeping powers to the Executive Branch and law enforcement, was passed by Congress a mere 45 days after the September 11th attacks, our elected representatives for the most part have proved that if it's a choice between staying in office and defending the Constitution, they'll choose the former.

As John Whitehead of the Rutherford Institute (hardly a "liberal ideologue") put it, "The Patriot Act drove a stake through the heart of the Bill of Rights, violating at least six of the 10 original amendments -- the First, Fourth, Fifth, Sixth, Seventh and Eighth Amendments -- and possibly the Thirteenth and Fourteenth Amendments, as well."

Most of our Congressional delegation just voted for the National Defense Authorization Act, which includes language on military detention that codifies into law some of the more disturbing excesses of Executive power. While members justified this on the basis that they weren't legislating new powers, as Benjamin Wittes, a legal expert at The Brookings Institute writes: "The codification of detention authority in statute is a significant development ... because it puts the legislature squarely behind a set of policies on which it had always retained a kind of strategic ambiguity … Congress has now given that endorsement, and that is no small thing."

When we see the same reps who, before they were elected said, "Members of both parties in the House must refuse to play along with the same tired politics of fear and false choices," once in office playing along like the people they criticized, it's demoralizing.

But, as I told my son, because we love our country, we can't give up the fight. Our voices and our votes matter. We have to keep holding Congress' feet to the fire. And if that means protesting in the streets, well, so be it.

May 2012 bring liberty and justice to all, not just the 1 percent.

CAROLYN LUMSDEN

Carolyn Lumsden has been with The Hartford Courant since 1992 as an editorial writer, op-ed editor and now editor of the Opinion pages. She was previously a reporter for the Associated Press in Massachusetts and a copy editor for Random House, the New York publisher. Carolyn has a master's degree in communications from Stanford University and a master's in legal studies from Yale Law School, where she was a Knight fellow in 1998-99. She has twice been honored with the Sigma Delta Chi award of the national Society of Professional Journalists, for editorials published in 1995 and 2017. In 2015, Carolyn was honored with the Yankee Quill Award, the highest individual honor bestowed on journalists in New England by the Academy of New England Journalists.

Is 'Grammar School' Ironic?

By Carolyn Lumsden The Hartford Courant April 26, 2009

Copy editors have thankless jobs. They fix writers' copy and for their efforts get called names.

But I understand. Once upon a time, I too was as clueless as the columnist who has described me in print - affectionately, of course - as "the evil one-eyed editor." I graduated from college not knowing "between you and I" was wrong, and was offended when corrected. That slight started me reading grammar books, and first was the little bible "The Elements of Style."

So it caught my ear when a crabby Scottish professor griped on National Public Radio's "Talk of the Nation" recently that Americans have little formal grammar instruction. Most of what they know, he said, they get from "The Elements of Style," celebrating its 50th anniversary this month.

A remarkable statement. Come to think of it, I had more schooling in Spanish grammar than English until "Elements" got me addicted.

Linguist Geoffrey K. Pullum of the University of Edinburgh blasted the late "Elements" authors E.B. White and William Strunk as "grammatical incompetents" who got some of the rules wrong. He said the book is dangerous because it is "just about the only grammar they [students] ever see in their whole education."

I checked the state's curriculum guidelines. Grammar is recommended in grades 1 and 8, and there it stops. The word doesn't appear in the state's high school guidelines. That doesn't mean it's not taught, but it would be comforting to see at least a mention.

So as not to pick only on Connecticut, I looked at test questions on the Massachusetts Comprehensive Assessment System, which students must pass to graduate from high school. The questions all concerned reading comprehension. No grammar or punctuation quizzes.

Maybe it's no wonder, then, that Fortune 500 companies spend $3 billion a year training employees in basic English, according to an NBC report.

The millions of copies of "Elements of Style" sold in the past half-century do prove that many Americans love their language. So do such best-sellers as Lynne Truss' "Eats, Shoots & Leaves." (Which talks about British grammar, a different beast.) There are several passionate grammarians in The Courant's circulation area who catch our slip-ups and will undoubtedly grade this essay. (I won't be offended.)

But I think most Americans (and schools, too?) are afraid of grammar. It's a bit like math. The formulas are hard to remember, and in grammar's case, they're often illogical and change depending on what audience you're writing for. The nuts and bolts don't begin to interest many people until they're out of school and have to write in their jobs.

Way too often, writers fail to appreciate their invaluable ally. I speak, once again, of the maligned copy editor, the drill sergeant of the newsroom, the person who protects columnists and letter writers and novelists from embarrassment.

Here's "Talk of the Nation" host Neal Conan speaking to Professor Pullum on April 16: "Those of us who work in the journalism business have of course been terrorized in our time by ferocious copy editors." One wonders what mistakes Mr. Conan was terrorized for. The editors likely did him a favor.

If copy editors are such ferocious terrors, it's because they are the thin blue line against babble. Schools seem to have ceded the job to them and to Messrs. Strunk and White.

Vile Words? Are They The Real Problem?

By Carolyn Lumsden The Hartford Courant June 22, 2008

This past week, I went back in time to put invective in perspective.

Hartford Mayor Eddie A. Perez's anger at nasty-grams posted on The Courant's online comment boards, beneath stories on crime in the city, prompted me to visit the Connecticut Historical Society Museum to see just how civil conversations were a few centuries ago.

The kind staff of the wonderful Historical Society let me handle several Connecticut Courants from 1800. The four-page blue-gray newspapers look quaint with their Page 1 ads for horses and timepieces. But the rants against Thomas Jefferson were far from quaint.

"Murder, robbery, rape, adultery and incest will openly be taught and practiced, the soil will be soaked with blood, and the nation black with crimes" if Jefferson is elected president, predicted a writer who signed himself as "Burleigh" in a front-page editorial on Sept. 15, 1800.

The Republican candidate was "an enemy to the United States, and wishes its destruction," the Federalist mouthpiece Burleigh wrote in another editorial that year. He described Jefferson as a "libertine" and an "atheist" and asked readers, "Are you prepared to see your dwellings in flames, hoary hairs bathed in blood, female chastity violated, or children writhing on the pike and the halberd" if Jeffersonians take power?

Goodness.

The attacks turned racist in a handbill from around that time that called

Jefferson "a mean-spirited, low-lived fellow, the son of a half-breed Indian squaw, sired by a Virginia mulatto father."

Despite all this, Jefferson won the election.

This little history lesson is not to defend The Courant for failing to catch and cull some vile, cowardly and anonymous comments about Hartford (and the mayor) from our message boards these past few weeks. It's just to show that, well, 'twas ever thus.

I don't expect that to console Mayor Perez. He vented his anger with a demonstration Friday afternoon at the newspaper, which happens to sit across from an entrance to I-84. One editor, watching the scene out the window, noted the irony of the mayor using his free-speech right to protest the newspaper's free-speech right by blocking workers from exercising their freedom-of-travel right to get on the highway and go home.

To me, the mayor's fuss is beside the point. His temper tantrum over messages that few people saw until he publicized them is distracting the city and the region from the more serious conversation about 90 shooting victims so far this year in Hartford. Isn't that what we should be talking about?

Looking For The Truth About Wisdom

By Carolyn Lumsden The Hartford Courant July 20, 2008

Change can be a bummer.

Thursday I went back to Yale Law School. The Gothic halls were more beautiful than a decade ago, when the school was under renovation and I was there on a one-year fellowship.

But the pay phones near the cafeteria were gone, victims of new technology. It was shocking to see holes in the booths where the phones had been. They had been my lifeline, my solace. After a bad class, I would call home and huddle over the mouthpiece and wail, what was I thinking, going back to school at 45?

That's how Reinhold Neibuhr fans must feel - in need of a little consolation. God grant them the serenity to accept the possibility that the great theologian may not be the father of the famous Serenity Prayer, adopted by Alcoholics Anonymous in mid-century. Yale Law librarian/scholar Fred R. Shapiro has questioned Mr. Niebuhr's authorship in an article in this month's Yale Alumni Magazine. He found the prayer popping up in newspapers several years before Mr. Neibuhr reportedly wrote it. I returned to New Haven this past week to see how Fred did his detective work.

Back in 1998, Fred worked among the dark stacks of the temporary basement library while the splendid light-filled permanent library on the third floor was closed for repairs. I remember him as wearing glasses and looking preoccupied.

Well, no wonder. It was a radical time for librarians. Online databases of old newspaper and book pages were springing up, and they could be searched by computers in seconds, unlike the laborious microfilms and -fiches that had to be loaded on machines to be read.

Fred would soon use these databases to challenge the 150-year-old "Bartlett's Familiar Quotations" with his "Yale Book of Quotations," published in 2006 - and which he immodestly but accurately calls "revolutionary." He would include hundreds of modern American quotes that stuffy old Bartlett's has ignored, such as "Nuts!" (Gen. Anthony McAuliffe) and "Today I consider myself to be the luckiest man on the face of the earth." (Lou Gehrig).

And he would shatter many quote myths. On a whim I looked up "The opera ain't over until the fat lady sings." Fred had found that the line commonly attributed to TV sports icon Dan Cook in 1978 was coined two years earlier by a Texas Tech publicist, Ralph Carpenter. Bartlett's had it wrong.

The Internet can do enormous harm in passing off lies as truth on popular sites like Wikipedia. But Fred has used ProQuest and Google Books and NewspaperARCHIVE.com to nail down facts in ways scholars never dreamed of doing before.

He found in them several early versions of the Serenity Prayer. Such as this 1938 Courant article quoting Constance Leigh, superintendent of the Newington Home for Crippled Children: "that we may have the courage to change what should be altered, an understanding and serenity to face what cannot be faced, and the wisdom to recognize one from the other."

This was five years before Mr. Niebuhr wrote the prayer, according to his daughter, Elisabeth Sifton.

In her rebuttal in the alumni magazine, Ms. Sifton objects to Fred's hunch that the great minister might have unconsciously adopted a folk saying as his own. Search engines aren't perfect, she says. Her father could have been preaching those lines long before he wrote them, and his audience could have repeated them in their own speeches and writing.

She has a point. But why no attribution to Mr. Niebuhr? Harder than acquiring the grace to accept a thing you can't change is having the wisdom to know whether what you're accepting is true. Fred Shapiro's groundbreaking detection, while making us wiser, isn't making such decisions any easier.

CARRIE MACMILLAN

A lifelong Connecticut resident, Carrie MacMillan wrote feature stories and columns for the Republican-American in Waterbury, Conn., for 11 years. Her work, which spanned health, general news, personality profiles, arts & entertainment and ruminations on marathon running, marriage, friendship and parenting, garnered more than a dozen awards from local and national news organizations. Carrie now writes for Yale School of Medicine's web site, where she enjoys continuously learning and reporting on fascinating doctors, patients and medical advances. She lives with her husband, two sons and a crazy dog atop a steep driveway in Oxford. Carrie graduated magna cum laude with a degree in English from the University of Connecticut, and tries to find time to write the occasional freelance piece.

"First Day Of School More About Future … And Past,"

By Carrie MacMillan Republican-American Waterbury Aug. 28, 2015

My oldest son starts kindergarten next week. This isn't going to be one of those "Where did my baby go?" reminiscences.

I know exactly where the last five years went.

That's partly because I've been trying to practice what many strangers have achingly told me over the years: "Enjoy them while they are little; it goes too quickly."

But it's mostly because I've been acutely aware of the months, weeks, hours and minutes that passed excruciatingly slowly. Potty training comes to mind.

Yet, as I fill Colin's crisp L.L. Bean dinosaur backpack with crayons and glue sticks, those trying memories are fading. In no time, I'll be one of those mothers who scratches her head when talking to an anxious parent of a toilet-training kid and says, "Yeah, I think my oldest potty-trained himself at 18 months? Or was he 4? They'll let you know when they're ready. Cherish them when they are young! Pass the chips."

Getting Colin to sleep through the night was no easy feat. But surely, in a few years, I'll shrug when a new mother talks about sleepless nights and say, "We were lucky, Colin was always a good sleeper," completely forgetting the long spell when he woke up at 5 every morning, refused naps and had meltdowns all day long.

On the other hand, the months in which every word was elongated in a sing-song voice, and each truck on the highway was celebrated — loudly — felt fleeting. My husband and I coined the term "Colinism" to mark funny things he said. "A couple few minutes," was a favorite.

Just the other day, he was reading a book about dinosaurs, which, in his words, were however many "meateaters" — not "meters" — long. During a children's sermon in church a few months ago, the pastor asked what it meant to pray. "It's when an animal eats another animal," Colin replied.

When it comes to starting school, I am following Colin's lead and trying not to dwell on the moments that will never return. He brims with pride and jumps in place at the mere mention of sharp pencils, a desk of his own and a school bus to ride. He's eager to learn, make new friends and get a little space from his younger brother. And because of that little brother, my husband and I get to hold on a little longer to the joys and frustrations of toddlerhood. I can't fathom what is going on in Colin's head when he imagines what school will truly be like. But I remember my first day of first grade. I was nervous. The school bus looked impossibly immense when it pulled up to the bottom of our driveway on a busy road in a small town.

My brother — two years older and usually more a menace than a protector — held my hand and walked me down a long ramp in Kent Center School to Mrs. Ackerman's carpeted classroom. I found a laminated rectangle with my name on it and took a seat at a desk the color of a manila envelope.

I settled in and loved school throughout the next 16 years — yes, even high school.

It may be naive to hope Colin has the same experience I had. I know there are rough patches I am whitewashing out of my time in school. But I am thankful he is not daunted by this new experience lurking next week.

OK, I lied. Reminiscing is inevitable in parenthood. Children grow up too fast and too slow. I suppose all parents are forever toggling between "fast-forward," "pause" and, occasionally, "rewind."

"Missing Mother Mightily"

By Carrie MacMillan Republican-American Waterbury May 14, 2006

When my grandmother died, I saw my mother cry for the first time. I was 9, and it scared me. But over the next 14 years, I don't remember seeing her cry again not when she was diagnosed with breast cancer and not when doctors told her there was nothing else they could do.

My mother didn't know how to deal with the loss of her mom. So, I shouldn't be surprised that I don't know how to cope with hers.

It's been nearly five years now. It doesn't get any easier, and holidays like Mother's Day don't help.

Maybe if I had children of my own, I'd enjoy it. But for now, I know my mom a woman who laughed on her deathbed would not want me to mope.

She'd prefer I celebrate her. But it's risky to indulge in her favorite activities, which included slathering herself in baby oil and baking in the sun on her lake-front property beneath a cloud of her own cigarette smoke.

She appreciated the irony in getting breast not lung or skin cancer.

I think I know how she'd want me to describe her. "Tell them I'm pretty," she'd suggest. Or "tell them I look great in a bathing suit." (She was both gorgeous and shapely at 53, the age she died.) Or perhaps, "Tell them I'm smarter than you."

All would be said with a touch of fun sarcasm. She possessed a clever sense of humor unmatched by anyone I know. It was a little sick, yes. A little twisted, sometimes. But also, innocent. And in the end, useful. Her wit made her two-year bout with cancer easier for everyone.

When my mom was diagnosed, she called it "The Big C." When her hair fell out and she needed a wig, she went to a salon called Above the Rest. She quickly dubbed it, "Without a Breast."

She loved people, especially her three children's friends. She'd send my college roommate a $5 bill, then wait a few days, and send me $3. After I brought a boyfriend home, she'd ask, "Did he say I'm cute? Oh, good."

It didn't stop after she became really ill. While hospitalized for her mastectomy she scouted eligible single doctors for my older sister.

Occasionally, she'd come across someone who didn't quite get her sense of humor.

At my college graduation, she met my boyfriend's stepmother for the first time.

At a reception at the student newspaper where we worked, my mom said, "Thank God, I don't have to read any more of these Daily Campus articles! She just kept sending them."

Later, my boyfriend's stepmother asked him, "Does Carrie's mother not support her career in journalism?"

Of course, she supported me. It was her way to poke fun at everything. I was fair game because our humor clicked. She nicknamed me "Cruella" for my sometimes steely reserve. "How long must you stay with us for Thanksgiving? Must you come?" she wrote in a letter to me during my freshman year at American University.

When I gained the freshman 15, she didn't suggest I cut back on Belgian waffles. Instead, she joked about how she, too, had put on weight in her latest attempt to quit smoking. "Dear Tubby, Are you fat, too? We'll be so cute together when you're home," she quipped.

After I transferred to UConn she wrote, "Must I write letters to you still? I'm getting sick of it." She wasn't really. The cards kept coming. Halloween, Saint Patrick's Day, Easter. While I studied in Russia, I was the only student in the program who got a letter nearly every week.

Sometimes she'd write one zinger.

"Saw the good daughter today. I don't think she cares for you that much. Agree?" she'd teasingly ask.

I received my last piece of mail from her less than a month before she died. She'd lost her short, salt-and-pepper hair for the second time. The cancer had spread to her liver and was heading for her brain. Still, she wanted to congratulate me on the job I was about to start. She signed the card in the name of the editor I had gladly left behind and wrote, "I want you back."

In a moment of seriousness two days before she died peacefully at home, she gathered us around her bed. She told us she loved our father, but that the best thing in her life was us kids. She didn't want to die, but mostly, she didn't want to leave us behind.

In the next breath, she regretted not having had time to pick out dad's next wife.

I hope I continue to remember my mom's slightly husky voice over the telephone. I can visualize her tossing a tennis ball, over and over, for the dog. She'd pause to inhale from her cigarette, leaving a ring of bright pink lipstick on the stub.

Like her letters, she favored short and sweet calls. "Can I go now?" she'd ask, if I called right when she got home from work. The dog was running circles around her legs and there was laundry and gardening to do, and naturally, some rays to catch.

Invariably she'd find time to ask, "Do you miss me?"

"Yes, mom," I'd say, sometimes with impatience.

But, of course, I missed her.

I'll always miss her.

So when I need to feel my mom's presence, no matter what day it is, I re-read some of her letters and cards.

They're guaranteed to make me laugh and sometimes, cry. She would want the laughter most of all.

"The Unthinkable Can Happen All Too Easy"

By Carrie MacMillan Republican-American Waterbury July 15, 2017

I left my lunch at home on Friday. I did the same thing on Wednesday.

On both occasions, I was harried to get out the door, simultaneously peeling small children from my legs, admonishing the dog, calling out final instructions to my mother-in-law or husband.

Still, I can't remember the last time I left behind my lunch, other than last week. With a 4-year-old and a 21-month-old to transport to daycare or leave with a grandparent, I'm always amazed I even make it out the door in the first place.

Last week, a 15-month-old from Ridgefield died after he was left in his father's hot car all day. The father reportedly says he forgot to drop the child off at daycare, and then forgot the child was in the car.

When I heard that story, an immediate combination of horror, relief, sympathy and fear swept over me. If you believe the father, which I am inclined to, it's a relief to realize the child was not intentionally harmed. Caring for young kids is all consuming, so consuming that it can become easy to lose sight of the goal, which is to protect them. I suspect I'm not alone in wondering, 'Could I ever forget my child like that?'

I'd like to think not, but sometimes I forget to blow out a burning candle for hours. Sometimes I turn left to go home instead of going straight to pick up the kids from day care. At a swimming pool the other day, twice I averted my gaze for 30 seconds, not knowing where one of the kids was. Although many other adults were nearby, I felt that momentary twinge of panic — and guilt.

Getting everyone ready in the morning is a chaotic scene of changing diapers and sheets, making breakfast, brushing teeth, negotiating clothing choices, packing lunches, walking the dog and stopping fights. That doesn't include being awakened by a screaming toddler whose teeth are coming in, assuring a 4-year old that it was just a dream, or nudging the panting dog out of my face at 5 a.m.

By the time I get to work, my day feels half over. My energy is sapped. It rebounds and recommences with the evening rush of dinner and chores. But the moments when I am the most prone to absentmindedness are in the morning. Getting out of the house must play out like a well-rehearsed production of a Broadway show, but since two members of the cast either can't seem to talk or reason, it never does. That's why lunches and cups of milk get left behind. And if there is even a slight change in the routine, it's more likely to happen.

The other night, I was giving my boys a bath as my husband prepared to go out for a run. He knew I was expecting one of our neighbors.

"What are you going to do if Julia comes over?" he asked me, as I lathered up one boy's head and pushed a Thomas train toy to the other.

"Oh, I don't think she's even going to come," I said.

"But," he said, pausing, and I suddenly got what he meant.

No, I assured him, I would not leave the boys unattended in the tub to go answer the door. If she comes, I promised, she'd leave what I needed on the front step. I had told her to do so if I wasn't home.

As he headed out, I shouted, "Maybe leave the front door open a crack, so if she does come, I can yell for her to come in."

He liked that option.

It's not that my husband doesn't trust me. And I wouldn't have left them in the tub to get the door, especially since the younger of my sons enjoys dipping his head underwater. Rather, it's that nagging "what if" in the corner of every parent's head.

In today's world, with Amber Alerts sounding a piercing siren on your phone and horror stories of women attacked in parking lots, it's easy to feel unsafe.

But the place we want to feel the safest is in our home. In many cases, our car is an extension of that — the vehicle that transports us from work to school to day care to swim lessons and beyond.

Today's babies are tightly strapped into rear-facing seats because that has proven to be the most secure option in a crash. Police officers professionally installed all of our car seats. Yet I know the car is the most dangerous place my kids will be.

The thought of a child dying in a car seat because he was left there, forgotten perhaps because a parent had a lot of other things on his mind, is frightening. I'd like to call anyone who does that a negligent parent. But I read that the Ridgefield dad curled into fetal position when his son was pronounced dead at the hospital.

I can't imagine living with that. But I can imagine how it could happen.

KAREN MAMONE

Karen Mamone has worked in newspapers and magazines in Connecticut, North Carolina, Florida, and Ireland and the UK for 40 years. She taught print journalism in a London City and Guilds certificate program in Dublin and covered the Irish stage for "The Stage and Television Today" for six years.

Mamone attended University College, Galway (Ireland) and later, as an older student at Central Connecticut State College. She left two months before graduation to take a full- time newspaper job. Her terrier Poppy didn't get his degree either.

Letters from Clatterbridge
On The Road To Mary Robinson
The Ladies On The Bus Consider The Myths of Ireland

By Karen Mamone Northeast The Hartford Courant Feb. 3, 1991

This month, former Courant reporter Karen Mamone marks her fourth year of sending occasional letters from her home in Ireland. Her cottage is near the village of Kilmeague, about 30 miles from Dublin.

The 7th of November, Election Day, fell on our usual shopping day, the one morning each week when the red mini-bus ferries me and the rest of the car-less and stay-at-home ladies of Ballyteague into Newbridge for the grocery, post office, and picking-up-the-pension run. I was glad it worked out that way, because I wanted to hear the grass-roots reaction to the candidacy of Mary Robinson, the first woman ever to run for president of Ireland.

She had been gaining steadily in the polls, but I wondered if this articulate, liberal constitutional lawyer could win against a party hack of the good-ol'-boy school in this traditional male bastion, this land that has rejected divorce and abortion. Even though the polls had predicted the 1986 referendum on divorce would pass, and despite a pre-election scandal involving her opponent, I knew better than to underestimate the conservative leanings of the plain people of Ireland.

Anyway, I wanted to hear what the ladies had to say. I didn't plan to bring it up. I just wanted to hear, or overhear, comments not edited for foreign ears.

The usual chatter started up as the bus turned up the hill toward the village. But it was about the weather, Beila's flu, Granny Connolly's funeral Mass (bad, bad, too short, and the priest mumbled).

"Have you been down this road?" Ned, the driver, asked me as we detoured onto a narrow lane outside Kilmeague. A road narrower than most driveways, overgrown, and full of turns – a boreen, the Irish diminutive little road.

I had, but said no so I wouldn't spoil his fun. Ned apparently had a story to tell. This is Molly Dix Lane, he said. Years ago, when the coffins were carried on pallbearers' shoulders to Crosspatrick graveyard on the hilly slope below Allan, the earthly remains of crony old Molly Dix were transported from her cottage down this long winding lane. But the branches of an overhanging tree caught the edge of the coffin and knocked it to the ground.

Our Molly it seems, was so shaken by the fall that she woke up and lived for another seven years. Before her second funeral procession, her husband walked ahead with a slash hook and took the precaution of hacking down every tree branch and hedgerow limb that protruded into the road.

Everybody laughed, although they all knew the story. And they started recalling other strange country goings-on. What about Mary Robinson, I wanted to ask. But they had other women in mind. Another Mary, the one who cursed Back Lane. I heard about the hanging a few months ago. A man in his 40s was discovered hanging from the attic rafters of his house. (All the neighbors, in perfect accord with neighbors everywhere, said he was a nice, quiet man who kept to himself.)

I didn't remember he lived on Back Lane. It all started about 40 years ago, said Nellie, who is old enough to remember. The county council, the local government body, built a dozen small cottages on Back Lane, just across the canal from me in Allenwood. A crazy old lady named Mary Malone applied for one of them, but was turned down in favor of young couples with small children. So she put a curse on the houses, Nellie said.

In the past few decades nearly every household on Back Lane has been visited by tragedy or hardship: four suicides, two car crashes, a motorcycle accident, a drowning, a shooting, and dozens of miscarriages and stillbirths.

"Do you believe the old lady cursed the houses?" I asked Nellie. She shook her head and took a deep drag of her unfiltered Players. "I couldn't say for sure. Maybe it's just a pisheroque."

I had forgotten about the other Mary, and asked Nellie about other pisheroques, folk beliefs, and legends. This country is full of them, like if you refuse to give milk to a needy neighbor, your own cow will go dry.

Other than media-spread myths like the snake-in-the-coat-sleeve, and the albino New York sewer alligators, it's a new experience hearing legends retold in ordinary conversation. I lived in and around Hartford for 25 years and can't remember ever hearing a local legend or folktale. Maybe the odd scene of a grisly murder noted, or a spooky house of indefinite origin, but nothing so elaborate or immediate. I recall, as a teenager, some sinister association with a perfectly ordinary house on a Peter Parley Row, but I think now it was my own mental connection with Boo Radley in "To Kill a Mockingbird" (I had the same problem much earlier when I confused hall monitors with hall monsters).

No, our local folklore involved sexual proclivities of Berlin Turnpike strippers, the slippery dealings of used car salesmen, and whether that tall-fenced house really belonged to a Titanic survivor who dressed as a woman to escape.

Here the gossip is more lyrical. Fairy rings and pookas. Curses and dead awakening. Fairies, by the way, I was informed, are fallen angels with the morals of mere mortals; not bad enough to be damned, nor good enough for heaven.

Neither are fairies the property of the older believer. Geraldine, the 30-ish wife of a friend who lives across the bog, still swears her car ended up in a ditch late one night because a giant pooka ran across the road in front of her. Others suggest that on that same evening, there was, as the Irish understate their national vice, "a drop taken."

Still, I can imagine Geraldine putting a curse on a road and making it stick.

Mary Robinson won the election, by the way. I finally asked, as the bus pulled into the parking lot of Dunne's stores, what the ladies thought of her.

"I'm going to vote for her just to spite me husband," said Safie.

My neighbor May organized a carpool to the voting place at Allenwood School after tea. "Sure we girls might as well go for one of our own," she told me in the car on the way over. "She can't be any worse than that shower they've got in there now." (Shower: an indefinite pejorative.)

Funny things is, when her inauguration day came (after a nauseating number of "here's to you, Mrs. Robinson" headlines) all the ladies on the bus were terribly annoyed with her. They thought the Irish-designed coat and dress outfit she wore for the ceremonies was too short. "For them skinny knees and all," Betty said. "It was a disgrace, making a show of herself that way."

Thanks For The Mammaries

By Karen Mamone Northeast The Hartford Courant, July 20, 1986

Perhaps the most encouraging thing that can be said about my form is that it is anatomically correct.

At its worst (generally the second and fourth Wednesday of each month), it could stop Jane Fonda in mid-squat. At its best, it has a number of swellings and contours and lumps, and a few of them are in the appropriate places.

Despite fairly regular thoughts that perhaps it should be remodeled into a more acceptable total acreage, I tend to take a somewhat tolerant attitude toward my form and expect others to do likewise.

But I hold no one responsible for his nerve endings. I am not particularly bitter toward the few souls roaming the planet who would be happy men today if their reasoning were not tainted by testosterone poisoning.

This, however, is not about me. This is about breasts. And memory. This is about the memory bra.

In a few months, Japan's leading manufacturer of women's undergarments will introduce a revolutionary new product to American chests – a brassiere that remembers the shape of its wearer. The memory bra, which has been selling like rice cakes in Japan, will hit the shelves of Bloomingdale's in New York wearing a $28 price tag, according to the folks at Wacoal Corp.

They say the bra's key feature is "NT wire," made of a metal alloy of nickel and titanium that provides the garment with s "shape memory" function.

"The metal alloy," they say, "has a special feature remembering the original shape, so that our new product...will keep the shape of a breast in good form forever."

It's that last phrase that worries me. It seems to raise a whole lot of questions. I spend a good part of every workday on a monumentally complicated machine with gobs of memory. I have a typewriter at home that has a one-line memory.

My own memory is pretty good, but, frankly, I've been looking forward to the day when that will no longer be the case.

Now, my age roughly coincides with the number of years Jack Benny admitted to. That is old enough to notice from time to time (daily, actually) that certain vital body fluids seem to be on the wane. Old enough to have empirical evidence about the effects of gravity which are somewhat more gripping than Newton's habit of tossing vegetation off bell towers. And I do seem to remember – albeit vaguely – that certain of my appendages once inhabited decidedly more spritely locations.

Or so it seems.

Now, the folks at Wacoal (which you have to admit sounds a good deal more like a Nebraska insurance company than a lingerie manufacturer) say that if I rush right down to Bloomie's the very moment the memory bras hit the street and promptly introduce it to my current contours, it will register my various circumferences and radii and imprint the necessary information on its NT wire forever and ever.

And even after washing, the memory bra returns to "the original breast line shape" when you wear it, according to a Mr. Nokio Nakamura.

Now here's the problem. The memory bra never met my original breast line. I can barely remember it. How can a bra have a better memory than I do?

Perhaps I should keep an eye out for a 22-year-old who seems to have my original breast line and ask her to put the bra on for a while.

"Pardon me, Miss, but your bosoms seem to resemble what mine looked like a few years back. Would you mind..."

The Cricket's Solo

By Karen Mamone Northeast The Hartford Courant Oct. 26, 1986

Few eyes are as keen as Thoreau's. It was he who noticed, walking through a swampy wood near his Concord home, the skunk cabbage never completely surrenders to the oncoming winter.

He saw, even as its broad mantle of leaves withered and collapsed with autumn frost, that nascent hoods were forming for the next spring push to the surface. "They see over the brow of Winter's hill," Thoreau wrote, "they see another summer ahead."

We're way behind the skunk cabbages. We tend to miss even the current season, let alone foresee the stirrings of the next.

Somebody wise and witty – and probably French – said life is what happens when you are otherwise engaged. There's ample proof of that on days when somebody says to you, "I just don't know where the summer has gone, I never even got to the beach."

We nod in agreement, reinforcing the notion that some mysterious meteorological conspiracy is responsible for summer lasting only 36 days this year instead of the usual 90.

It was there all along, of course, the regulation Gregorian summer with its requisite number of days. Sure, it rained on some of them, so we just voided them out, rejecting as unseasonable anything but San Diego skies.

And on the first blanket night, we complain that we didn't get any autumn at all this year, as if without an official Fall Foliage Sunday Drive to Avon or Vermont, we were forbidden by law to look around us.

Right now – without maps and tourist board guidance – fall is happening outside your door. It is an epic drama. All you need to do to participate is stop being otherwise engaged.

The first hard frost, whenever it comes, is more momentous than almost any other event in the natural year. Even leaf-fall pales beside it. The treed landscape becomes naked in stages, but the first frost is as sudden and killing as a tidal wave.

Of course there is sadness in it, as everything you have known and nurtured is imprisoned one morning in a rime of white crystals. The captives are left withered, slimy black, and unspeakably dead: First the limp bodies of plants imported from warmer climes – tomatoes, marigolds, melons. Then even hardy perennials, until the whole world, save scraggly pines, seems mouse brown and mole gray.

But autumn is not all death. And not death at all, really. Even the marigolds will be back in six months – and that is a kinder arrangement than most deaths we mourn. No, outside your door right now is an elusive, fragile transitory time when the sky is alive with bird migrations, when ferns and lichens shine without the competition of their tartier relations, when the last brave dandelions and asters bloom, when the snowy tree cricket stops so the meadow cricket can sing solo.

I have always been fond of keeping records of when things begin and end, perhaps to remind myself that, in nature, there are no finite episodes, only parts of a cycle.

Last year the tree crickets stopped singing Nov. 1, but the final plaintive chirp of the meadow crickets didn't come until the 15th. The last hardy dandelion bloomed next to the dumpster in the parking lot on Nov. 15, and the milkweed burst its pods on the day before Thanksgiving.

The spring-blooming dayflower that grows in the weedy strip beside my sidewalk surprised me with a second flowering at the end of October. Like its first cousin, the spiderwort, the finely detailed bloom lasts only a few hours. The legendary plant taxonomist Linnaeus named the dayflower,

Commelina communis, with its two prominent blue petals and a small, inconspicuous faded one, for three Commelin brothers. Two were notable botanists, and one died young, before accomplishing anything in the science.

The club mosses stay green all year. They look like tiny pine trees, and if you study them long enough to let your eyes adjust to a new scale, they become whole forests in miniature. A wood louse passing through looks like an armored dinosaur in a primeval wood. It is the earthy smell of the club moss that scents forests in autumn. Shade-loving haircap mosses and the velvety pincushion moss that might be growing behind the garage or garden shed are also easier to find in the fall, without the lushness of summer to distract.

The careful eye also can find the intricate lichens – like the British soldier lichen, with its erect grayish stems capped with bright scarlet "hats." They are so courageous they'll even grow on granite.

Birds' nests you missed amid the foliage suddenly appear when the last leaves are gone. Only the eagles and ospreys return to the same nest, so you can bring one built by any other species inside for closer examination.

And the masterful architecture of a hornets' nest can be appreciated with little anxiety – as many as 2,000 perfectly uniform combs covered in the finest gray parchment. If you're inclined to pull one down, though, be aware that some inhabitants may still be in residence. As the cold weather progresses, each queen will begin to leave home, seeking out individual hibernation quarters in old logs or sheltered crevices. The rest of her subjects will die off as the hard frosts come, and only she will re-emerge in the spring, to rule again.

VIVIAN MARTIN

Prior to becoming a college professor, Vivian B. Martin worked as a newspaper reporter, freelance magazine writer and, in the late 1990s, for companies on that then-foreign place called the World Wide Web. As a reporter she worked for The Hartford Courant and Connecticut Law Tribune, covering issues ranging from city housing to business. As a freelance magazine writer, her work has appeared in Black Enterprise, Women's World and Scientific American. From 1997 to 2003, she wrote an op-ed column for The Courant, a number of which were published in newspapers around the country. Her book publishing includes writing mass market (Astrocycles), scholarly book chapters, and co-editing a book on research methodology, Grounded Theory: The Philosophy, Method, and Work of Barney Glaser (co-editor, Astrid Gynnild). She was cofounding editor of Teaching Journalism and Mass Communication. Among her current projects is a book that is part memoir, social history and critique as it maps the reconfiguration of racial attitudes from the 1960s through Obama. Vivian is the chair of the journalism department at Central Connecticut State University. She received her Ph.D. from Union Institute and University.

Why Smart People Don't Vote

By Vivian B. Martin The Hartford Courant Aug. 10, 2000

You know the drill: Someone tells you he or she is not going to vote and you offer up the usual list of reasons why everybody should. You talk about civic duty, the need to be part of the solution and the fact there have been elections and referendums decided by one vote. If the errant citizen happens to be black, I dig even deeper and evoke memories of civil rights workers who died fighting so that blacks could vote. I've managed to pry a few people off the couch with that one.

Yet my canned lecture wasn't good enough recently when my sister said she would not vote in the much-watched U.S. Senate race in New York. Since she thinks Democrats and Republicans have similar ideologies and tactics, she will not reward Hillary Rodham Clinton or Rick Lazio, the congressman from Long Island, with her vote.

Maxine Martin isn't someone who needs a civics lesson. She may march to her own drummer -- actually clarinet and tenor sax (she's a jazz musician) -- but she follows politics in the news media and is among the minority of people in New York City who answer summonses for jury duty. She's been turning out for the little and big elections since she became eligible to vote more than 20 years ago, so I really wanted to know what had gotten into her.

"I'm not knocking voting at all," she wrote during a flurry of e- mails we were exchanging on the subject. "I still believe in it if you really believe in the person for whom you're voting. But if you're lukewarm about somebody, or just voting for someone because you don't want someone else to get in office, then I don't believe it's a good idea to vote."

Once it was clear to me that Max (a) was not suffering from post-traumatic stress after watching Apollo Night at the GOP convention and (b) will vote this fall but pass on the Senate election, I was able to entertain the notion that not voting can be a responsible civic act.

"If we don't vote, then maybe we'll get someone who works harder at getting our votes. It's like buying a commodity. I don't want to just pay for anything. I'll spend [or vote] on the best product," wrote Maxine, who teaches in East Harlem part time. Those who are quick to counter such views with the usual "every vote counts" diatribe need to be more aware that there are educated, responsible people who look on the current political system and say, as Maxine wrote, "OK, what else do you have for me? What we have now is just not good enough."

Jack C. Doppelt and Ellen Shearer, professors at Northwestern

University's Medill School of Journalism, conducted a national survey of 1,001 people and subsequent in-depth interviews. They found the usual group of know-nothings among non-voters. But they also uncovered a sizable group of non-voters who are knowledgeable about politics and civic affairs. The professors, authors of "Nonvoters: America's No-Shows," found that three out of 10 of the non-voters fit a category of people they called "Doers." As one of five categories that the researchers outline, Doers are under 45, young, well educated, involved in their communities and read and/or view much political news. Not voting is a deliberate choice for them. Some aren't registered to vote; others only vote when they want to get rid of a candidate.

Some non-voters may sound like spoilers. But spoilers for whom? For party bosses who think the U.S. Constitution exists to further their party's interests? For all the lobbyists who work against the interests of ordinary people?

The political establishment refuses to adopt some of the measures that would turn more of the 100 million-plus adults who don't vote (more than half of the voting-eligible population) into voters. Campaign finance reform certainly would give more meaning to the votes of ordinary citizens. The presidential primaries held earlier this year showed that open primaries, which would allow the growing blocs of independent and unaffiliated voters a voice, increase voter participation. Yet half of the states in the country do not admit unaffiliated voters to primaries. And the political parties whose efforts led to the 7-2 Supreme Court decision that overturned California's "blanket primary" system, which allowed registered voters to cast their votes for any candidate regardless of party, are out of step with the California voters who approved blanket primaries.

Meanwhile, those who oppose admitting Ralph Nader to ballots and some televised debates this fall foster the cynicism that keeps voters away. If our political system is to turn non-voters into voters, it needs to offer them more than canned lectures.

A New Diversity In The NAACP

By Vivian B. Martin The Hartford Courant July 31, 2003

I thought I knew who the "colored people" in the National Association for the Advancement of Colored People were. So when M. Saud Anwar, founder of the Pakistani-American Association of Connecticut, suggested that the NAACP should be at the forefront fighting the discrimination that people of color like Pakistanis have experienced since 9/11, part of me said, "Whoa!"

The NAACP was founded by a multiracial coalition working with the luminous intellectual W.E.B. Du Bois and crusader-journalist Ida B. Wells-Barnett, and people of any color can join. Yet I am not certain that the issues Anwar, a physician and activist, is concerned with should be high on the group's agenda. The Connecticut State Conference of NAACP Branches is concerned with poverty and educational access in the inner city and the black-white achievement gap. Anwar, a South Windsor resident, is concerned about the nearly 60 doctors from Pakistan that he says are being denied admission to the United States for residencies and other short-term medical assignments. Anwar is talking to lawyers on behalf of 15 of them.

As I listened to Anwar lay out his case over coffee recently, I was thinking that the processing of visas for anyone coming into this country should take longer these days. Prior to 9/11, some people in the Immigration and Naturalization Service weren't doing their jobs properly. Yet the process needs to be monitored to avoid discrimination against Muslims and others from the Middle East, and Anwar shouldn't have to start a "National Association for the Advancement of Brown People," a path he briefly considered, to do that.

To his credit, Anwar didn't flinch when I pointed out, in a manner much friendlier than some African Americans do when they discuss this issue in private, that prior to their post-9/11 problems, Pakistanis and others of color weren't looking to join with African Americans to fight racism. Racial profiling was just something that happened to black people.

But now Anwar, sharing the results of surveys he has done of the state's Pakistani community, says Pakistanis and African Americans have more common interests than some might think. "I'm looking to help empower the NAACP by renewing it," says Anwar, who says he will join a state branch. "Their work is not done."

American blacks, of course, know this. But the time may be ripe for a diversity initiative within the NAACP. James Griffin, president of the Connecticut State Conference of NAACP Branches, says any policies that single out Pakistanis are discriminatory. NAACP chapters have supported challenges to aspects of the USA Patriot Act because of concerns about civil liberties and racial profiling. But some of the alliances they have forged are not easy.

Heaster Wheeler, executive director of the NAACP branch in the Detroit area, where the nation's largest Arab American community resides, says Arab Americans never bothered to show up for community forums on racial profiling until after 9/11. "And then we [blacks and the NAACP] couldn't get a seat at the meetings."

"We will always be against racism and discrimination, period," he says. But he adds, "Many people think they know what the agenda for the NAACP should be, but African Americans have a unique experience that will always make our issues different."

Anwar's decision to join the NAACP in Connecticut is partly a result of his knowing other Pakistanis who have joined chapters in other states.

Although small numbers of Indians, Hispanics and others of color are NAACP members in this state, Griffin says that most of the state's 6,000 to 7,000 members are black. If some of the newer groups showing interest in the NAACP join for more than their special interests, this could be an interesting transition to productive relations between African Americans and other communities -- and a departure from the tensions between American-born blacks and immigrant groups that have come to the country and, in part because they weren't black, leaped over American blacks in status.

Many of the recent immigrants of color are able to prosper and move around so freely because of the civil rights struggles of American blacks, a history that Anwar says inspired him and others in his native Pakistan. Perhaps there's a certain poetic logic in Anwar and other Pakistanis joining up with the NAACP to help take the fight for civil rights on its next leg.

Welcome, colored people.

In the Final Analysis, Opinion Makes A Difference

By Vivian B. Martin The Hartford Courant Nov. 20, 2003

This is the last time I will speak to you through this column. After 6 1/2 years, the editorial page editor is dropping it as part of other changes.

For me, the timing is just right. Within a few months, God and dissertation committee willing, I will be a media scholar, with extra initials behind my name and theories to espouse. But I am not turning my back on the doing of journalism. I'm getting back to half- started writing projects, including a series of essays on race and politics sparked in part by some ideas I addressed in this column over the years.

I will miss this perch on occasion. For journalists, the op-ed is a rare treat. Those of us who started out as reporters pretty much shut out all thought of expressing opinions in our work. In op-ed writing, the stronger the opinion the better, and it takes time to get used to the idea that you can get away with saying some pretty fool things if you want.

Op-ed writing is a little like parallel parking; the writer has to angle things just so and work in some tight spaces that are getting tighter (op-ed columns around the country have shrunk from 750 or 800 words to under 700). It is a workout in thinking, language precision, compression and showmanship.

It's both a privilege and a responsibility, and I feel blessed to have had the chance to do it regularly.

Prior to writing for this page, I had not thought much about the opinion side of journalism and probably viewed it as more luxury than necessity. But I now believe that insightful commentary is needed more than ever. During fieldwork for my dissertation on how people negotiate news each day, I spoke with a 50-year-old woman who was mourning the cancellation of Bill Maher's "Politically Incorrect" in the midst of post-Sept. 11 sensitivities.

"I get my thinking news from him," explained this woman, who would pursue further study of such issues as the Palestinian cause and Bush tax cuts after hearing Maher speak about them. Maher's humor commentary differs from the pieces on a newspaper's op-ed pages, but the woman used his show in a way similar to what others have told me they do when reading opinion pieces. If the commentary is thoughtful or provocative with purpose, and if it isn't too predictably ideological, it helps people think.

Sitting at Starbucks last week with a former IT hotshot who has been out of work for 27 months and who, along with his wife, is moving north, I wondered how the couple's story would end. The IT worker, who like many in his field lost his job because of offshoring to India and other realignments, was in good humor. He shared that a long stretch of unemployment can increase self- knowledge even as it brings on financial ruin. But three, six, nine months out -- how do these stories, multiplied by hundreds of thousands, change the country we're becoming? At a time when the war in Iraq could be remaking not just the Middle East but the world as we know it, and when huge domestic issues such as Medicare and Social Security hang in the balance, readers need commentary that brings perspective to the big issues of the day.

Some people prefer that columnists, news articles and most everything else they encounter reflect their views. Political scientists debate whether there is more ideological divisiveness among regular people or whether it's just the political elites who intentionally talk past one another for political advantage. From the reader responses I've received over the past 6 1/2 years, I know that there are some mean and just plain stupid people out there. And as an African American woman, I've heard from people who would complain that I was playing the "race card" if I wrote about liking Rocky Road ice cream.

Most of you who got in touch are far more humane and thoughtful than that. Your e-mails and phone messages on issues ranging from working to popular culture to war kept me writing this column at times when I was thinking of moving on. The philosopher John Dewey wrote about the "eclipse" of the public, the problem of the public recognizing itself and its common concerns. But many of you, from all spheres of society and backgrounds, checked in to say you were reading, listening and reflecting.

Thank you for recognizing our common concerns. Thank you for reading me.

LISA MCGINLEY

Journalism is Lisa McGinley's early love and later career. For The Day of New London, from 1995 to semi-retirement in 2016, she served in one or another combination as arts and features writer, reviewer, columnist, religion reporter, city editor and deputy managing editor. Since then she has been a member of The Day's editorial board and writes editorials and columns. Managing the news staff and coaching young reporters as they went from rookies to professionals was the best job in the world. Writing opinion pieces is the other best job in the world.

New London Is Still Her Haunt
Kermit and Walter and Gwen

By Lisa McGinley The Day New London Nov. 20. 2016

It isn't easy being green — or brown, or any kind of minority, which was what Kermit the Frog really meant.

The subject of minorities preoccupied this year's presidential election. Some were to be walled out, some deported. Minority citizens were courted in blocs for their votes.

Gwen Ifill, the "PBS NewsHour" managing editor and co-anchor, who died Monday at age 61 after a private struggle with cancer, was two kinds of minority, a woman and an African American. She was a PK — preacher's kid — whose parents came from Caribbean nations. She delivered the nightly news and hosted "Washington Week in Review" with the intelligent steadiness that marks the great news anchors as people we come to trust.

Americans are still arguing about what the news media did or had done to them in the campaign. Was the media biased, duped, unable to get the big picture? Media figures became part of the story, thus surrendering a claim to objectivity.

Gwen Hill was too ill in the days before the election to cover it as she had previous campaigns, but she would have been as unlikely to earn that scorn as Walter Cronkite would have been.

On the "NewsHour," Ifill and co-host Judy Woodruff didn't glam up the news. Colleagues didn't shout over one another. Guest experts on the show usually look like regular people, not celebrities, yet they turn out to be the very people on the planet who know all about the subject at hand. And there are always at least two: the one for and the one against.

Because her news operation researched its facts and presented them evenhandedly, viewers learned over time that they would not be hearing a retraction the next day. What she presented held up.

When the subject was one that a viewer could measure against his own experience, it passed the personal knowledge tests. Like Cronkite, in his day the most trusted person in America, she was an honorable journalist. Her report was her word.

Kermit the Frog, of course, was no reporter or even a human. But puppeteer and Good Human Being Jim Henson gave his froggy surrogate a goofy voice to channel the kinds of truth that children need to hear. From Kermit they learned that what they suspected was true: It isn't easy being green, but it has potential.

In their own lives they could see he had given it to them straight, and they remembered it. When Henson died unexpectedly in 1990, young adults called home in sorrow: "Mom! Mom, Kermit is dead!"

Being free gives Americans the right and the need to expect the truth. When we're uncertain or fearful, we are a minority of one. We need someone who understands the situation and won't mislead us.

By presenting all sides with candor and courtesy, such a person also becomes a model of how to agree to disagree. Gwen Ifill, as a moderator of civil debate, didn't allow it to get personal, precisely by the strength of her own personality. She struck a tone of civility that kept the focus on the facts.

Civility doesn't call names. Green doesn't attack Pink. If they don't respect each other, under the moderating influence of Gwen Ifill at least they learned to respect the process.

Kermit and Gwen and Walter all provided the news their audiences needed. It's sad to have lost Ifill just when we needed someone like that more than ever.

Still, they left us their example. In the months to come Americans will do their own fact-checking and gut-checking about what they hear. As they do after every election, they will watch and learn whom to trust and whom they cannot trust.

Hurricane Lessons

By Lisa McGinley The Day New London Aug.17, 2004

Being newly 6 that August, I wasn't analyzing the weather that led up to my first hurricane. Summer swayed between sultry and sunny. Days were for the beach and dusk was when little kids listened from creaky cottage beds while grownups chatted on the dark porch below.

On weekends, when my father was down from Hartford, we would sail on the beautiful Bonnie, the Atlantic class sailboat he owned with my uncle Bud.

Atlantics are the quintessential sailboats. The 30-foot sloops have the grace and lines of the 12-meter yachts that race for America's Cup, but are small enough for a three- or four-person crew to race, with a 6-year-old for ballast.

At Niantic Bay Yacht Club, where the Atlantic fleet skippers have gone on to Fiberglass hulls and national renown, a half-dozen wooden Atlantics sailed in the 1950s. By unspoken arrangement the owners each chose a different color for hull and spinnaker, making them easy to tell apart through binoculars. Leventhals' was navy; Rices', red; Millers', hunter green. Bonnie was pure white.

On Saturdays, when my father skippered, my mother allowed me to go, bundled into a musty canvas lifejacket that in memory I can still smell. My job on board was to keep out of the way and duck when my father yelled, "Coming about!"

On Sundays, in recognition of Bud's passion to win and the salty language that he used to do it, I was kept home.

When we were not sailing, the boats rode at mooring in Niantic Bay.

There they were, sitting ducks, when Hurricane Carol ripped into the Connecticut shoreline on Aug. 31, 1954, with little warning from weather forecasters. The only way to protect the fleet would have been to tow the boats up the Niantic River and hoist them out of the water. There was no time.

Carol is my mother's name, and even a child could appreciate the irony that a storm with her name was attacking the beach, the cottage and, most brutally of all, Bonnie.

Other hurricanes have since taught me that the day after the storm almost always glows with brilliant sunshine, as if the world has been painfully, penitentially cleansed by its ordeal. On a September day like that I followed my father down to the beach. Saltwater still flooded the streets. Sand lay everywhere in heaps, and in it, like broken eggshells, were strewn pieces of white hull.

I picked up one. My father carried another that was large enough to recognize.

I don't know what he was thinking. I have never asked him. Perhaps he was just glad his family was safe.

But I can remember my tears.

My Bonnie lies over the ocean, My Bonnie lies over the sea. My Bonnie lies over the ocean, Oh, bring back my Bonnie to me.

My father and his brother bought another Atlantic. They named her Bonnie, too, and sailed her for the next six years.

In September 1960, Hurricane Donna attacked, and although it did not pulverize the second Bonnie, it snapped her "spine" near the keel. My father gave up. Bud bought a different kind of boat.

My sister's name is Donna.

Conscience Money Could Help Opioid Crisis

By Lisa McGinley The Day New London Oct. 23, 2016

People are dying of opiate overdoses in houses, cars and doorways, and the state's new battle plan is going to need the resources for a public health crusade.

Gov. Malloy and the Connecticut Opioid Crisis Response (CORE) Team, led by doctors from the Yale University schools of medicine and public health, have come up with a strategy to address the crisis that resulted in 697 fatalities last year.

Health insurers helped to develop the three-year plan, but there is another party that should be at the table.

To mount an all-out crusade against opioid abuse, pay for life-saving emergency services, and get the addicted into proven treatment plans, the state and its partners will need the companies that make and market opioids to step up — not with pious plans for future research but with dollars earned in the overselling of painkillers that are far more addictive than the makers have wanted to admit.

A voluntary effort to compensate for unintended consequences would not be a first.

Alfred Nobel found a way to ease his conscience for the mortal damage caused by his invention of dynamite. He put the profits into a perpetual awards program for innovators who improve the human condition: the Nobel prizes for peace, medicine, and life-changing work in other fields.

The Mashantucket Pequot and Mohegan tribal nations, operators of the two casinos in Connecticut, contribute to the Connecticut Council on Problem Gambling for treatment and awareness of gambling addiction.

Neither example pretends that harm can be undone, yet they are more than salves to the conscience. Both attempt to counteract the bad effects and perhaps lessen future abuse.

The U.S. is fighting a man-made epidemic that didn't exist 30 years ago — over prescription, overuse and overdosing of opioid drugs. The PBS News Hour reported recently that Stamford-based Purdue Pharma, maker of OxyContin, had reported $30 billion in sales since 1996.

So who seem like the right ones to help Connecticut save lives and prevent addiction? Who is making the money right here in the state? This stuff isn't coming from offshore drug lords.

Purdue Pharma has a bad reputation for misleading prescribers about opioids' addictive properties in the run-up years to the epidemic. The privately held company pleaded guilty to criminal charges in 2007 in connection with its practices, and now, according to its website, seeks to fund a researcher who will investigate ways of "sparing, tapering and discontinuation" of opioid use.

In July, Pfizer Inc., which has less of a position in the painkiller market than other pharmaceutical giants, agreed to a statement of ethical marketing principles. Pfizer is helping Chicago in its lawsuit for compensation for costs of emergency services related to overdoses, The Washington Post has reported.

There are other lawsuits, and even more governments will likely try to recoup the costs of responding to an epidemic of emergencies with a single, traceable, preventable cause.

Why wait for the lawsuits? Makers of painkillers could avoid the legal costs and do the right thing now, when the state's CORETeam urges increased access to treatment with methadone and Suboxone; recommends making naloxone (Narcan) readily available for emergency treatment of overdoses; wants to ensure prescribers of painkillers follow guidelines and limits; and is committed to making the public aware of how big this epidemic is, and what can be done about it.

Meanwhile, Connecticut will be tightening its belt to deal with budgetary shortfalls. If the CORE plan is not supported, it will fail. If it does fall to the state to pay for it all, some other need will suffer.

As the Associated Press and The Center for Public Integrity reported last month, the opioid industry has been spending heavily in this fall's Congressional campaigns. How about spending some of that on grants to prevention programs or for municipal naloxone supplies? Why do drug makers even need to be asked?

MEG MCGUIRE

Meg McGuire, formerly Meg Angus-Smith, has been a journalist for 30 years in New York and Connecticut. She started in weekly newspapers and moved to full-time work in dailies 25 years ago as Lifestyles Editor at The News-Times in Danbury and then the Middletown NY Times Herald-Record. She knows about the tectonic changes in journalism firsthand, having been part of what was euphemistically called a "reduction in force" in 2008. Now she's working to find new ways to "do" the news as an independent online publisher of Delaware Currents covering the Delaware River, its watershed and its people.

Bending A Gender Custom

By Meg Angus-Smith The News-Times Danbury Jan. 28, 1992

The 15 bachelors were dressed to kill, the 100-plus women were splendid in everything from jeans to sequins.

The men ranged in age from 20s to 40s. The women spanned a broader spectrum, spiked do's to gray hair.

The women were there to gape, gawk, giggle and bid on the guys. It's called a bachelor auction.

Several charities have hit on this as a way to raise much-needed money. The Cancer Society is planning another for Valentine's Day at the Hilton.

This one, at the Holiday Inn on Newtown Road – in the same room where Rotarians sedately gather – was sponsored by ESCAPE, an arts organization that wants to involve young people, the disabled and senior citizens in arts projects.

Everyone enjoyed themselves, nobody died, and the auction raised $4,000 for this worthy cause. So what's bugging me?

As I flipped through the cute catalog after the "show" was over, each page held my scribbled notes describing the furious bidding that shot as high as $400 for two "stud-muffins," a phrase used by the auctioneer, disc jockey Bill Trotta (who sported a blue sequined jacket).

After every bachelor's name, I had scrawled a dollar amount. Some less than a hundred, for date packages that usually included dinner, dancing or a show.

If men buying women is repugnant, not to mention illegal, why is women buying men cute? Some of these guys stripped to show their hairy or hairless chests, to the evident satisfaction of both themselves and the audience.

Why does a bachelor auction work, when a "bachelorette" auction makes my stomach turn over?

Suppose, just to push the Outer Limits quality of this whole exercise, suppose a man had bid on one of these men?

Yep, sure is dangerous territory, this buying and selling of people. No matter how good the cause I can't say I'm happy with anyone buying anyone. Or any group nailing some arbitrary monetary value on any human being, male or female. Who wants to deal with the ego of the guys who "earned" the most? Or who's going take the time to reassure the men who didn't score high?

But no matter how hard I try to sneer, there's something else happening here.

The whooping and hollering that you might think would accompany such displays of male pulchritude were certainly loud, enthusiastic and appreciative. But not, in any way, sleazy.

The most adventurous, and perhaps demanding, date package was for a weekend skiing in Colorado. Perhaps it was the "overnight" implication that cooled the bidding.

There was a note of delight in the squeals of girlish glee that punctured the evening. They relished the turning of the tables, tiptoeing near a mighty taboo.

"It's about time that men had women judging them," said Valerie Osterhoudt, 32, one of the evening's successful bidders, who clearly enjoyed turning the tables.

There are no hard and fast rules for how we play this gender dance.

It struck me that even a mass of women, fired up, are just not that threatening. Picturing the scene of a woman up there, and catcalls from a male audience makes me nervous and scared.

There's often a touch of hostility in even the most routine male approach to the female, and though a walk in the other guy-ette's moccasins should make us more sympathetic, there's simply no way to catch the quick dread of the comment that masquerades as a compliment delivered in a semi-snarl by a stranger.

Whether the tables are turned or not, the fare can be ruinous to some. But hey, you can't categorize real life.

Michael Swartz, 23, one of bachelors, admitted to a few "butterflies" before the auction, but was all smiles afterward. "It's fun."

Ignorance Can Never Be Bliss

By Meg Angus-Smith The News-Times Danbury March 3, 1992

We Americans have a rather broad streak of prudery, spliced with voyeurism that is more dangerous than it looks.

It seems to be really hard for some people to handle the not terribly complicated fact that female breasts are both fun and useful – sometimes at the very same time.

Not too long ago, Denise Perrigo – a mother whose body was working exactly according to designer specifications – expressed concern that breast-feeding her 2-year-old felt good.

Perrigo, 29, was worried -- an occupational hazard with parenting – and decided to ask someone if it was Ok to become stimulated by breast-feeding.

So she called a nearby volunteer bureau in Syracuse, N.Y. to find a phone number for those gurus of the breast, La Leche League.

Unfortunately, the volunteer gave Perrigo the number of the Rape

Crisis Center, where another volunteer apparently equated the question – and that Perrigo was nursing a 2-year-old – with sexual abuse.

Next thing Perrigo knew, her child was taken into custody by the New York State Department of Social Services, and Perrigo was in jail.

In a scene that sounds straight out of a nightmare, Perrigo says she kept on thinking if she just explained it better, they'd understand. As she said: "We could get this whole mess straightened out, and that could be the end of it."

That was a year ago.

Her child was taken from her, and though criminal charges were quickly dismissed, the DSS pursued abuse and neglect charges with awesome assiduousness.

After eight months in foster care with only chaperoned visits from her mother allowed, the little girl was permitted to go to her grand parents, Perrigo's parents. It took so long because they never agreed with the DSS contention that there was abuse.

The nightmare continued as judges heard the case and dropped the charges, only to have DSS come up with a different collection of charges to extend its custody.

In November, the little girl, now 3, was finally able to come home.

Experts say an average length of time to nurse a child for the rest of the world is about four years. Now, I don't want to institute an international standard here, but I do want to know where are our brains?

"If it wasn't so serious, it would be laughable," said Ralph Cognetti, the Syracuse lawyer who is preparing Perrigo's lawsuit against the DSS and others. Right you are Ralph.

If it feels good for grown-ups to play with breasts, why ever should those very same nerves not function when breasts are doing the job they were intended to do?

Why are we likely to arrest some woman for doing with her breasts what should be done with them – sustaining life?

And how come the poor woman did not know that the job has a few benefits?

As a matter of fact, I think it's very clever that the breast-feeding system is designed to encourage the mother, when a lot of other child-care systems – natural and otherwise – seem not particularly interested in the well-being of either parent.

We Americans have a real problem with sex. Oh, we like it well enough. Or at least I think we do. We're prone to giggle and snort and generally act like schoolboys – and girls – over any mention of things sexual.

We howl over obscenities in art, and yet drool over the juiciest gossip available on any politician. We don't want our teen-agers to have condoms, yet use sex to sell every imaginable teen-age dream. We fight any attempt to let real sex education in our schools, avoid the topic in our homes, and arrest a woman because no one understood how her body was supposed to work.

Anita In Wonderland And Doubting Thomas

By Meg Angus-Smith The News-Times Danbury Oct. 15, 1991

I'm not interested in any canonizing the woman, nor in vilifying the man involved in the bitter agony taking place in Washington.

Though I must confess my heart swelled as I saw Anita Hill alone before an array of white men in suits, taking on the beating heart of privilege, and forcing the pontificating games players, for a brief moment, to touch the real, messy world of life as it is lived, not as it is imagined in the halls of the Capitol.

I wonder if there is any good to be wrung out of this public torture? Can we, despite the best efforts of our elected representatives, find a truth in all this?

Perhaps.

Never after this, can the accusation of sexual harassment be dismissed out of hand by anyone, least of all by investigators into the background of a potential Supreme Court Justice.

There lies the crime. That weeks ago, the people in charge of these investigations, mostly men, thought it didn't matter. That it wasn't serious.

Which compounded the error of 10 years ago, when Anita Hill thought it mattered but couldn't bring herself to address it in any way that would leave a footprint for us to see her outrage.

And in 10 years have we learned anything? Bringing these accusations, she faced a hostile world that doubted her credibility and even her sanity.

With your hand on your heart, can you say that the world would have been MORE receptive to her charges 10 years ago?

As her voice held strong against a rising tide of her own emotions, she acknowledged the weakness of her position.

She tried to educate these men in the weary vagaries of gender relations from the point of view of the weaker sex. Yes, weaker. The Alice in Wonderland quality of the hearing was never more obvious, as the glare of media attention and constituent interest forced these guys to a teach-in on an issue that they may never have taken seriously before in their lives.

I cannot presume that every woman has a harassment story to tell. I will say, when the subject comes up, everyone I know has at least one. Few have had a recourse to law. Fewer still want to. Though many are grateful that the law treats the issue seriously and recognizes that this matter cannot always be resolved between two people.

And it's still not too late for all you guys who are making little jokes today about how careful you'll have to be about relations with women. Yes, you will have to be careful. Why does that surprise you?

How could anyone think of themselves as grown-up and not realize that there is no relationship without its thorns.

Even in the apparently superficial world of professional interaction.

Neither women, nor blacks, are monoliths. There is no type to run true to. Clarence Thomas is one of many blacks who are teaching us that they don't march to a lock step of opinion.

Anita Hill could help us learn that not all women are fire-eating feminists, ready to litigate at the drop of a hat, nor are they meekly grateful for any sort of attention that comes from a male.

Pry the handlers off this case, kick out the public relations people, defrock the self-righteous of the right and left, and what we're left with is two people who contradict as many stereotypes as they create.

Two real people, as capable as any of the rest of us of misunderstanding the rhythm of our delicate gender minuet. A dance defined mostly by missteps.

Many long-standing worthwhile relationships have started only on the incessant urging of one side or another. There is room for coaxing, even for being a nuisance.

All sorts of professional conversations verge on the blue, and often plummet into the vulgar. Wrenched from its context, the remarks repeated by Hill sound horrible. But I've heard worse, and not just in a bar.

Most times, most people manage the give-and-take of vulgarity and incipient romance with good grace. Sometimes, an explosive situation is rendered harmless by a ribald comment.

I hope that will never change.

The key is the relationship. And only the two people involved can begin to understand its chemistry.

What must change is the urge that the powerless feel not to make waves. If the give-and-take is taking too much and giving nothing, they must be empowered to speak out, even if some people think they are too sensitive, or silly, or self-important.

They, and they might be us, must be given the freedom to be wrong, too. Without castigation or recrimination. Just because someone says there has been harassment doesn't mean there has been, nor does it smack of a plot or hysteria.

What it does mean is that there is a situation where one person, usually a woman, has had to endure treatment that she found distasteful from someone with the power to make her life miserable.

And that exists in situations that you and I may be able to laugh off, or not even notice. We are not experts in this field. Relationships are defined solely by the individuals involved.

The whole Senate business of white hats and black hats, good old boys and naughty girls, demands there be two sides to a story: the right side and the wrong side.

Baloney.

I can't, and won't, see a hero or a villain. I see victims, men and women, of a way of looking at the world that limits us all.

The truth of sexual harassment that may or may not have occurred 10 years ago may never be found. The harassment that happens right here in

Danbury is right before your eyes, if you'll let them be opened.

It's not something as simple as a "behave yourselves, guys.'

Men and women both have to exercise responsibility for the way they wish to be treated. And give each other room to learn.

FAITH MIDDLETON

Faith Middleton, then Faith Vincent, wrote these columns as a young 20-something "Family Editor" for the Journal Inquirer of Manchester.

She is an institution in New England broadcasting and is an inductee of the Connecticut Women's Hall of Fame. She has twice received the George Foster Peabody Award, the industry's highest honor. Her broadcast career spans three decades as host of The Faith Middleton Show *on Connecticut Public Radio WNPR where she has conducted more than 12,000 interviews exploring "the richness of life." When Middleton was fourteen, both of her parents died, only one month apart. She moved in with her twenty-seven-year-old sister and her family in Manchester. While she wanted to attend college, there was no money for tuition. But through scholarships--in 1971, Middleton graduated from Eastern Connecticut State University with degrees in English and Sociology and was editor of the school paper. She has worked at the Willimantic Chronicle, the Journal Inquirer, The Providence Journal and was editor-in-chief of Connecticut Magazine. She was selected as NPR's first Senior Journalist in Residence. She is now primarily doing her "food schmooze" program on WNPR. In addition to her Peabody awards, she is the recipient of the prestigious Ohio State University Award, the Mark Twain Award for distinguished journalism, and the Connecticut Bar Association Award. She has been named "Best Talk Show Host" by the editors and readers of* Connecticut Magazine *more than a dozen times.*

Isn't It Obsolete?

By Faith Vincent The Journal Inquirer Manchester May 17, 1973

The reigning Miss America really hit on something last week when she said publicly swimsuit competition is an unnecessary part of today's pageant competition.

It is not only unnecessary, dear heart, it is a throwback to the days when women were judged on nothing more than beauty and or the states they represented. I will not begin to debate now whether this still exists today.

A pageant veteran myself after appearing in several, judging a few, and covering the Miss America extravaganza in Atlantic City, I can and will testify that a good deal of what goes in the pageant circuit is unnecessary.

Pageant officials have lately defended the swimsuit side by arguing that "the girls" demonstrate how they would behave "under pressure."

It is difficult and a true test, they say, for her to walk that runway in front of all those people. That evidently, is 20th Century pressure.

What these officials refuse to admit is that nearly every moment of the competition is filled with unbearable pressure, including the sleepless nights worrying about the next day's hurdle. Appearing at a judges breakfast or teas is far more nerve-racking and a better indicator of "momentary character" than swimsuit strutting ever could be.

I should state here that I am an ardent pageant supporter when permitted to say so. But I will criticize, as is my privilege in this column from time to time, because pageants have the tremendous potential to mean something to women.

When the officials begin thinking about doing away with all the nonsense – the beef on the hook business, the petty little questions, the evening gown splash – and begin really judging on intelligence, character and accomplishment, they will have been a part of something that matters, not something that sells.

The pageants are still "beauty contests" though pageant officials break out in hives when you mention the phrase. They insist we refer to them as "scholarship pageants" because they pay for college educations and the like.

The officials, though, would do well to spend a little more of their time viewing such programs as "Woman Of The Year" which appeared Monday night, or talking to the Shirley Chisholm's the Margaret Mead's, the Eleanor Roosevelt's, who would not be caught anywhere near Bert Parks.

How Very, Very Odd Mr. Barenburg

By Faith Vincent Journal Inquirer Manchester July 13, 1973

Some curious things are happening at Paramount Pictures these days.

Paramount, the studio now filming F. Scott Fitzgerald's, "The Great Gatsby," is also the studio that has been telling newspaper reporters they are banned from the set during any shooting in Newport, R.I where Paramount film crews have been on location.

Oddly enough, though, a full page spread on the Newport action appeared today in Women's Wear Daily, the fashion world's trade paper that has, coincidentally, been pushing pretty heavy on the "Gatsby Look" in fall fashions.

I happened to be one of the reporters – in fact, the first – to call Paramount a month ago to make arrangements to spend a day on the Newport set. Their press agent, Bruce Barenburg, assured me he would make the necessary arrangements and phone me with all the details.

Weeks later, and still without a return call, I phoned the studio to see what was going on.

It seems Barenburg hadn't gotten around to telling me that the press had been banned from the Newport set – for reasons, at this point, unexplained. The agent said only "magazines" promising not to release their stories and photos until March, 1974, were being given clearance.

I told Barenburg that was quite odd because I had just read Women's Wear Daily's story on the filming.

He said Women's Wear Daily was getting "special treatment" and I probably wouldn't consider it odd if I knew the "real story."

I phoned a Paramount executive later in the day who said it was all very simple, really, that with the set being so "complex," they could not accommodate all the papers asking for interviews. "We tried to be as fair as possible."

When pressed, the executive admitted Women's Wear Daily was, in fact, the only paper allowed on the set. After all, he said, Women's Wear Daily was just a small trade paper with very little circulation outside New York.

What the executive did not mention was WWD's heavy push on the Great Gatsby look in fashion, which, to my personal way of thinking, really began making headlines in this "small paper" not long after Paramount announced it would do the film.

Not to mention that full-page advertisement on the page preceding today's Gatsby story in Women's Wear Daily which just happens to mention that "look right out of F. Scott Fitzgerald."

I wouldn't be at all surprised if the Great Gatsby look didn't hit its peak in popularity in the fashion world just about the time the movie comes out in March.

Will wonders never cease?

The Sugar Syndrome

By Faith Vincent Journal Inquirer Manchester May 31, 1973

Nothing is more irritating to those blessed with any good sense about nutrition than America's constant preoccupation with sugar.

Perhaps some of the most discerning news on the subject came recently from an interview I witnessed featuring a University of Connecticut dentist who studies tooth decay in very young children.

He said he has examined many infants and found their teeth to be riddled with cavities – even before they have pushed up through the gums. How is it possible? More and more parents, it seems, are in the habit of dumping a teaspoon or two of sugar into baby's formula or orange juice bottle to make it more palatable.

The doctor pointed out that sugar so affects a human's system that a child's teeth can be weakened during pregnancy as a result of the amount of sugar consumed by the mother.

What we seem to forget is that there was a time when sweets (sugar) were not used to the extent they are today.

People seemed satisfied to absorb natural sugars from the fresh foods they ate and made. Their taste buds and minds were not conditioned to believe anything loaded with sugar gives extra energy.

Thanks to people like Dr. Carlton Fredericks, who got his start years ago in Connecticut, there are still some of us around who never did fall into the sugar and white bread syndrome.

One of these people is Adele Davis, a popular and sometimes controversial nutritionist who frequently delivers a scorching diatribe on America's unwitting preoccupation with sugar.

Ms. Davis seems to hit upon something when she says the tremendous increase in ill health has paralleled our consumption of sweets.

She also gives us food for thought as to why this may have come about.

The multi-billion dollar refined food industry has gained such power, she claims in her book, "Let's Get Well," that it keeps people in ignorance and literally controls the health of our nation. She states further that this industry controls a vast amount of nutritional research and it either ignores or fails to report nutritional information that would hurt profits.

Her most scorching slam against the sugar industry comes in the remark that the industry's relentless advertising campaigns reach like the life-crushing tentacles of an octopus into every home in America.

I live in one of those homes in America where it takes a lot of reading and constant reminders to overcome the desire for sweets loaded with chemicals and empty calories.

In fact, I keep many of the books I read on the subject of nutrition in full view – they are a reminder that we can stop poisoning our systems before the damage is irreversible.

Kathy O'Connell was bashful about photos. She did not use one with her columns. She was not, however, bashful about what she wrote.

KATHY O'CONNELL

Kathy O'Connell, in a short life, was for 20 years an arts writer and editor at the Middletown Press, arts and feature writer for the Hartford Advocate, and a copy editor and columnist at the Record-Journal in Meriden. She was 54 when she died in 2007 after a short illness. Born in Philadelphia, Kathy was a member of St. Joseph's University's first female graduating class in 1974.

How Do You Solve A Problem Like Scalia?

By Kathy O'Connell Record-Journal Meriden April 13, 2004

Somewhere about the 30th lap of a set of 54 in the pool at the YMCA one day last week, after learning that federal marshals in Hattiesburg, Miss., had ordered two newspaper reporters to erase tapes of a talk being given by a justice of the U.S. Supreme Court at a high school there, the song entered my head.

I offered apologies to Leonard Bernstein, Stephen Sondheim and Arthur Laurents. But the song stayed, to the tune of "Maria" from "West Side Story": Scalia! What is it with Justice Scalia? Seems every little thing To which he tries to cling Is wrong! Scalia! Say it loud and the liberals are praying! Say it soft, it's like jackasses braying Scalia! Scaleeeeeeeah, Scalia! What is it with Justice Scalia? The flap in Mississippi was apparently touched off by a rule Antonin - Nino to his fishing buddies - Scalia had set down that he does not do television.

That's fine by me. Television, like booze, pills, cheese blintzes, black raspberry sherbet and Thin Mint Girl Scout cookies, is really a drug in disguise.

But when federal marshals order newspaper reporters to erase tapes (haven't those young whippersnappers ever heard of notebooks and pencils?), well, it gets my Irish up. Way, way up.

Every working day, I hear reporters, mostly young but smart and tenacious, tell stories of the public officials who carp, whine, moan and sometimes yell at them because unflattering things have made their way into the paper.

They're sometimes told, these hardworking men and women of the allegedly free press, by municipal officials that they have no right to quote them without their approval. They're Republicans and Democrats, liberals and conservatives.

Many of them, alas, are educationists who think that how they decide to spend taxpayers' money on the latest fads in training brains and raising self-esteem is nobody's bidness, as the fabulous Molly Ivins likes to say.

But others among them are members of city and town councils, elected officials who, by law, are supposed to be accountable to those who pay their (usually modest, but nonetheless) salaries.

Maybe because of television - the commercial venues of which are regulated by the government - it's gotten into the heads of entirely too many public servants that they can call the shots in the print press.

Nope. Sorry. It doesn't work that way.

In my nearly 30 years in this profession, it seems as though we go through a Constitutional flu season every 20 years or so.

There was Watergate and the Pentagon Papers. Then came Iran-Contra. The government wished the press would mind its manners. Now we've got the Sept. 11 investigation. The White House wishes it would all just go away.

Trouble is, when you mind your manners in this bidness, you very often keep people in the dark, when it is our duty to help bring them into the light.

It's times such as these those of us in this increasingly difficult business need to shine the First Amendment in the squinty little eyes of self-inflated public officials, no matter how high up in the hierarchy they happen to be.

It doesn't matter that a sitting justice of the Supreme Court thinks he's above the law. A desire to suppress the press doesn't make it law. It just makes it stupid.

Darn, now I've got another song running through my head, this one by Richard Rodgers and Oscar Hammerstein II, from that otherwise treacly musical about the von Trapp family: How do you solve a problem like Scalia? How do you tell him that the press is free? It could be that Poppy Bush Doesn't want to get off his tush To tell sonny boy Nino deserves a push To get the point How do you solve a problem like Scalia? How do you hold an oiled eel in your hand?

What Are You Afraid Of? Stand Up To Censorship!

By Kathy O'Connell Record-Journal Meriden Sept. 29, 2005

As entirely too many citizens don't know but should, this is Banned Books Week. Ban books, here in the allegedly freedom-loving US of A? You've got crackpots on both sides of the aisle: those on the right want to protect kids from references to homosexuality or just sex. Those on the left want to make sure we all feel guilty that we oppressed everyone who wasn't like us.

The very idea that there needs to be a week honoring certain books is scary, but necessary. It's real, a threat to freedom so deep and serious it leaves passionate readers and other information junkies shivering in our shoes. Not out of fear, mind you, but anger. When I got my first library card in 1958, I had been given a key to a golden kingdom. The woman at the desk asked if she could help. I like horse stories, I said. Into my hands fell "Black Beauty" and other books. I was delirious with delight. Never mind that at home there were dozens of equally enthralling tales: Nancy Drew, the girl detective; Cherry Ames, the brave nurse; Vicki Barr, the airline stewardess; the Hardy boys; an obscure but engrossing series on the lives of the saints published by what was then Farrar, Straus and Cudahy. Nothing was kept from me for not being age-appropriate. My parents, especially my mom, insisted that reading, no matter what it was, was a great and noble pursuit.

So what's up with these amateur thought police who want to protect us, especially if we're kids (and I still am one at heart), from ourselves? The idea that certain adults want to restrict any child's reading because it might lead to temptation (oh, the horror!) or is politically incorrect is, well, whacked. While thinking that books can change children's lives is quite correct, that there are "dangerous" titles out there is simply insane. A while back there was a woman in Wallingford who was horrified that her child was "required" to read a Harry Potter book. This mother was worried reading such stuff of magic would turn her beloved into a Satanist. Or something. Oh, please.

Reading Jack Kerouac's "The Dharma Bums" at 15 didn't turn me into one, nor did reading Eldridge Cleaver's "Soul on Ice" a year later make me a gun-toting revolutionary. Unrestricted reading instead turned me into a glutton of sorts. I looked forward to rainy, cold and dismal days when I could haul a pot of tea up to my room and read, and read, and read. My first real job, with a paycheck, was in my town's smallish library - like so many, a former bank; the strong floors held up to the weight of the books - sorting and shelving. I'd look at each book and page through it before I put it in its place. More often than not, they were slim volumes on self-improvement or how to make more money, or lose weight. In each cart, however, there were gems. I discovered the brilliant silliness of S.J. Perelman. I came across more titles by my two hands-down favorite writers at the time, Louisa May Alcott and Mark Twain, than I knew what to do with.

Gloryosky, Letita, don't keep books from your children because you're afraid of what they might bring about. Keep in mind that censorship, in any form, is not really about protection. It's about cold, blind fear.

Meriden Needs A Starbucks Like A Duck Needs Tap Shoes

By Kathy O'Connell Record-Journal Meriden Jan. 27, 2004

"Why don't you get Mary, Bill and the girls Starbucks gift certificates for Christmas?" the eldest of my three older sisters suggested as we were discussing what to get for whom. "They love Starbucks." I ended up getting them instead a really cool family game from a really neat store, O'Doodles, on Germantown Avenue in the Chestnut Hill section of Philadelphia. Because Chestnut Hill is decidedly upscale, just a few doors down from O'Doodles is a Starbucks. There are a few others sprinkled around the area, to the point where you can't swing a frazzled cat without bonking a barista on the head.

A barista, for those who must know, is the pretentious name Starbucks gives the people who make the coffee, which comes in equally pretentious sizes: tall, grande, Venti (they trademarked that one), solo and doppio. They also boast at least a dozen different kinds of coffee, which I can understand, but only up to a point. I draw the line at Special Reserve Estate 2003 - Sumatra Lintong Lake Tawar. I've ground up my share of Sumatra beans. Kenya AA and Jamaican Gold, too. When you brew it, it tastes like, well, coffee.

It's rumored that some folks are poking about downtown Meriden with an eye on opening a Starbucks, but parking, apparently, is a problem.

That, however, is the least of it. What with both the Lord & Taylor and the Eddie Bauer stores at Westfield Shoppingtown Meriden set to close, the whole idea of dropping an entity as relentlessly upscale as Starbucks in the middle of a decidedly struggling city makes about as much sense as putting foie gras on a diner menu. Not that it can't be done, mind you. It's just not the nature of the beast.

Before anyone thinks I don't believe Meriden is worthy of having a Starbucks, consider its citizens. They're mostly working people who aren't at that rarified end of the economic scale where they can afford to view coffee as a cult object.

It's why you don't see a lot of blue-collar vegans. These people have much more important things to do than cultivate a lifestyle. One of them is simple survival.

Then again, it seems that divide, between those just trying to make it and those self-absorbed enough to settle for nothing less than a tall skinny half-caf organic shade-grown Mexican bean, keeps getting wider. As someone who spent a year working with the very poorest of the poor in scenic places such as Paterson, NJ and Syracuse, N.Y., the growing pervasiveness of what I call L'Oreal Syndrome - "because I'm worth it!" - is deeply disturbing to me.

Take, for example, the burgeoning market in gourmet goodies for pets. You can now also buy greeting cards for one dog to give another, or a human, even though it's well known that dogs can't read. While the relationships people have with their animals are very real and worthy of respect - anyone who's ever had to euthanize a pet knows the loss is painful - they, too, have their limits. Over Christmas, one store was advertising designer polo shirts for pampered pooches that cost three or four times as much as polo shirts for people.

Really, now.

I'm not saying Meriden shouldn't have a nice place to have a cup of coffee; it already does, for me in the form of the Friends of the Library Bookstore, where I meet a fellow writer for some java and jawing about twice a month.

Fischer's is nice too, and if you haven't checked out La Aguadena Bakery, you don't know what you're missing.

These are all local places, not chains, which is a very good thing. They're unique, and run by people who understand their community well enough to know anyone willing to pay exorbitant prices for coffee just because it has a fancy name and tastes a little different than the ordinary kind is gullible as all getout.

That kind of upscale, I don't think we need.

KYRIE O'CONNOR

Kyrie O'Connor worked for 14 years at The Hartford Courant rising to assistant managing editor for features. O'Connor led the creation and redesign of many of the newspaper's feature sections. She left in 2003 for the Houston Chronicle where she became deputy managing editor/features. At the Chronicle, she wrote a daily memo to her staff about trends in popular culture and discoveries she made about life in Houston, eventually turning the memo into "MeMo", one of the Chronicle's first blogs. She later became editor of the San Antonio Express-News and is now retired. She has been a frequent panelist on the National Public Radio show "Wait, Wait ... Don't... Tell Me." Born in Rochester, NY she graduated cum laude from Wesleyan University in 1976.

Hillary Clinton Shouldn't Hide Behind The President

By Kyrie O'Connor The Hartford Courant Jan. 12, 1996

By rights, I should be Hillary Rodham Clinton's biggest fan. She seemed right from the first to have so much going for her that I respected.

She was blazingly smart, with an education from the finest schools. She got a law degree, a husband, a child. She hung onto her own name until it became -- when her husband lost the governorship after his first term -- politically untenable. She worked really hard at her job. She was an articulate speaker, a compelling public presence.

I respected all those things. When she was deemed to be insufficiently domestic, I cheered. Great! Burn the aprons! In fact, when she capitulated,

I reviled every faux-domestic photo op (opening a White House oven and such) and every cookie recipe.

But something still bothered me about Hillary Clinton, and considering that even the likes of Bob Dole and Phil Gramm are married to accomplished professionals, it may be the kind of problem that's likely to come up more often in the future rather than less.

And when Bill Clinton offered Tuesday -- or, rather, when his crafty media-relations team offered -- to pop New York Times columnist William Safire in the snoot for calling Hillary Clinton a "congenital liar," I was reminded of how much this whole thing bugs me.

Isn't that the problem with Hillary Rodham Clinton?

She hides behind a man.

This dynamic, brilliant, driven woman agreed at some crucial point in her life (perhaps by default) that he -- not she, not both -- would be the politician, the office-seeker, the office-holder.

Fine! A man has a right to a career! But having decided that, did Clinton have the privilege of trying to be more than the wife of the one who ran?

That's the problem.

She seems to want a share in the power that comes with public office, the ability to shape public policy -- such as health care -- and the clout to fire people -- such as the White House travel office staff.

Clearly, being a successful woman in a decorative role, a woman who can't practice her chosen job and can't really go for another in the private sector, must be misery.

But that's the only role Hillary Clinton has earned, after all. If it drives her crazy, I don't know what to do about that. This isn't a situation with an easy solution.

All I know is I wish she'd tried harder than this to find one, and when I read about lost papers turning up hither and yon, and hear Republican senators alluding to much worse, I wonder if any of this derives from the initial self- thwarting she chose.

No one voted for her. No Senate confirmed her.

In the closest modern parallel, both in relation and talent, John F. Kennedy made the very controversial appointment of his brother Robert

F. Kennedy as U.S. attorney general. And noises were made about some similar option for Hillary Clinton.

Maybe it was wrong, or maybe she -- a woman, a wife -- couldn't have been confirmed to any appointed federal post. But maybe she could have tried.

And that's the nut.

Did she try for anything except what she seems to have thought came to her with the marriage certificate and the law degree?

You can't hang onto a man and ride him right up to the highest office in the land and expect equality of respect and power.

For that matter, you don't do it if the guy has a bagel-shop franchise.

I thought this was a lesson privileged women learned a while ago, and it's one women without privilege have known all along.

If you want any kind of power, you don't look to a man to get it for you. As frustrating as it is, you own yourself or you don't own anything. You want half the bagel shop, buy in. You want to run the country, run for office. It's hard. It's not fun, and it's not fair.

Hillary Clinton must know that.

But the funny thing is, if she'd gone for office herself, she'd be just the kind of person I'd like to have the chance to vote for.

The Chicago Gummi Bears And The Green Bay Omphalos It's Time For You Gridiron Guys To Get A Makeover And A Little Imagination

By Kyrie O'Connor The Hartford Courant Jan. 25, 1998

After today, the year is tundra. It stretches out, treeless under a low gray dome of clouds until late March, then a false, fleeting flurry of basketball excitement, then on and on. I am Fred Flintstone driving on the tundra. Over and over, I pass by the same meaningless puck, hoop, home plate, puck, hoop.

You see, I love professional football. The year begins when the preseason begins, with all its illusion and gentleness, and I love the march of the 18 weeks -- its Sundays and Mondays and by-weeks -- the playoffs, even the Barnum tawdriness of the Superbowl, when the year ends, leaving half a year for existing.

But as much as I love the game, there is one thing I do not love: These guys -- hulking, gross, mystical, clothed -- don't know how to dress. The NFL suffers from two vices, failure of imagination (Guys love archetypes, hence the Village People. Cowboys, Vikings, Giants. If women played football, the Superbowl would feature the French Maids vs. the Nurses) and the guy-like belief that if you put any two colors together on a uniform, such as orange and navy, they will look good. So herewith some ideas for addressing both failings. And if you think I'm wrong, consider the Buccaneers. They dressed like glasses of Tang for years and lost miserably, and then they got real uniforms, and they made the playoffs. See?

MOST DEEPLY NEEDY: The Tennessee Oilers. The what, the who? Change the whole thing. Capitalize on your growth industry. The Tennessee Elvises. Home uniform is the Vegas Elvis, shiny white satin, number spelled out in rhinestones, vampire high collar, muttonchops on helmet. Away uniform is Young Elvis matte black leather look, smoldering, pompadour and sideburns on helmet. The sneer is, fortunately, part of the game face.

The St. Louis Rams. Is that what the jewel of the Mississippi is known for, the quality of its sheep? Chances are the NFL target audience has a different association having to do with large horses with inexplicably hairy feet. Call the team the St. Louis Brews. Home uniform is shiny silver and white (subtle drop-shaped condensation marks would be nice) with blue-and-red detailing, working pop-top on silver helmet. Away is the long-neck look shiny brown top to bottom, with a trompe l'oeil bottle cap on the top of the helmet. Feeling kicky? Embroider a church key on the sleeve.

The Arizona Cardinals. Oh, yeah, right. Arizona, the Bird and Prelate State. Continuing to name teams after what the state is most famous for, I suggest the Arizona Slightly Passé Decorating Trends. Dusty pink shirt, dusty turquoise pants (reverse for away). Dopey little kekolo guy on sleeve. Helmet looks like a throw pillow. When the Southwest Look goes really far south, make 'em all wear matelass slipcovers.

ALSO IN NEED: The Baltimore Ravens. The team with the most inspired name has the worst uniforms. Dahlink, we have a menacing bird here, a dark and demented poet, the Gothic possibilities endless. Black, glossy, with iridescent feathers. On the headgear, the holographic illusion of the straight and scissor-like beak. Up the outside of the leg, the word "nevermore."

The Pittsburgh Steelers. Why does one of the most honorable teams in football dress like bumblebees? Suit up like men of steel, burnished and stainless, with visible riveting. No stripes, no logo, no numbers. Let the other guys figure it out. You're the Steelers.

The Chicago Bears. Look, men, you weigh, collectively, more than the Sears Tower and you play in a climate that could freeze a fireball. Once a year, say the week after you've been eliminated, show a little good humor about your situation. Go out on the field like a variety pack, some in citrus yellow, some in clear green, some in jolly orange, some in Life Saver red. Once a year, would it kill you to be the Gummi Bears? If anyone snickers, pound 'em.

And, next to last, the Connecticut... The Connecticut what? Say we were to have our Native American benefactors buy us we'll use this example for poetic justice the Panthers. What is the Nutmeg State noted for? Well, the Marthas doesn't sound like a winner, but how about the Connecticut Preps? The look: yellow polo-collar jersey, printed illusion of pink crewneck tied nonchalantly at neck. Pants, green with multiple embroidered turtles. No helmet it would muss the carefully mussed hair.

If you think this is a wussy concept, consider the last time you picked up a driver or a racquet against one of these guys, with his 15 extra pounds and his slight stammer. Then remember the flawless swing, the dead-on serve. Those preppy guys will kill you every time. And that, sir, is what we want.

Finally, the Green Bay Packers. The G on the helmet is an omphalos, a snake eating its own tail, alpha merged with omega.

Or maybe it stands for Green, which is even more subtly wonderful, when you think about it. We will not tinker with Green Bay, which is glyptic, ineffable, serious yet insouciant, lambent, plangent, a quiescently frozen confection.

Green Bay is perfect. Behind the G, the od is invisible.

TOP 10

By Kyrie O'Connor The Hartford Courant Sept. 19, 1999

Fall Fashion Preview

To go in search of 10 wonderful, can't-miss fashion items for fall, I took Size 2 with me. (Calling her Size 2 is a bit of an exaggeration. She's the sort of person who pulls something off the rack and says "Ooooh! This comes in a 0!") Size 2 is also 19 and does most of her shopping in New York. If you averaged us together, we'd be 31 and a size 4, and we'd shop in Westport.

One of us would consider this an upgrade. Nevertheless, we found much to delight in and much to agree on. It's a lovely season to be 31.

1. If you want to look new instantly, stash the backpack. Banana Republic has a lovely sleek black leather one-shoulder crossover bag in black leather for $130, and you can find nylon versions, as well as crossovers that look positively sport-utility, almost anywhere.
2. The shoes that will make you happiest are likely to be in some sort of gray fabric. You can get everything from smooshy gray fleece slip-ons ($49.95) to smashing mary janes ($72) at Nordstrom. But since you must have black shoes, Ann Taylor has the chicest, city- friendly, little black leather flats ($78) with the squarest square toe and a little platform.
3. Your sweater choices must be simple and sophisticated, but that's the easy part. Choosing is hard. Again this fall, you can't go wrong with three-quarter sleeves or a bateau neck. In fact, the neckline is the focus of interest. If it never occurred to you that the clavicle is an erogenous zone, it will now. J. Crew has a silk fully fashioned bateau-neck in baby blue, khaki, black or cranberry ($68).
4. But the big surprise is that Abercrombie & Fitch has evolved from the lacrosse look to something you can consider even if you've already taken the chemistry final. There's a charmingly fuzzy merino wool/acrylic/nylon sweater to be worn over a cami or tank top in baby blue, soft olive or gray ($49.50). No huge number on the back.
5. If you have an office job, you will be looking for outfits that have the stature of the classic man-style suit without making you feel like

a girl Gregory Peck. Ann Taylor has a highly plausible gray heather rayon-polyester tunic top (again with the bateau neck!) and long skirt for $68 and $78. It will send you swooping into the boardroom with such confidence you might forget to prepare your presentation, in which case, we regret to report, no outfit can save you.

6. Size 2 reminds me that some people have a night life. Express has a heaven-on-earth floofy ball-gown skirt in waltz length ($68) or floor length ($98) in, among other choices, a sweet baby pink. You can go with an ice-beaded shell ($49) or, better, a tiny cardigan over a strapless top. Instant Gwyneth.
7. If you persist in having interesting evenings, Size 2, all I can do is shrug. It's all you can do, too. Shrugs and other sleeve-configurations are everywhere. Perfect for clubbing: Shrug the shrug indoors, don it for warmth as you exit. Esprit has a cotton/poly shrug-and-tube set in pink or black for $49.
8. We all have to accessorize, and accessories forgive you on fat days. Pendants look new this year, and so does anything in turquoise. Ten Thousand Villages in West Hartford has a nice round turquoise pendant suitable for all ages for a mere $22.95.
9. If you find yourself with a pressing need to unbreak your heart, nothing works better than lots of black leather. Esprit's got a classic smooth zip-up hip-length jacket that may succeed in persuading you that you were too good for him anyway. At $198, it's cheaper than three therapy sessions, and it won't make you revisit your childhood.
10. But for comfort and elegance, the place to splurge this season is on a wrap: massive, squishy but not overwhelming. Hayseed in Litchfield offers a nest-lining-soft wrap in richest red cashmere, $550.

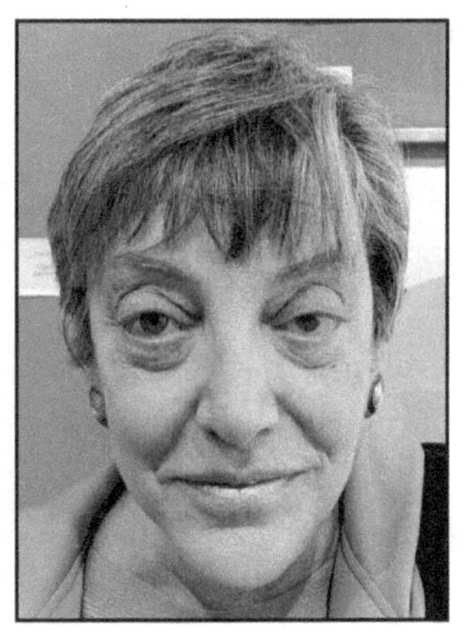

MAXINE OLDERMAN

Maxine Olderman was born in New Haven in 1952. She graduated from Amity High in Woodbridge and from Connecticut College in New London where she was elected to Phi Beta Kappa with a double major in art history and English. She has worked as a copywriter at a radio station and a film reviewer at the Yale broadcast station. She free-lanced for a variety of publications in the New Haven and Westport areas including the magazine New Haven, New Haven County Woman, Business Digest, Westport Today and as a fulltime art reviewer for the New Haven Register. She also worked as a design associate at the DaSilva Gallery in Westville. Now semi-retired, Olderman continues to work as a substitute teacher.

Six Sculptors In Search Of Themselves

By Maxine Olderman New Haven Register Nov. 6, 1988

Like Pirandello's classic play, "Six Characters in Search of an Author," the exhibition "6 Sculptors/6 Spaces" at the John Slade Ely House is a search for self-expression, not only through the sculptures, but through each artist's use of the space allotted the works.

Presented in the framework of the charming Ely House, each artist was given carte blanche on the space. Walking from room to room is like seeing six separate one-person shows.

For all the sculptors, the use of the inner space of the gallery is as sculpturally significant and exciting as the pieces themselves.

Gallery curator Ray Smith believes artistic freedom is the key to providing the proper psychic soil for nurturing artists, especially those whose works are not often displayed publicly.

"I envision the Ely House as a center for artists ... particularly developing emerging artists, and I prefer to show those people who are not instantly recognizable locally," Smith said.

"I want to give them a place to stretch and develop as much as they can. I encouraged each sculptor to create a special environment for his pieces and the installations are all very personal."

Smith's philosophy has proved successful in the show - it is the most engaging exhibit in the area for some time. It is a must-see, even for those who may not consider themselves fans of modern sculpture.

It is rich in scope, texture and mood, and with the exclusion of one sculptor - Val Kropiwnicki, whose work is rife with jagged steel edges and black ghostlike images - each artist has a sense of humor, subtle or overt, that is sometimes intellectual and frequently hilarious.

The work of Chris Shields, in particular, encompasses a world that is at first glance sterile and self-important but which proves, upon closer examination, to be quite inventive in its execution.

Irreverent look: In the spirit of "many a truth is made in jest," his installation, "Origin of the Specious," is an irreverent look at Darwinian concepts of evolution and the concept of man as an intelligent being who delights in flaunting this intelligence.

Shields' installation is a showroom of paleontological humor. An artist's statement accompanying the work states that as man evolved, he "could sit squarely atop the food chain and utilize his enlarged cranium in pursit of Truth, Beauty and the Appian Way."

Three human skulls, complete with serious-looking shards and fragments reeking of historical import, line one wall. Above each is a biography that describes the men, realistically named Tiaba, Chiang and Uknobe.

These plaster skulls seem freshly dug, until one studies the biographies; one proclaims that the gentleman's contribution to humanity was "humming" and another's last words were, "Are these mushrooms edible?"

The humor does not diminish the artistry at work. Indeed, in Shields' work there is the chance frequently to reflect that man, in all his pompous grandeur, may not have evolved quite as far as he would like to believe.

An abrupt shift of mood and time brings us to the work of sculptor and ceramicist Dolores Marchese.

Seemingly real: Displayed in a cozy room amid the artist's own pieces of Victoriana, including Oriental rugs and marble-topped tables, her sculptured clay people are at once colorful, playful and quite real.

They seem, in all their rosy-cheeked splendor, to be so legitimately invested with life that they may very well gather for tea and crumpets after the spectators have left.

Marchese has cleverly exploited a wonderful niche in the room, which is rich in architectural coziness and lead-paned windows, to highlight three women swinging in space under hanging plants. Bursting with fuchsia, bright blue and pink, these happy little ladies gaily swing in time to a rich inner melody that resonates through the room.

"The Seated Bride," clutching dried flowers in her hands and adorned with flowers in her hair is so endearingly portrayed that she will steal your heart and imagination. Perched on the edge of her chair, it's as if she has a real beating heart.

All of Marchese's works are magical and enchanted, including her brightly colored still lifes, which are hung in the room along with her "family" made of polychromed clay. It is a room one would like never to leave.

Sexual abandon: Matt Pozorski, a sculptor from New Haven, has created the exhibit's most massive and ambitious work, "The Four Horsewomen of the Apocalypse." Done in steel and wood, his four women ride atop nuclear missiles with great sexual abandon in a kind of macabre merry-go-round.

Skillfully executed with the use of nails, screws and steel projectiles to define or flesh out parts of the female anatomy, Pozorski's phenomenal piece is a visual oxymoron ... it is sexual yet anti-erotic, frightening yet funny, tense and free. His achievement as an artist is that the viewer is forced to confront these conflicting sensations simultaneously.

The rest of Pozorski's work focuses on his exploration of his two primary images, the Hero and the Goddess. It is through these archetypes that he has developed his artistic connections between life, sex and death.

His fanciful use of materials, including pieces of rubber tire, nuts and bolts, and thumb tacks for eyes in his delightful large-scale piece "Merrubbermaid" does not diminish the agelessness of this rather medieval image of woman done in oak and steel.

A Giacommetti-like, anorexic figure of wood and steel, bears the delightful title, "I Wuld Kill for Thighs Like That."

Pozorski's "Drowned Sailor," in the shadow of the looming female "Valkyrie" with spidery legs of steel, recalls the heavier import of his "Four Horsewomen." It underscores his statement of the often fine line between sex and violence.

Minimalist geometry: To enter the world of Mary Pace's installation is to clean one's visual palette and explore the efficent use of geometry. One room formally explores the use of black line and form on the gallery's white walls that "cuts" the space in a minimalist sculptural manner.

Her other room is colorful and full of funky projected shapes that create their own chiaroscuro of light and shadow. She has succeeded in her mission "to eliminate a lot and to establish a basic vocabulary." Many of her works draw on an elemental vocabulary of design and clarity.

Jutting, jagged: Entering the rooms of Val Kropiwnicki's installation brings on a disconcerting shift of mood. His jutting, jagged steel-edged sculptures beg to be described in staccato -- cold, tough, mean and raw.

Yet beneath the surface -- even in the eerie triptych "The Father, Son & Holy Ghost" -- there is the whisper of sadness trying to "steel" itself against the cruel realities of life.

Kropiwnicki's work, a reflection of the pain of a loved-one's death, is moving and disturbing because it forces the viewer out of his complacency. Indeed, many of his works, with their guillotine-like blades, could actually inflict injury, as if he is telegraphing the message that his art is like life itself.

A particularly successful piece, "Shattered Flagg (White Fence)" done on paper in charcoal, crayon and steel is like a miniature glimpse of the film "Ordinary People." An orderly suburban home, with symmetrical plantings and manicured lawn is shrouded in a black ghostly shadow.

It is, like all of his pieces, a poetic and sensitive work and even his device of covering the radiators in the room of his installation with dark green parachutes gives the usually charming Ely house the look of a M.A.S.H. unit. His ability to juxtapose ordinary images with dramatic impact is compelling.

Finally, the works of Bob Keating, a landscape designer and sculptor, resides appropriately enough in the Ely House's sculpture garden. They will remain there throughout the winter. Smith anticipates the contrast between the black of Keating's steel and stone constructions and the pure white of snow.

Keating's playful and masterful works, which blend with the environment, use the exterior landscape in much the same way as the other artists use the interior of the gallery.

He has exploited the richness of natural detail to highlight the line and movement of his works. All four of his pieces seem to have sprung naturally from the ground.

6 Sculptors/6 Spaces is the first in a series of four ambitious shows that Smith is bringing to The John Slade Ely House. For most of the sculptors it is their first major exhibition. It is a privilege to see the work of these exciting artists in various stages of development and exploration.

All six are from Connecticut; three are from the New Haven area. Smith would like to see the show become a tradition. If 6 Sculptors/6 Spaces is any indication of the quality and richness to come in subsequent shows, viewers are in for rare artistic treats.

En Route To Nicaragua, Show Finds Some Of City's Soul

By Maxine Olderman New Haven Register June 25, 1989

Artists - unlike, say, economists and politicians - are considered to be the most directly connected to a community's soul, to be more closely allied to the subtext of its feelings. Given that, several local artists were asked to interpret New Haven life as part of a cultural exchange with its Sister City of Leon, Nicaragua.

"New Haven Artists Interpret New Haven," on display on the fourth floor of City Hall, commemorates five years of mutual exchange between the cities. The artworks will travel to Nicaragua in the fall, the second such exhibit to be shown in Leon.

It is no small responsibility to capture the essence of a city through artistic means, and not all of these artists have shown a pretty picture.

Several works vibrate with political and socio-economic anger. Fethi Megilli has contributed a print of a somber young black man. The caption reads: "They treat you like a child on those minimum-wage jobs. And there is no way you can make it on that kind of salary. It is just a dead end."

Mark Aldrich's collage in ironic red, white and blue features a pair of legs beneath a staircase and the warning: "Run, Don't Walk."

Amy Unikewicz has produced the show's most chilling piece, best described as a post card from hell. Using a post card format, Unikewicz sends her greetings to Leon from Dixwell Avenue, "home to numerous drug busts."

She writes, "you should be glad you're not here. I'm scared to death to go outside." Perhaps sharing horror stories of poverty and crime enhances sisterhood. But this strident message doesn't work as successfully as others, which cry out for an arm-in-arm search for freedom.

Don Wunderlee's sculpture of papier-mache and wood is an expression of hope. A small figure caught in a spirited moment of movement is projected from a peace symbol with the wonderful inscription: "Give Peace a Dance."

Wunderlee wrote of the piece: "Many people in New Haven have had wonderful experiences in Nicaragua. This piece reflects that positive energy and good will."

The work that best reflects the sense of sisterhood is an intriguing effort of a group who began the work on the New Haven Green last summer during the city's 350th birthday celebration. Mark Aldrich, Lynn Johnson, Jo Aerne, Jeff Sokolowski and Steve Jones are among the collaborators on the four-panel panorama, a recreation of the New Haven Green and the Green in Leon. The depiction of East Rock bears their signatures, like graffiti on the rocks. With delightful disregard to true locations, it moves from Ingalls Rink (a whale) and the harbor, to mountains near Leon. Painted in the naive style of Grandma Moses, it's a fresh, lively piece that truly captures the spirit of cultural and social exchange.

Photographs are some of the most impressive offerings in this show. A lovely photograph by Wes Thomas shows a woman bathing her infant son outside, with the round-bellied child sitting Budda-like. A photograph by Joy Bush, "Summer Night" of three people, two sitting on a bench, with one standing behind them, across from the Shubert theater on College Street is great fun. Each person's expression reflects a special contentment, and even the manikins in the store window behind them seem to enjoy the soft summer air.

Kathi Milani's photo of three firefighters in action is full of strength, struggle and a universally human experience. Stephanie Fitzgerald's "Saturday Morning Dance Class" is simply delightful. Eight little girls, in tights and leotards, arms outstretched, search for the perfect plie. Robert Goulet poses theatrically beneath the Shubert's marquee bearing his name in Sara Waskuch's photograph. It gives New Haven an odd but humorous Las Vegas ambiance.

Susan Klein's silk screen is one of the most memorable works. Titled "In the Wake of Route 34," it depicts an abandoned tire store, a melancholy evocation of an area and a business that has outlived its usefulness. It is a beautifully drawn portrait of urban renewal in red, yellow and black.

Despite its strengths, "New Haven Artists Interpret New Haven" is a disappointing show in some ways. As one means of explaining who we are and what makes us unique in this city, the works seem to miss much that makes the city rich and colorful. When the show goes to the Cultural Center in Leon, some of the works will be given as gifts.

One wishes the show had been broader - more of the diversity of New Haven's architecture, Yale, ethnic neighborhoods and summer festivals. Certainly urban blight and crime should not be ignored; they are as much a part of the city as great pizza. But it feels as if some of the real heart of the town is missing.

TRACEY O'SHAUGHNESSY

Tracey O'Shaughnessy is an award-winning columnist, art critic and associate features editor for the Waterbury-Republican-American. A sought-after speaker and journalist, she writes about society, culture, religion and women. A two-time recipient of the national Society of Professional Journalists award for her columns, she also speaks widely to corporations, civic and religious groups. Her column has won praise from the American Society of Newspapers Editors, the New England Associated Press News Executives Association, the American Academy of Religion and the American Association of Sunday and Features Editors. Her art criticism has won her four first-place awards from the Society for Features Journalists. A native of Massachusetts, O'Shaughnessy is a graduate of Wesleyan and American universities and has taken additional classes at Georgetown University and Yale Divinity School. She has been at the Republican-American since 1994. According to WNPR's Faith Middleton, "Tracey isn't just one of the best contemporary writers writing in Connecticut or New England right now, she's one of the best contemporary writers writing anywhere right now. She's a wise and attentive observer who can translate and articulate the human condition in a way that resonates. . . Fuzzy things, ever universal, become sharper in her description of them."

"Tracey O'Shaughnessy is a New England treasure. Her writing is at once nuanced and vibrant." — New England Society of Newspaper Editors

REFLECT: Fewer Firms Give Paid Maternity Leave

By Tracey O'Shaughnessy Republican-American Waterbury July 29, 2012

How worried do you figure Marissa Mayer is about her maternity leave? She's 37 years old, holding the top spot at Yahoo and is set to become the first CEO of a Fortune 500 company to be pregnant. Her selection as CEO comes in the middle of a hoary debate about women "having it all," a discussion we never seem to resolve or tire of. Because they are the baby-bearers, women have become the standard bearers for the notion that they can balance work and family with the poise of the Flying Wallendas.

Earlier this year, a former State Department official, Anne-Marie Slaughter, set off a blistering cat fight by writing an article for Atlantic that said women need to stop fooling themselves. The idea that women could have it all was bunk, she wrote. Pretending that raising kids and working is a snap only makes it harder for women who can't quite swing it.

"The minute I found myself in a job that is typical for the vast majority of working women (and men), working long hours on someone else's schedule, I could no longer be both the parent and the professional I wanted to be," she wrote, "at least not with a child experiencing a rocky adolescence." Those who have managed to work at high-powered jobs while having children, she told The New York Times, "need to admit that we are the exception and not the rule. We need to stop congratulating ourselves and focus on the reality for most women."

And what is the reality for most women? Working women still earn about 75 cents to a working man's dollar, a gap that holds true across identical occupations, the Bureau of Labor Statistics reports. The biggest gender gap in the country is in the male-dominated financial activities industry, where women earn 70.5 cents for every dollar men make, the BLS reports. In other words, before they even have children, women lag behind their male counterparts, even as they outpace them in educational achievement.

It's also true many women still work in jobs that require them to be tethered to a desk, or a classroom, making the juggling act for them far more challenging than for women who are given the flexibility to work from home.

Mayer has said she plans to work at home after the birth of her child, a privilege high-powered women enjoy and low-wage women do not. The food services manager at Target doesn't get to work at home. Nor does the social studies teacher at the middle school. Mayer's income and her position will afford her a measure of control that most working women lack.

Mayer's total compensation from Yahoo will be more than $60 million. She won't be sweating the $30,000 she'll pay for a nanny. Meanwhile, Child Care Aware of America reports the cost of having two kids in child care exceeded the median annual rent payments in every state.

No wonder so many women don't go back to work after having children. They can't afford to.

But the biggest immediate difference between Mayer and the rest of the bassinet-and-briefcase crowd will be the state she lives in. California is one of the few states that guarantee paid maternity leave.

That's paid maternity leave.

Connecticut provides unpaid leave up to 16 weeks at large private companies, up to 24 weeks for state employees, and all can be required to use their accrued vacation time during their leaves of absence.

The United States likes to congratulate itself over the Family and Medical Leave Act, which guarantees workers up to 12 weeks of leave without imperiling their job or benefits. But with nearly two-thirds of Americans now living paycheck to paycheck, 12 weeks without dough is untenable.

The United States is the only major industrialized country not to guarantee paid maternity leave nationwide. It is one of only three globally not to offer paid maternity leave. The other two are Swaziland and Papua New Guinea.

Mongolia grants paid maternity leave.

So does Google, Yahoo's chief competitor, which offers 18 weeks of paid maternity leave, according to CNN Money. Lucrative companies that consider their female employees valuable — like, one suspects, Yahoo — offer paid leave. But most companies do not, a situation that has grown worse as the labor market tightens. While 27 percent of companies surveyed by the Families and Work Institute offered paid maternity leave in 1998, only 16 percent do now.

Will Marissa Mayer's position at Yahoo change that? Will her tenure shatter the breast-pump ceiling and make it possible for women to deliver the next generation and nurture them, too?

Let's hope so. We could use a victory in the Mommy Wars.

Seismic Shift In American Marriages

By Tracey O'Shaughnessy Republican-American Waterbury Jan. 31, 2010

My friend is a Sugar Mama. She's got a six-figure job, a mansion in a stately Boston suburb, a house on the Vineyard— and a husband to stay home with the kids.

This arrangement has given her pause over the years. There have been acute spasms of guilt when she was ready to ditch the whole stiletto-and-Blackberry thing for Silly Putty and Build-a-Bear. But her less-marketable husband could never pull in the Croesus purse that she does, and so the couple has decided to do what many others have done, have one parent stay in the cave and the other slay the dragons.

Except that in my friend's case, the woman is the dragon slayer.

And in the eight years that she has been pulling this off, a lot of women have joined her.

A new study finds that married women are making, as Katie Couric might say, a lot of jack.

The study, from the Pew Center for Research, found that more women are marrying men with less education and lower earnings. Men, increasingly, are marrying women who are better educated and make more money.

The Pew study followed news that the number of working mothers who are sole breadwinners in their families rose last year to an all-time high, while the number of stay-at-home dads inched upwards. The U.S. Census reported that in most of the homes with women as breadwinners, both parents had worked until the recession, which sliced with particular ferocity into male-dominated jobs like finance and construction. The Bureau of Labor Statistics reports that 78 percent of jobs lost during the recession were held by men, and that women's wages have risen by 1.2 percent more than men's over the past two years.

Anybody who had been following education trends was unlikely to be surprised at the findings; women have been outpacing males in college enrollment for some years now. College degrees tend to increase earning power, even in a landscape when women still earn 78 percent of what men earn. At some point, those women were going to marry, produce children and face the thorny question of who was going to sacrifice what.

It seems hard to believe that only a few years ago, hard-core feminists were lobbing grenades into the "Mommy Wars," lambasting uber-educated women for "opting out" of the labor force to spend time with their children.

Fewer women are able to do that today; the Census reports that the number of stay-at-home moms declined from 5.3 million to 5.1 million last year.

All of this is a seismic shift in American marriage; only 40 years ago, teachers, stewardesses and others were summarily fired if they got married.

"Marriage is a different deal than it was 40 years ago," Pew economist Roger Fry, told USA Today. "Typically, most wives did not work, so for economic well-being, marriage penalized guys with more mouths to feed but no extra income. Now most wives work. For guys, the economics of marriage have become much more beneficial."

Marriage has always been a good bet for men. As Elizabeth Gilbert points out in her new book, "Committed," married men live longer than single men; married men accumulate more wealth than single men; married men are far less likely to die a violent death than single men; married men report themselves to be much happier than single men; and married men suffer less from alcoholism, drug addiction, and depression than do single men.

And now it's even better.

None of this means that men are "opting out" of wingtips for Webkinz. Stay-at-home dads represent a mere 1 percent of the population. And many women agonize over the wrenching decision between maternity and material needs. But certain aspects of marriage and society are sure to change. In spite of their increased involvement with housework, men still lag significantly behind women in household chores.

The National Science Foundation reports that while married women with more than three kids spend about 28 hours weekly on housework, married men spend only 10.

More critically, as Gail Collins points out in her new book, "When Everything Changed," for all feminism has accomplished, it has left the question of caring for children in the dustbin. Women still wrestle with questions of child care that continue to baffle, dishearten and divide them.

Most women are not Sugar Mamas. But in two-thirds of American families, according to the Shriver Report, they are either the primary or co-breadwinner.

Most of them haven't the luxury of a stay-at-home dad. For those women, sprinting from work to home, where they confront the "Second Shift" of laundry, cooking and shuttling kids to and from activities, the news that women make more money and are educated better is an abstraction cloaked as a victory.

They don't feel empowered; they just feel tired, and harbor a sneaking suspicion that if men bore children, this question would already be solved.

No Party Or Class Has The Monopoly On Lechery

By Tracey O'Shaughnessy Republican-American Waterbury Nov. 26, 2017

My, my, what a cornucopia of creeps our benighted country has dished up for us this holiday season.

And so refreshingly bipartisan!

Who says we are a polarized country when our pantheon of perverts comprises so many politicians, publishers and pundits from such a wide array of society? The political autocracy, media plutocrats, technology titans and Hollywood's reliable randy libertines have all contributed so handsomely to the national level of disgust that it's hard to single out any particular class, party, industry or partisan for having a monopoly on lechery.

Oh yes, they are all men.

Even the "progressive" men, like the formerly debonair broadcaster Charlie Rose, now accused by more than eight women of groping, exposure and lewd behavior. So much for champions of feminism. Their hypocrisy reeks of a particularly noxious smugness.

The biggest story this fall has become the swelling parade of satyrs outed for raping, abusing, exposing or forcing themselves on so many women. Not tax reform. Not health care. Not the boarder wall. But the relationships between men and women in the workplace. We have not come a long way "baby."

Firstly, it cannot be declared loudly enough that most men do not grab, grunt, gyrate or grope women without the slightest provocation.

We just need more of them.

And they need to speak up a little louder. As New York Times columnist Charles Blow writes, "We have to re-examine our toxic, privileged, encroaching masculinity itself," he writes. "And we have to focus on the fact that society itself has incubated and nourished a dangerous idea that almost unbridled male aggression is not only a component of male sexuality, it is the most prized part of it."

Indeed, it is one thing to learn that one smarmy Hollywood producer was a boor, ordering up women to his hotel room as though they were egg-white omelets, but the procession of men accused of sexual harassment or rape has seemed to scoop up moral detritus like a hurricane-swollen river.

An entire herd of them -- on the left and the right -- has now been branded as predacious pigs. Politically, they are as disparate as Fox News' Bill O'Reilly and NPR's Michael Oreskes; as Charlie Ross and Mark Halperin; and as Donald Trump and Bill Clinton. Occupationally, they run the gamut from actors to comedians, media titans, producers and publishers.

Some, like Louis C.K. or Al Franken, offer tardy acts of contrition so fulsome as to prompt biliousness. Others, like Kevin Spacey, bumbled his apology to then-14-year-old Anthony Rapp by using it to announce his coming-out party. The conflation of homosexuality with pedophilia is a canard the gay community has long fought. Thus, Spacey's bungling announcement managed to draw the ire of the gay and straight community, even as it deflected from the real damage his alleged actions did to his accusers. Their numbers have now grown to 20.

So, call it plainly. These men were piggish predators who, as Times columnist David Brooks writes, have "morally obliterated" their victims. Moreover, he writes, "By treating such behavior as 'locker-room talk' or laddish behavior, they helped smooth the ground for all the predators to come."

All of that brings me to that rip-roarin', straight-shootin' cowboy of Christian virtue, Roy Moore.

The Alabama candidate for Senate has been pointedly accused of preying on many young women, including a 14-year-old, when he was in his 30s and serving as a district attorney.

The allegations, reported by The Washington Post, are detailed and deplorable. Moore, an evangelical Christian, has denied them all and Alabama's state auditor compared Moore with Joseph and Mary. "There's just nothing immoral or illegal here," he said. "Maybe just a little bit unusual."

This is biblical malpractice of the most iniquitous sort. Leaving aside Big Christian Tenets like the virgin birth, the baseness of this analogy falls somewhere between ignorance and blasphemy.

A Christian should know better. And when Christians do not know better and prattle about with excuses like "It's between him and God," they damage the brand.

Not long after Moore's vigorous denials, an Ohio state lawmaker known for his stalwart support of "family values" and opposition to gay marriage resigned after officials acknowledged he had sought or engaged in relationships with gay men. All of that might have been just fine -- though it might have proved disturbing to his wife -- had he not preened about as a defender of "a committed natural marriage." Whatever that is these days.

Sadly, these kinds of sanctimonious blowhards cause secular observers to look at Christians as holier-than-thou hypocrites.

The duplicity in the left-leaning media follows a discouraging parallel. We can't possibly put credence into reporters whose behavior subverts their credibility.

Is it really so hard to keep your hands to yourself and just do your job?

So, this holiday season, as we digest this repast of debauchery, we might want to ask ourselves what it takes to change our mind. Because if we cannot change our mind, in the light of new revelations or evidence, we cannot grow as human beings or as a society.

I wish I could say that I did not like and admire many of those who have lately been exposed as serial harassers. Many fought for causes in which I believe, produced glittering prose, pointed punditry and thoughtful, expressive work.

But I cannot look at these figures with the same respect I once did.

It's just too hard to digest.

AMY PAGNOZZI

Amy Pagnozzi has been an award-winning columnist for The Hartford Courant, the New York Post and the New York Daily News, and has served as executive editor for the Doe Fund, which administers to the homeless in New York City. She studied English literature at Queens College and also studied at Thomas Edison State University. A native of Branford, CT, she lives in New York City.

Tuning Out Racism Not The Answer

By Amy Pagnozzi The Hartford Courant April 9, 1999

When a San Francisco health club threw up billboards that said when the aliens come, "they'll eat the fat ones first" a month or two ago, the backlash began immediately.

Portly people assembled beneath the signs, dancing and waving placards that said "Bite My Fat Butt," and bam -- TV, newspapers, politicos jumped on the bandwagon. Antidiscrimination laws protecting fat folks got drafted.

OK, so Hartford is not San Francisco, or New York, or Boston -- but it's my hometown, and I want those "Picozzi and Slave Boy are Back" billboards off I-84.

Don't tell me you haven't noticed them, because for more than eight months they've been a blot over Hartford -- five billboards in all, rotating from location to location.

I don't care if "Slave Boy" (a.k.a. Curt Kaplan) is really white. So what if the rear-view photo of Picozzi and Kaplan was not intended to mislead?

(Apparently it's a happy coincidence that Kaplan's hair is kinky in the back and straight in the front.) So what if WCCC radio claims it is making a pun? (Picozzi and Kaplan were fired from another station. Now they're back. I get it -- I still don't like it.)

We've got a downtown chock-full of people of color. You forgot to think about them, driving past "Slave Boy" billboards en route to work? And all you people driving past, you forgot to say anything?

I guess this is what some folks in Hartford mean when they say they are blind to race.

Five of those billboards have been hanging around for close to a year without a peep from Hartford's politicians, its NAACP chapter, or this newspaper. Sure, Greater Hartford NAACP President Russell Williams flinched when he saw them, but he didn't do anything.

"I felt awkward for sure and it certainly is something that caught my attention," Williams said. "There are a lot of issues and they mostly seem to deal with levels of insensitivity -- when it comes to the treatment of minorities. It seems nobody understands why the actions are the way they are."

It also seems few people in Hartford speak plainly about race, Williams included (and I'm not saying he doesn't have his hands full with other matters -- police abuse, fiscal desertion, segregated schools).

In New York, people talk about it too plainly. Here, people pride themselves on their lack of prejudice, says sociology professor Noel Cazenave of the University of Connecticut. "There is very, very intense denial. If you talk about racism, if you bring up the subject, you are liable to being called a racist," says Cazenave, whose course "White Racism" is part of the statewide core curriculum.

"It's just not considered civil in this region to be straightforward." As people of color progress, they, too speak "The Language of Success," which Cazenave defines as "accommodation, the language of getting along -- obscure, evasive language."

Or, as the Rev. Henry Price of the Greater Hartford African American Alliance put it, "Any time you raise the race issue, somebody says 'There you go again,' or accuses you of reverse- racism, or calls you P.C."

For months of Sunday brunches at Hal's diner, where the Alliance meets, there was talk of the billboard. "Lots and lots of back and forth -- people particularly didn't want that sign up there in Pope Park," says Alliance President Rev. Nora Wyatt. But nobody phone- zapped WCCC. Nobody wrote letters. Nobody even borrowed a cherry picker in order to cover that shame with paint.

"Picozzi and Slave Boy are Back." I know it bothered lots of you, because I asked. Your bellies lurched and you looked down politely -- the way you might at a cocktail party if somebody's breast popped out of her dress.

"You've got it, the Negroes of Connecticut have been well conditioned to look down," laughs Cazenave.

But I had spoken to whites as well.

Somebody tells you they're blind to race, it usually means they're blind to racism.

Take Picozzi, a nice enough fellow. As a 50-something member of the Brown Sugar generation whose listeners are overwhelmingly 18-to-49-year-old Caucasian males, he just doesn't get it: A) he explains, Slave Boy is white; B) Kaplan was given that name as an intern, when he was running around saying "Yessir, yessir, getting coffee;" C) He was given a chance to shed the handle when they landed the new job and declined. (WHCN, the station that fired them, made Kaplan use his own name "because they were really really offended by Slave Boy. I don't know why," says Picozzi.)

Well, all I can provide is a little context: D) The "Lethal Weapon" movies; E) The Pink Panther movies; G) "Huckleberry Finn" (yeah, Jim's the moral center, it's a classic, but there's still this little squirt bossing him); H) "Wheel of Fortune." I) The Lone Ranger and . . . Tonto -- that name now eponymous with racism.

What tokenism is to the workplace, Tonto-ism is to the media -- whether you're talking books, movies, TV, video games or radio. Individuals (including Picozzi) say "My best friend is black" to prove they're not prejudiced. The institution appoints a sidekick.

You think Tonto had it bad? Tune into WCCC some morning and try Quivers-ism. I defy you not to feel degraded, hearing Robin laughing manically at Howard Stern's racist jokes.

It is in this atmosphere that "Picozzi and Slave Boy" exist -- not the moon, not Michael Picozzi's backyard, but here, hovering over us as we drive downtown gulping gall with our coffee. And anybody who says "get a sense of humor" or calls you PC is feeding you more. Hold that head up, not down, because you are properly civilized.

WCCC can be reached at (860) 246-9084. I guess I don't need to tell you to be polite.

Dogs Behave As Well As 14 Children

Amy Pagnozzi The Hartford Courant July 10, 2001

On Sunday night, I visited Nicole and Andrew Graff of Killingworth, curious to see their menagerie -- giving them no notice other than to say I was on my way.

When a town's zoning board suddenly creates a new regulation limiting the number of dogs that can be kept on residential property without so much as a single public hearing, you figure on finding some sort of emergency situation.

Four dogs and no more, Killingworth says. The Graffs have 14. And some of their neighbors complained about noise, apparently.

So why is it that even when I was almost on top of their house off of Route 148, I could barely discern any barking? Am I too used to city life? Too hard of hearing?

Nor could I see a single neighbor's house from their newly built Victorian, which sits on nearly nine landscaped acres, next to a state forest measuring 72 more. Even in the Graffs' backyard, I had to look around to see where the barking was coming from, what with 20 grand worth of chain-linked dog runs surrounding the house.

There wasn't anything you wouldn't want to put your foot in accidentally, which I've got plenty of in my backyard with just two dogs.

As for the basement kennel, equipped with dog-sinks and hair dryers, washing machines, three freezers -- even canine futons, cedar chips stuffed within their cotton batting -- it was laboratory clean.

No noticeable chaos or cacophony anywhere -- nothing, in my opinion, to justify the zoning board's April cease-and-desist order against the Graffs, giving them just weeks to whittle their litter from 14 to four.

And when I called Killingworth Town Attorney William Howard on Monday to get the zoning board's side of the story, his secretary said: "Bill told me to tell you he's not available for comment."

Nicole Graff allows: "Sometimes you can hear our dogs barking from the neighbors' houses, but it's way, way in the distance."

The Graffs' Middlesex Superior Court appeal of the town's order forbidding them to have more than four dogs is scheduled for a July 31 return date. "It's unconstitutional," charges Nicole, 33, a law clerk in Hartford's Appellate Court who takes her bar exam in two weeks.

Before choosing to live in Killingworth, she called the town clerk and the zoning officer to make sure there weren't any such restrictions.

"A couple of weeks after we moved in, the rules suddenly changed," Nicole says.

The town declared there was a "customary limit" of four dogs per household, based on its research finding that of 250 licensed dog-owners, only five had more than four dogs.

Though I never much liked that grade-school exercise Lifeboat, in which you pick off some passengers for the supposed greater good, I'm going to take a crack at it. Given all the Graff dogs being on borrowed time till the court decides their fate, we may as well start now, beginning with Earl.

Earl's a blind dachshund who bumped into stoops, trees, etc., before Nicole bought him a "brother" dachshund named Val, crating them together so they'd bond, putting bells on Val's collar for Earl to follow.

Though he gets around pretty well now, I figure the Graffs have plenty of sighted dogs; we can toss Earl overboard.

Then there's Von Steuben, their German shepherd. Nicole took him in when he looked like a possum-mutant -- bald, scabby and swollen from some rare variety of mange.

Poor Von swallowed so many different drugs in the eight months of vet-hopping it took to find the Boston specialist who cured him, he's still not what you'd call a credit to his breed. Splash, into the sea he goes.

Then there's Massimo, the 6-year-old Italian mastiff. A compulsive barker during his puppy days, a couple of snips by a veterinary surgeon turned him into a compulsive squeaker.

Sure, he's regal to look at -- but he emits a constant low-level noise like a rubber porcupine squish-toy. By eliminating Massimo, they get the added bonus of having to hear only nine of their beloved pets squeal out their death throes as they go down for the count.

Death? Why is Pagnozzi talking about death when the town of Killingworth merely ordered the Graffs to get rid of 10 dogs, never suggesting anything about killing them. Because the aforementioned pet specimens didn't strike me as highly adoptable.

Not that Killingworth's regulation would make any more sense if the Graffs had only show dogs.

The Graff dogs go to bed like little angels between 8 and 9 o'clock, marching instantly into their kennels the moment Mommy Nicole tells them to. Excepting of course the dog whose turn it is to sleep in the Graffs' bedroom, which they do on rotation. "Not on the bed, they're not allowed on the furniture," Nicole says.

Of course not -- especially since Andrew Graff, 31, is allergic to dogs, not to mention the couple's five cats and 33 assorted parrots, cockatoos and macaws, all of whom he loves for his wife's sake. Nicole grins, cracking wise and sounding just like a lawyer-to-be and the animal lover she's always been:

"Andrew knew even before we went out on our first date that the pets were a pre-existing condition."

Govenor Missed A Good Opportunity To Educate

Amy Pagnozzi The Hartford Courant Sept. 24, 2002

Okay, today, we're going to play a little game. It's called Stump Adam.

Amy: Adam, thank you for taking time away from your busy schedule in the governor's office to be with us.

Adam: You don't want me -- I'm just the lowly office guy. You want Chris Cooper, the governor's spokesperson.

Amy: Suppose I play with you AND Chris AND the governor -- wouldn't that just be ideal?

Adam: I'll just tell Chris.

Amy: Sure you will -- this won't take long. LGBTI. What do those letters mean to you (hint: more than a bad hand of Scrabble). The clock is ticking, Adam …

Adam: Stump Chris instead of me, and I promise I won't tip him off what you're asking.

Amy: OK, we'll save the "I" for later. Go for LGBT and I'll even give you the context: language Gay PRIDE rally organizers wanted Gov. John Rowland to include in his proclamation of the weekend just past.

Adam: Lesbian, gay, bisexual and transgender.

Amy: Very good. Now we've just got that "I."

Adam: I give up.

Amy: It stands for intersexed, as in … ?

Adam: I'm not guessing.

Amy: Just give it a few seconds …

Adam: No!

Poor Adam. Don't feel bad. This really nice guy named Vinny who works at The Polo Club, this really cool transvestite bar on Maple Street? He didn't know either. Even I wasn't sure -- and I pride myself on this kind of stuff.

And it's not easy to find out. Try www.dictionary.com. … Nothing. OK, Dr. Dictionary? No? Let's try intersexuality? Oh, here it is, an article in Discover Magazine about intersexed babies. And here's a whole website, ISNA.org: "Intersexuality is a problem of stigma and trauma, not gender."

ISNA.org: That's the website of the Intersex Society of North America, and what they have accomplished in less than 10 years is amazing.

As is the story of Cheryl Chase, a society founder and an international advocate whose story may be better known than "intersexed," the word she popularized for more stigmatizing terms like hermaphrodism or genital birth defects.

Countless media projects and scholarly articles detailed Cheryl's story: As an infant, she was subjected to surgery that made her body reflect the male gender appointment her doctor had assigned. By 5, she realized she was indeed female. She has since lived her life as a woman and gender activist. In

1999, the Supreme Court of Colombia issued a historic decision establishing human rights protections for people born intersex, leaning heavily on a 10,000-word amicus brief she presented.

It's quite an accomplishment, bringing together untold new numbers of intersexed people, making society more aware of their prevalence, while simultaneously shifting the focus of those who provide their health care.

When the child's psychosocial well-being became the primary concern, it was easier to see how many of those early surgeries were performed for no other reason than making parents and society comfortable with what they perceived as gender deformities.

It was rather like doctors' handling of children born to mothers prescribed thalidomide: Seeing thumbs, toes and other digits in unexpected junctures, surgeons trimmed neatly around them as if crimping bits of crust on a pie or pastry.

Whether the digits discarded were functional and whether such a child might find practical use for them wasn't questioned.

So, you may well ask: Aren't the intersexed just as likely to be heterosexually as homosexually oriented? How does it happen that the intersexed come to be included with gay, lesbian, transgendered and bisexual?

By default, of course -- minorities simply tend to gravitate toward other minorities, much as people of mixed ethnic parentage, regardless of complexion, may choose to identify as people of color.

In that respect, I feel rather inclined to give the governor a slide.

Had Rowland asked what intersexed means, he would absolutely have been doing an educational service for all of the people of Connecticut.

Unfortunately, the proclamation Rowland was given to sign was bereft of initials his staff perceived as extraneous.

"The omission of initials was in no way meant to infer that the governor was trying to avoid acknowledging anyone or being less supportive of their civil rights," said Chris Cooper, his official spokesperson.

So, John Rowland supports equal rights for hermaphrodites?

"The governor feels that all people's civil rights must be preserved, regardless of gender or sexual orientation or lifestyle," said Cooper.

So what's Johnny R saying? Yay to the gay, thank the heavens for lesbians, hi! to the bi! And who's not intersex?

Because if that's what he's saying, I would like to formally welcome John Rowland to the Connecticut gay pride movement. I'll be waiting at the next tea-dance -- that is, if his dance card isn't too full.

NANCY PAPPAS METCALF

Nancy Pappas Metcalf was a reporter and editor on multiple beats at the Hartford Courant from 1973 to 1986, including a stint as the paper's dance critic. She then worked for more than 20 years as a health writer, editor, blogger and frequent media talking head at Consumer Reports magazine until her retirement in early 2015. She was a four-time National Magazine Award finalist and winner of three SDX awards from the Society of Professional Journalists, among other honors. She lives in West Hartford with her husband, former Courant music critic Steve Metcalf. They have three adult daughters, plus sons-in-law and grandchildren. She is a native of Iowa and a graduate of Wellesley College and the Columbia University School of Journalism.

Dance Program Reveals Tharp's Sense of Humor

By Nancy Pappas The Hartford Courant May 29, 1981

After looking at two sassy, assorted collections of Twyla Tharp's dancing this week at the Bushnell Memorial, I am dazzled by her authoritative control over her material, enchanted by the unexpectedness of so much of her choreography, hugely entertained by her wit, and, sometimes, dismayed by the ideas she chooses to express.

For Wednesday night's program, Tharp chose to open and close with really funny dances.

"The Rags Suite from the Raggedy Dances," the opener, is a 1972 creation for a duo – in the instant case, Shelly Washington and John Carrafa. Its opening part, set to Scott Joplin's "Fig Leaf Rag," is an extended joke:

the dancers walk on, then off, then on again, within the space of about five seconds. They dance, they twitch their faces and shoulders as they cross the stage and exit the other side. They run around behind the stage out of sight. They enter again, this time a little drunk. They exit. They run around behind the stage again. They enter, now with nervous pit-a-pat feet. They get cramps in their legs. They fall asleep standing up and are awakened after a few seconds by the crash of a piano chord. And so forth. All this happens with perfect comic timing.

Now the music changes abruptly to a set of Mozart variations, the ones that sound like "Twinkle Twinkle Little Star." During the first statement, of the simple unadorned tune, the dancing is small, sparkling, restrained. Subsequent variations, each with a particular embellishment, are embellished choreographically as well. One is danced jerkily, another with high-legged, swoopy steps that turn into pratfalls. As this section progresses, the dancers move more and more independently of one another, until, by its end, they've ceased communicating entirely and are shouting totally different scripts, rather like one of those Robert Altman film sequences with overlapping conversations.

A second, brief Joplin rag, danced with funny, fine, flailing arms, concludes the piece.

The finale, "Eight Jelly Rolls," dates from the same period. This 1971 creation uses Jelly Roll Morton's piano music, marrying popular dance styles like the jitterbug and the Charleston with Tharpian shrugs and bounces. It contains what may well be the funniest thing I've ever seen in a dance – an extended falling-down-drunk sequence, danced Wednesday by Christine Uchida. It goes like this: as five black-tied women dance a crisp, unison vaudeville routine, Uchida, staggeringly intoxicated, attempts to join in. She goes east when she should go west, stops, does a terrific long take, then heads west just as the rest have turned east. Charlie Chaplin should have done so well as Tharp. The bit has to last at least five minutes, and at no point does it lose its comic momentum or run out of freshly hilarious new ideas.

Both the "Rags Suite" and "Eight Jelly Rolls" make use of Sharps signature movement vocabulary – the famous connected sequences of nervous quirks, smirks and jerks. But she is perfectly capable, it turns out, of virtually abandoning this lexicon if she feels like it, which she did last year when she made "Assorted Quartets," one of the pieces on Wednesday's bill.

This piece mainly moves in two distinct modes. The first, brisk and concentrated, features well-disciplined turns and militarily stiff, fast kicks and steps. The other looks like a game of some kind, although the rules aren't evident – the dancers run, stop, push each other, then start the sequence again. It looks like fun, with a few combative undertones.

Combativeness is hardly an undertone in "Short Stories," a 1980 piece on Wednesday's program. Set to rock and roll tunes by Supertramp and Bruce Springsteen, it features, among other things, a truly unpleasant passage in which Mary Ann Kellogg's unconscious body is tossed like an inanimate object among three men, and finally left for dead in the middle of the stage. The others in the dance – the three men and two other women – stare at it stupidly for a minute, and then resume the activity they had engaged in before the mayhem: making out, dancing cheek to cheek, and getting in fights with each other. It's all very well-made, and the dancers, as usual, execute it to perfection, but it's nihilistic and I wish I didn't have to look at it.

Staging, Bold Choreography Electrify Dworin's 'Lighthouse'

By Nancy Pappas The Hartford Courant Sept. 6, 1986

Judy Dworin has been a steady, nurturing presence on the Hartford dance scene for 15 years now, building the dance program at Trinity College and working behind the scenes to encourage and unite the region's struggling dancers and choreographers.

Along the way she has, naturally, made and presented in public an assortment of more or less conventional modern-dance works on varying themes and topics.

In short, nothing in her background prepares one for "Lighthouse," the stunning exercise in performance art that she and a group of collaborators presented Friday night at Trinity's Austin Arts Center.

Much of the work's impact stems from Dworin's daring decision to seat the audience in folding chairs on risers on the stage, at the rear, facing out toward the front of the stage and the empty auditorium.

The piece opens with the entire place in pitch darkness, as the dancers, actors and musicians call to each other from all over the place, with the audience at the center of the conversation. Then the lights go up in the auditorium, and we see four dancers slowly "swimming" over the rows of seats.

After a playful opening sequence, during which we begin to expect, this will be a pleasant, mild evening of inconsequential modern dance, things suddenly turn tense and threatening. As if hypnotized by the single light bulb swinging pendulum-like across the stage, the dancers turn psychotic, overturning chairs and attacking one another. In the evening's most riveting moment Nusha Martynuk clings like some ferocious animal to Dudleu Brooks, in spite of his violent efforts to shake her off.

Allison Friday – the "outsider" of the piece – gets trapped and wrapped in a fish net and left for dead. Her four tormentors, Martynuk, Brooks, Carter McAdams and Kathy Borteck Gerstein, stride away and slowly disappear into a bottomless black pit (actually it's the orchestra pit being hydraulically lowered but it looks terrifying from the onstage vantage point).

In the piece's final image, the dancers retreat to the auditorium as it is raked violently with searchlights. Then all is black, until the dancers reappear as eerie, disembodied-looking, illuminated heads peering over the backs of chairs.

Andre Gribou, a pianist, and Emily Metcalf, a cellist, have crafted a well-matched accompaniment featuring not only conventional live music but also appropriate sound effects and wordless vocalizations.

Dancers Give Daring Performance

By Nancy Pappas The Hartford Courant April 26, 1986

In an astonishing assimilation of a totally foreign dance technique, the Hartford Ballet Friday delivered a haunting and daring new piece of choreography by three of the founding members of the Pilobolus Dance Theatre.

In "Land's Edge," choreographers Alison Chase, Robby Barnett and Jonathan Wolken for the first time made a new dance for a company other than their own – one that has never experienced Pilobolus's strange blend of Gothic mime and the use of the body as a purely abstract sculptural medium.

Yet the Hartford dancers seemed perfectly at home in this strange new world of movement.

The piece opens with four couples whirling slowly beneath a starlit sky, to the gentle sound of the lapping surf. Suddenly, the waves wash a mysterious, unconscious woman (Judith Gosnell) into their midst.

The rest of the lovely dance tells what happens then, to the woman and to her surprised and, at times, unwilling receiving party. This group includes a pair of men, identically done up in turn-of-the-century suits; the hunched, ragged village idiot played brilliantly by Ted Hershey, and four women, more or less indistinguishable from each other.

They pick the woman up and dance with her as if she is a rag doll. Slowly the idiot, nuzzling her with his face, restores her to consciousness, and they form a tentative attachment, these two lost souls. The others alternate between indifference to the goings-on and efforts to separate the pair. Finally, however, the stranger is welcomed into the group, and the dancing resumes under the stars.

The evocative, melodious sound track by Paul Sullivan – complete with Pilobolus's trademark whispers, creaks and clock chimes – is an integral part of the narrative.

This, however, is but one of three very interesting new dances choreographed specifically for the Hartford Company by outsiders.

"Gazebo Dances," which opens the bill, is by William Whitener, a dancer with the Twyla Tharp company. In what seems a reference to George Balanchine's famous abstract ballet, "Concerto Barocco," Whitener has costumed his dancers in simple white rehearsal garb and assigned himself the challenge of deploying the extremely large cast of 17 in a formal series of combinations. One imagines it is a dance that could be put into binary language by a skilled computer programmer. The effect is calm and clear.

Joyce Zel and Wayne Davidson furnish the very capable accompaniment, a four-hands piano piece by John Corigllano.

Finally, Christian Holder, the former Joffrey Ballet dancer, has created a winsomely sassy ballet, "Swing Suite," to a medley of Duke Ellington tunes. It has no visible larger purpose than to please and relax, and that is enough, for so it does.

BARBARA PARENT

Barbara Parent has been a feature writer and columnist for the Record-Journal in Meriden since 1984. She also has worked at the Waterbury Republican-American, the Southington News, and the Southington Observer. Among several writing awards, she received the Distinguished Media Award from the American Cancer Society of Connecticut and first place for feature writing from the CT Society of Professional Journalists. A native of New Britain, she graduated from Newington High School in 1961 and has lived in Southington more than 40 years. Among her three children is Bryant Carpenter, long-time sports editor of the Record-Journal. Barbara has six grandchildren.

Different Kind Of Teenage Sleepover

By Barbara Parent Record-Journal, Meriden Jan. 15, 2008

The morning of the sleepover I cannot find the video that is as crucial to tonight's get together as the Lipton Onion Soup dip was to our teenage sleepovers.

"A Summer Place" is our tangible youth, like our laughing faces frozen in time on the black and white amusement park photo booth strips.

This night is not the usual meeting for the four of us. No movie theater tonight. No restaurant dinner tonight. No gab session for just an hour or two. No day at the tag sales or an arts and crafts festival. Tonight we are not 60-somethings. Tonight we are teenagers, our lives uncomplicated, free and breezy as we never recognized at the time that they were.

Over what seems as if forever that we have been friends, the four of us have danced at sock hops and at weddings. We have babysat and gone on to hold our own babies. We have supported one another through the angst of teenage breakups and through divorce. We have watched our children grow and watched our parents die. We are grandmothers laughing like school girls.

We are akin to all girlfriends universal. In laughter or in tears, we hold on to one another. We are girlfriends like all girlfriends who came together no matter where their beginning. A friendship formed as little girls on the playground or waiting at the school bus stop. As middle-schoolers or high school classmates, college roommates or neighbors. As new mothers walking our babies, or volunteering at our children's school or place of worship. Friendships formed as co-workers or playing bingo at the local senior center. We become friends sitting with one another on the bleachers at a Little League field or in a high school gym. We meet through marriage and remain friends even after we are no longer in the same family. Girlfriends prompt those e-mails that fly around the internet about bonding and friendships, menopause and a dozen other issues. Girlfriends are the lifeline to one another, the sister some of us never had.

Girlfriends. They are the bakers of cakes and the preparers of casseroles. They are the babysitters and the drivers. They are the listeners, the confidants. The kinship of women nurtures and supports and is what makes women strong.

I locate "A Summer Place" behind a stack of Disney VHS tapes and at one point think, "Cinderella" might be more appropriate. Joan always says we friends grew up in a time of, "Happily ever after." Life was to be like the stories in our Little Golden Books. Somewhere along the way we dispelled the notion we were weaned on in the 50s. Those who did not come of age in that era often scoff at it, and we are guilty of it too as our eyes roll instead of tear at the dialogue between Sandra Dee and Troy Donahue. We giggle at Percy Faith's theme, fading in and out to the point of irritating and our laughter borders on sacrilegious. It is sad that a movie regarded at best as the anthem of our youth is reduced to corny in our maturity.

But then, gone too are the pajama parties that had us sleeping on the floor, sneaking in boys and cigarettes and setting our hair in bobby pins.

Gone is a time when the very worst thing that could happen was to have your steady boyfriend ask for his ring back. And yet, tonight's sleepover transcends 50 years. It is the same because we are the same. Girlfriends hurriedly exchanging places to capture our image before the click of the photo booth camera.

After breakfast we linger in the driveway our reluctance to leave one another more pronounced than usual. We hug our goodbyes as we always do yet this morning hold on as tight as we can. The tears we did not shed last night fill our eyes.

Chemotherapy and radiation begin tomorrow for Joan.

Lunch With The Girls

By Barbara Parent Record-Journal, Meriden April 7, 2016

Sherrill, Rosemary and I meet for lunch in downtown Niantic. The day is lovely, breezy but not that bone chilling wind that is so prevalent in these parts and one that my brother rarely encounters at his home in Florida and never fails to let me know during our phone conversations. If I should mention that to Sherrill and Rosemary over our Cobb salad, salmon topped Caesar, and the fisherman's platter they would say serves me right because I was mean to him when we were teenagers.

Let me clear up one thing right now. They each have two sisters. Neither one had, what I thought at the time, a pesky younger brother who tattled on her.

Sherrill ponders "broiled or fried" before ordering the seafood platter. The whisper of whole bellied fried clams of our teenage years at the Log Cabin in Newington escape from our lips with a collective sigh.

"Not at our age," Sherrill says, passing on the fried. Ah, of course, not at our age. Our meals arrive and I notice that Rosemary's Cobb is garnished with thick slices of avocado.

"Good fat," I remark and at the same time wonder if I should have asked prior to ordering, if my salmon was farm-raised or the preferred, wild caught.

The three of us choose our meals with an eye toward eating healthy, the catch words that make me shudder but alas, try to adhere to. My eyes, however, devour wide brioche rolls stuffed with fat hamburgers, triple decker clubs and sides of French fries that pass by on trays carried like crown jewels by servers dressed in black and white.

The late writer and director, Nora Ephron was passionate about food and during an interview said that sitting down to a meal should always be enjoyed at the moment as if it were the last as one would not necessarily know the meal is indeed their last.

The way I look at it, Ephron, who scripted Meg Ryan's classic climax scene in "Harry Met Sally," knew what she was talking about.

Another blow to past lunches: a cup of tea and two glasses of water are set at our plates. When did we stop ordering white wine? It's all too, well too, too, too something.

Conversation rolls around to health insurance. Circumstances dictate different scenarios and we moan and groan about Medicare regulations and co-pays and prescription tiers and who would think it would come to all this, but it has. Sherrill warns I should get the shingles vaccine and that's when I blurt out that Lois Lane knows that Clark Kent is Superman.

The two of them look at me with stunned expressions and I think they too are shaken, as I was, by this incredible news thus rendering them speechless. Well, what kid watching the "Adventures of Superman" in black and white on an 18-inch TV screen wouldn't be. How many adolescent girls wanted to be the Daily Planet's star reporter and the boys, cub reporter Jimmy Olsen. What made it all so believable was that we could grow up and realize our childhood dream unlike say a career as Cheyenne, Wyatt Earp, Annie Oakley or Jim Bowie.

"How do you know that Lois Lane knows Clark Kent is Superman," Sherrill asks in an incredulous tone.

I tell them it was the movie, "Batman vs Superman." I watched what had evolved in the adventures of our childhood superhero during the last 50 years while we were absorbed with our own lives. Things have certainly changed, I tell them. But all is good. Superman gets around even though these days phone booths are few and far between. And, Lois. Well our Lois looks damn good for her age and finally ditched the hat and pocketbook.

Of Black Olives, Sour Cherries And Wild Violets

By Barbara Parent Record-Journal, Meriden April 2, 1989

The priest is just beginning the graveside service when my cousin Billy and I exchange a quick smile across the blanket of flowers covering the casket that separates us.

He's so handsome, I think and recognize his face as a mirror of my father's from photographs taken 35 years before. Our fathers are brothers and that is the way with genes, or so I recall from a fleeting moment of paying attention in some biology class from a long time ago.

My eyes wander to my father's three sisters, and I see the similarities in their faces and hope some of it is reflected in mine.

I try to concentrate on the hereafter but my cousin Beverly catches my eye and we mouth a silent, "Hello" and without warning I'm thinking about violets and black olives.

We spent our childhood days, my cousins and I running through the wild violets that grew in the side lot of our grandparents' house.

We scrambled up the cherry trees that stood in the back yard, stuffed our mouths with the ripe sour fruit and spit the pits out at one another. We were half the ages our children are now, our parents were younger than we are today. Each Sunday they would bring their families to our grandparents' house, the house in which they grew up.

We cousins rolled in the blanket of violets that overran the terrain. We climbed the trees so easily it was as if the limbs had grown just to supply us with ladders. We descended upon the festive weddings that were so plentiful in our large family. We devoured black olives and stuffed our pockets with candy-covered almonds then gather in a corner and giggle ourselves silly.

Italian families such as ours have big weddings. We twirl spaghetti on our forks, and scoop sausage and peppers into thick slices of Italian bread. We cousins can hardly contain ourselves until the cellophane wrappers are removed from the trays of cookies made by all the aunts and great aunts. We drink root beer from glass bottles and if it is a summer wedding we take our bottles outside and put our thumbs on the neck, shake with all our might and let go and the soda squirts out all over our dress-up clothes.

We don't get in trouble because our parents are dancing the tarantula and drinking Chianti and don't have us under a microscope watching our every move.

There are photographs taken 35 years ago by my father's uncle who posed each family and made up a set of 5 x 7 black and whites for each.

My cousin Anthony is maybe 9, standing dressed in his little-boy suit next to his sister Linda, her hair in pipe curls and a smile so wide it looks as if her face will split in two.

Beverly and her two sisters are wearing wide-brimmed straw hats and carrying black patent leather pocketbooks. Even though the photographs are black and white I know the dress I have on is a dark green dotted Swiss because it was my favorite. My brother is wearing suspenders to hold up a pair of pants that have perfect creases down the center of each leg.

Such was just one of long ago Sundays and I hold tight to the memories as the priest's final words bring our aunt's funeral service to a close.

We no longer spend our days, my cousins and I, running through the wild violets that grew in the side lot of our grandparents' house. At family wedding receptions, fewer now as the generations age, we sit at tables and drink our cocktails, behaving like the grownups we have become.

CAROL KING PLATT

Carol King Platt is a former contributing editor at House & Garden and for 23 years wrote a weekly garden/lifestyle column for The Day of New London. Her work has also appeared in the New York Times, The Record-Journal Meriden, Traditional Home and Better Homes and Gardens. She takes as her topics the classic themes of great literature - that is to say, Life, Death, Sex and Rhododendrons. Carol lectures regularly about garden design and flower arranging and has designed gardens in Connecticut, New York, Massachusetts and Rhode Island. Carol is the past chair of the Landscape Design Council of Connecticut, and is a member of The Connecticut Unit of the Herb Society of America and the Wallingford Garden Club. Carol lives and gardens with her husband, Rose and Rhododendron guy, Ted Platt at Rose Cottage in Wallingford.

Fine Living

By Carol King The Day New London Jan. 1, 2006

There used to be a commercial on HGTV for a "lifestyle" channel that you had to subscribe to called "Fine Living." It really bugged me when the announcer said something like, "In Italy, they have a saying, 'Live like you are making a movie.' That sounds to me like, "Live your life like it's a show for other people to watch."

Then the Fine Living commercial showed attractive people jumping out of an airplane (for fun, not because of engine failure) and diving off of high cliffs into tropical pools. There was also a scene where a small crowd gathered to watch as a beautiful couple got out of a classic European sports car in front of a fancy restaurant. The only thing missing was Carly Simon's song, "You're So Vain, (I Bet You Think This Song Is About You)" playing in the background.

That commercial made me consider what "Fine Living" means to me, because it sure isn't jumping out of a perfectly good airplane. Nor do I want to dive off a cliff or even own a vintage Ferrari. To me, "fine living" means being lucky enough to live in a comfortable home with a pretty garden, eat decent meals and to be able to enjoy them with friends.

I'm not being facetious when I wonder, "Is this too much to ask? Is it too much trouble?" When people see our garden, some of them say, "Looks like a lot of work," (but in my mind I hear, "You are nuts...") When my husband built a beautiful corner cabinet, he heard the same thing. "Looks like a lot of work..." ("He's out of his mind.") It's as if there is something peculiar about working hard at something you like to do and enjoying what you've created.

I once read, "Life is too short to stuff a mushroom." Well, shoot, I really like stuffed mushrooms and I'd be disappointed if I never again went to a party where somebody had bothered to make them. For me, stuffed mushrooms have become a metaphor for the dilemma between the desire for "fine living" and the amount of trouble required to acquire it. Any "fine living" decision requires effort, whether it's expending the time and energy to "stuff your own mushrooms," or making enough money to hire somebody to do it for you, or make or do whatever else it is that seems good to you.

My sister, Kitty, who lives in a lovely neighborhood in California, says that whenever she goes to a cookout or even to a dinner party at somebody's house, the food is always served on plastic plates, even for adults, though everybody owns regular plates that would make eating a meal a whole lot easier. Kitty says her friends say, "Oh, plastic plates are just so easy." They think she's odd, or possibly peculiar because she uses her everyday plates or even her good china when she entertains (but then Kitty was raised on the East Coast, so what do you expect?)

Though plastic plates are an environmental disaster, the sturdy good looking ones are expensive and you have to remember to stock up on them like you do toilet paper and kitty litter. Apparently, it's worth it to be able to just shove them in the trash instead of sticking them in the dishwasher.

Of course, it's admirable that a working couple with children has enough energy to entertain at all.

Maybe, for some people, using regular dishes for company is too much to "pay" for the "fine living' pleasure of entertaining at home. Though I like to have a clean house, I'd rather do almost anything than housework. Sometimes the house gets messy and it bothers me. However, this past summer, we had a lot more company than usual: my husband's skating friends, my landscape design group, relatives for lunch, friends for coffee or brunch, family birthday parties and people who dropped by to see the garden.

At first it seemed like we were on a treadmill, always straightening up the house, putting away garden tools, finishing projects and feeding people. After awhile though, it became sort of a routine to keep things presentable. In addition, entertaining got easier and less stressful, not to mention more fun and we got to know some really nice people better. After guests went home, we enjoyed the fruits of our labor-the cleaner house, the tidy garden, the pleasant memory, the leftovers-and we felt really good.

Maybe for us, entertaining people we enjoy on a more regular basis is the key to fine living in our own home. That dumb Fine Living Channel commercial suggests that we should live self-consciously, always aware of how our lives look to others. I think it is better to live consciously, aware of how to live, period. What makes us satisfied with our lives and our homes? How and what do we like to eat and with whom? Which "fine living" issues are important enough to spend time on and which aren't? How much kissing and hugging do we need? What does it mean to live in our own moment rather than in others' perception of us? I ponder these things as I stand at the sink, stuffing mushrooms. I've never made them before.

Single Houseplant: Honest, Quiet, Slim and Beautiful, Too

By Carol King Platt The Day New London May pre 1999

Remember when dating sites were in the Bargain News and the Classified section of newspapers instead of on line? It made for great reading if you needed a giggle. Single Generic Females never listed qualities such as liking expensive restaurants, fancy hotels, large diamonds and designer shoes. No-ooo… It was always romantic fireside chats and long walks on the beach in the spring rain that S.F.'s were seeking.

In other words, "I'm a cheap wet date with dripping hair and a runny nose." I guess I'm just not romantic. However, there are some beings who really would love some quality time spent in a refreshing spring rain. They are your SGHP's, or Single Green House Plants. After a long winter spent sitting around in dry heated rooms with nothing to do but work on their dust mote collections, houseplants can be pretty scruffy looking.

Books on houseplant care say that SGHP's should be placed in the shower to rinse their foliage clean and flush the excess salts out of their soil. The problem is, houseplants are very messy bathroom guests. They splash soil on the shower walls and they never clean their leaves out of the drain. They drip muddy water all over the bathroom floor and they never ever hang up their towels.

Yes, sir, a couple of SM and/or FGHP's showering together can really trash a bath. It is much easier to wait for one of those lovely, gentle, showery days, when the temperature is above 50 degrees. Take your winter-weary houseplants out on the deck or patio and let them rinse off and soak up the rain. (Don't be tempted to speed up the process and squirt them with the hose. The cold water will send them into shock.)

When they are all clean and flushed out, look them over for pests and give them a haircut if they need it. Cut off all the dead stuff. Long vining houseplants such as ivy, pothos or philodendrons can be cut back if they are leggy looking.

Remember to bring them back inside or to a sheltered place before the sun comes out because a sudden blast of sunshine will give them a sunburn, just when they are getting ready to be gorgeous. The combination of the lengthening spring days, a rain bath, a good hair cut and some fertilizer will stimulate your spindly spinster HP's to grow into beauties that will never have to advertise for attention.

If a houseplant has been in the same container for several years, it may have grown too big for its pot. While some plants such as sansevierias like to wear tight shoes, most plants need a little room to wiggle their toes. Spring is the best time to "pot them on," or move them to the next larger size pot.

On the other hand, this might make the plant too large for the end table where it lives, or else the new pot will be too large for the antique jardiniere that you have carefully selected to complement your decor. In this case, simply remove the plant from its pot, trim off some of its roots, plop it back into the same pot and add fresh potting soil to fill in the space.

Or, you can divide the plant into two smaller plants. Your choice.

So now that your plants are clean, groomed and wearing new pots, where should they spend their summer vacation? A plant that thrives in a bright sunny window will fry in bright sunlight outside. Sun lovers will be happiest in a spot that gets filtered morning sun. A plant that needs only moderate light inside should summer outside in a shady location. All houseplants need a location protected from wind, and one not so secluded that they will be forgotten by everybody except slugs.

Some year, I hope to build an ideal houseplant vacation spot under the shelter of my south facing deck. Kind of a Club Med for plants, it would have shelves along the house walls and hooks for hanging plants. The light lovers would live near the front and the shade lovers would lounge along the back wall.

Any houseplant vacationing there would be very happy. Also healthy, caring, sharing, honest. Enjoys star gazing. Long green hair.

July Fireflies

By Carol King Platt The Record-Journal Meriden June 28, 2005

The fireflies arrived early this year. My husband says it is a case of premature illumination. Actually, they didn't arrive, like migrating birds, from far away. They have been in the garden all along, living a beetle-type existence. It isn't until they became sexually mature that they became, well, flashy.

Since The Record-Journal is a family type publication, I wasn't going to write about the life cycle of the firefly - a really pupating subject-until a third grade teacher told me that even her 9 year old students know all about the firefly facts of life. She doesn't think the information will adversely affect their dating habits.

From the beginning of its life to the end, a firefly is a bright little thing. Even as an egg, it has a slight glow. The larva hatches from the egg wearing two tiny sidelights which have no purpose that scientists can find, not even to signal turns. The larva, or glow worm, is a beneficial insect because it crawls around in the grass for two summers, looking for slugs, worms and small bugs to eat. Soon after its second winter, the glow worm builds itself a small underground room where it stays for 15 to 20 days listening to inspirational music such as the Doors', "Light My Fire" and the ever popular Debbie Boone's, "You Light Up My Life."

In the meantime, its insides are rearranging themselves from a crawling around-in-the-grass-type insect to a Flying Fortress with floodlights. At this point, I must issue a warning. CAUTION: The following paragraphs contain sexually explicit material containing violence and cannibalism, and may offend some (woosie) people. There are many different species of fireflies in the garden, each with its own flash code. The males cruise the sky flashing their strobe lights, showing off and bragging. The females lounge around in the grass emitting suggestive and inviting blinks. When a male and a female of the same species flash the same signal, the male flies down closer and closer to the female on the ground and finally they mate, flashing all the while. Though this may sound like splendor in the grass, to the voyeur, it just looks like two greyhound buses parked back to back on the street with their blinkers on.

To complicate matters, some hungry and cannibalistic females are able to mimic the flash codes of other species. It's kind of like calling out for a pizza. She just flashes 555-LOVE and an amorous male arrives on her doorstep, just in time for dinner. In self-defense, some males have learned to emit flashes which will confuse the cannibalistic female, causing her to give herself away. This is why there is so much flashing going on out there on a summer night, but very little action.

The males, which often outnumber the females 50 to 1, are flying around wondering whether they are going to get lucky, or get eaten. Biologists estimate that while it may take a male firefly seven days to find a mate, a female can mate and be back in her burrow in six minutes, unless she has a craving for a midnight snack.

By the end of August, the light show is over for the year. Thank goodness the fireflies will be back next summer. I love to see the lightning bugs. I always hope to see them. But I can tell you one thing. I'd rather see than be one. (With abject apologies to Ogden Nash.)

BARBARA ROESSNER

Barbara Roessner retired in July as executive editor of HearstCT Media, which includes several daily and weekly newspapers in Connecticut. Previously, she was managing editor, projects editor, writing coach, opinion columnist, magazine writer and chief political reporter for The Hartford Courant. She began her journalism career at the Record-Journal in Meriden after she received a bachelor of arts degree in Greek and Latin from Wesleyan University. She received the university's Distinguished Alumni Award. She was a Koeppel Journalism teaching fellow at Wesleyan, a Knight Journalism Fellow at Stanford University, and a strategic communications consultant at Harvard, Village Voice Media Company and the Aspen Institute. A Pulitzer Prize-winning editor, she has twice served as a Pulitzer juror.

---

6 Year Old Boy A Victim Of Grown Ups' Political Correctness

By Barbara T. Roessner The Hartford Courant Sept. 29, 1996

Sitting on a school bus at the height of the Clarence Thomas hearings, it didn't take a clairvoyant to sense trouble ahead. Goo- goo eyes, air kisses, paper planes bearing declarations of devotion. Pinches, pokes, nudges and noogies. To the adult eye, it was a veritable sex orgy on wheels -- third-grade style.

I couldn't decide whether to stand up, shout "Halt!" and deliver a lecture on the insidious origins of gender inequity or simply pray that none of these future leaders of America ever got nominated to the Supreme Court.

For I feared then what we know now. Taking the issue of sexual harassment seriously while maintaining a degree of rationality -- that is, responding to it with concern, but not hysteria -- requires a level of common sense seldom displayed by the general populace. Fine lines and shading are not our cultural forte. Inevitably, the kids on the school bus would get nailed.

Sure enough, the subsequent sagas of Bob Packwood, Paula Jones and Tailhook have morphed into the sorry tale of one Jonathan Prevette, a 6-year-old with thick glasses and a goofy grin who kissed a girl on the cheek and was immediately threatened with a week's suspension from his North Carolina elementary school.

The case of the first-grade Casanova represents everything that is ridiculous and absurd and extreme about the phenomenon of "political correctness." It's also a classic case of what happens when we adults become sensitized to an issue -- whether it's sexual harassment, bigotry, violence or a host of other very real and very serious social ills -- and we impose our newfound sensitivities on our clueless kids through harsh, life-altering punishments.

Time and again, I've seen it happen. An overzealous, misguided and just plain stupid junior high sports team spray-paints anti-Semitic or racist graffiti on the property of the opposing team; they get charged with hate crimes. A kindergartner gets caught with a butter knife in his school backpack and is expelled for carrying a concealed weapon. A high school student circulates a lewd joke about the president's wife and is accused of producing and distributing "pornography."

There's just not enough room these days for the boneheadedness of youth. With increasing frequency, it seems, the good talking-to becomes a permanent black spot on a school record. A stern reprimand becomes a criminal charge. A detention becomes an expulsion. And yes, a peck on the cheek becomes sexual harassment.

The story of Jonathan Prevette's alleged offense struck a particularly resonant note with me. When I was in first grade, a boy made me kiss him. He twisted my arm until I consented, out of physical pain and pscyhological fear, to press my lips against the side of his face. It was a crude display of power, coercion and submission. He was the master and I was his prisoner.

It was, unequivocally, sexual harassment.

What strikes me most about the incident now, though, is that while it occurred in the Dark Ages of the '50s, it was handled in an eminently enlightened and appropriate manner. I told my parents. They told the principal. The principal told the kid's parents. Everybody got called in for a meeting. We talked. The kid was verbally rebuked by the adults. He was contrite. I felt protected and safe. It never happened again.

Today, no doubt, an officer of the law would be summoned. At the very least, a psychologist and social worker would pounce. The kid's school record would be forever marred by vague but alarming language about his "unwanted sexual advance." He might be referred to juvenile court. Surely, I'd be treated for trauma. Perhaps my parents would sue for emotional damages, and I'd be rich.

One thing's for sure. Jonathan Prevette had better think twice before aspiring to the Supreme Court.

Taking The Money And Running From Our Problems

Barbara T. Roessner The Hartford Courant May 10, 1998

We here in Connecticut think of ourselves as a pretty civilized folk educated, thoughtful, forward-looking, progressive even. We've got money. Green lawns. Good schools. Clean government. A tradition of enlightened public service.

We should think again.

Our children are in a downward spiral here in the richest state in the nation, plunging headlong into a place that doesn't look anything like the landscape we carry around in our heads. A grim place without adequate housing, food, clothing, schools or the prospect of a decent-paying job the flip side of our self-satisfied self-image.

In the past couple of weeks, we've learned that Connecticut once again has the highest per-capita income in the nation by far.

We also learned that its child poverty rate is rising faster than in any other state by far.

That means that every day we've got more millionaires, more mansions, more Mercedes and more kids who are growing up without the most basic tools of life. And every day, the two ends of the spectrum move farther apart.

Take any 15 kids in a typical Connecticut classroom today; three of them are poor. And one of the three is newly poor pushed from stability into chaos within the past 10 years at the same time that more rich people are getting richer.

No other state in the nation not Alabama or Mississippi or any of those other faraway places with notoriously conservative politics and little wealth has neglected its neediest children quite so blatantly, so consciously or so maliciously in the past decade.

Maliciously? Yes. Because unlike Alabama and Mississippi, Connecticut has bucks, and we know better.

We're No. 1 in wealth, and we've got the strictest welfare "reform" rules in the nation. We've got one of the best educated populaces in the nation, and one of the country's most notoriously deteriorating public school systems right here in our capital city. We've got the chiefs and lieutenants of the most lucrative businesses and industries in the world living right here in our midst, and we can't seem to create the kind of jobs that afford a living wage.

Most malicious of all: Ten years ago, we had the second lowest childhood poverty rate in the nation; now we're 29th.

"We're in free fall in terms of childhood poverty. You have to put your mind to it to make that happen," says Paul Gionfriddo, a former state legislator and now head of the Connecticut Association of Human Services.

"This is Connecticut," Gionfriddo says slowly. "This," he says incredulously, "is the late 1990s. This is a rich state."

Why, then, is this happening?

Simply put, our own selfishness and shortsightedness. Our own willingness to take what we can for ourselves in the short run, regardless of the consequences. A self-serving and myopic electorate that chooses and tolerates self-serving and myopic political leadership.

One small but glaring case in point: As the economic apartheid in our state accelerated indeed, as the news of it hit the newspapers, radio and TV the governor and the state legislature decided to dole out election-season tax rebates.

That's $115 million 50 to 100 bucks in each taxpayer's pocket that could be going to desperately needed day care, job training and education programs.

But hey, this is Connecticut. We're enlightened, trendsetting, smart, forward-thinking. We'll take the quick cash, and let our children be damned.

Home Is Where The Issues Are

By Barbara T. Roessner The Hartford Courant Nov. 10 1996

Bill Clinton has a way with women. He knows what we want, and he knows how to give it to us. That's why we elected him. Again.

Four years ago, he was a bit tentative in his come-on. He talked about mothers and fathers and kids and the difficulties of getting by in a stressful, confusing, enormously demanding world. Mostly, though, he talked in generalities about the economic frustrations, the financial stagnation, the working-harder-for-less phenomenon of the "middle class." He seemed to be talking to us, sort of.

In 1996, he left no doubt.

Time off the job for teacher conferences and doctors' appointments. A ban on tobacco ads aimed at the young. Tax credits for college tuition. School uniforms. Teen curfews. Minimum hospital stays for child-bearing.

In 1992, it was the economy, stupid.

In 1996, it was the "soccer mom." And there was nothing stupid about it.

Relegating us to a sports metaphor (at least it wasn't war), and placing us on the sidelines, in a helpmate role no less, wasn't exactly brilliant. But talking our issues, and in our language -- this was genius. Women of all races, ethnicities and classes went overwhelmingly for Clinton on Election Day. And I'm convinced it's not just what he said, but the way he said it.

Micro as opposed to macro. Real rather than ethereal. Concrete instead of abstract. Dead-on, not around. It's fascinating to listen to the (overwhelmingly male) pundits bemoan the downsizing of the American political agenda during this presidential election. "Policy McNuggets," they've dubbed Clinton's approach to the issues. "Minimalist," they scoff. To hear them tell it, the president's pandering to the domestically minded women voters, courtesy of Dick Morris' hit 'em "where they live" strategy, has trivialized and demeaned the political discourse.

Well, I hear a distinct echo here of the old feminist rally cry: The personal is political. I hear the voters, and especially women voters, saying the minutiae of our lives do matter. They do have a place in the political arena. And contrary to the pundits, I think the resultant trend toward driving the issues home to where they can be seen and felt and absorbed in an immediate, pragmatic form is a wonderful way to re-engage the citizenry in a system from which they've been increasingly estranged.

This new politics of increments doesn't mean we no longer care about the bigger issues, the grander questions, the intellectual conflicts. It does mean we don't have a whole lot of time to debate "the role of government," or other similarly ephemeral exercises. We're too damn busy getting through the day. And staying awake long enough to get our kids into bed. This isn't about philosophy. It's about life.

If Clinton wooed and won the women's vote, it's because he successfully integrated the larger world with the smaller one. He synthesized the landscape and the garden plot. He wove together the macro and the micro, and made it whole. He connected.

Haley Barbour's post-election analysis is that the Republicans failed to convince women the national debt is important.

Nonsense. It's important. It's just not quite as important as getting the mortgage up to date, the college tuition bills paid, the kids' braces covered. And yes, the teacher conferences, the medical appointments -- and the soccer games -- attended.

"President Clinton understands the struggles that families go through," the television ad claimed, showing file footage of Clinton signing the Family and Medical Leave Act.

Well, that sure beats a pledge of allegiance to the nebulous "family values."

Will 1996 go down in the history books as the election in which the issues were diminished, or finally made real?

It depends who's writing the history.

SUSAN SCHOENBERGER

Susan Schoenberger is a writer, editor and copy editor with a long history of working for news organizations, including The Baltimore Sun, and The Hartford Courant. She is now the Director of Communications at Hartford Seminary.

A Watershed Year, her debut novel, won the William Faulkner-William Wisdom Creative Writing Competition in 2006 under the title Intercession and was published in 2011. Susan's second novel, The Virtues of Oxygen, was published in 2014. Her short stories have been published in Inkwell, Village Rambler and Bartleby Snopes. Susan has three grown children and lives with her husband Kevin and their dog Jackson in West Hartford. When not working or writing, she likes to read, run and talk about updating the house. She is extremely opinionated, as are most women she knows, and an unrepentant eavesdropper.

In The Heart Of Friendship

By Susan Schoenberger The Hartford Courant Jan. 17 2016

Karen didn't wear sunscreen. Theresa and I would badger her on our annual Cape Cod weekend, but she ignored us. "You'll wish you did when you get old," we said, but old wasn't in the cards for Karen.

She started 2015 with a swelling of hope, a job promotion, a stunning new house that she'd finally finished decorating, her family close. In April, on her 55th birthday, she was diagnosed with Stage IV breast cancer. By October she was gone. It was unthinkable, and yet, here we are, starting 2016 without her.

Theresa Sullivan Barger, Karen O'Brien and I met in the late 1990s as copy editors for The Courant, three ink-stained veterans of the newspaper business then working part-time as we raised our families. Right away, we recognized something in each other. It was a general willingness to get out of the house, and maybe not insignificantly, to drink wine. But if we were the characters from "Friends," all three of us would be Monica, so it was a responsible amount of wine -- for the most part.

We loved each other as good friends do, a casual kind of love reflected in small gifts and get-togethers, gossip and griping. Such a love doesn't come up in conversation. It skims along the surface. It's there, but no one needs to talk about it, and that is a comfort in itself.

When journalism kicked us out of the plane at 30,000 feet, we fell together, skydivers gripping each other's forearms on the way down. We all reinvented ourselves in middle age, pulled the parachute and landed somewhere safe, but not without each other's help. This was the practical side of love, which is less mundane than it sounds.

Resumes, references and job referrals flew around in flurries of emails. In the depths of the recession, when jobs were like rare gems, we became a sort of ego protection society. Pre-interview, we would pump each other up over lunch or on long phone calls. "You can do this," we said. "You're totally qualified." Post-rejection, we nursed each other's bruised pride like defensive parents: "They're idiots. You deserved that job. If anything, you're overqualified."The thing is, we truly believed it.

Karen's illness changed our love again. When a friend grants access to existential questioning, to the slow and painful process of the body turning on itself and breaking down, to final thoughts and wishes, the love seeps into your soul, where it should be.

This is when all those conversations we had with Karen over coffee, on the beach and in the office took on flesh and blood. On visits to the hospital or rehab, we met in person the once-estranged brother, the gregarious in-laws, the beloved nieces and nephews. We witnessed our friend's husband cradling her thin frame, squeezing in next to her on the narrow hospital bed. We cried with her heartbroken sons, held hands with strangers, hugged until we were suffocating.

Love for the dying becomes fierce and protective. We berated medical professionals for any perceived or imagined carelessness. We cursed the dark rooms and the lousy food. We said "I love you" out loud because we had to, because it might be the last thing our dear friend -- the one who knew best that listening is one of the highest forms of love -- heard from us.

Sometimes the love became tangled up with anger, about tests that didn't happen, about decisions that might have prevented a downturn. We could have dwelled in that anger, but we learned to acknowledge it and move on. We even appreciated that this is where life happens most viscerally, not where the rubber meets the road, but where the rim scrapes the curbstone. Where the sparks fly.

Dust to dust, they say at funerals. But don't tell me that my friend Karen is dust. She is the voice that gently explains when it's time to accept the unacceptable, she is the easy laughter I can still hear when I close my eyes, she is the stubborn one who never wore sunscreen. And she is love, the whole variety pack. I tell you, she is love.

Frozen Out: A Job Put 'On Hold' Is Like A Job That Never Existed; At Work

By Susan Schoenberger The Hartford Courant June 15, 2009

After months of sending out resumes and hearing nothing but the echo of an empty inbox, I received a surprising call from a recruiter who asked if I was interested in applying for a job in the marketing department of a law firm.

An actual job with an actual salary? Was I interested?

I raced down to the recruiter's office, where I learned that the firm was looking for someone with "strong editing skills." They weren't concerned about law-firm experience or even marketing experience. They wanted a word person. As one of thousands of word people with a little too much word-free time on their hands, I was absolutely elated.

The downside was that the salary was mediocre for a full-time job, but I rationalized that I would be learning new skills and setting myself up for a career outside of journalism, which is stalled in the kind of purgatory that takes years to escape. If I got the job, I decided that my three kids would just have to adjust to a new schedule and a mom who couldn't pick them up and drop them off 17 times a day.

A few weeks later, the firm set up an interview. I allowed myself a rare mall visit and spent $200 on a clearance-rack J. Crew suit. I studied for the interview, combing the law firm's website and drilling my patient lawyer-neighbor about what the job would involve.

At the first interview, a lovely human resources employee talked up the benefits of the firm and said it hadn't experienced much of a downturn in business. I sat in the spacious conference room with its moneyed decor, and despite every effort to keep them in check, my private hopes began to jump around like a metal detector over a gold ring in the sand.

At a second interview, I immediately connected with the delightful head of the marketing department, and my hopes bounced around again. I started to picture myself working outside the house once more, heading off to a job with a purpose, a challenge, a group of colleagues who would laugh indulgently when I asked them what "tort reform" meant.

A few days later, the recruiter called to tell me I was one of two finalists for the job. She told me to prepare for a phone interview with a regional marketing person, who would help make the final decision. I combed the website again and rehearsed my answers to tough interview questions like "What's your greatest weakness?" (Correct response: I sometimes care too much about the quality of my work.)

A week or so later, I got the call. The recruiter said I had beaten out the other finalist. There it was, the gold ring in the sand. The firm would send me a formal offer in the next few days.

This set off the flurry of phone calls and e-mails required to completely rearrange my life. I canceled a creative writing class I had been scheduled to teach and started organizing carpools. I got a bus schedule. I ransacked my closet, looking for clothes that would get me through the first few weeks.

A few days went by and I still hadn't heard from the firm. That's when I got the second call, the one from the recruiter telling me that the job was, unfortunately, "on hold."

What was that now?

I spent the next five days with my life "on hold." It was too late to uncancel the class, but I wasn't sure if I should unravel all the other schedule changes. Mentally, I was already working full-time, doing laundry at midnight and talking into a wireless headset at the grocery store as I directed my family around like an air traffic controller.

Needless to say, a job put "on hold" in this economy might as well be a job that never existed in the first place. The recruiter finally told me that the law firm had decided to freeze hiring for the foreseeable future.

I went through my rationalizations in reverse: I wasn't sure I wanted a full-time job anyway; who wants to work for a boring law firm; the salary wasn't enough to justify the family upheaval; I can wear flip-flops again instead of law-firm-appropriate shoes. Nine days out of 10, I'm fairly sure everything worked out for the best.

But in that place where my private hopes still reside, a part of me wishes the job hadn't dissolved like a mirage as I got closer to it. It's no fun to go back to Square One, which, of all the squares, is the least cheerful and most unsatisfying, and I'll probably never find out what "tort reform" means.

March To Prevent Another Columbine

By Susan Schoenberger The Hartford Courant April 20, 2000

It was a year ago today. Image after shattering image of high school students running from their school, hands behind their heads, bodies cringing as gunshots exploded around them. It made me physically ill and it made me cry repeatedly for days and days.

Weren't we all that way? My friend's husband joked that she had Columbine High School diagrammed on the wall in their house. It affected everyone, but it seemed to terrify mothers the most: the idea of sending our children off to school and never seeing them alive again.

The mother of one Columbine victim, interviewed recently on the radio, said she couldn't believe she hadn't seen her daughter in a whole year. Hadn't seen her. She hasn't even begun to face all the days and years that lie ahead.

The whole scenario is unthinkable, yet it happens again and again. And what have we done about it as a society? Virtually nothing.

What have we done as individuals? Surely, we all thought, now Congress will pass reasonable gun control measures. But that hasn't happened either. Apparently, the vast majority of Americans who believe in gun control haven't made themselves clear.

So what's next? Do we need another Columbine or another first- grade death? Absolutely not. What we need is to make enough noise to be heard over the Charlton Hestons of the world. The NRA may have millions, but we have something more powerful: millions of votes.

On May 14, which also happens to be Mother's Day, a march has been organized in Washington. They're calling it the Million Mom March, but I hope that doesn't put off the millions of men and women who believe in gun control but don't fall into the category of mother.

Rallies are also being planned around the country for people who can't make it to Washington.

The organizers have a Web site (www.millionmommarch.com) and a toll-free number (888-989-MOMS) and they've tried to get the word out. But it's not easy to get people there. I can't even count the number of women I know who would love to go to Washington but just can't get it together. Sometimes it's childcare, or money, both legitimate reasons.

Others say they can't spend Mother's Day away from their children. But look at it this way: If your children are old enough, you can explain why it's more important for you to be counted in Washington to make their world a safer place. If they're not old enough to understand, celebrate Mother's Day another time.

Still others need to be with their own mothers that day. Not everyone has a mother like mine who said, "That's great. Maybe I'll go, too."

But if you can't go to Washington, find a local rally (some local information is on the Web site, but ask around) and add your voice and feet to the cause. This is one case where the saying holds true: If you're not part of the solution, then you're part of the problem.

Most of the time, I'm proud to be part of this country. My grandfather used to gather us up around the flagpole every Sunday evening as he took

Old Glory down. He would sing "God Bless America," his eyes wet with tears. I tell my children that being born in the United States is like winning the lottery.

But the proliferation of guns (there are more guns in the United States now than people) puts my kids into another kind of lottery. Will they be the next victims? It could happen.

So I'm going to Washington. I'm taking my one vote and my two feet, because I don't want to feel helpless. I don't want to sit on my hands as the gun lobbyists blame everyone but themselves for gun violence. I don't want to feel my skin crawl in another argument about what the Second Amendment really means. What matters is now. And I don't want to live through another Columbine.

SANDI KAHN SHELTON

Sandi Kahn Shelton is the author of seven bestselling novels and three non-fiction books about parenting. These days she writes novels under the name Maddie Dawson. Her latest, Matchmaking for Beginners, came out in June 2018. She has three kids and four grandchildren and lives in Connecticut with her husband, Jim. She used to be the humor columnist for the New Haven Register and Working Mother magazine, where these columns first appeared.

Good Morning To All You Out There In Radioland

Sandi Kahn Shelton New Haven Register May 4, 1997

My daily life normally consists of basically three things: pouring and then wiping up juice for kids; staring at a computer screen, coaxing words to spring onto it; and driving back and forth across town with various children in the back seat, all yelling that they're going to be late.

But now there's something new that's been added to my life. Nearly every day now, I get to talk on the radio.

Let me tell you: this is the weirdest thing that has ever happened to me, even counting the time that I found the bag of kitty litter in the dryer when there was no way it could have possibly gotten there.

Radio stations from all over the country - places like Moberly, Mo., and Lufkin, Texas - call me up and want me to tell them things. The phone rings, and some guy yells in my ear in that unmistakable Morning Disc Jockey Style: "SO! SANDI KAHN SHELTON, IS IT TRUE THAT YOU'RE THE

FUNNIEST MOM IN AMERICA, AND WHAT DO YOU THINK ABOUT THE SITUATION IN ZAIRE?"

This is all because I have a book out. Apparently, here in America, when you get a book published, your name goes in some secret catalog that only radio personalities subscribe to, claiming that you will do almost anything on the radio.

Believe me, it has been an interesting experience, trying to figure out my feelings about Zaire on live radio, while relating this to my own life, of course.

Mostly I see it as my daily dose of adrenaline. You know - see if the brain cells can kick into gear at a moment's notice. The most interesting thing about it is that there is never any clue what kind of radio show I'm suddenly patched into. Often, it will be a thoughtful program about books, analyzing trends and discussing the higher ideals of motherhood.

But just as often, there will be some shock jock on the other line who's never heard of children and wants to berate those of us who have them.

"Why does anyone bother to get kids, when they just grow up and hate you?" one disc jockey asked me the other day.

I wasn't sure what to say, so I told him about the time the kitty litter was in the dryer and then asked him if he's given any thought to Zaire lately.

Another guy, from Burlington, Iowa, said to me last week, "You write a lot about appliances. What is it with appliances anyway?"

So I explained how hostile appliances are and that you have to be careful about trusting them too much, because it is scientifically proven that they are not on our side, and when I got all finished, he said, "Well, that doesn't make any sense because appliances are inanimate objects and they have no feelings."

We were both silent for a moment, and then I said, "Well, maybe your appliances have no feelings, but mine are horrible."

I don't think it's any accident that practically the next day, Iowa washed away in a flood. They told us on the news that it had to do with a lot of rain, but I think it's a pretty safe bet that it was all the washing machines there letting go at once.

He's just lucky he didn't ask me about the hostility of car engines. The whole place could have become immobilized.

Another interesting thing I've learned about radio stations is that the whole industry runs as haphazardly as say, my own life. Often one will be scheduled to call, and the call just won't happen. Then, later, there I'll be, pouring and wiping up orange juice and taking the dog out to pee, and suddenly the phone will ring, and there I am, needing to talk about motherhood.

The other night I was climbing into bed, exhausted, and the phone rang, and it was a Boston station, insisting I had an appointment to be interviewed for a solid hour on my theories of parenting.

It sounded suspiciously like my cousin Noah's voice.

"Noah, you know I don't have any theories after 11 p.m.," I said.

There was a stunned silence on the other line. "Are you able to do this interview?" said the man at last.

"You mean, this is really true?"

It was true. But at 11, I begged for a few stipulations: no questions about Third World nations. And could we agree at the outset that appliances don't love us? He said OK.

The Young Will Do Anything To Tame Hair

By Sandi Kahn Sehlton New Haven Register July 3, 1988

On the bathroom counter there are: Clean Sculpting Gel, Super Hold Sculpting Gel, Styling Mousse, Dippity Do, No More Tangles, Firm Setting Lotion and Freeze and Shine Super Spray.

None of these products belongs to me.

They belong to the two children of the household, who seem to be transfixed with the idea of lacquering their hair in place.

I suspect they would even pour laundry starch on their hair, if they only knew what that was. I have lately lived in fear that they would seize upon the Krazy Glue as a possible permanent solution to the problem of floppy hair.

I don't see that having floppy hair is any major human deformity. That's sort of what makes hair different from other body substances, like skin or bones, for instance. It blows around, it ripples, it shines, it feels nice to run your fingers through. I tell these children that hair is supposed to move.

But try to explain that there is an appeal in having dry, windswept hair. I have said things like, "Who wants to look like they just came out of the hot wax section of the automatic car wash anyway?" Sometimes, for fun, I have said, "So what's so great about getting your hair to stand up on end for hours at a time?"

These insults mean nothing to my children, mainly because they have seen photographs of me at my worst, back in the days when I wore my hair long and parted in the middle. This was admittedly a hideous style for most people, even though there was no other possible hair style to be considered when I was in junior high school.

My mother, who was perhaps ahead of her time in being a hair-cementing aficionado, used to argue that my hair shouldn't be permitted such license. It needed and wanted to be disciplined, she said, as though hair were a battalion of hooligans who had gotten out of line and desperately needed someone to call a halt to their collective misbehavior before they committed a truly heinous crime.

"Look at that hair!" she would fume. "It just does whatever it wants to. It's just crying out to be tamed."

This was not an effective argument to use with me, since I was at an age when all I wanted was to be untamed. I was proud that at least my hair was able to accomplish the look of this, when I had so miserably failed.

My mother had certain torture devices for "taming hair" - huge clips with metal teeth that trained your hair to sit upright in a wave formation. This training session took place while you slept, but heaven help you if you should roll over and get your scalp caught in one of these vise grips.

I now understand that she was forced to resort to these primitive, mechanical methods because all the wonderful mousses and sculpting gels hadn't been invented yet. Her main weapon against flying hair each morning was a single, pitiful can of Adorn hairspray.

I have had to face the truth: I am caught between two generations that believe that hair should resemble a ceramic mold, while I can't help but feel sorry for every little hair that is caught in its resin trap.

So I sit alone, thumbing through a magazine while the children explain to haircutters just how they want their hair to look. The conversations between people and their hairdressers should be private, I think, even if these are minors bargaining for new kinds of sidewalk materials to be plastered to their heads.

I can't help but overhear the 12-year-old explaining to his haircutter - a young woman who looks like she whipped up her hair in the blender just minutes ago - that he'll be away at Boy Scout camp, and he doesn't think he'll be able to take his whole battery of hair-care products along. Could she suggest something that will hold his hair in place in a permanent sort of way?

I cringe, waiting to hear her suggest Krazy Glue or perhaps something from the Plasticrete Co. in North Haven. Instead, she tells him there's only one way to solve such a problem.

She gives him the standard military haircut.

His hair, I fear, may be permanently tamed. He thinks it's great.

Is It The End Of The World As We Know It

By Sandi Kahn Shelton New Haven Register Nov. 30, 2012

If you thought you'd get out of Christmas shopping this year due to the fact that the Mayan calendar (and presumably the world) ends on Dec. 21, Marie McDaniel has some news for you: the planet is going to stick around for a while longer.

She's quite sure of it.

McDaniel, assistant professor of history at Southern Connecticut State University, is teaching an online course this semester called "Apocalypse Then: End Times in American History." She claims that the Mayan Calendar doomsday prediction, while interesting, is just the latest in a whole series of end-times predictions.

The Mayans had a complex way of thinking of time, McDaniel pointed out, but they never predicted the end of the world on Dec. 21, 2012. That date was simply thought to be the end of one cycle of time, which would be followed immediately by another. But the whole idea of that as doomsday gained traction just the same, and these days you can hardly find anyone who hasn't at least heard of the impending apocalypse just a few weeks from now.

"These ideas come up all the time," McDaniel said. "Throughout American history, we go back to this again and again."

Jessica Kenty-Drane, associate professor of sociology at SCSU, is so confident that the end of the world isn't coming this month that she's created an entire syllabus for a new course for the spring semester, called "Apocalypse Now?"

So far 28 students have signed up to examine the ways that we have a steady diet of fear and apocalyptic thinking. "I want students to look at how much of what they hear and talk about is apocalypse-themed," said Kenty-Drane. "As Rosie O'Donnell said, fear has become the most valuable commodity in the news."

So just what is it about being human that makes us want to run around like Chicken Little, perpetually declaring that the sky is falling?

McDaniel's course starts with a look at the Book of Revelations in the Bible, perhaps the earliest and most graphic of the end-times predictors.

"If you believe that God started everything, then you believe that God can end everything," she said. "And when things in society get harried or uncertain, it makes sense to say that God is in control. The Book of Revelations is popular, less because of what it actually says and more because of what is going on in any given time."

In many cases -- such as with the Puritans -- the idea of a judgment day, or apocalyptic end of the world, helped to control society. "It helps if you keep reminding people that God can come at any time, and that secularity is sinful," she said.

As American history unfolded, versions of the apocalypse were seen in times of warfare, of great industrialization, in upheavals with ethnic strife, she said. "People saw these things as examples of God's retribution," she said.

She said she has difficulty convincing her students that this kind of thinking didn't end with people from earlier times, that it's actually still with us today. "The students look at the people in the past and think of them as religious and superstitious," she said. "But we are no different. Americans today fear terrorism, nuclear war, pandemics. Each generation has its fears and catastrophes. How we interpret them is related to the culture we're in now. We have the same beliefs. We just call it something else."

There are, in fact, people who interpret events from the news as being foretold in Revelations. Remember Harold Camping, the Christian radio broadcaster, who last year declared that the world was going to end with a violent Judgment Day on May 21, 2011 -- and then when the world didn't end, he recalculated and said the end would actually come on Oct. 21, 2011? Thousands of his followers believed him and gave away their worldly possessions in anticipation of the end.

"There are people who believe that there are signs around us that show the apocalypse as described in Revelations is already coming," McDaniel said. "They see earthquakes, big storms, illnesses, the dying off of birds and bees, and asteroids and believe that these are signs that God is displeased with us. These people believe in the 'rapture,' when the people who are saved will be taken up to heaven before the trials and tribulations come and wipe out the evils of their culture."

"For some people, the idea of a Judgment Day, when the world ends, is good news," said Kenty-Drane. "They're sure that they're going to be OK, that God will punish the people who are bad. When there's a religious component like that, people believe that they can survive via their faith."

In Kenty-Drane's course next spring, students will be asked to notice all the apocalyptic threats they're exposed to, and do a critical analysis of how likely any of them is.

"If we can take away the end-time narrative, then many of these threats are actually solvable," she said. "We need to get to work on the real threats that beset earth: climate change, overpopulation, world hunger, the spreading of disease. That's harder than deciding that we will be saved if we have faith that God will protect us."

Apocalypse stories, though, run deep in human beings: that's the conclusion McDaniel has come to. "They're as deep as our creation stories and myths. We want to know what's going to happen. But no one knows the future. We can't know the future. All we can do is to make predictions based on the past," she said.

For those who want to go into the business of making predictions about the end of the world, McDaniel has a bit of advice: "Be vague. And if you're going to predict an apocalypse, by all means, don't make it a certain date."

Otherwise, no one will ever listen to you again.

LISA SIEDLECKI

Lisa Siedlecki has spent nearly four decades stringing words together for a living. Since her very first gig as editor of her high school newspaper (New Fairfield High School, Class of 1980), Lisa spent part of high school and college as a stringer for The New Fairfield Citizen News; became the Managing Editor and then Editor in Chief of The Echo, the weekly newspaper at Western Connecticut State University; and then earned an internship at The News-Times in Danbury in her junior year. After graduating from WestConn, with a B.A. in English/Writing, and a concentration in journalism, she spent 18+ years as a reporter and columnist at The News-Times, covering several local towns and then writing three different columns, including Approaching Sanity, a humor column. After a short stint where she syndicated Approaching Sanity in six local newspapers, Lisa joined the staff of Walnut Hill Community Church in Bethel, where, for eight of her 13 years there, she was Communications Director. She was Director of Corporate Communications for Origami Owl Custom Jewelry. She is director of marketing and communications at The Jericho Partnership - a local faith-based non-profit that serves the needy community of Danbury. She's also a drummer on Walnut Hill Community Church's worship team, and is part of the duo "Ellipses," which plays the local coffeehouse circuit. She and her husband, Mike, have six grown children between them, two grandchildren, and a very playful Husky-Shiba Inu named Lexi. They live in Southbury.

Lottery Fantasy, Lottery Reality

By Lisa Siedlecki The News-Times Danbury Dec. 1, 1996

Right this very minute, I could be a millionaire and not even know it.

Of course, in a few minutes, when I go check my lottery ticket numbers against the lucky six that were drawn, my balloon of hope will burst like a Bazooka bubble and I'll be pulling little damaged pieces of hope off my lips, nose and chin.

But let's not jump ahead. Right now, allow me one of my favorite daydreams: savoring the possibility of having correctly selected, against all calculable odds, six of six numbers from a field of 40.

For now, we discount the reality that I usually can't pick one of 36 numbers on a roulette wheel; that the only thing I've ever won strictly on the basis of luck is a cow-motif sugar-and-creamer set where the milk comes out of the cow's mouth; that I'm lucky like Garfield is perky.

Yet, come Tuesday and Friday – the nights Connecticut Lotto is drawn – I sometimes splurge for a ticket or two. After all, you can't lose if you don't play.

Here's my rule about buying tickets: If the jackpot is under $10 million, I only buy a ticket with change; in other words, if I'm buying $15 worth of gasoline with a $20 bill, I'll ask for two Quick Pick tickets. That way, I went in with one bill, but I come out with a nearly full tank of gas, two lotto tickets and three George Washingtons to tuck inside my wallet. I feel like I'm ahead already.

If the jackpot, however, is over $10 million, it's OK to go to the store with the express purpose of buying a Lotto ticket.

It used to be, when I bought a ticket, I'd stay up to watch the news to see what numbers were drawn. But now I have discovered a much more preferable way to play Lotto: The all-day daydream method.

I buy a ticket, and then wait until the next morning's News-Times to see what numbers were drawn. That way, for the entire day and night, I can imagine what life will be like after I win.

"This is the last time I'll be pumping my own gas," I say to myself as

I stand in a downpour, refilling my empty tank. "Next week my personal assistant will be standing in this godforsaken line," I mutter while the person in front of me at the grocery store is unloading his 47th can of cat food.

And then there's the happy matter of breaking the good news to my husband. (This is my favorite part.) I call him at work and say this: "Honey, stop whatever it is you are doing, walk immediately into your boss's office and tell him he's a germ-infested, foul–smelling devil spawn who has Sweet Tarts where his brains should be, then come on home. Trust me."

Upon his arrival, I've got a filet mignon dinner on the table, a bottle of Don Perignon in the cooler, the candles are lit and I'm wearing a bustier fashioned entirely out of $20 bills.

"Go ahead," I say, "you can rip 'em. We've got plenty more."

Just before I get the paper to check the numbers, I perform a mental assessment of how we'd really spend the money. Yes, we have bills. And, yes, we have relatives, whom we like. So the first chunk would be spread around there.

My nature dictates another chunk would go to charities, but after that, this saint becomes a sinner. Atlantic City, Cancun, fancy car, nice house, very large-screen TV, massive stereo system . . .

But first, here are the numbers I've got: Game One: 3, 12, 28, 31, 38. Game two: 12, 14, 17, 18, 20, 44.

Now as the bubble of hope expands, let's go check the winners: 8, 14, 19, 24, 38, 44.

Just as I suspected. Pop . . . sssssssssssssssssssssssssss.

It Feels Good To Lend A Hand

By Lisa Siedlecki The News-Times Danbury Sept. 28, 1997

I'm the Dave Matthews Band; they're the Glenn Miller Orchestra. I'm the Macarena; they're the Charleston. I'm blue jeans and "business casual;" they're house dresses and slacks. I'm Jerry Seinfeld; they're Milton Berle.

There's no denying it, we're different, me and the folks at the Bishop Walter Curtis Congregate Home in Bethel. Separated by a generation – or, more likely, two – you can bet these senior citizens and I don't sing the same tunes in the shower.

But put us in a room with a group of caring souls, a disc jockey, a bunch of cameras, and the makings for some wickedly decadent ice cream sundaes, and – wow! – can we click. We're not really so different after all.

I can sing along with Frank Sinatra, they can do the Chicken Dance. And we can all do some serious damage to a bowl of chocolate ice cream with caramel, hot fudge, whipped cream and a cherry on top.

That's how it was one Wednesday a couple of weeks ago, the day United Way set aside for caring, when I put aside my dignity, and along with the volunteer center's Karen Nourse, attempted to dance the Charleston. Our goal was to make some senior citizens happy campers for the afternoon.

If success were measured in smiles, we scored a dilly. Faithful readers of this column have heard me rant recently about such things as covering grade-school textbooks, ridding the world of dust mites, and nearly getting thrown up on at Walt Disney World. But today there will be no ranting, no complaining – no matter how good-natured – and none of my usual smart-alecky humor.

That's because there was nothing to complain about, not with all those beaming aces. Without a doubt, the Bishop's place was a good place to be that day.

Oh sure, I can rage on about how poorly I did the Charleston, if you can call flailing my arms and legs that way the Charleston. But even embarrassing myself while the cameras clicked was more than worth the results.

"I've lived here for eight years," said one resident of the Bishop Curtis congregate called Augustana, "and this is the best party we've ever had here. You are all so nice and so much fun."

A bunch of us from The News-Times were there, and we were joined by a group of employees from Caldor. We were a small platoon of the large army of volunteers that fanned out around Greater Danbury that day, dispensing a helping hand, a smiling face, a dose of caring. We fixed roofs, we painted walls, we cleaned up yards and gardens.

The United Way Day of Caring is the kick-off to the year's campaign, and for 1998 the goal is to raise $2.9 million through one-time donations and weekly payroll deductions. That'll go a long way to make life easier for a lot of Danbury area people who need a little boost – or a big boost.

Funds will go to homeless shelters and AIDS cooperatives; it will to Ann's Place, the Home of I Can Cancer Support Services; it will go to day-care centers and senior citizens congregates. A lot of people will get a leg up, but they aren't the only ones who benefit from a day like the Day of Caring.

I, along with a room full of others, made a bunch of people – elderly, sometimes lonely people – smile and laugh. And I did the Charleston. I was bad, for sure, but I felt so good.

Stepping Out On My Stylist

By Lisa Siedlecki The News-Times Danbury Oct 20, 1996

My heart is heavy with guilt. I must unburden myself with a confession. I have cheated on someone with whom I have a very close and intimate relationship. Someone whose fingers have tenderly and meaningfully run through my hair. Someone with whom I've shared my deepest fears and headiest desires, not to mention complementary wines.

I'm talking, of course, about my hair stylist.

Oh, God in heaven, forgive me. I'm not even sure what made me do it. A moment of weakness? Unlikely, since I made – Gasp! – an appointment. An underlying feeling that she somehow wasn't fulfilling all of my needs? Doubtful. She's served me well.

As I search my soul – and oh, how I've searched – I've come to the realization that, plain and simple, I needed a change. The excitement of someone new. Someone who could look at me from a different perspective and see something no one else had seen before. And then bring out in me a confidence and self-assuredness – and, yes, an innate sexiness – I'd never felt before.

The truth is, I've done this before. The Stylist Switch. And I never feel good about it. I always feel like I'm betraying a sacred trust, because, as we well know, the bond between a woman and her stylist is sealed with Krazy Glue. It's stronger than the bond between some husbands and wives.

Face it, we put our "look" in the stylists' hands. We go to them when its time for our proms and our weddings and our reunions. One slip, and it's our reputation that's in the toilet. From their perspective, the pressure of being responsible for someone's image must be a little overwhelming.

Therefore, when a match proves successful, it is indeed a union no one should put asunder.

So then I go and commit hairdresser adultery.

I feel as though I should say confession before the Rev. Vidal Sasson. ("My child, perform three perms, two foil wraps and one manicure for your penance. And, oh, throw in an Act of Contrition for me, will ya, hon?")

The worst thing about perpetrating such an indiscretion is the inevitable time when you will come face to face with your ex-stylist – and endure the moment when she sees you with your New Haircut.

Of course, without exception, that will be the precise 24-hour period you are having the Preeminent Wretched Hair Day – where the gel spontaneously liquefied and the mousse ran screaming from your bathroom – and you know she is thinking, "She left me for THAT?"

So you stand here, shifting from one foot to the other, telepathically summoning a gale-force wind to kick up suddenly and tame every unmanageable curl on your head, transforming you to a '90s-version Farrah Fawcett.

"H-H-H-Hi," you stammer, running your hand through your mane, unable to look her in the eye.

"Gosh it's been months, and you know, I've gotten like ONE haircut since you (a bald-faced lie) and, boy, as you can see, its, like, reeeeeeally overgrown, and, ya know, I should give you a call."

She walks away, laughing the way she laughed as she worked her magic on your hair while you talked about the previous four-to-six weeks of your lives. And she's muttering, "Serves you right, leaving me for that hatchet job, you hairy hussy."

Then, immediately, it occurs to you: What if your relationship with your new stylist doesn't work out? Could you go crawling back? Would she take you? Could it ever be the same? And what about trust?

Oh, my heart is heavy with guilt indeed.

LYDIA HUNTLEY SIGOURNEY

Poet and author Lydia Huntley Sigourney was born in 1791 and died in 1865. Gordon Haight (Yale University Press) wrote "a curiously appealing" biography of her, "Mrs. Sigourney: The Sweet Singer of Hartford," in 1930. The Courant's review of the book notes her "sugared verse and moral essays." Nonetheless she "established a reputation which has made her a fixed figure in Hartford literary and social tradition." Sigourney Street is named after her. She wrote poetry for The Courant for decades. Rival publishers competed for her work.

Sigourney went abroad in 1840 where she was received by William Wordsworth, and Thomas Carlyle and was presented at the court of Louis Philippe. Between 1840 and 1850, Sigourney published fourteen more collections of her poetry.

Haight wrote, "Mrs. Sigourney practiced constantly in her own life the lessons of sobriety, thrift, patience and virtue that her poems taught." Her son died at 19, the same year her husband died. Her daughter married and then moved to New York State and Lydia Sigourney wrote a poem that begins:

Bid not farewell, -- love pass from my door
As one whose returning an hour may restore;
No passing phrases, but let the smile speak
Bright from the blue eyes, and fair o'er thy cheek.

Call thy young children in from their play,
Cover their faces up, lead them away.
Methinks my enfeebled heart 'wildered and lone,
Dreads the going more than the gone.

From the first life throb, when on my breast
One bright Sabbath morning they laid thee to rest,
We have dwelt undecided, like sapling and spray,
But newer loves govern thee, Lie these away.

The Ladies of Hartford, in Connecticut, to the Ladies of Greece

(Lydia was the secretary of the Greek Committee of Hartford when Greece was attempting to separate from Turkey's Ottoman Empire. Her letter was printed in the Connecticut Courant April 8, 1828).

Sisters and friends – from the years of childhood, your native clime has been the theme of our admiration. Together with our brothers and husbands, we early learned to love the country of Homer and Aristides, of Solon and of Socrates. That enthusiasm which the glory of ancient Greece enkindled in our bosoms has persevered a fervent friendship for her descendants. We have beheld with deep sympathy the horrors of Turkish domination, and the struggle so long and nobly sustained by them, for existence and for liberty . . . Sisters and friends, our hearts bleed for you. Deprived of your protectors by the fortune of war, and continually in fear of evils worse than death -- our prayers are with you in all your wanderings, your wants and your grief... We are the inhabitants of a part of one of the smallest of the United States and our donations must therefore of necessity, be more limited, than those from the larger and more wealthy cities...our little children have cheerfully aided, that some of you and your children might have bread to eat (clothes) to put on. Could you but behold the faces of our little ones brighten, and their eyes sparkle with joy while they give up their holidays, that they might work with their needles for Greece...we extend across the ocean, our hands to you in the fellowship of Christ. We pray that His cross and the banner of your land may rise together over the Crescent and the minaret, that your sons may hail the freedom of Ancient Greece restored.

In a separate "report to the public" Sigourney reported the committee "collected in money, and received in materials, upwards of $1,200" producing 1800 garments and 100 barrels of kiln-dried meal. The committee acknowledged: the Choral Society "for the avails of their concert amounting to $137;" the Hartford Female Seminary, Washington College, East Hartford, West Hartford, Wethersfield, Newington, Glastonbury, Captain Beebe of the steamboat Amazon "for conveying gratuitously to New York…and to several gentlemen of Hartford for their kind advice and assistance."

Beautifying Schoolhouses

By Lydia H. Sigourney (1831)

I hope the time is coming when every isolated village schoolhouse shall be as an attic temple, on whose exterior the occupant may study the principles of symmetry and of grace. Why need the structure where the young are initiated into those virtues which make life beautiful, be divorced from taste, or devoid of comfort?

Why should they not be erected in fine, airy situations, overshadowed with trees and embellished with shrubbery? Why should not the velvet turf attached to them be bordered with hedges divided by gravel walks, tufted with flowers? Why should not the thick mantling vine decorate the porch . . . and convolvulus look in at the window, touching the heart of the young learner, with a thought of him "whose breath perfumes them and whose pencil paints?"

Why should not the interior of our schoolhouses aim at somewhat of a taste and elegance of a parlor? Might not the vase of flowers enrich the mantelpiece, and the walls display, not only well executed maps, but historical engravings or pictures, and bookshelves be crowned with the bust of a moralist, or sage, orator, or father of his country? Is it alleged that the expense thus incurred would be thrown away, the beautiful objects defaced.

This is not a necessary result. I have been informed by teachers who had made the greatest advances towards the appropriate and elegant accommodation of their pupils, that it was not so. They have said that it was easier to enforce habits of neatness and order, among objects whose taste and value made them worthy of care, than amid the parsimony of apparatus, whose very pitiful meanness operates as a temptation to waste and destroy.

She penned a poem in tribute to George Goodwin

who owned The Courant from 1778 to 1836, it's longest serving owner. He died in 1844. Her poem ends with this:

Would that our sons, who saw thee onward move
With step so vigorous and serenely sage,
Of thee might learn to practice, and to love
The hardy virtues of an earlier age.

On June 11,1860 on the occasion of the 85th Anniversary of the Battle of Bunker Hill

where Connecticut Gen. Israel Putnam was hailed as a hero, The Courant published half a page on the day-long ceremonies held at Putnam's grave in Brooklyn, CT, including Sigourney's poem, which was read aloud that day:

Roll back, roll back, ye fourscore years!
The battle scene restore,
The rushing hosts, the reddening skies,
The canon's deafening roar;
What chief your patriot band inspires
With his own iron will?
Who leads undaunted to the charge?
Putnam of Bunker Hill.

Through all the long and weary course,
Of war's disastrous day,
If freedom's vestal flame grew faint
'Neath fortunes adverse ray
New courage, kindling at the past
Through every heart would thrill,
As memory from her tablet cried,
Putnam and Bunker Hill.
Oh, little sons who yet shall rise,
Your country's pride and stay
To throw an Aegis o'er her breast
When we have passed away;
Oh, fair young creatures – yet unborn –
Who home's loved sphere shall fill,
Teach to your listening babes the words,
Putnam, and Bunker Hill.

Here on this sacred spot, a tomb
We pledge ourselves to raise,
Which for the millions yet to come,
Shall guard his name and praise.
Speak Cenotaph! At morn's first ray –
At noon – at evening still;
Through the eternal marble say,
Putnam, and Bunker Hill.

She honored Hartford Poet William Cullen Bryant

on his 70th birthday, when she was 73, less than a year before her death.

Published in The Courant Nov. 19, 1864.

Honor to him, the loved of all,
The master of our Western Lyre,
Who o'er his Country's heart hath thrown

The melody with which his own
Hath ever dwealt – shaping its tone
To heavenly choir.
Honor to him, whose early years
The old Homeric fire display'd.
And now to Wisdom's Ripen'd truth,
Doth bring the sun-beam of his youth.
Without a shade.
All hail to him whose genial strain
Nor bitterness, nor satire knew,
But from the charms of Nature's face.
And Virtue's majesty and grace
Its impulse drew.
All hail! – and still through lengthen'd days
May his pure thoughts unsullied flow.
And in the alembie of the mind
Mingling like molten gold refined
Through future ages, on mankind
Their wealth bestow.

CLAIRE SMITH

Claire Smith was the first woman to cover a major league baseball team when The Hartford Courant assigned her to cover the New York Yankees in 1982. She spent more than three decades as a newspaper reporter and columnist. She began her career at the Bucks County Courier Times in Pennsylvania, went on to the Philadelphia Bulletin and came to The Courant when the Bulletin folded. She covered major league baseball at The New York Times from 1991 to 1998 when she moved to the Philadelphia Inquirer and then ESPN. In 2017 She became the first woman, and fourth African-American, voted into the writers' wing of the Baseball Hall of Fame as the recipient of the J.G. Taylor Spink Award, presented annually since 1962 for "meritorious contributions to baseball writing." In her speech, which she directed to her son Joshua, Smith cited previous winners of the Spink award, including Ring Lardner, Damon Runyon and Grantland Rice. She graduated from Temple University.

Sox Fans Temper Enthusiasm With Historical Reality

By Claire Smith The Hartford Courant May 13, 1982

The Boston Red Sox are the best team in baseball, playing at a 21-10 clip, their best start since 1946. But not all Red Sox fans around Hartford are planning October trips to Boston's Fenway Park yet. They know that a great Red Sox start does not a pennant make.

Ask any true Boston fan and they'll recount tales of success in April and May that too often have led to heartbreaks in August and September.

"I'm on standstill in a way. I'm up in the air," said a leary Michael Bell of Hartford, a construction worker and long-time Sox rooter. "I followed them for 10 years and that's what causes me now to have my doubts. I don't want to get burned."

Bob Ross of Hartford, a Southern New England Telephone worker, agreed. "I'm happy for them, but I'm not getting excited," he said with a laugh. "I've been a fan for too long."

Still, Ross says the Sox might surprise a few people. "We all think this is their year...we think every year is their year," he said.

That's what even the most cynical fan thought in 1978 when the Sox got off to a 19-10 running start and in the middle of July led the American League East by 10 games. That dream was shattered by a division playoff loss to the Yankees, a team that was sitting 14 games back on July 14. Only the year before the Sox broke a lot of hearts by ending up two games out despite a league record 219 homers, thanks in part to a nine-game swoon in July. In 1972 the Sox blew an entire season by finishing one game behind the Tigers after dropping two of their final three games in Detroit.

"They do well for a couple of months and they fall away," Jules Langlois of Hartford, a retired factory inspector, said with resignation. "That's what happens every year, so you can't get excited."

But even with history staring them in the face, there are fans who refuse to heed the word of the cynics or doubters.

"I'm getting my hopes up," said Ken Gelber, a salesman from New York, said confidently. "I think this is going to be a good season."

The difference, Gelber said, "is that the Sox are getting help from unexpected places."

"Dennis Eckersley is the real surprise," he said, referring to the Boston pitcher who was a disappointing 21-22 for the past two seasons combined. Eckersley is now 3-2 with a very respectable 2.38 ERA. "I gave up on him two years ago, but he's doing well."

Even Ross admits to some early season shock from a team picked by many experts to finish no higher than fifth. "Carl Yastrzemski is surprising me by still being around," he said. "And the pitching has been very good. I think the Red Sox are surprised by it, too. If they keep playing the way they're playing, they'll be right up on top."

Gelber thinks that if the Red Sox do land on top, it will be because of second year manager Ralph Houk. "He's won a few pennants already," Gelber said. "He'll get them rolling."

And, says Hartford iron worker Dick McCartney, once the Sox show their fans they intend to keep right on rolling into October, the doubts will melt away. "The fans will get excited," he said. McCartney, a graduate of Pittsfield, Mass. High School signed with the Red Sox in 1958 and played minor league ball for several seasons. "They just don't want to bring it out too early, but the foundation is there. They're not committing themselves yet. But I'll commit myself. I think they've got a good ball club."

S. Murphy of Hartford, a hotdog vendor, also thinks the fans will warm to the Sox as the season goes along. "When you're in a bar it's safe to say 'I'm a Yankee fan'," Murphy said of the other team favored in these parts. "Everybody loved the Sox, but when the Yankees caught on to a little success, everybody became a Yankees fan. When the Sox win, then you'll see the fans."

Randolph Exits Yanks A Winner

By Claire Smith The Hartford Courant Nov. 30, 1988

Willie Randolph received the news that the Yankees no longer required his services on Thanksgiving eve. The irony of that surprising, unwelcome message was not lost on the dean of the Yankees, one of the handful of survivors who can remember the pennants, World Series championships, the good days.

"I was disappointed and hurt, but in no way was I bitter," Randolph said from his home in Franklin Lakes, N.J. "When I received the news I remembered the meaning of the (Thanksgiving) season. It was time to give thanks for the 13 years, for my family and friends."

In one sentence Willie Randolph perhaps showed why he was the most underappreciated Yankee. He always showed a team not only how one can survive the most difficult of times, but how to do so with dignity and class.

Willie Randolph will turn 35 in June and is five years older than his successor free-agent signee Steve Sax. Randolph has been slowed by injuries, and the Yankees felt that second base should be on the cutting edge of their clean sweep in search of a return to the postseason, not seen since 1981. The baseball decision cannot be judged any time soon.

The Yankees' method of dealing with one of their most loyal employees, as usual, leaves a great deal to be desired. Whether it's a Dallas Green touch or a George Steinbrenner touch also is subject to speculation. But Randolph knows what Tommy John now knows and what Ron Guidry may soon learn: loyalty didn't buy them so much as a cup of coffee this winter, let alone an invitation to come back.

Other players joust with Steinbrenner, defy him, sue him. Then, after bitter seasons, they are usually run out of town. Randolph, for years underpaid by baseball standards and under appreciated, did his best to get along, for the good of the team, as well as his peace of mind. In the end he got shown the door, too, in a particularly heartless fashion.

But Randolph is not bitter. Rather, he knows it's time to look ahead. Randolph, about to enter his 14th season but his first full one outside of New York, feels like a rookie again. Granted second-look free agency by the arbitrator's ruling in the second collusion decision, Randolph is considering all options.

"I'm very excited," Randolph said. "A little nervous too. I want to know as soon as possible where I'll be playing, what the division race will be like."

Where is still very much a question. Randolph won't reveal who the suitors are, but he says he feels wanted. "Who knows?" he said cryptically, "Maybe I can just go across town."

Well, whether it's the Mets, or the White Sox or maybe even the Dodgers, one thing is certain: Randolph knows there will be less pressure. For years now, after pennant winning stopped in the Bronx, Randolph wondered if the feeling would ever return. "I never looked at it as maybe the grass was greener somewhere else," Randolph said, "but I wondered, sometimes, if it might be more fun."

So Randolph looks ahead and leaves it to the Mattinglys and Winfields to fend off the distractions only Yankees know so well. Sure Randolph will look back. Former Yankees always do because they cannot help but think of their good friends when headlines blare about discord in the Bronx Zoo.

Randolph will also look back on occasion just to see how the Yankees fare without him. Players like Randolph do that, too, because they feel they made a difference. And Willie Randolph did make a difference. Every time he stepped on to a field he made the Yankees a better team.

Last season when injuries cut his effectiveness and eventually his playing time, the difference in the team was measurable. Not one game would pass without someone saying or thinking, "Willie Randolph gets to the ball in the hole" or "Willie Randolph turns that double play." Such things were always taken for granted on the days Randolph played. On the days when he was absent, it was almost as if the team bided its time awaiting Randolph's return. And when he did return, the Yankees, more often than not, took off with Randolph.

Randolph's mark was not limited to the field. He was named co-captain along with Guidry in 1986. Last season he really grew into the role. He was a quiet leader, following much in the footsteps of Don Baylor and Phil Niekro. Randolph is not given to boasting, but even he wonders, now, who will make Rickey Henderson play, who will buck up Dave Righetti and all the other sensitive types when the pressures that never broke Randolph, start bending the others.

"I never walked around announcing what I can do for a club," Randolph said, "but I took pride in trying to get to know each player and letting them know I was concerned about them."

Don't look for that to be replaced by Sax. He'll have his hands full trying to learn the difference in playing in baseball's Twilight Zone as opposed to baseball's Disneyland. He may fill Randolph's shoes offensively, but he'll be lucky to hold his own defensively. That's about it. And Sax, Green and Steinbrenner had better hope it works. Because there's no turning back. The Yankees fans know that; the players know, too.

"They can't look for me anymore," Randolph said.

That's not boasting. That's fact.

(Postscript: Randolph played 145 games the next season, 1989, with the Los Angeles Dodgers, hitting .282. He retired after one year with the New York Mets in 1992).

Baseball's Decision-making, Minority-level Hiring 1-for-35

By Claire Smith The Hartford Courant Dec. 12, 1988

One-for-35.

Frank Robinson knows he would not have made it to the major leagues, let alone the Hall of Fame, if he had too many 1-for-35 streaks. That's why Robinson, though satisfied with the overall efforts by Major League Baseball in its pursuit of fair hiring, is extremely disappointed at the lack of progress at what he considers the decision-making level.

Thirty-five is the number of managers, general managers and club presidents who have been hired by major league clubs since April 1987, when then-Dodgers GM Al Campanis galvanized a movement by questioning whether blacks had the "necessities" to hold upper management positions. Of the 35 changes, only one has been filled by a black – Robinson, who was named manager of the Baltimore Orioles six games into the 1988 season.

Nine major league clubs made no changes in any of the three key positions. The Yankees have changed president, GM and manager a total of six times since the Campanis incident without hiring a minority. The Red Sox have made one managerial change and the Mets have made no changes.

Only two positions in the majors were filled by Hispanics.

Cookie Rojas, born in Cuba, was hired to replace Gene Mauch as Angels manager in March; he was fired before the season ended. Nick Leyva, recently named Phillies manager, is of Mexican-American descent.

When Campanis spoke, baseball had one Hispanic manager, Mexican-American Pat Morales, who was fired during the 1987 season. With the addition, subtraction or whatever measure prevails, Robinson sees the overall gain as meager and his disappointment immeasurable.

"Manager, general manger, president – they are decision-making positions," Robinson said. "So I am very disappointed on hirings at that end of the spectrum. Something has to be done. Baseball has to focus in on it. One thing I know is that, a year from now, we cannot have another one-for-whatever. Something has to be done. If not, something is really wrong. If that happens, it will take some real hard looking into as to what our (The Baseball Network, and organization that lobbies on behalf of former players who are minorities in their quest for employment opportunities in baseball) course of action will be."

"That's not a threat. We would just have to reassess. I think we've been very patient, very cooperative with Major League Baseball. We will continue to be. But there's no hiding the disappointment at this time."

Unlike Henry Aaron, Robinson does not criticize the efforts by Major League Baseball carte blanche. "There's been significant progress made in the two years on other levels," Robinson said, "I'm very pleased about that."

Like Commissioner Peter Ueberroth, Robinson points to the gains made since December 1986, when Ueberroth advocated taking a hard look at the game's across-the-board hiring and granting of licenses and concessions, which historically had excluded minorities. After the Campanis incident, Ueberroth instituted a "fair hiring" program at two distinct levels: one dealing with former players and the other dealing with front office, clerical and support personnel as well as licensing and concessionaire contracts.

Last week at the winter meetings Ueberroth announced that, in the past 18 months, minorities were hired to fill 36 percent of all new baseball positions and that baseball's minority base has risen from 3 percent to more than 10 percent during that period. On the field in 1988, approximately 10 percent of uniform management positions in the major and minor leagues are held by minorities, Ueberroth said.

Baseball also could be on the verge of naming a minority as National League president. In April, NL President A. Bartlett Giamatti will replace Ueberroth as commissioner. Of the three candidates for the vacated presidency, two are black: attorneys Simon Gourdine and Gilroye A. Griffin Jr.; Phyllis Collins, vice president and secretary for the National League, reportedly is the other candidate.

"I'm really interested to see what happens there," Robinson said. "But to comment on the specifics before anything happens would be an injustice."

Robinson admits he senses a growing resentment over the inclusion of minorities from other sports. Gourdine was deputy commissioner of the National Basketball Association for 12 years. The Orioles and Dodgers have hired vice presidents whose backgrounds are in pro football and basketball; Calvin Hill and Tommy Hawkins respectively. And Robinson said he supports women's rights and therefore cannot find fault with Collins' candidacy. Therefore, Robinson said, as president of the Baseball Network, it is only natural he would want all possibilities along those lines considered.

But Robinson said, "I'm very pleased with all the candidates. I have no quarrels with any of them. All three are outstanding people."

Robinson said he also has no problem with how Ueberroth or baseball's upper echelon have tackled the problem. "The commissioner, the league presidents, some of the owners are very sympathetic to the cause," Robinson said. "They are still working very hard. Some of the owners are still playing hardball, however. The attitude is 'Nobody's going to tell me who to hire'."

Therein lies the battle, Robinson believes. The last bastion of the "old-boy" network is still holding strong. Though some minorities, such as Mets first-base coach/hitting instructor Bill Robinson and Orioles minor league manager Bobby Tolan, were interviewed for big-league managerial openings this past season, Frank Robinson alone was hired. And Robinson already was in what he considers the decision-making tier, serving as assistant to Orioles owner Edward Bennet Williams when the now deceased Williams asked him to take over the team in early April.

Robinson took great pains to point out that minorities, especially within the Baseball Network, have no quarrel with most of the men who eventually filled the managerial positions. "Doc Edwards, Jim Lefebvre, Jeff Torborg, Art Howe – they are people who have been around, paid their dues," Robinson said. "All I ever really quarreled about is that only one minority was hired after such a tremendous turnover.

"We always seem to be one step behind. Last year we could not get interviews. This year we got interviews, but no jobs. A lot of people say that's progress. Sure, that can be a positive step, nothing to thumb our noses at. It's a step, but a very small step. Interviews can also camouflage a lot of stuff. Names can be tossed around to give the impression there's been a change of thinking when maybe there hasn't been."

Robinson is pleased that former Reds great Joe Morgan has taken himself off the roll of candidates so that his name cannot be "used" when most everyone knows Morgan has no desire to return to baseball. Robinson also is pleased that some organizations have done more than interview. The

Orioles have made a significant effort, spearheaded by Williams, who was alarmed at the lack of blacks, not only in management, but among players throughout the system. Then there's Houston, which just hired Bob Watson as an assistant general manager. Watson, Robinson said, applied for and won a legitimate position, which had been vacated last winter when Bill Wood was elevated to GM.

"That's a very significant hiring, something I don't believe most people realize," Robinson said. "The man was given an opportunity and won the job. That's all anyone wants. Is a chance, a legitimate chance."

There still are problems, one which may have occurred only to Frank Robinson. "One thing that has always bothered me is the 'Robinson syndrome'," he said. "After Jackie Robinson broke the color barrier, then Frank Robinson broke through as manager. It was me and only me, even though I knew there were other qualified people out there. Now it's Bill Robinson. Too many times his is the only name you hear being considered for an interview. I want to see more people considered for these jobs. The more names you see, the more likely someone, somewhere will break through."

Before Campanis spoke in 1987, lost his job because of ill-chosen words and sparked a movement, Robinson spoke that spring and said he thought the door had closed tight behind him after he had been fired as Giants manager in 1984.

Asked if he had changed his mind, Robinson thought for a moment, then said yes, with reservations.

"I don't think the door was ever really open," Robinson said. "There had to be a crack, I guess, because I squeezed through. But even to this day, I don't know that it's ever been open. That's what I'm still waiting to see."

JACQUELINE SMITH

Jacqueline Smith, Hearst Connecticut Media editorial page editor of The News-Times in Danbury and The Norwalk Hour, began her journalism career as a part-time Hartford Courant correspondent with a high school education. Mid-career she earned a B.S. in Journalism from Southern Connecticut State University, summa cum laude; and a master's degree in writing with honors from Wesleyan University. She has taught Journalism at the University of Hartford and SCSU. Her first full-time reporting position was with The Day of New London, where she won first place in the New England AP News Executive Association for her investigations into wrongdoing in the management of the Electric Boat Division of General Dynamics Corp. in Groton. Jacky was a business writer and columnist for the New Haven Register. As a reporter at the Record-Journal in Meriden, her investigation into the dearth of minority teachers in the Wallingford School district, outlining how officials skipped over black and Latino candidates, earned her first place in the National Education Writers annual competition. She also served as city editor and assistant managing editor at the Record-Journal, managing editor of The News-Times and editor of the New Milford Spectrum. Her columns and editorials have won several first, second and third place awards from CT SPJ and from New England journalism organizations. She and her husband, James (the editor of this book), have four daughters.

Time Now To Say Goodbye

By Jacqueline Smith The News-Times, Danbury Sept. 10, 1990

"The time has come," Sarah said to her melancholy Mom. Even just joking about this moment – which she had all summer long – would instantly summon motherly tears. So we knew the inevitable as we stood outside the dorm they call "the jungle."

The time had come to say goodbye to my firstborn and let her begin a new chapter of her life, as a freshman at the University of Connecticut. Without me.

Sarah was less than three years old when, at the beach one clear afternoon, she saw a jet zoom above. She watched so intently that she fell backward as the white trail crossed overhead. Pointing a tiny finger, she exclaimed, "Look Mommy, a scratch in the sky!"

This wonder, this exhilaration of discovery, will continue to be with her in college. And what horizons she will see. We give the gift of a college education to our children and know they will grow. We are proud of them. But pride also carries the pang of letting go.

These confident 18-year-olds can hardly fathom that we remember when they did not exist.

So they easily dismiss our perplexity at the warp time took – their childhoods gone too quickly. And now that they are away at college, family life will never be quite the same. No "sweet dreams" said to each other before bedtime every night.

But the parental sadness at a child's leaving is more than maudlin musings. It's the realization of lost opportunity, laden with guilt and regret. While these babies were growing, so were we. As young parents, we too often put our needs and wishes first. We spent time building a career. It seemed more important to fly off on a business trip than to take seriously a young girl's question: "Mommy, why do you have to work so much?"

And unlike our parents' generation, we children of the '60s found divorce a more acceptable option to an unhappy marriage. We worried about its effect on our children, but we told ourselves they would be OK if we were happy. So, Sarah Flinn and her sister Rebecca, and later, her stepsisters had to make the difficult adjustment to their parents' divorces and remarriages. As for many of our children, it became part of growing up.

I took the afternoon off from work the day before Sarah went away to college. She spent the day, though, saying goodbye to her Bethel friends. So I sat in her quiet bedroom and got lost. I absorbed all the details that made the room so Sarah-ish – the graduation photos of friends tacked on the bulletin board she had decorated to match her wallpaper, her teddy bears arranged in a corner.

Sometimes, when she was younger, the stress of school would keep her awake at night. I would sit on the edge of her bed and, pressing my fingertips to hers, making sure they were aligned just right, I would tell her to collect all of her worries and send them out to me through our special connection. I would take care of them. Sarah would squeeze her eyes shut, round up her worries and give them to me. Soon, she would be relaxed, then asleep.

Sarah hasn't needed Mom to ease third-grade multiplication anxiety for quite a while. But I hope the fingertip connection is still there.

My little girl, who knew butterflies were really "flutterbys," now stood outside her dorm and knew "the time had come." I knew it, too. But I was not ready. Tears filled my eyes. When I hugged her goodbye, though, anyone could see she is taller than I and obviously ready for her life on a college campus.

It wasn't until I was in the car driving back to Bethel that I realized she had quoted, perhaps subliminally, her favorite Dr. Seuss book. Before she learned how to read, before she took the first step away – kindergarten -- Sarah would climb onto my lap and we'd read in union, for the zillionth time:

"The time has come, the time is now...Marvin K. Mooney, will you please go now?"

Elks Keep Dishing Sexual Discrimination

Jacqueline Smith Record-Journal Meriden Feb. 18, 2000

"I don't care to belong to any club that will accept me as a member," Groucho Marx wrote in 1966.

His witticism makes me think of the Polish Elks.

That seems to reflect their convoluted logic. But let's face it, the Polish Elks here in Meriden are not yet up to the mid-60s. They're stuck back further in time.

They are hawking tickets for a "stag" dinner March 2 to honor one of their own with kielbasa and golabki. Stag means men only, though the Polish Elks say, sure, they'd sell tickets to a woman.

"We wouldn't lock them out," said one good-natured organizer.

But women probably wouldn't want to come, they say. Some members said that women might be uncomfortable surrounded by mostly men. "I know women who did come, and then when they found out it was mostly men, they left," one organizer said.

Oh, and then men might have to watch their language in the presence of women. We can't have inhibited Polish Elks, can we. That would sure spoil the party.

The Polish elks see nothing wrong with their attitude. It's just been that way for a long time, 114 years.

This is how sex discrimination perpetuates. Women have worked hard for equal pay and for the more obvious ways of equality with men, such as the opportunity to vote and to play sports.

It's the less obvious, the unquestioned ways of society that are harder to root out.

Subtle sex discrimination is difficult to document, wrote Nijole V. Benokraitis in "Sex Discrimination in the 21st Century," because "many people do not perceive it as serious or harmful.

"It is often not noticed because most people have internalized subtle sexist behavior as 'normal,' 'natural,' or 'acceptable'."

That's why the Polish Elks can't see the problem with their exclusionary attitude. Technically, the private group is within legal rights because although they say the event is stag, they would let women buy tickets.

Even the two women on the city council have disappointedly tepid comments about the Polish Elks excluding them.

"It's traditionally been a men's night out, a Polish men's night out, and it should be respected as that," said Councilor Patricia D. Lynes.

A technical right, however, doesn't translate to a complete right. The message to society remains the same as it has year after year after a hundred years: men only.

We could shrug and say these Polish Elks eventually will get the message as the other groups of Elks have (the Italian Elks ended their men's-only night last year) or maybe some of the 300 or 400 men expected next month will see the light and say no.

What we cannot shrug off, though, is that two of our city leaders stand at the forefront of this stag event.

Mayor Joseph J. Marinan Jr. will give a proclamation on behalf of the city (the whole city or only the male portion?) to the evening's honoree and Police Chief Robert E. Kosienski will be master of ceremonies, as always.

What does this say about one of our leading department heads? About 10 percent of the Meriden police department are women, yet the police chief says to the public through his action that it's OK to leave women out of some events.

The old-time Elks were "very chauvinistic" admitted a past exalted ruler (that's the Elks' title), but it's "changing."

Oh, yes, that's right. They do welcome some women – they let the Elks sister organization, the Emblem Club, serve them dinner.

Women, it's time to let the men get their own kielbasa and golabki. Tell your daughters we are not here just to serve men.

Who Really Wins Here?

Jacqueline Smith The News-Times, Danbury June 6, 2015

Lori Jackson Gellatly did everything she could, everything she knew of, to protect herself and her twin toddlers when she got a restraining order against her estranged husband, Scott Gellatly.

He was abusive, she wrote in requesting the restraining order. She was fearful.

Lori sought the safety of her childhood home in Oxford and the comfort of her parents, Doug and Merry Jackson, my next-door neighbors. Doug installed an alarm system and put new high-wattage lights outside; Merry went door to door along the wooded street and told neighbors to be on the lookout for Scott. He has a gun, if you see him call the cops; he shouldn't be here -- Lori has a restraining order. They did everything they could.

But early in the morning of May 7 last year, before 6 a.m., after Doug left for work but before neighborhood children would be waiting for the school bus at the bottom of the hill, Scott showed up at the Jackson home. With his gun.

He shot to death the woman he once loved enough to marry, critically injured his mother-in-law, and even shot the dog, Nika, that was trying to protect the women, police said later.

The twins, about 18 months old at the time, were upstairs, unharmed, as their mother lay dying in the kitchen and their father fled.

This happened the day before a court hearing to determine whether the temporary restraining order could become permanent. This is the most vulnerable time for a partner seeking the order. Yet Scott -- and anyone in that situation -- legally could carry a gun.

Doug and Merry Jackson did everything they could, but they couldn't stop a killer with a gun.

What could stop such senseless heartbreak is to close the loophole in restraining orders and when someone fears for her or his safety, allow police to collect weapons right then instead of waiting a month or so for a permanent order.

That simply makes sense.

Doing all they could, Doug and Merry Jackson, and Lori's sister Kasey Mason who now is raising the twins, went to Hartford, urging legislators to pass a bill closing the loophole. But the Jacksons, and representatives of the Coalition Against Domestic Violence and other supporters were not the only ones talking.

The Connecticut Citizens Defense League, a grassroots organization advocating for gun rights, didn't like the bill. They said it would infringe on a gun owner's right to due process. And some legislators paid heed. Some argued that protection already exists through a "risk warrant" -- after making a complaint to the police who then go to a judge for a warrant to seize firearms. This is cumbersome and not enough protection.

The bill stalled in the Senate as the midnight Wednesday end of the session arrived. The proposed bill "would make it easy on the word of a single person, without the chance for rebuttal or explanation, to take away a person's firearm, something that is their protection and their pastime and something that is of great value to them," reasoned state Rep. Joe Markley, R-Southington.

What a specious argument. A gun owner's right to carry a gun, to pursue their "pastime" at all costs, is more important than someone's right to live? I don't think so.

And, I submit, it's not even in the gun owner's best interest to have a gun handy when emotions are raw and restraint may be weak. Something "of great value to them" indeed could be lost.

Scott Gellatly is in prison now, charged with killing his wife, and what good did it do him to keep his gun? He can't have it now.

JANE GROSSMAN STERN

Jane Grossman Stern specializes in books about travel, food, and popular culture. She writes a regular column for Hearst CT Media. With her former husband Michael Stern, they are best known for their Roadfood books, website, and magazine columns, in which they find road food restaurants serving classic American regional specialties and review them. Starting their hunt for regional American food in the early 1970s they were the first food writers to recognize that this food was as worthy to report as was the haute cuisine of other nations. Their book Square Meals (Knopf 1985) put comfort foods like mac and cheese, meatloaf, and mashed potatoes on the culinary map. Jane grew up in New York City where she attended the Walden School and received a BFA in graphic design at Pratt Institute in Brooklyn. Jane earned an MFA in painting from Yale. In addition to their food writing, the Sterns have written books on American popular culture, including The New York Times bestselling Elvis World (1987) and The Encyclopedia of Bad Taste (1990). In all, they have written over 30 books. They were staff writers for Gourmet magazine for 18 years. They are regular guests on American Public Media's public radio program, The Splendid Table. They have won numerous awards, including James Beard awards. The couple divorced in 2008. Jane Stern now lives in Ridgefield. They still write as a team. In 2011 they published The Lexicon of Real American Food and Jane Stern published a book on her little known but long-standing career as a tarot card reader.

'Bar food' Elevated At Cask Republic

By Jane Stern Connecticut Post May 8, 2018

Trying to always keep an eye on my budget, I have begun to enjoy the plethora of bar foods and happy hours in our area. Long ago bar food was a chafing dish filled with mini egg rolls and saggy jalapeno poppers. Unless you arrived first, opening the mostly empty silver chafing dish was a depressing sight. After a drink or two it almost didn't matter, it was "free food."

Bar food has become one of the main reasons people now dine out. With entrees even at middling restaurants skyrocketing toward $30 or more, a decent-sized appetizer or "small plate" is a guilt-free alternative.

I will be reporting on some of the best affordable bar food I have found. Cask Republic is the first.

Cask Republic has three locations, two are in our area: Norwalk and Stamford. Like the original New Haven location they are visually welcoming and tasteful. The wooden tables are generous, the bar well stocked and sparkling, the staff friendly and yes the food ... very nice. Cask Republic has a menu filled with an array of "small plates" and the ones I sampled were worth the trip.

Like many hip restaurants, Cask Republic has a selection of craft cocktails. Bartender-invented creations of oddball liquors, exotic bitters and strange fruits. Honestly, I have yet to meet a craft cocktail I liked. Please give me a Tanqueray and tonic, or a decent whiskey sour with a bright red cherry and I am happy. I do not want to play "guess the ingredients" with a glassful of booze that may be inventive but tastes dreadful.

So I ordered a mojito, not the one with strawberries and rhubarb in it, but just a regular old mojito. It was very good, fresh mint, good rum, lots of ice. I had arrived at Cask Republic in a rather foul mood; it was pouring rain outside and I just paid my taxes, but halfway through the mojito the world took on a rosy glow.

My appetite sparked, I surveyed the menu. Cask Republic offers 15 small plates, a broad selection designed to please most palates. The waitress suggested I order what I wanted and she would orchestrate when the courses were ready to be served. There was no rush to eat and leave, and this type of timed serving put a big load on the kitchen. I was impressed by the offer. This is not an "eat it and beat it" place; Cask Republic encourages you to dine and drink at your leisure.

The first small plate I ordered was shrimp and grits. It was not the traditional South Carolina version, but had two large tiger shrimp, a mound of Mexican cotija cheese grits and an andouille sausage vinaigrette. I was prepared to not like the sausage vinaigrette, which seemed unnecessarily "inventive," and something you might put on a salad, but it was wonderful, providing a tangy and spicy bump needed to the bland cheese grits. Granted, two large shrimp seems rather sparse, but the whole dish once assembled was quite luxurious.

Then came two large blackened fish tacos dressed with cilantro crema and classic pico de dallo salsa. The fish was indeed "blackened" and was surprisingly spicy. I would only suggest ordering the tacos if you like a real kick in the tastebuds and a need for a jump-start.

There was no rhyme or reason to the dishes I ordered. I just ate what looked intriguing. The truffled gorgonzola fondue with homemade potato chips first struck me as skimpy, but then I remembered it was a "small plate" and in this context seemed perfect. At least two handfuls of homemade potato chips were served next to a coffee cup-sized cheese fondue. It was perfect food for getting soused, easy to eat, not a lot of chewing involved, relying on hands rather then utensils.

One dish that took me by surprise was the dull sounding Roasted Vegetable Flatbread. In my book vegetables are OK, flatbread, meh, but this version was one that would convert a skeptic. It was brash and punchy topped with caramelized onions, "12-hour" roasted tomato, a goat cheese cauliflower puree and salsa verde. It was perfect with the mojito and was healthy, well-proportioned and filling.

Cask Republic has a vast selection of interesting beer and what is more perfect with a beer than a Bavarian soft pretzel sided with cave-aged Amish cheddar and grain mustard ale sauce. Not too long ago I was stuck at the Frankfurt Airport in Germany waiting for a connection. I was happy for the free time bestowed on me because it gave me time to scout out the big soft pretzels I saw for sale as I rushed to my gate. To my dismay the pretzels were tasteless and terrible. I can't explain why the pretzel in Norwalk was better than the pretzel in Germany, but it was. Maybe all airport food is awful, but big soft pretzels should be an easy offering.

I ended my feast with a very decadent plate of crisp pork belly bites. It was made with grilled apples, pickled jalapenos and a sweet barbecue glaze. It required a second mojito, after which I stumbled out on the rain-soaked streets of Norwalk. My bad mood had lifted; taxes and inclement weather is a given, but good bar food is a find.

At Uncle Leo's, Doughnuts Are The Pride of Connecticut

By Jane Stern Connecticut Post April 10, 2018

Often during mud season I wish I lived elsewhere. The snow is gray, the slush is everywhere and aside from some hopeful buckets collecting sap from maple trees, this "fifth season" is drab.

But wait, it's not all bad! I am celebrating mud season for two reasons. Ridgefield (where I live) has been voted (once again) as the safest town in the entire USA and miraculously the best doughnuts in the land are a mile from my house.

The best doughnuts are to be found at Uncle Leo's Not Just Coffee & Donuts, a popular local spot. Uncle Leo's has been in the Georgetown section of Redding for more than a year. When it first opened I popped in and chalked it up to yet another place to grab a cup of coffee and an egg-and-cheese sandwich.

Uncle Leo's is on Main Street. Main Street is always in flux; restaurants come and go quickly, the local fire department holds its fair here every summer, and the best scenery is the old Gilbert and Bennett wire mill, which is still waiting for its debut as something other then a crumbling old building, both majestic and sad.

If you grew up in Connecticut, you are possibly unaware that doughnuts are a major New England obsession. Living here, one just takes them for granted. Like pizza, I could make a case for our state having the best of the best. The problem is that every 5 feet there is a Dunkin Donuts, and where there isn't a "double delta," there are the tricked-up new places that lure millennials in with rococo doughnuts frosted like wedding cakes and stuffed with discordant elements like bacon and peanut butter.

So hosannas for Uncle Leo's where there are not a million same-tasting choices and over-the-top weirdness is not the signature. The doughnuts made here are classic New England style: plain, cinnamon sugared, yeast risen, chocolate and cream filled. Not only is the kitchen at Uncle Leo's not out to prove how clever they are, but I can honestly say that the lack of silliness and super-high quality makes these the best I have eaten.

If I had to invent a genre for them, I would say they are "workingman" doughnuts, as honest and timeless as the old mill across the street. They are designed to be eaten when bought (not pumped full of preservatives) and have no taste of old frying oil, a fate that some of the once-great doughnut emporiums in Fairfield County have suffered.

In addition to doughnuts, Uncle Leo's has good egg sandwiches. It is hard for me to get worked up over an egg sandwich, which is why I ignored the place for so long. When I went in for my doughnut fix, the man in front of me on line said, "I would like a Heart Attack." What? I perked up and followed his lead and ordered my own Heart Attack. An Uncle Leo heart attack is not for the lean-cuisine crowd, it gets its morbid name from the fact that it is a cardiologist's nightmare. Eggs and cheese and sausage and bacon in close proximity on a bun.

I was surprised that sausage and bacon proved such a brilliant combo; I thought they would cancel each other out, but I was wrong. I am no longer a single "pig meat" girl; I like sausage and bacon together.

If you do not want to start your day with a Heart Attack, there are a dozen other breakfast sandwiches available, including a breakfast stromboli, a table of crust into which is tucked your meat of choice.

Veering away from breakfast I tried the lunchtime daily special soup chicken gumbo. It was sturdy and well made, as was the warm roast beef on a roll with a container of "au jus" for dipping. There are numerous cold-cut sandwiches and daily hot meals offered, nothing cutting edge or super fancy, just good plain food.

If you have lived in Georgetown for any length of time (or are a member of the local fire department like I am) you will probably know most of the other customers there. It truly is where the locals eat.

Inside the cafe are three little tables that fill up fast. Most diners take their food to go. In nice weather, it is easier to get a seat; there is a pleasant, spacious patio with tables and chairs to sit at.

I am delighted to see Uncle Leo's as popular as it is, because nobody goes down Georgetown's Main Street accidentally. You go down Main Street because you already know what is there. It is a hidden-away street at once folksy and mysterious. Georgetown has changed only slightly since I first moved here.

Decades back, I remember an astonishing number of bars and liquor stores on Main Street. There was also an old-style barber shop and a TV repair shop that would replace the blown-out tubes in your old set. It took weeks to get the TV fixed, and lugging the TV in its heavy mahogany cabinet was a chore. This all seems as outdated as the Old Wire Mill.

The legendary Georgetown Saloon is closed and I see only one liquor store now, but the blue collar charm of the town is still there. Ignore the expensive steakhouse with valet parking next door to Uncle Leo's and treat yourself to Connecticut's humble pride: great doughnuts.

ERNESTINE STODELLE

Ernestine Stodelle, a pioneering modern dancer who performed with Doris Humphrey and José Limón was known as the most knowledgeable dance critic in Connecticut, writing as a freelancer for the New Haven Register. She had a multifaceted career in modern dance as a performer, author and teacher. In 1929 she joined the seminal dance company started in 1928 by Ms. Humphrey and Charles Weidman and was often paired with an up-and-coming Mr. Limón. After performing into the 1930s, she helped dance scholars in her later years reconstruct and preserve many of those early modern works, created long before dances were routinely recorded or notated. In addition to writing a book about Martha Graham, "Deep Song," and other works on dance, she ran dance studios in Connecticut well into her 80s. She died at 95 in 2008.

Star's Performance Is Cause For Rejoicing

By Ernestine Stodelle New Haven Register Jan. 30, 1989

Certainly an artistic event, but also because it was a benefit performance for the Connecticut Hospice, Rudolph Nureyev's first appearance in New Haven was a cause for rejoicing. Seldom is our city host to the caliber of dancing that graced the Shubert Theatre Sunday night.

A generous program, rich in three different styles - classic, romantic and modern - proved that the virtuoso performers of the Paris Opera Ballet can stand alongside the great Soviet dancer and be as proud of their technique as he is of his Kirov background. Together, the Gallic spirit and Nureyev's finely tuned theatrical taste let us see first-rate dancing and excellent, if not always perfect, choreographic choices.

The only disappointment lay, to my surprise, in the last piece on the program, an effortful attempt at comedy by former Paul Taylor dancers Daniel Ezralow and David Parsons. With a master like Taylor and the inspiration of an actor-dancer like Nureyev, and the litheness of his partner, the versatile Laurent Hilaire, the choreography could have avoided triviality.

Classicism was magnificently represented in the first two Pas de Deux: the duet from Don Quixote, performed with a dash of Spanish suavity and more than a dash of technical flair by Elisabeth Platel and Manuel Legris; and the delicate, romantic duet between Aurora and her Prince from Tchaikovsky's "The Sleeping Beauty." The last was exquisitely rendered by the sensitive Isabelle Guerin and the aforementioned Hilaire. Here was dancing with superb control.

Nureyev's first appearance was in Balanchine's "Apollon Musagette," set to Stravinsky's famous score. Though the Russian superstar was showing strain at moments, the interpretation of a work that was revolutionary in its day was faithfully transfigured by three Parisian dancers, Claude De Vulpian, Carole Arbo and Platel as the Muses of Song, Drama, and Dance, respectively.

But it was in the Mahler "Songs of a Wayfarer" that Nureyev broke through the restraints that seemed imposed upon him into a truly inspired performance. Maurice Bejart's choreography, though stilted at times, reaches into the depth of the music's profound statement, and the great performer in Nureyev proved once again his extraordinary artistry at conveying emotions that go beyond acting and even dancing.

For one thing, Nureyev's facial expressions are so intense that they are spokesmen for his entire body. One is lifted, one is thrilled at such wholeness of acting. Hilaire was as excelled as his partner, but one had all eyes for the Slavic Nureyev.

The Bournonville danced by the company of two men and six women was indeed a joy, with typical freshness and precision in the best Bournonville style, including those Danish experts that all critics have come to love.

Limon Dancers Probe Humanity's Penchant For Self-destruction

By Ernestine Stodelle New Haven Register 7, 1988

There is no doubt that the movement style of the Jose Limon Dance Company, now performing at the Joyce Theater, is unique in the contemporary dance world of virtuoso dance athletics.

Limon dancers are trained by their artistic director, Carla Maxwell, who worked with the great dancer-choreographer, in movement of a heroic nature: expansive, fluent, incisive when dramatic, ecstatic when lyrical, and above all, rich in meaning.

Limon sought, in his own words, "to probe the human entity for the powerful, often crude beauty of the gesture that speaks of man's humanity."

During the 17 years since their founder's death, the Limon Dance Company has wisely invited other gifted choreographers to stage works that have expanded the range of their inherited repertoire.

As a result of contributions by Murray Louis, Susanne Linke and Anna Sokolow, in particular, the company's potential has been explored in various movement styles. Now comes a new work for the company that brings them back to the very source of their founder's creative impulses.

Czechoslovakian-born Jiri Kylian's "La Cathedrale Engloutie" ("The Engulfed Cathedral") fits the Limon company like a glove. In fact, if the program didn't note that the ballet was first performed in 1975 by the Netherlands Dance Theatre, of which Kylian is artistic director, one would believe Kylian composed the work specifically for the American dancers - the choreography is so deeply intertwined with the company's movement style.

"La Cathedrale Engloutie" takes its theme from a fifth-century legend about a cathedral off the coast of Brittany, which became inundated by the tides as an act of God's vengeance for the evil ways of the populace.

Using Claude Debussy's impressionistic piano score - played by Richard Justin Fields in conjunction with recordings of waves crashing on a rocky shore - Kylian has created a quartet of extraordinary power. Danced superbly by Bambi Anderson, Michael Blake, Stuart Gold and Nina Watt, the legend's uncanny mysteries unfold in tableaux of visual splendor.

When the curtain rises, an aura of gold, as of the sun, suffuses the scene as the four dancers gaze offstage with terror at a slowly disappearing vision. Then, with devastating reality their own engulfment begins. Image after image of tidal force sweeps across the stage engulfing the couples. They first move successively, like waves breaking, then as if inundated themselves by tons of water.

Wheeling forms rise and fall, battered by gravitational suction; arms, legs helplessly shoot out, overpowered by the surge of ocean tides.

No longer definable in terms of individuals, the choreographed images we witness suggest great swirls of human helplessness. These give way to a kind of retrospective look into the evil that has brought about the devastation. The decadence is revealed in terms of sexually suggestive duets in which the two couples interchange partners lasciviously. Yet the tidal forces around them do not cease. It would seem that Kylian is symbolically submerging his characters in the social mores of their times.

All these dynamic images - so kin to Limon's conceptual thinking as well as to his sweeping movement choices - cause one to think that Kylian is also of the breed of big imagists. Here, indeed, is an indictment of man's tendency toward self-destruction.

Jose Limon's masterful 1950 duet, "The Exiles," set to Arnold Schoenberg's Chamber Symphony No. 2, Op. 38 was performed with great sensitivity by Carla Maxwell and Gary Masters. Drawn with grandeur, Adam and Eve are the exiles who represent man's tragic fall from grace.

They also, in Limon's imagination, find the strength to discover their own resources for survival, and thus the Biblical myth - before our eyes - becomes a metaphor for 20th-century man.

Maxwell and Masters are Limon dancers of long vintage. Their performance was tender, exceptionally sensitive, and worthy of the creator's belief in dance "as a vision of ineffable power."

The program closed with Limon's "There is a Time," performed by the company.

Noguchi Found The Heart Of Stone

By Kate F. Jennings and Ernestine Stodelle New Haven Register Jan. 8, 1989

THOUGH Isamu Noguchi, the prolific Japanese-American sculptor, has died, the legacy of his elegant, intuitive sculpture continues to give light.

Of his contributions to the parks and museums of cities in both hemispheres, New Haveners have only to walk across the Yale campus to find a Noguchi creation: "Sunken Garden" at the Beinecke Rare Book and Manuscript Library. The marble garden, completed in 1964, displays the complementary design instincts of Noguchi and architect Gordon Bunshaft, of Skidmore, Owings and Merrill.

Open only to the sky, it is an object of contemplation for passers-by, who can peer over the waist-high granite walls surrounding it, and for readers in the adjacent underground study room who can glance through glass doors at its pure white forms.

Three large, abstract shapes share the garden's pristine space: a huge, precariously tilted cube, a monumental circle with a cut-out oval center, and the pointed top of a pyramid barely emerging from the marble floor, on which striated curves suggest interplanetary orbits. Sunlight vibrates throughout the sculpture garden, brightening the Beinecke's ground floor offices and warming the austere stone surroundings.

"It's a very serene, intellectual garden," said Sasha Newman, curator of European and contemporary art at the Yale Art Gallery. "It has a soothing beauty; it's sympathetic to the viewer.

"It's very site-specific (to the Beinecke Library). He creates an environment.

"We've taken him somewhat for granted," Newman said. "We get embarrassed by the modernist tradition, by the attachment to materials. (But) he glorifies that, getting at the heart of the material. It's a wonderful push-pull between the traditions of the East and the West."

Noguchi once wrote about the garden: "The landscape is purely that of the imagination, it is nowhere, yet somehow familiar. Its size is fictive, of infinite space, or cloistered containment. Looked at from above, this garden is contained by the massive frame of granite that surrounds it. The drama is being silently enacted, inexorably."

Cultural synthesis: Noguchi was born in 1904 to a Japanese father and an American mother. The duality of his heritage, upbringing and education seemed to present challenges and opportunities rather than conflicts. He met these by creating works that synthesize both cultures - the contemplative, selective, humble spirit of the East and Western art's openness, sense of scale and experimental nature.

Noguchi's first significant mentor was Constantin Brancusi, in whose Paris studio he worked as an assistant during the late 1920s. Brancusi's sculpture used sophisticated, simplified lines, stripping away an object's individual features until only the essential structure remained. The pureness of the white stone of the "Sunken Garden" recalls Brancusi as well. Noguchi wrote, "My memory of Brancusi is always whiteness … he wore white, his beard was white, he even had two white dogs."

Whether the species was bird, fish or man, this reductive approach produced symbolic sculptural entities whose purity of form and natural inspiration would be an enduring influence upon Noguchi.

After Noguchi's return to New York in the 1930s, he supported himself with a series of commissioned portrait busts, entering whatever sculpture competitions were available to find an audience for his more inventive ideas. His commercial portraiture success, however, gave him access to artists from other disciplines, among them, Buckminster Fuller and Martha Graham, with whom he would maintain lifelong, working friendships.

The AP plaque: The first important public competition Noguchi won was for a commemorative plaque above the entry to the Associated Press Building at Rockefeller Center in New York. This gleaming stainless steel relief, completed in 1939, draws the viewer's attention in a way not unlike the seductive lure of Rockefeller Center within the city itself. The five figures in "News" overlap and crowd one another, conveying a sense of speed, mobility and intensity appropriate to the plaza below where people converge and blend in the surrounding courtyards.

The mechanistic forms of the newsmen and the industrial material chosen for the piece recall Bauhaus ideals of this era and reveal Noguchi's ability to incorporate a multiplicity of changing artistic currents throughout his career. The graceful, economic details, such as the swirl of paper descending from a typewriter carriage, are characteristic of Noguchi's originality and its application to site specific sculpture.

With "Sunken Garden," Noguchi was in his most placid, philosophical mood. But there was another side to the man little known to pedestrians and museum-goers: Noguchi the designer of stage decor for the dance. As the creator of forms that functioned as integral parts of dynamic stage action, Noguchi had no peer.

Working with Graham: Though the sculptor contributed decor for the George Balanchine ballet "Apollo" in 1948, it was his epoch-making collaboration with modern dancer Graham that changed the potential of stage environment for the dance. Noguchi's collaboration with Graham resulted in a cornucopia of stage set designs whose lean, biomorphic contours echoed the concerns of the surrealist movement. Together, Noguchi and Graham were able to fuse materials that could not have been more dissimilar: one, solid, geometrically conceived earth-related forms in metal, stone, wood, travertine; the other, the live, dancing body with its high-voltage feelings.

He modestly explained their relationship: "With Martha, there is the wonder of her magic with props. She uses them as extensions of her anatomy."

Between 1935 and 1967, Noguchi designed more than 20 settings for Graham productions as diverse as the solo "Frontier" and the evening-long masterwork, "Clytemnestra."

Throughout the 32 years of the collaboration, the sculptor's aim - "to wed the total void of theater space to form and action"- succeeded again and again. With mastery of theatrical design, he captured the symbolism implied in Graham's concepts in his scenery's concrete imagery. Though primarily abstract, the three-dimensional forms Noguchi created had a life of their own as meaningful spatial objects.

When Graham tackled the drama of the biblical Judith in 1950, she required a tent and a wealth of props to tell the tale of the Hebrew widow who seduced and killed her people's enemy, the Assyrian Holofernes. Noguchi supplied a standing support of crossed wooden beams terminating in an upward-jutting phallic form. It served as the General's tent when covered with a draped cloth. The over-sized jewelry that Judith donned prior to the seduction scene emphasized the drama to come.

Creating environments: Following an extended pilgrimage throughout Europe, India and Japan in the early 1950s, Noguchi began to focus his energies on plans for sculptural environments, gardens and playgrounds. Here, the harmonious interaction of human forms, landscape space and sculptural mass could be expressed and engineered for the future.

Noguchi described his concepts for these sites: "I am excited by the idea that sculpture creates spaces, that shapes created for that purpose (i.e., as counterpoint for architecture), properly scaled in a space, actually create a larger space. There is a difference between actual cubic feet of space and the additional space that the imagination supplies."

In the early 1960s Noguchi purchased a factory building in Long Island City, N.Y., to escape the costs and limitations of Manhattan studio space. He later bought a second building, where the Isamu Noguchi Garden Museum, planned and financed by the artist, opened in 1985.

"Noguchi was always moving forward, trying out solutions, working on something new," said Alan Wardwell, the museum's director. "His most recent sculptures are placed outside the museum to greet the visitor first. He was never content to repeat or rely upon successes of the past."

Noguchi's own words underscore his questing spirit, "After each bout with the world, I find myself returning chastened and contended enough to seek, within the limits of a single sculpture, the world."

HELEN UBIÑAS

Helen Ubiñas is an award-winning columnist for the Philadelphia Inquirer, Philadelphia Daily News and Philly.com. She was a longtime reporter and columnist for the Hartford Courant, where she was awarded numerous honors, including a team Pulitzer Prize for breaking news in 1999. Ubiñas was born in New York City. She received her bachelor's degree from Boston University and her master's degree from Trinity College.

In 2000, she became the Courant's first Latina news columnist. In 2007, she was one of 12 US journalists awarded the prestigious John S. Knight journalism fellowship at Stanford University. She's also received several awards since becoming a columnist in Philadelphia, including first place in column-writing at the 2014 Keystone Press Award. In 2017, the National Society of Newspaper Columnists awarded her top honors for her columns.

Real Life, When Your Name's Not Rowland

By Helen Ubiñas The Hartford Courant Dec. 11, 2003

Given the circles he travels in, it wouldn't surprise me to learn the governor has lost touch with how the other half lives. You know, the half that pays full price for vacations and golf outings and concert tickets, the half that isn't eligible for the six-year deferred-payment plan for home improvements.

So I thought I'd remedy that: John Rowland, meet Pedro Valentin.

Actually it's a re-introduction, governor. Maybe you remember him? You met a few years back when you presented him with an award for his work at the state Department of Administrative Services. Valentin still has the picture. Everyone is looking pretty pale from the harsh winter weather, except you, of course. You, governor, look as tanned as George Hamilton. Maybe you just got back from one of those discount vacations at a rich friend's house?

You and Pedro actually have a lot in common. He's been fretting about home improvements, too. Of course, his repairs are on his first -- and only -- home in Lebanon, not a lakefront retreat like yours. It's on a lovely dead-end street, modest, but very homey. He's done all the work himself, on weekends or whenever he's had a free moment to grab supplies from Home Depot. Funny, he's never seen you there. Didn't you say that's where the cabinets for your cottage came from? Oh wait -- that was one of your little misstatements, wasn't it?

For a guy who learned how to do stuff from the do-it-yourself channels, Valentin's accomplished a lot. Things were shaping up, until your administration laid him off in April. And then everything stopped. Suddenly his wife was the sole provider and he was collecting just $126 a week from unemployment and not much more from his part-time job teaching art at a local college.

Anyway, the new garage is just a shell. He buys a half-dozen or so bricks whenever he can afford it, just so he can keep guests from killing themselves on the unfinished walkway. And since the holidays, even those have had to wait.

Thanksgiving was nice, but it was definitely pared down. Usually, all friends had to bring to the Valentin house for dinner was themselves. This year, it was potluck.

Now there's Christmas to think about. His 5-year-old son wants Santa to know he likes Thomas the Tank Engine. Valentin told his relatives, just in case Santa can't manage Christmas gifts on top of the mortgage and the utility bills.

And then there's the tree. If worse comes to worst, Valentin said, he'll cut down one of the pine trees growing out front and bring it inside.

"Or maybe I'll just string lights on it, and we can all look outside for the Christmas spirit," he says.

The plan was to take his son and wife to Florida sometime this winter -- but that's not going to happen. Not unless the Tomassos come through the way they did for you, governor.

It's been stressful. And you, better than anyone, understand stress, don't you, governor? What with everyone on your case over a few perks? Valentin's blood pressure is skyrocketing; his asthma is back. The man could really use a hot tub. Think the folks who work for you could buy him a spa just like the one they gave you, Guv?

He can't sleep, and admittedly that's when he thinks of you the most. OK, then and when he's getting his hands all sticky from trying to glue the broken mirror he can't afford to get repaired back on his car.

Truth is he doesn't begrudge you or anyone else the good life. Isn't that what this country is about? he asks. But a long time ago, when his dad drove him to his first job washing dishes and reminded him that a pot has two sides, an inside and an outside, and both have to be washed, he learned that you have to earn your own way.

He still prides himself on being raised that way. On working hard and never taking a handout, and on always trying to do the right thing. What do you pride yourself on, governor?

Cowards: Look Into The Eyes Of Yet Another Life You've Erased

By Helen Ubiñas The Hartford Courant Feb. 25, 2005

You cowards who shot into that crowd of kids on Tuesday night. You should know what you did.

The kids piled into the hospital to say goodbye to Lorenzo "Morgan" Rowe because of you. Friends, girlfriends, his boys. They were sitting in the waiting room, hanging outside, crying and laughing and then going silent until finally one of them cried out. "Why?"

Why, they asked the adults around them, should we be good? You tell us to do the right thing, to stay in school and out of trouble and things will work out. But then, Morgan was good; good grades, good kid, all he was doing was walking down the street after a Weaver High School basketball game Tuesday night. And now he was dead. Why?

How do you cowards answer that? What do you say?

The mothers looked frozen in the waiting room Thursday, panicked as they talked about how it could have been any of their kids that night, about how it still could. "They're angry," one mother said, watching the teenagers in the other room. She hears them talking in corners when they think no one is listening about retribution. "Yours is coming," they say.

The problem, said another mother, is not that they're angry, but that they're not afraid. Not afraid of walking into Morgan's room. Not afraid of staring into his swollen face, at the tubes inserted into his mouth. Not afraid of dying.

That's why even after Morgan's father, Lorenzo Rowe, knew that his son was gone, that the only thing keeping his son's chest moving were the machines he was connected to, that he had to make a decision about donating his son's organs, he let the kids keep going into the room. There was a line at one point. They sat and stared as though they expected him to wake up any minute.

"It looks like he might, right?" one girl said.

But last rites had been given him hours ago and doctors were just waiting until after midnight Thursday to wheel him into the operating room to give someone else a chance at a life you took -- if his father could just sit still long enough to sign the papers.

"Five minutes, just five minutes," Lorenzo Rowe said. He wanted to drink some tea, grab a cigarette. He had been like this all day, his girlfriend, Robin Abrams, said, looking for an excuse not to have to deal with it.

"It's not fair," she said. "He was shortchanged, the world was shortchanged."

In the parking garage, Rowe kept saying he was fine, but you should have been there to see the way his hands shook when he described his son, that smile he had, the one girls didn't stand a chance around. His love affair with

X-Box and 50 Cent. He's thinking about playing something by him at the funeral. The quick way he picked up chess.

"He even beat me a few times," he said, laughing.

That's why the first night when doctors asked him about donating Morgan's organs, he thought they were crazy. Morgan was going to wake up. "He was going to snap out of it."

He still believed that the next day, too, when he went to see his mother, Morgan's grandmother, and she told him in that quiet way that maybe, just maybe, he should think about it. "Maybe Morgan can live through someone else."

But the swelling was down, he thought. He looked like himself, not like he had the day your bullet traveled from your gun and into the middle of his head. The bullet is still there.

And so he took one last shot, put his lips up to his son's ear and whispered, "I got your X-Box, come and get it."

But Morgan wasn't going to come and get it. And he's not going to University High School for Science & Engineering like he planned. He won't be that engineer he dreamed about being. And sometime around 7 p.m. Thursday, his father had to admit that to himself and sign the papers. "To give someone else a chance," he said, his hands still shaking.

And you, you cowards, need to know that.

A Boy Survives: And A Hartford Mother Hopes People Step Up, Speak Out

Helen Ubiñas The Hartford Courant August 13, 2003

He just fell. And at first, the people standing around the little boy didn't think the unrelenting popping noises had anything to do with him collapsing onto the pavement like a rag doll.

Firecrackers, they figured; they were at the annual West Indian Parade, after all.

But then they saw blood gushing from 7-year-old Tyrek Marquez's head, and a woman who had been standing nearby said everyone suddenly started screaming and running, crashing into one another as they desperately sought cover from gunfire that never seemed to stop. After the initial spray of shots, she said, it was as if anyone with a gun started using it, including a man she saw firing from behind his back as he ran away.

As she fled, the woman saw a man in a wheelchair frantically trying to roll himself to safety, but there didn't seem to be anywhere to hide. She took refuge under a truck, sharing the cramped space with another bystander who, so afraid, threw up all over the woman's shoulder. But it was the image of the little boy crumbling to the ground, she said, that she hasn't been able to shake. And that's why on Tuesday afternoon she found her way to the Connecticut Children's Medical Center on Washington Street, seeking out his mother, September Chatfield.

"I'm sorry," says the Hartford woman, grasping a card she has come to deliver. "I feel so bad for leaving him there."

After a short pause, Tyrek's mother, sitting in the waiting room right outside the hospital's intensive care unit, tells the woman it's OK. Her son is strong. He's alive, and as long as she and others aren't afraid now, when it really matters, when people need to come forward, it's OK.

You hear that - all of you who pray at the altar of the "No Snitch" culture that has helped destroy this city? This mother is asking you to do the right thing, to step up, to speak up. There still haven't been any arrests in the parade shootings. It's a humble enough request, isn't it, from a mother and an innocent young boy who deserve justice?

Chatfield had been waiting outside a store for Tyrek when he was shot Saturday. Tyrek had grown tired of being at the parade, so she let him go to a friend's aunt's house nearby. But when she went to get him, they told her that he'd just gone to the store.

"I hope you're not at the parade," a friend called just moments earlier to say. There was a shooting. Not long after, Chatfield says, the two boys Tyrek had been with came screaming and crying down the street.

"Tyrek got shot," they told her. They thought he might be dead.

"Shot." "Dead." The words rang in Chatfield's head as she and her boyfriend rushed to the hospital, Chatfield crying and praying and banging on the dashboard all the way.

She called St. Francis Hospital and Medical Center, where he had initially been taken, but they couldn't tell her for sure if Tyrek was there. They were treating multiple victims of the parade shooting, including 17-month-old Zinia Jackson, who was shot in the leg.

This can't be true, Chatfield thought. This can't be happening. Chatfield, who was born and raised in Hartford, knows better than most how the streets could suddenly, cruelly, claim the city's most innocent. Her home, on Enfield Street, sits right between the empty lot where 14-year-old Aquan Salmon was shot dead by a police officer in 1999 and the plot of ground where two years later a stray bullet tore into then-7-year-old Takira Gaston's face.

Any mother trying to raise children in Hartford fears the frightening reality of tragedy touching her family, but Chatfield says she always hoped and prayed her own would be spared.

She knows how dangerous it can be to speak out, even if it's the right thing to do. But this is different, she says. This is an innocent boy, a boy too young to have allegiances to anything other than maybe the New England Patriots and the New York Knicks.

At the hospital, police asked Chatfield what Tyrek had been wearing. She'd just bought him the clothes he wore that day to the parade, but she suddenly went blank on the white T-shirt, the orange plaid shorts and the Nike Uptown sneakers he'd wanted so badly.

"Oh my God," she remembers thinking. "They're going to tell me my son is dead."

He wasn't, but she says doctors told her they had to operate to clear his head of broken bone fragments and to see if the bullet that entered the back of his head and exited near the side had done any damage.

For four hours, Chatfield waited, at first in the family room, where she called her mother, a woman whose spirituality she suddenly yearned for.

"Ma, get down on your knees right now." Chatfield didn't answer right away when her mother asked what was wrong. "Ma, get down on your knees right now and pray for my son."

Later, Chatfield paced the parking lot, wondering if just around the corner some doctor would appear to tell her that Tyrek was gone. Doctors suggested she go home, get some rest, but other than leaving for a quick shower and change of clothes, she's been by Tyrek's side. It's been hard, she says, with a newborn and three other children at home.

"But I'm not leaving my son."

Chatfield didn't know it, but around the same time she and her family were thanking God that Tyrek was breathing on his own Monday, city officials were talking tough in the name of Tyrek and other innocent victims shot during the parade. They were forming a "Shooting Team" with state prosecutors to investigate gun crimes, they told the TV cameras. They'd share their "most watched list" of people who pose a safety risk with the state's attorney's office. There would be, Mayor Eddie Perez triumphantly declared, a 9 p.m. curfew for people 18 and under beginning Thursday night.

When I fill her in, Chatfield doesn't seem impressed. The shooting, she says, happened way before 9 p.m. And she's not sure anything can save the city now.

"They've let it get too far," she says.

She hasn't talked to Tyrek about what happened; they're not sure he remembers. But it's unlikely he'll ever forget. Even after he's transferred into a regular room today, he's looking at months of physical therapy for his left side, which was left weakened after the shooting. Doctors still want to run tests to make sure the bullet didn't affect his spine.

In his room, a trio of "Get Well" balloons hover over his bed and a mini football lies on his pillow, which is stained with blood. For a while, he sleeps soundly, with the help of pain medication. But when he wakes, he reaches out for his mother.

"Ma," he cries.

"What is it, Ty?" she asks, holding him close. "What's wrong?"

"Ma," he cries again. "My head hurts."

DEB WALDMAN

In nearly 40 years as a professional writer, Deb Waldman has written for a wide variety of publications including People, Parents, Sports Illustrated, Sports Illustrated for Kids, Glamour, Chatelaine, National Geographic World, The Washington Post, and Publishers Weekly. She has also written or co-written eight books and had her work published in a number of anthologies. She has written magazine and newspaper articles about everything from boy scouts to strippers.

She got her start writing for her high school newspaper, the Utica, NY Free Academy Corridors, and went on to study journalism at Syracuse University, where she wrote for at the university's newspaper, The Daily Orange. Her first job was at the Cape Cod Times. After nearly six years as a newspaper reporter, she went to Cornell University to earn a Master of Fine Arts degree in creative writing. She has also taught writing and journalism at Cornell, Ithaca College, St. Lawrence University, and Grant MacEwan University, and has been a music critic for the New Haven Register.

MUSIC REVIEW: Lewis And The News' Tight Show Provides Clean-cut Fun

By Deb Waldman New Haven Register May 3, 1987

It was "Hip to be Square" at the Hartford Civic Center Friday night.

Not only was that the most wildly received of the 20 songs Huey Lewis and the News did during their two-hour concert, it was also the theme for the evening.

Opening act Lonnie Mack, a country-flavored R&B guitarist, set the tone when he and his band banged out a number called "The Oreo Cookie Blues." The audience loved it.

No members of the tatoo, spike and spandex crowd that frequent many Civic Center rock events were in evidence. This was strictly clean-cut fun - kids came with their parents, parents came with their partners.

The air in the arena was clear, the sound clean and the lighting so bright it was possible to see Lewis' eyes widen with excitement from the middle of the arena.

Lewis was happy, his band was happy and the Tower of Power horns more than lived up to their name. When they weren't pumping life into songs like "Trouble in Paradise" and "Hip to Be Square," they'd swing their horns back and forth like synchronized tin soldiers with movable arms.

The horn players, who bopped on stage 40 minutes into Lewis' show (just in time to help out on "Power of Love") provided a polish and punch rare in many rock concerts.

Lewis didn't have to depend on the brass to carry the show, though. His own band showed real flair, especially for crooning, doo-wop love songs. The horns left the stage when Huey and the boys harmonized on ditties like "Naturally" and "Stuck With You."

Perhaps Lewis is at ease with those sweet songs because he's such a good guy himself. On stage, he seemed as friendly as a neighbor who'd lend you a rake or a lawnmower if you asked politely.

Still, there was something disconcerting about his performance. Though he wailed on the harmonica, danced in front of the drummer and occasionally ran to the back of the stage to serenade the folks in the obstructed-vision seats, his hair remained perfect, his very tight Levis didn't rip and his baggy red shirt didn't seem to gather any sweat.

That's hip.

MOSTLY MUSIC: The Face Behind The Faces At Toad's

By Deb Waldman New Haven Register Aug. 29, 1986

Richard Forrest Harlow stood in the middle of the sticky dance floor at Toad's Place one afternoon, surveying the paintings on the wall.

"Huey Lewis," he said. "Tough face. He really does have a tough face to do. He really does have a nondescript face. Not ugly, but nondescript."

Harlow ought to know. He did the painting. For the last five years, he has done all the paintings at Toad's Place - the ones in the window that advertise upcoming bands and the smaller works that make up the Wall of Fame inside.

"I don't have to wait to have a show in a gallery," he said. "My work is shown every night at the club."

Harlow starts painting immediately after a show is confirmed. The posters are usually 4 feet long and 2 feet wide and take about two hours to complete. He likes to use photographs for reference. When that's not possible, he goes to a nearby record store for inspiration or uses his imagination.

"It's a challenge for me," he said. "Robin Trower is a real prime example. I did a design of a guitar with banners hanging from the guitar with his name coming off the banners."

Harlow, 37, began drawing when he was growing up in Shelton. "By the time I was in first grade, I had perspective down - ovals for bird baths rather than circles."

The birdbaths were put on hold after high school, when Harlow participated in protest marches, did artwork for a local underground newspaper called "View from the Bottom," made and sold rock 'n' roll badges and shirts and played in a band called The Plan.

Ultimately, he said, he would like to do promotional artwork for a record company. For now, however, he is happy working in his studio upstairs at Toad's Place. "They pay me to paint," he said. "How can I argue?"

Besides, the perks - bringing his son to a soundcheck to breakdance with Cyndi Lauper, chatting with Graham Parker, and listening to Marshall

Crenshaw tell stories - are hard to beat. And he knows his work is appreciated.

"I did a poster for The Alarm," he said. "It was their first tour, and they came into the building, and usually I like to get the posters autographed during sound checks, so when people show up for the show, it's already autographed and it looks nice. And when I went to get the autograph, Twist, the drummer, said 'Oh! You're the artist fellow. We've heard about you.' ... I knew I was achieving what I set out to do - to get my name circulated in the industry."

Members of The Alarm, it seems, weren't the only ones who liked the poster. "Someone stole it," he said. "Just walked off with it."

Singer/producer Dave Edmunds didn't get such a bad deal on a Harlow, either. "He had me paint a duplicate poster and ship it over to England," Harlow said. "I was kind. I only took $25."

ELSEWHERE:

... Bleached Black have signed a record contract with Relativity Records and a new release is tentatively planned by the end of the year.

... Former Earl's Watch-men Sal Paradise, Chuck Evans, Bob Norr and Mike Posser have reformed as Subdueds. More details will be published as available.

... There will be a homecoming of sorts at the Grotto tonight for Connecticut residents Arti Dixson and Mark Epstein, now playing with Mark Elias. Elias is opening for The Reducers.

... Joey Melotti and Brian Keane, also known as the Joey Melotti Duo, will be at The Foundry tonight and Saturday. Melotti and three other as yet unconfirmed musicians will be at The Foundry on Sunday, under the name The Joey Melotti Quartet. "What happens is these guys are in and out," Melotti explained. "Sometimes I don't find out till a few days before."

KATHARINE WEBER

Katharine Weber is a widely published novelist and autobiographer and was a columnist for the New Haven Register. Before her appointment to the Richard L. Thomas Visiting Chair position at Kenyon College, she was an adjunct associate professor of creative writing at Columbia University's School of the Arts (2006-2012), Kratz Writer in Residence at Goucher College (2006), a lecturer in fiction writing at Yale (1996-2003) and a visiting lecturer in fiction writing at Connecticut College. She is the author of six novels and a memoir. Katharine is an editor at large for Kenyon Review and is on the Editorial Advisory Board of American Imago. She has served on the board of the National Book Critics Circle and is an associate fellow of Calhoun College at Yale University. In 1996, Katharine was named one of Granta Magazine's "50 Best Young American Novelists." Her novels have been named New York Times Notable Books three times, have twice been longlisted for the Impac Dublin Literary Award, twice shortlisted for the John Gardner Fiction Book Award, twice shortlisted for the Paterson Fiction Prize, and twice shortlisted for the Connecticut Book Award, which she won in 2007 for Triangle. Her novels have been translated and published in 16 languages.

About 13% Of America Can't Read This

By KatharineWeber New Haven Register June 1, 1986

If you are illiterate, you were unable to read recent newspaper accounts of the alarming 13 percent illiteracy rate among adults in this country.

And if you are among that 13 percent that the U.S. Census Bureau has deemed lacking in "functional competency" - perhaps someone is reading this column aloud to you - then you were spared another recent newspaper story about a school board in Kingston, Mass., that had dropped a summer reading program out of fear that the books would "bore students." (The board later reversed the decision after attracting a great deal of unwanted publicity.) The reading list included titles by Mark Twain, John Steinbeck, Charles Dickens, Alan Paton and Bernard Malamud.

One member of the Silver Lake School Committee voted against the reading list because she "had not heard of half the books on the list." The chairman of this august body that is allegedly charged with overseeing academic activities within the school district claims to have favored the controversial reading program. But he stated that he could sympathize with the students' lack of interest in the proscribed reading list because, "You're not reading because you feel like reading when you get into high school. You have to buckle down."

Another recent survey, this one conducted by the non-profit Educational Testing Service of Princeton, N.J., and backed by federal funding, reveals that between 62 percent and 80 percent of American 17-year-olds demonstrated "unsatisfactory writing skills." The study said that there is "clear cause for concern about the writing proficiency of the nation's students."

In response to these last statistics, Education Secretary William J. Bennett said, "This important report shows that the second of the Three R's is in appalling poor shape among American young people. The reform movement that has begun to show real progress in reading had best now begin to pay some close attention to writing."

Now, before coming to any conclusions about these three related news items, let me first point out that if the secretary of education persists in calling writing "the second of the Three R's," then it is no wonder that there is a substantial illiteracy rate in this country. (Actually, factoring out adults who are literate in their native languages, the national illiteracy rate is closer to 9 percent.)

Secretary Bennett needs to pay some close attention to his own writing. He should have said "appallingly poor shape." And "had best now begin" is an unusual and pretentious construction. "Had better" would be better; "ought to" would be best. (Statistics on the illiteracy rate within the Cabinet are unavailable.)

Taken altogether, these recent findings reveal a disregard for more than the simple mechanical abilities that allow us to read and write at the most basic level. There seems to be very little expectation that reading and writing serve a greater purpose than the utilitarian communications necessary for good grades, good jobs and competency in the workplace and the world of commerce. We have simultaneously lowered our standards for use of language and turned away from the pleasures of reading and writing.

I suppose a case can be made for other priorities and values. Who am I to impose Bernard Malamud on someone who only wants to learn the skills required to earn a fat salary as a commodities broker, buy a condo and retire to the Sun Belt? There are many people who sincerely believe that a good old-fashioned liberal education is irrelevant.

The desirability of perfect grammar and spelling is not the issue; neither is this intended as a general lament over the slippage of values. What is declining, according to the evidence, is both respect for the structure and use of language, and a turning away from dependence on the written word as a source of information and knowledge.

In the case of words, familiarity does not breed contempt. To the contrary, it breeds respect and love. Love of words and books is a marvelous thing to cultivate in a child. Shrugging and allowing that no one is expected to enjoy reading, anyway, suggests both ignorance and a complacency about that ignorance. If parents are more often to be found zoned-out in front of "Moonlighting" than curled up with a good book, a very distinct message is absorbed by their children.

In some cultures, when scholarliness was next to godliness, this attitude used to be called laziness.

Life Is Risky For An Animal 'At Liberty' In The Country

By Katharine Weber New Haven Register Nov. 17, 1985

Dear Unknown Bethany Neighbor:

Last night I killed your dog. Actually, last night you and I together killed your dog.

There was nothing I could do to prevent what happened. He raced out into the road in front of my car, and there was a car right behind me, and another coming toward me in the opposite lane. In the seconds before my car struck him, I exclaimed to my 4-year-old daughter, "Brace yourself – we're going to hit that dog!"

But even though I knew it would happen, the soft "thump-thump" as the car struck his body was a shock. If one were to run over a little child, the impact would be identical. In an instant my car had become a machine that had crushed the life out of something. I had obliterated something that had been alive, something with a brain, and feelings, something capable of loving and being loved.

I wish I could tell you that he never knew what hit him, but that would be a lie. He knew. He was still alive when the car behind me ran over his body. Then he was surely dead.

I stopped my car and spoke calmly with Lucy, who was tearful. Then I got out and talked for a moment with the driver behind me, who had also pulled over. She thanked me for doing the right thing by neither braking nor changing direction. We looked back up the road at the still form that was barely visible in the growing darkness. Car headlights would shine up over the crest in the road and then the cars would swerve around the body.

It would have been dangerous to try to move him; the combination of darkness, speeding cars, and the crest in the road would have made it a particularly risky task. And he was clearly dead. And I had a very shaken child in the car and family supper to prepare.

So we left your dog lying dead in the road with cars speeding over the bloody remains of his body.

Did you love him? He was a not quite fully-grown Doberman, I think. Maybe it was a she. I didn't see a collar, but maybe there was one. I couldn't take the chance of approaching the body to make sure, because, as I have said, I didn't want to get run over by one of the cars speeding along the dark road. The middle of Amity Road at nightfall is no place for woman nor beast.

Did a child cry last night? I'm so sorry. My child cried last night. I cried last night.

Why was your dog off his leash and out of your yard?

Maybe he escaped. Maybe it was the first and only time he was at liberty. I will never know how your dog came to be running across Amity Road last night at the moment that I drove by with my daughter after her dance class.

Did you curse the vicious dog-killer who murdered your beloved pet and didn't even stop? Were you angry because I didn't personally come to tell you that your dog had been brutally crushed beneath the wheels of two cars? I couldn't very well go door-to-door looking for you. I did report the accident right away at the police station just up the road.

According to the town clerk's office there are 664 dogs with licenses in Bethany. There is no breakdown by breed. So while I suppose I could have made an effort to track you down, it wasn't really something I was inclined to do today. By now you know your dog is dead. His body wasn't there when I drove by this morning.

Is there a lesson to be learned from this? I couldn't have done one thing differently. You could have. There is a law in the state of Connecticut that makes it illegal for dogs to wander unleashed off of your property. Dog owners are informed on the back of the dog licenses issued by our town that they are liable for prosecution if they allow their dogs to roam on public highways. Where was your leash or tether, your fenced yard, your closed gate?"

If your dog was a Houdini, then increased vigilance would have been the answer. Pets, not unlike small children, sometimes require round-the-clock supervision.

Yes, Bethany is the country. Lots of people assume that those rules can be safely ignored out here. But country roads, as you may have noticed, are usually lined with carnage. Life in bucolic Bethany is mighty rough on woodchucks, skunks and opossums. Where were you when your dog died?

When you let your pet go "free," you sentenced him to death. And you made me the executioner.

A Jewish Yule Greeting

By Katharine Weber New Haven Register Dec. 22, 1985

Being Jewish in the summertime doesn't, in itself, distinguish one from other people. The experiences and associations of warm weather, like gardening or sports, or beach-going are universally shared. There is no moment when one's choice of suntan lotion or tennis racket is automatically a statement of separateness, off difference.

This time of year there are countless little moments of confrontation for Jews like me who spend most of the rest of the year in a happily homogenous state. It begins in September with Rosh Hashanah and Yom Kippur. To decline an appointment on Yom Kippur can be a statement of what is otherwise not obvious. If one is Jewish in the way that I choose to be, it is a statement of what is sometimes not even obvious to oneself.

I am Jewish. I do not celebrate Christmas. Yet the world around me is festooned with twinkling lights and charming decorations that signify the celebration of the birth of Jesus Christ. There are countless arguments that trees and Santa Claus aren't religious symbols, that they are traditional holiday decorations. While there is a difference between a wreath and a nativity scene or a Christmas tree and crucifix to me the difference is slight and one of degree not definition.

The Supreme Court and I are not in agreement on the issue. I am disappointed by recent decisions upholding the placement of crèches on public property. On the other hand, I am pleased by the Connecticut ruling earlier this month that forbade the placement of a lighted cross on the front of Greenwich Volunteer Fire Department headquarters. To me these things are all manifestations of the celebration of Christmas. And Christmas isn't an American tradition, it is a Christian one. Ronald Reagan's words to the contrary, ours is not a "Christian nation." Ours is a nation that has a strong Christian tradition and that is not the same thing at all.

At this time of year I feel like Scrooge. There is no clear answer to the Christmas dilemma. One Jewish friend advises, "Always be en route to someplace else. Traveling is the answer. Spend the days in airports. Go someplace exotic where they don't celebrate Christmas." Yet the lights are beautiful, the music is appealing, and the spirit of Christmas can be delightful. Perhaps what forces the issue into perspective is having small children. When one is a parent there are a lot of basic questions concerning values and beliefs. Having grown up in a household with mixed – although primarily Jewish – backgrounds, I am determined to place myself and my children in a more specific cultural context. My husband is Jewish. This family is Jewish. Not for us the peculiar hybrid phenomenon of Jews with Christmas trees. I speak with the fervor of the converted, having grown up with Christmas trees that were purchased annually in a bargaining ritual conducted by my father in Yiddish.

I am quite deliberately not even beginning to address the religious beliefs represented by this choice of affiliation because our identity is not particularly predicated on those beliefs. It is a cultural identification and one that comes with a lot of baggage. If you need to know my religion before you invited me to your country club or offer me a job, then there is no question in my mind that I have elected to choose the right label.

Perhaps the experience of being Jewish in America ought to include a more casual acceptance of Christmas, but it seems to me that the problem lies in the general perception that the experience of Christmas is universal, like Thanksgiving. I don't deny anyone the right to celebrate religious holiday, but I would like to feel like less of a stranger in my own territory. Last week when I went shopping for Hanukkah presents with my 4-year-old, two different shop clerks told her that Santa would bring her something because she was such a good girl. The second time she looked at me with a small smile and said, "They don't know we're Jewish, do they, Mommy."

At this point I think that I make my friends nervous. I know what they are thinking. Do you wish her a Happy Hanukkah? Do you invite her to a Christmas party? Do you let her children help decorate the Christmas tree? Do you just ignore them until after the holidays?

Wish me a Happy Hanukkah. Wish me a Happy New Year. Wish me a happy holiday. Invited us to your parties – we love all of the food of the season. We enjoy your Christmas trees too. We give Christmas presents to our friends who celebrate Christmas. Just bear in mind that Christmas isn't for everybody. And to those to whom it applies: have a Merry Christmas.

www.ingramcontent.com/pod-product-compliance
Lightning Source LLC
Chambersburg PA
CBHW062015190726
48284CB00012B/66

* 9 7 8 1 9 4 0 8 6 3 1 0 8 *